Dictionary
of the History of
the American Brewing
and
Distilling Industries

Dictionary of the History of the

WILLIAM L. DOWNARD

American Brewing
and
Distilling Industries

GREENWOOD PRESS
WESTPORT, CONNECTICUT • LONDON, ENGLAND

Library of Congress Cataloging in Publication Data

Downard, William L
    Dictionary of the history of the American
brewing and distilling industries.

    Bibliography: p.
    Includes index.
    1. Brewing industry—United States—History.
2.   Distilling industries—United States—
History.   3.   Brewing industry—United States—
Dictionaries.   4.   Distilling industries—United
States—Dictionaries.   I.   Title.
HD9397.U52D68   338.4'76631'0973   79-6826
ISBN 0-313-21330-5 lib. bdg.

Library of Congress Catalog Card Number: 79-6826
ISBN: 0-313-21330-5

First published in 1980

Greenwood Press
A division of Congressional Information Service, Inc.
88 Post Road West, Westport, Connecticut 06881

Printed in the United States of America

10 9 8 7 6 5 4 3 2 1

COPYRIGHT
ACKNOWLEDGMENTS ____

The author and publisher gratefully acknowledge permission to quote from the following:

The Alcoholic Republic: An American Tradition by W. J. Rorabaugh. Copyright © 1979 by Oxford University Press, Inc. Reprinted by permission.

Brewers Almanac 1974. United States Brewers Association, Inc. Reprinted by permission.

Tax Briefs. Copyright © 1977 by Distilled Spirits Council of the United States, Inc. Reprinted by permission.

Every reasonable effort has been made to trace the owners of copyright materials in this book, but in some instances this has proven impossible. The publishers will be glad to receive information leading to more complete acknowledgments in subsequent printings of the book, and in the meantime extend their apologies for any omissions.

To our parents,
    Bill and Millie
        and
    Bob and Katie

CONTENTS

PREFACE

The history of the American brewing and distilling industries is marked by the existence of a great number of firms in each industry. One source estimates that 22,000 distilleries (albeit many of them small stills) operated in the U.S. in 1802; and at one time or another approximately 3,000 breweries have been extant. Given the size of the industries, at least in sheer numbers, this historical dictionary is not comprehensive with reference to company histories; but, I trust, it is representative.

It contains entries on the institutions, personalities, special legislation, events, and terminology of the history of the American brewing and distilling industries. Certain general articles serve as a key to other specific entries. There are histories of nineteen urban brewing centers (see Appendix IV) with cross-references (indicated by "q.v.") to firms having separate entries in this dictionary. Also, entries on the Kentucky distilling industry and Peoria distilling industry will act as a guide to firms in those areas. Other similar general articles are Brewing Process, Brewery Workers' Movement, Federal Liquor Regulations, Kentucky Distilleries and Warehouse Company, Prohibition, Taxation of Distilled Spirits (Federal), Taxation of Malt Liquors (Federal), Whiskey-making Process, and Whiskey Trust.

The general guide for selecting brewing firms was as follows: (1) all, or as many as possible, presently existing companies; (2) major firms in 1877, 1895, and 1973; (3) selected important and interesting firms in the nineteen urban brewing centers; and (4) companies of special historical interest. *One Hundred Years of Brewing* (Chicago and New York, 1903; Arno Press Reprint, 1974), a publication of H. S. Rich and Company, is an invaluable, generally very reliable, and incredibly comprehensive history of brewing that contains literally hundreds of brief company histories. This source, plus Manfred Friedrich and Donald Bull, *The Register of U.S. Breweries, 1876-1976* (Trumbull, Conn., 1976), made it possible to select and recount the histories of many firms for inclusion in this dictionary. The *Register*, for instance, lists more than 2,000 firms, tracing name changes and closing dates.

Decisions on which distilling firms to include in this work proved less problematical than brewing entries. There is no source comparable to *One Hundred Years of Brewing*, and generally there is less material available on the history of American distilling. Most present-day firms are included plus many of the Kentucky and Peoria, Illinois, distilleries. In all, brief histories of approximately 180 breweries and 100 distilleries are included in this dictionary.

The Index will act as a guide to finding information on many topics and personalities included in various entries under other headings. The abbreviation "q.v." following a term or phrase indicates a cross-reference to the preceding word or words.

A special note is appropriate on the spelling of the word "whiskey." Canadian and Scotch whiskies usually omit the *e*, and thus would be spelled whisky. American practice utilizes both versions. Federal regulations on whiskey omit the *e*, whereas most publications—academic and otherwise—include the *e*—thus, "whiskey." I have used whisky in referring to Canadian and Scotch types, but whisk*e*y in all other cases.

In preparing this work, I have become indebted to the people who provided help and support. Most of the currently operating brewing and distilling firms I contacted provided valuable historical information. The cooperation of company officials in providing requested information is appreciated. The individual entries, I hope, will reflect their input and serve as a small repayment for the inconvenience incurred. Saint Joseph's College (Indiana) granted me a sabbatical leave from my teaching duties, and the library staff, headed by Robert Vigeant and H. Don Kreilkamp, aided me in procuring materials. Jerry Caroon of the Milwaukee County Historical Society and Claire McCann of the University of Kentucky Libraries provided important help in the early stages of research. William Vollmar, records administrator at Anheuser-Busch, was invaluable as a resource person and also contributed some research of his own. Philip Katz, senior vice-president, Research Services of the U.S. Brewers' Association, gave me free access to the association's considerable library holdings. The Distilled Spirits Council of the U.S. also provided access to its collection and forwarded various publications of the organization. I am also thankful for the assistance of the personnel at the following libraries: The John Crerar Library (Chicago), Chicago Historical Society, Kentucky State Historical Society, Louisville Public Library, University of Illinois Library, Purdue University Library, New York Historical Society, New York Public Library, Massachusetts Historical Society, Historical Society of Pennsylvania (Philadelphia), Peoria Historical Society, Library of Congress, Historical Society of Western Pennsylvania (Pittsburgh), and the Hamilton County Public Library (Cincinnati).

Thompson Willett, president of the Willett Distilling Company, was very helpful in providing source material and giving me a "feel" for the industry.

William Samuels, Jr., president of Maker's Mark Distilling Company, introduced me to H. W. Coyte of Paris, Kentucky. Coyte has written personal histories of many Kentucky firms and is an accomplished and careful historian—albeit nonprofessional and unpublished. He checked my sources and Kentucky histories, and contributed material of his own. A number of people provided helpful criticism on the technical terms. Sam Cecil, at Maker's Mark, and Sterling Long, a microbiologist at National Distillers, corrected some of my errors on distilling terminology, while Peter Blum of the Stroh Brewery Company straightened out a number of my brewing entries. I accept full responsibility for any errors remaining in the text.

A number of my students also contributed. Mark Salkeld, Mike Haynes, Kit Hartnett, and Anne O'Donnell deserve mention. Karen O'Brien typed a considerable portion of the early drafts. A former student, Ray B. Merritt, was also helpful with the typing. Along the way many friends and relatiyes helped keep me going by maintaining a friendly inquisitiveness about my progress.

Art Stickney of Greenwood Press was a constant source of help, constructive criticism, and encouragement. My wife, Sue, aided me in the research and did the bulk of the typing. When the opportunity arose to take on the job, I demurred, but she urged me on. I am glad now that she did.

INTRODUCTION _____

THE AMERICAN BREWING INDUSTRY

The origins of beer and brewing probably date from the time of the Egyptians around 2000 B.C. The god Osiris is often credited with the invention of the beverage. The use of grain (often barley) in brewing and the fermentation afterward have been practiced in most societies. Egyptians allegedly influenced the Greeks, and Western civilizations brewed the beverage during the medieval period in Europe. Thus brewing was a well-developed process by the time of the first English colonial settlements in America in the early seventeenth century.

Early settlers, including the Pilgrims of Plymouth colony, drank beer as a matter of course. In England, beer was the "universal beverage," largely owing to unsafe drinking water. Because of the brewing process, beer generally proved healthier than water, and even though the water in New England proved relatively wholesome and safe, beer drinking continued to be popular.

The beer of the colonial period was different from modern beers. Ale, porter, and stout, in the English tradition, were the predominant types. Barley and water were the most necessary ingredients, while hops added flavor to the brew. Initially, ales were unhopped, but by the seventeenth century ales and beers alike generally contained hops. Overall, the English brews were brewed with top-fermentation yeast and were lusty, fairly dark, and high in alcoholic content.

In contrast, lager beer (q.v.), introduced by German immigrants in the 1840s, was lighter, more effervescent, and more highly hopped than the English beers. Also, the fermentation process utilized a special yeast that settled at the bottom of the vats, and brewers "lagered," or stored, the beer for a time as fermentation proceeded. Modern lager beer, making up more than 90 percent of all beer consumed, is more lightly hopped, a bit lower in alcoholic content, and lighter and drier than its nineteenth-century counterpart. Conversely, today's ales contain a greater quantity of hops and are heavier than lager.

During the seventeenth century, the Dutch in New Netherland, and the

English colonists of Virginia, Massachusetts Bay, Rhode Island, Connecticut, New Jersey, Maryland, and Pennsylvania consumed beer on a fairly regular basis. Commercial brewing at home began, but most colonies also imported the brew from England. Pennsylvania had a commercial brewhouse in 1685, and there is evidence that William Penn himself might have had a brewery on the premises of his mansion in 1683. In the southern colonies, rum remained somewhat more popular than beer, owing in part to the lack of barley and hops.

In the eighteenth century per capita consumption of beer declined, but the volume increased. Philadelphia, which exported a considerable amount to the southern colonies, shared the position of brewing center with New York City, which would be the nation's largest urban producer until the late-nineteenth century.

After the Revolutionary War, consumption of rum, whiskey, and other distilled spirits outran the consumption of beer. One reason seemed to be the relative ease in growing rye and corn for whiskey-making as compared with the scarcity of malt and hops for brewing. In the early 1790s Secretary of the Treasury Alexander Hamilton noted in his Report on Manufactures that the quality of American malt liquors did not measure up to European products, but that competition among domestic brewers might result in a greater volume and quality of malt, hops, and beer. Thus he urged that import duties be levied on malt liquors. Virginia had passed such a duty in 1786, and it seemed to provide some encouragement to the local industry. Hamilton also stressed the value of malt liquors as moderating influences in comparison to ardent spirits. Such reasoning evidently figured in the passage of the Excise Act of 1791 (q.v.), which levied a domestic tax on distilled spirits, but left malt liquors untaxed.

Despite the efforts to encourage production of malt liquors, the industry lagged in the early-nineteenth century. In 1810, 132 breweries produced approximately 185,000 barrels for a population of about 7 million. Stanley Baron, in his study, *Brewed in America* (Boston, 1962), notes that "the American production was far from impressive in 1810, but by early 1820 it appeared to have deteriorated completely." Americans were consuming whiskey at a greater rate, and beer sales slumped. A slight increase in consumption occurred in the late 1820s and into the 1830s at a time when grain farmers began to market their crops directly instead of making whiskey, but the real growth of the industry would wait until the 1840s when lager beer (q.v.) began replacing ale, porter, and stout as the primary American brew.

Between 1840 and 1860 German immigrants changed the nature and importance of the American brewing industry. Lager was introduced in the early 1840s, was immediately popular among the German immigrants, and gradually built a similar appeal among non-German beer drinkers. The greatest strides occurred in the 1850s. The number of breweries grew from

431 in 1850 to 1,269 in 1860. New York and Pennsylvania remained the largest brewing states, but westward migration into the Old Northwest states of Ohio, Illinois, Indiana, Michigan, and Wisconsin encouraged western brewers.

As a food product, beer is perishable, and before the adoption of the pasteurization (q.v.) process, it was necessary for localities to produce their own beer. Some transporting did occur prior to pasteurization and refrigerated rail transport, but the stability of the beer was often a problem. Thus the number of firms continued to expand in order to meet local demand. The emergence of the national brewer and subsequent concentration of the industry occurred after 1880 as bottling, pasteurization, and refrigerated transport facilities encouraged some brewers to market their beer nationally.

In the meantime, the industry was dominated by German brewers who had often learned the trade in a German country, emigrated from the native country for economic or political reasons, and entered the brewing business in cities like New York, Philadelphia, Cincinnati, Detroit, Milwaukee, St. Louis, and any number of small towns across the nation. Eberhard Anheuser, Adolphus Busch, Christian Moerlein, Frederick Miller, Gottlieb Heileman, Bernhard Stroh, Joseph Schlitz, Frederick Pabst, Christian Schmidt, and David Yuengling were just a few of the new brewers, among the hundreds of German immigrants of the mid-nineteenth century.

After 1860, the brewing industry made impressive gains owing to a number of factors. Temperance (q.v.) forces had successfully campaigned against whiskey consumption, which decreased substantially, and mechanical, chemical, and biological innovations of the period gave the industry a modern look. Ice-making machines, steam power, hoists, pumps, lifts, pneumatic malting (q.v.), pasteurization (q.v.), refrigeration (q.v.), research in yeast cultures, and bottling (see Bottled Beer) improvements were among the changes in brewing science and technology.

The period also saw brewers organize the U.S. Brewers' Association (q.v.) in the aftermath of the Internal Revenue Act of 1862, which placed a tax of $1 on each barrel of beer sold. The organization would act as an industry-wide agency to promote the interests of brewers—primarily the lager brewers. And, in the 1880s it served as a unified front when dealing with the brewery workers' movement (q.v.).

One of the most notable late-nineteenth-century trends in the industry was the increasing concentration of companies. The national brewers grew at the expense of local concerns as the average production per plant increased from 3,084 barrels in 1870 to 22,458 barrels in 1900. Competition, price wars, and overproduction also encouraged British investors to attempt brewery consolidations (see Consolidations, Brewery) in the 1890s. A number of such forays into American brewing succeeded, but no large national brewer sold out to a British syndicate. In many cities, local brewers formed their own mergers to meet the same problems; one example was the Pittsburgh Brewing Company (q.v.).

Concentration and individual brewery closings continued until the adoption of nationwide Prohibition (q.v.) in 1920 virtually destroyed the industry. The abolition of alcoholic drink resulted in large measure from the activities of the Anti-Saloon League (q.v.), which used pressure politics to outlaw the saloon and drinking in the United States. The Volstead Act (q.v.), the enforcement legislation for the Eighteenth Amendment, declared that the manufacture and sale of beverages in excess of ½ of 1 percent in alcoholic content were illegal. Brewers either manufactured near beer (q.v.) to meet the restriction, or turned to new fields such as the production of malt syrups, ice cream, or soft drinks. Anheuser-Busch (q.v.) even went into the manufacture of bus and truck bodies. Most brewers—facing competition from bootleg beer and whiskey, beset by the economic problems of changeover costs, unused building space, and the lack of capital—went out of business. The Christian Moerlein Brewing Company of Cincinnati and William J. Lemp Brewing Company of St. Louis followed this route— evidently as a means of raising liquid capital for family distribution. Each brewery, operating as a closed corporation, was owned primarily by family members. In the Lemp case, many had entered nonbrewing fields and apparently saw little chance for successful alternative operation of the business.

However, many of the nation's largest breweries continued to operate, and by the mid-1920s there appeared some possibility that Prohibition might be repealed. Violation of the law was so widespread, and enforcement costs so high that organizations such as the Association Against the Prohibition Amendment (q.v.) steadily gained support. Anheuser-Busch, Pabst, Miller, Schlitz, Falstaff, and others held on and reopened in 1933 with the passage of the Cullen Act (q.v.), which permitted the manufacture and sale of light wines and beer up to 3.2 percent in alcoholic content. Later in the year the Twenty-first Amendment repealed the Eighteenth. By June 1933, 31 plants had resumed operation and the number grew to 750 in 1935.

In 1914 approximately 1,300 breweries produced more than 66 million barrels of beer, and in 1937, 720 breweries produced 58,750,000 barrels. Clearly, the trend toward concentration and higher productivity begun prior to Prohibition had resumed in the 1930s. Otherwise, the post-Prohibition industry experienced several changes.

At first brewers encountered stiff competition from the soft drink industry —in part because of the continuing depression that adversely affected purchasing power. Also, state and federal authorities passed new and elaborate regulations. Consumption patterns also shifted as packaged beer sales climbed in the wake of the saloon's demise. More Americans had refrigerators, thus increasing home consumption in bottles and cans. Canned beer (q.v.) was first introduced in 1935.

The most notable and far-reaching trend in the post-1940 period was in the concentration of breweries and consequent closing of many firms. In 1950 there were 407 plants; in 1960 the number had declined to 229; by 1970 the figure fell to 142; and by the late 1970s just over 40 firms remained in operation. The apparent causes of such consolidation stemmed from the expansion of some firms into multiplant operations, thereby realizing savings in transportation costs and other economies; and the adoption of technological innovations and efficiencies by the larger national brewers. In a competitive industry not noted for its high profits in the 1950s and 1960s, the failure of many smaller firms was perhaps inevitable. When some nationals decided on expansion programs in the 1950s, some observers predicted failure because of poor sales trends and the large debts being incurred. By the late 1960s it was evident that these decisions were the right ones.

In the 1970s the brewing industry faced increasing turmoil largely generated by Philip Morris's 1971 acquisition of the Miller Brewing Company. The company set out to overtake Anheuser-Busch as the nation's largest brewer and employed wide-scale advertising, brand expansion, and market segmentation to climb from 7 million barrels produced in 1973 to 31 million in 1978. In 1978, Anheuser-Busch, still the nation's number 1 brewer with 41 million barrels produced, and Miller accounted for 44 percent of American beer sales. The leading brewers spent increasingly more money on advertising, but the big battle was between the big two. Newspapers, magazines, and television specials spent considerable time and space on recounting the struggle, and consideration of how the smaller firms might compete. But one source estimated that if the nation's twenty or so smallest brewers were to close, there would be little impact on the industry because their capacity is less than 2 percent of total industry capacity. Strong regional firms such as Heileman's (q.v.), Olympia (q.v.), and Stroh's (q.v.) continue to be successful and small locals count on future success because of local loyalty, low transport and advertising expenditures, and the ability to find a special place in the market.

Note on Sources

The starting point for study of the history of American brewing is *One Hundred Years of Brewing* (Chicago and New York: H. S. Rich & Co., 1903; Arno Press Reprint, 1974). This is a monumental and generally very reliable publication by the editors of the *Western Brewer*, a trade journal. Over seven hundred pages long, the work contains a general history of brewing and technology in addition to brief histories of hundreds of American breweries. Manfred Friedrich and Donald Bull, *The Register of U.S. Breweries, 1876-1976* (Trumbull, Conn., 1976), was recently published in two volumes listing breweries by location in one and in alphabetical order in the other. The best general secondary work is Stanley Baron, *Brewed in*

America (Boston: Little, Brown, and Company, 1962). Thomas C. Cochran's *The Pabst Brewing Company* (New York: New York University Press, 1948) is valuable and broader in scope than the title indicates. Recently, Will Anderson, a collector of breweriana (q.v.), has written a number of books that are helpful to those interested in American brewing history. Most notable are *The Beer Book* (Princeton, N.J.: Pyne Press, 1973) and *The Breweries of Brooklyn* (Croton Falls, N.Y., 1976). William L. Downard, *The Cincinnati Brewing Industry* (Athens: Ohio University Press, 1973), is a study of an urban industry. Herman Schlüter's *The Brewing Industry and the Brewery Workers' Movement in America* (Cincinnati: Union of United Brewery Workmen of America, 1910) is valuable and also contains information on brewery concentration and consolidation. John P. Arnold and Frank Penman, *History of the Brewing Industry and Brewing Science in America* (Chicago, 1933) is worthwhile and contains much information on temperance and Prohibition. A brief treatment, Warren M. Person, *Beer and Brewing in America* (U.S. Brewers' Foundation, 1941), includes statistics and trends in the period from 1933 to 1939. The *Brewers' Almanacs*, published by the U.S. Brewers' Association, contain historical statistics on consumption, production, taxation, and legislation. For industrial trends since 1945 the most recent and comprehensive study is the Federal Trade Commission, *The Brewing Industry* (Washington, D.C.: Government Printing Office, 1976).

The Selected Bibliography contains references to further source materials.

THE AMERICAN DISTILLING INDUSTRY

The precise origin of distillation is impossible to chart, but, as in the case of brewing, the Egyptians knew of distillation. They passed on the knowledge to the Arabs or Saracens. Apparently, Egyptian alchemists discovered ardent spirits between 2000 and 1000 B.C. Other evidence indicates that distillation from grain also occurred in China and India in the pre-Christian era. The Arabs passed on the words "alcohol" and "alembic," the latter meaning a "still."

During the twelfth or thirteenth century, distillation was introduced into western Europe, but the practice was probably known in Ireland and Scotland before then. The Celts called their drink *usquebaugh*, meaning water of life. The word "whiskey" is derived from this designation. The art of distilling was possibly introduced into the British Isles in the thirteenth century by a Franciscan friar, Roger Bacon, who had spent some time in Europe. Distilled spirits were popular in this period and after, and English settlers in America brought with them a taste for such beverages.

The process of distillation involved heating fermented liquid in a still (q.v.), usually a copper pot with a long neck. Connected to the neck was the worm (condenser), which distillers immersed in a barrel or container of cool water. The alcoholic vapor rose from the pot still and condensed into liquid in the cool worm. In the 1830s, the continuous still improved on the pot still and was generally adopted.

English colonists engaged in distilling well before 1650. Evidence suggests that Virginia settlers distilled a variety of fruits into brandies (*see* Brandy). Likewise, the colonists of the seventeenth-century New England and middle colonies fermented and distilled a variety of products—notably apple whiskey (applejack), rum (q.v.), cider, and brandy.

In all, by the beginning of the Revolution in 1776, distilled spirits had been widely accepted in the American colonies. Colonial authorities often legislated to control the beverage, and there was a general but unsuccessful attempt to prevent Indians from drinking spirits; but the popularity persisted. The use of spirits, often rum, by the mid-eighteenth century was very common, and candidates for elective office learned that the voters performed more favorably if they were "treated" before casting a vote. Likewise, Gen. George Washington recognized his soldiers' desire for spiritous drink and made sure his men had supplies of it to warm and comfort them. However, he also expressed concern in 1777 that an overabundance of grain was being converted into whiskey, thus causing food shortages. Thereafter, some states passed acts to protect the grain supply. Rum, which was made from a base of molasses, and brandy, made from fruit, did not come under such restrictions.

The nature of American distilling changed between 1790 and 1830. Whiskey, produced from grain, gradually displaced rum as the primary distilled beverage. Irish and Scotch immigrants of the mid-eighteenth century had been involved in grain distilling for decades. Settling in the frontier areas of Maryland, Pennsylvania, Virginia, and North Carolina, they distilled spirits from a mash of rye, and some corn. After the Revolution, many of the immigrants moved westward and many settled in the Kentucky area. In the meantime rum was losing some of its market because of the relative availability of domestically produced grain as opposed to imported molasses. Also, restrictions on the importing of molasses from British ports, and the Embargo Act of 1807, which cut off all foreign trade, hurt the rum trade. As settlers moved west, it was cheaper and easier to produce and consume whiskey instead of rum.

The Kentucky country was being settled in the 1780s and 1790s, and many of the new arrivals were farmer-distillers (q.v.) of Scotch and Irish backgrounds. Among them, liquor was a way of life, and the conversion of grain into whiskey was both natural and profitable. A packhorse could carry four bushels of grain in raw form, but twenty-four bushels of grain in the form of whiskey. Similar logistics accounted for the popularity of whiskey in western Pennsylvania and led to the Whiskey Rebellion (q.v.) of 1794 in the aftermath of the Excise Act of 1791 (q.v.), which placed unpopular duties on whiskey products. Enforcement of the provision in western Pennsylvania encouraged many farmers to move to the Kentucky region—where there was also discontent and evasion but no rebellion.

After 1800, the locus of the American distilling industry shifted from Maryland and Pennsylvania into Kentucky, and in mid-century into Illinois as well. Many stills and distilleries continued to operate in other states and regions, but the climate and limestone water (q.v.) of Maryland, Pennsylvania, Kentucky, and Illinois presumably made those areas more conducive to quality whiskey-making and the industry would be centered there.

During the first decades of the nineteenth century, Kentucky distilling continued its expansion and in 1810 the state had approximately 2,000 stills with an output of 2.2 million gallons of whiskey. Pennsylvania's 3,594 stills produced more than 6 million gallons. The total number of distilleries in the nation was approximately 14,000 in 1810. Distillers making from 3 to 15 barrels per season were commonplace, but the amount of whiskey consumption encouraged farmers to turn their grain into spirits. Americans consumed nearly 5 gallons of ardent spirits per capita in 1810, and the popularity continued until the 1830s. Temperance (q.v.) forces gained strength in the 1820s and farmers also began marketing their grain directly. Nevertheless, the American market for distilled spirits remained strong.

The early nineteenth century also saw the emergence of "bourbon" (q.v.) in the Kentucky area. Pennsylvania and Maryland farmer-distillers used rye and barley as the primary grains in whiskey-making, whereas Kentucky farmers began to use their plentiful grain, corn, as the major ingredient in making their whiskey. Known at first simply as "whiskey," "western whiskey," "Kentucky whiskey," or "Kentucky goods," the beverage became identified as a regional product in the 1840s made mainly in Bourbon County—which encompassed a large portion of the state. Although other distillers in the state, and in Tennessee, produced whiskey from the mixture of corn and rye, it was not known as bourbon. By the late nineteenth century, the term "bourbon" was used to refer to a whiskey made from corn, rye, and barley malt, mixed in with pure limestone water, heated, distilled, and then aged in new charred oak barrels.

Who produced the first whiskey and bourbon in Kentucky has been a question of concern over the years. Evan Williams, Jacob Spears, and Jacob Myers have each been credited with being the "first distiller of Kentucky" (q.v.) in the 1780s or 1790s, and the Rev. Elijah Craig as the first bourbon distiller, but so many farmer-distillers turned out whiskey that a certain designation is virtually impossible.

After 1850, the number of distillers in Kentucky and across the nation declined as many firms enlarged their output. Peoria, Illinois, soon became a competitor of the Kentucky industry and was noted for its huge plants of the 1880s and 1890s. The city's 10 to 15 distilleries (*see* Peoria Distilling Industry) produced more whiskey than the 200 or so firms of the Kentucky distilling industry (q.v.). In 1881, New York had about 50 stills; Pennsylvania, 110; New Jersey, 57; Ohio, 75; Indiana, 36; Illinois, 50; Kentucky, 140; Tennessee, 44; and Virginia, 49. North Carolina had an abundance of small distilleries, and many small distilleries operated across the nation.

The large total production created problems in the 1880s and 1890s as did similar trends in other industries. Overproduction, intense competition, and price wars encouraged concentration in the industry. The result was the formation of the Peoria-based "Whiskey Trust" (q.v.) and other consolidations such as the Kentucky Distilleries and Warehouse Company (q.v.). These mergers attempted to control production, induce efficiencies, and raise prices and profits, but legal and financial problems minimized their success.

The "Whiskey Ring" (q.v.) was another but even less fortunate merger of the period. Around 1870 government officials, mainly centered in St. Louis, permitted distillers to produce whiskey without payment of the federal tax, which was $.50 per gallon at the time. The profits on the untaxed whiskey were then distributed among liquor officials and distillers. President Ulysses S. Grant's Secretary of Treasury cracked the ring in the mid-1870s but not before the White House was implicated in the fraud.

The Bottled-in-Bond Act of 1897 was another, and more fortunate, event involving federal legislation. Distillers generally distributed their whiskey in barrels so that a storekeeper or bartender could modify the drink in a variety of ways to save money; and consumers were often unaware of such tampering. A few distillers, such as George G. Brown (q.v.), bottled their product before 1890, but the Bottled-in-Bond law encouraged bottling so that a consumer could buy whiskey with the assurance that it met certain standards. The act required that for a whiskey to be bottled-in-bond it had to be one hundred proof (50 percent alcohol in content), a minimum of four years old, and made at one place and all at one time. After bottling, the container was sealed with a green stamp attesting to tax payment and compliance with federal regulations. Later, in the Pure Food and Drug Act (q.v.) of 1906 and the Taft decision (q.v.) of 1909, further definitions and standards were spelled out for whiskey.

The taxation (see Appendix VII) of spirits has been an important factor in the history of the industry as well as for federal revenues. Between 1802 and 1862 taxes were either temporary in nature or very low, and there was no tax from 1818 to 1862. Afterward the tax increased steadily, except for the Prohibition era from 1919 to 1934, until it reached the current rate of $10.50 per gallon in 1951. Beginning in 1862, the government established a bonding period (q.v.) enabling a distiller to store his whiskey for a time before having to pay the tax. The length of time has been increased from one to three to eight and finally to twenty years in 1958, thus giving distillers more time to find markets before paying the tax.

In 1909, there were 613 distilleries in the United States. By 1914 the number had decreased to 434, and in 1919 only 34 companies existed. During the 1920s, approximately 20 to 30 distilleries operated under medicinal permits issued in compliance with the Volstead Act, in which Congress spelled out its specific guidelines for compliance with the Eighteenth Amendment. The temperance movement of the nineteenth century had gained strength in the 1890s and groups such as the Anti-Saloon League (q.v.) successfully agitated for state and local legislation against liquor, and then focused on a national law after 1910. The political efforts of such organizations were given a boost by the wartime spirit of sacrifice, thus aiding passage of the Prohibition amendment.

After the repeal of the Prohibition amendment in 1933, the distilling industry revived but underwent considerable change. Distillers' trade organizations showed genuine concern for consumer trends and urged producers to comply with the welter of federal and state laws geared to prevent earlier problems. Many of the older distilleries closed, but any remaining stock and many of the brand names were purchased by large companies. One could still drink Old Crow, but in the 1930s it was being produced by National Distillers Products Company (q.v.). The older small firms had generally sold out. A few reorganized, such as Jack Daniel (q.v.) and the Beam Distilling Company (q.v.), and some, like Willett (q.v.) and Maker's Mark (q.v.), would establish new firms in the post-Prohibition period. The distilling industry, however, would be led by the large firms, Seagram (q.v.), Hiram Walker (q.v.), Schenley (q.v.), National Distillers (q.v.), and an older firm, Brown-Forman (q.v.).

Although the natural advantages of the Kentucky region were not as important in an era of mechanical and technical improvements, the major companies tended to locate in the state. Lawrenceburg, Frankfort, Louisville, and Bardstown were centers of the industry, but the new firms maintained plants across the nation.

Also, the larger firms have stressed a varied line of products to meet increasing consumer demands for rum, vodka, gin, and cordials. Thus many distillers have purchased import and marketing rights to various brands and products in an effort to comply with consumer preference—which has shifted from the almost total demand for bourbon and whiskey blends in the pre-Prohibition years to a general taste for bourbon, light whiskey, wines, and the various white goods such as vodka, rum, and gin.

Note on Sources

Historical information on American distilling is sparse in relation to sources available on the brewing industry. The most comprehensive work is

Gerald Carson, *The Social History of Bourbon* (New York: Dodd, Mead & Company, 1963). It is a general survey, somewhat light in tone, but well researched and written. The most scholarly account is Henry G. Crowgey, *Kentucky Bourbon* (Lexington: University Press of Kentucky, 1971). Crowgey recounts the history of the Kentucky industry from the 1780s to 1850. H. F. Willkie, *Beverage Spirits in America* (New York: Newcomen Society of England, American Branch, 1949), is a brief but valuable account. Another short history is Morris V. Rosenbloom, *The Liquor Industry* (Braddock, Pa.: Ruffsdale Distilling Company, 1937). *Forty Years of Repeal* (New York: Jobson Publishing Corp., 1973) is also a brief account and chronicles the histories of the major firms after Repeal. Oscar Getz, *Whiskey: An American Pictorial History* (New York: David McKay Company, Inc., 1978), contains much useful information, as does Stan Jones, *Jones' Complete Barguide* (Los Angeles: Barguide Enterprises, 1977). W. J. Rorabaugh's *The Alcoholic Republic: An American Tradition* (New York: Oxford University Press, 1979) is an important study of the consumption of spirits from 1790 to 1830.

Given the popular interest in, and the economic importance of distilling, the relative paucity of source material and histories is somewhat surprising. The temperance movement must have cast a shadow on keeping records on the "liquor traffic." An 1881 history of American industry, Albert S. Bolles, *Industrial History of the United States* (New York: Augustus M. Kelley Publishers, 1966; reprint of 1881 edition), indicates the problem. Brewing and distilling receive four pages of treatment in a 900-page book. Bolles states: "It is not intended here to go into the moral side of the question of this industry in the United States, except merely to say the moral side of it, which cannot be entirely ignored, prevents the industry from being classed among those which are beneficial to our beloved country. It would be better for the land and for our countrymen were the industry to decline. Three-quarters of the spirits produced can be spared. Modern science shows that the temperate use of alcoholic beverages is not bad for certain temperaments; but it also shows that even the temperate use is bad for the majority of men, and that vice, pauperism, discontent, crude ideas, and content, and the gentleness and grace of life, enter and take up their abode. Less than one-quarter of the alcohol and distilled spirits now manufactured in this country is really needed as chemical solvents in the arts" (p. 522).

The Selected Bibliography contains references to further source materials.

Dictionary
of the History of
the American Brewing
and
Distilling Industries

A

Acme Brewing Company. (San Francisco). *See* Wunder Brewing Company.

Acrospire. This sprout grows from barley grains during germination (q.v.). When the acrospire reaches approximately the length of the kernel, the barley (q.v.) is considered ready for drying.

Act Supplemental to the National Prohibition Act. Congress enacted this addition to the National Prohibition Act (*see* Volstead Act) in November 1921. The legislation specified how whiskey dealers, who had obtained federal licenses for distribution of medicinal whiskey to druggists, could replenish their supplies.
SOURCES: John Ed Pearce, *Nothing Better in the Market* (Louisville, Ky., 1970); *Statutes at Large of the U.S.*, vol. 42, pt. 1 (April 1921-March 1922).

Adams, Samuel (September 22, 1722-October 2, 1803). The famous Massachusetts revolutionary leader for the American colonial cause for freedom from England was a maltster, as was his father.
SOURCES: John P. Arnold and Frank Penman, *History of the Brewing Industry and Brewing Science* (Chicago, 1933); Stanley Baron, *Brewed in America* (Boston, 1962).

Adjuncts. Unmalted grains, sugars, or syrups are used as supplements in the making of malt beverages. These materials, principally corn, rice, wheat, sorghums, and brewing sugars and syrups, are added to barley malt in the mashing (q.v.) stage of the brewing process (q.v.). The practice of using adjuncts developed in the late nineteenth century as brewers discovered that the use of such carbohydrate material had two advantages. Adjuncts were more economical in producing quality extract, and, just as importantly, these supplements improved the taste and physical stability of beer and resulted in a lighter beer that appealed to American consumers. Generally, adjuncts make up about 30 percent to 40 percent of the wort (q.v.) but decisions vary from brewer to brewer.
SOURCE: Harold M. Broderick, ed., *The Practical Brewer* (Madison, Wis., 1977).

Advertising. Brewers and distillers turned to extensive and professional merchandising techniques in the nineteenth century. Until 1850, the most common methods for increasing sales were advertisements in newspapers, local directories, and distribution of show cards for display in retail outlets. After the Civil War, brewers and distillers began to use labels, trade names, and slogans on a wide scale, using newspapers, billboards, cards, window displays and similar devices to sell the product. Brewers became interested in industrial expositions and competitions and cherished the winning of medals at the exhibitions. The Pabst "Blue Ribbon" label is an example of the interest in award-winning advertising and was first used in 1892. Hiram Walker's "Canadian Club" is an example of an early use of a trade name that became very successful. Anheuser-Busch (q.v.) used the name "Budweiser" and displayed the name on souvenirs, pamphlets, playing cards, bottle openers, calendars, matchboxes, and many other implements. By 1900, advertising was an important feature in merchandising and many firms hired professional companies. For example, Pabst employed the services of J. Walter Thompson in the 1890s. After Repeal (q.v.) in 1933, advertising liquor took on a professional tone and was geared to encourage the "sociable" nature of the drink. Brewers sponsored sports events and used advertisements to stress the respectability of drinking in the home. In both brewing and distilling, as competition and costs increased in the late twentieth century, one of the main keys to profit was in marketing the product and huge outlays were being made, especially by the large national firms. In 1946, advertising expenditures in the brewing industry totaled $50.4 million but then increased substantially until 1965 when brewers spent $255 million. Between 1965 and 1973, the total outlay decreased, but major increases occurred in the late 1970s. Miller was noted for large expenditures on advertising in the 1970s, and in 1978 Anheuser-Busch alone spent $117 million ($2.58 per barrel) for advertising. Marketing and advertising formed the key elements in the so-called beer wars in which Anheuser-Busch and Miller continued to fight for the number 1 position (held by Anheuser-Busch). Much of the huge expenditures were in radio and television advertising.

SOURCES: Stanley Baron, *Brewed in America* (Boston, 1962); Gerald Carson, *The Social History of Bourbon* (New York, 1963); Thomas C. Cochran, *The Pabst Brewing Company* (New York, 1948); U.S., Federal Trade Commission, *The Brewing Industry* (Washington, D.C., 1978); *Value Line* (June 15, 1979).

Agencies. National brewers (q.v.) employed these distribution representatives especially after the Civil War. The agencies, or branch offices, ranged from small icehouses near rail depots to extensive offices and warehouses geared to distribute beer for a distant brewer. Although some brewers had established outlets as early as the 1850s, the movement toward national status after 1870 made it necessary for the large firms to expand the system.

By 1893, Pabst (q.v.) had forty such branches and Anheuser-Busch (q.v.) had thirteen agencies in Texas in 1884. Distillers also employed distributing agents, often called commission merchants (q.v.), or just wholesalers. It was common for a distiller to contract with an agent who would purchase the company's whiskey, and then market it through his own devices. Before bottling and the adoption of trade names in the late 1800s, bulk whiskey (q.v.) from one distiller probably appeared under many names.

SOURCES: Stanley Baron, *Brewed in America* (Boston, 1962); Gerald Carson, *The Social History of Bourbon* (New York, 1963); Ronald Jan Plavchan, "A History of Anheuser-Busch, 1852-1933," unpub. Ph.D. dissertation, St. Louis University, 1969.

Aging. Aging is the process of storage for distilled spirits, primarily whiskey, prior to bottling. Mellowing of whiskey usually takes place in oak barrels. The emphasis on aging began in the early nineteenth century, and the term "old whiskey" was commonly used in advertising. The length of the aging term depends on the qualities of the whiskey and the methods of the distiller, but whiskies benefit in varying degrees from the longevity of the aging period. By federal regulations dating from the 1930s, with the exception of corn and light whiskey, American bourbon whiskies must be aged in new charred oak barrels. Uncharred or reused charred oak barrels may be used in aging corn and light whiskey. During the aging, whiskey, which is naturally clear and colorless before maturation, takes on a reddish amber color. As the liquid interacts with the wood, it absorbs various substances, most notably tannic acid. Before the general adoption of aging, whiskey, especially blended whiskey, was often artificially colored with caramel. *See also*, Barrels, Whiskey, Bourbon Whiskey, Corn Whiskey, and Federal Liquor Regulations.

SOURCES: Henry G. Crowgey, *Kentucky Bourbon* (Lexington, Ky., 1971); Harold J. Grossman, *Grossman's Guide to Wines, Beers, and Spirits* (New York, 1977); Department of Justice, *Proceedings . . . Concerning the Meaning of the Term "Whisky"* (Washington, D.C., 1909); H. F. Willkie, *Beverage Spirits in America* (New York, 1949).

Albany Brewing Company. Originally founded in 1796, this Albany, New York, firm was one of the city's oldest breweries, and produced ale and porter until introducing a lager beer in the 1890s. James Boyd built the original plant, and the Boyd family remained involved with the firm for most of its history. From 1863 to 1872 it was known as Coolidge, Pratt, & Company and then as Albany Brewing Company (1872-89), U.S. Brewing Company (1889-1903), Consumers Albany Brewing Company (1903-14), and Albany Brewing Corporation (1914-16). The firm closed in 1916.

SOURCES: Manfred Friedrich and Donald Bull, *The Register of U.S. Breweries* (Trumbull, Conn., 1976); *One Hundred Years of Brewing* (Chicago and New York, 1903; Arno Press Reprint, 1974).

Albany brewing industry. The industry's origins in Albany date from the 1650s when Dutch settlers Volkest Janse Douw and Jan Thomase Witbeck built a brewery to supplement imported Amsterdam beer with a domestic brew. They sold out to Harman Rutgers in 1675, who sold the plant soon after because he had inherited another plant from his father. He eventually moved from Albany, but was instrumental in the Dutch origins of Albany brewing. Albany beer apparently had a favorable reputation, and the city could support a number of breweries. The modern period of the city's industry began with James Boyd's brewery in 1796. His company, later known as the Albany Brewing Company (q.v.), became a successful and long-lived brewery. Other prominent brewers were John Taylor of John Taylor & Sons (q.v.) and Peter Ballantine (*see* Ballantine Brewing Company), who operated a brewery in Albany in the 1830s before moving to Newark, New Jersey, in 1840. Albany was noted for the production of ale until the early twentieth century. The city, which numbered just over 90,000 in population in 1900, had about twenty breweries in the 1890s, but only a few survived Prohibition. They were the Beverwyck Brewing Company (q.v.), Albany Brewing Company, Dobler Brewing Company (q.v.), and Hedrick Brewing Company (q.v.). By the mid-1970s, no brewery operated in the city.

SOURCE: Stanley Baron, *Brewed in America* (Boston, 1962); *One Hundred Years of Brewing* (Chicago and New York, 1903; Arno Press Reprint, 1974).

Alcohol and Tobacco Tax Division, Department of Treasury. In charge of federal liquor regulations from 1952 to 1968, this agency was succeeded by the Alcohol, Tobacco, and Firearms Division of the Treasury Department. In 1972 further reorganization resulted in a change of name to the Bureau of Alcohol, Tobacco, and Firearms (q.v.). *See also,* Federal Liquor Regulations.

Alcohol Tax Unit. The successor to the Federal Alcohol Administration, the ATU oversaw federal liquor controls and regulations from 1940 until 1952 until reorganization as the Alcohol and Tobacco Tax Division (q.v.) of the Department of Treasury. *See also,* Federal Liquor Regulations.

Ale. A top-fermentation (q.v.) beer brewed from malt cereal, ale has a more pronounced flavor and stronger aroma than lager beer (q.v.) and is slightly higher in alcoholic content. Of course, ale is brewed with a top-fermentation yeast. Fermentation occurs at a higher temperature than regular beer. Ale apparently originated in England and before the use of hops, in the sixteenth century, the term was used to describe virtually all fermented malt beverages. It was popular in New England until the 1940s and remains a popular drink in Canada and England, but presently accounts for only a small percentage of American consumption. In the nineteenth century, Albany (*see* Albany Brewing Industry), New York, was a leader in all production.

SOURCES: Will Anderson, *The Beer Book* (Princeton, N.J., 1973); Harold M. Broderick, ed., *The Practical Brewer* (Madison, Wis., 1977); Harold J. Grossman, *Grossman's Guide to Wines, Beers, and Spirits* (New York, 1977).

Alembic. This is the name for an early still (q.v.), apparently deriving from Arab terminology.

Altes Brewing Company. *See* Tivoli Brewing Company (Detroit).

Ambur Distilled Products, Inc. This family-owned and operated business was founded in November 1933 on the brink of Repeal. Samuel Joseph established the firm in Milwaukee, Wisconsin. In 1976 the company moved to a new plant in Glendale, Wisconsin. The firm operates as a bottler, rectifier, and wholesaler of a variety of distilled liquors and also does private label bottling for customers. The major brands are Cottontail Brandy, Southern Jubilee, Ambur's Cordials, Landmark Gin, and Starka Vodka. Arthur Joseph is president and treasurer, and Lorraine Joseph secretary-vice-president.

American Brewing Association. A brewers' groups founded this organization in 1930 to promote the interests and public relations efforts of near beer (q.v.). The association merged with the U.S. Brewers' Association (q.v.) in January 1941.

SOURCE: Stanley Baron, *Brewed in America* (Boston, 1962).

American Brewing Company. (Rochester). This New York brewery, founded in 1889 by Fred C. Loebs, survived Prohibition but closed in 1950.

American Brewing Company. (St. Louis). Casper Koehler established this St. Louis company in 1859. It was also known under the names H. Koehler & Brother, Excelsior, and Henry Koehler Brewing Association before the various Koehler interests were merged in the American Brewing Association in 1890. The company joined the Independent Breweries Company (q.v.) in 1907, but continued after repeal of Prohibition in 1933 as the ABC Corporation, and other names, until closing in 1940.

SOURCES: Manfred Friedrich and Donald Bull, *The Register of U.S. Breweries* (Trumbull, Conn., 1976); *One Hundred Years of Brewing* (Chicago and New York, 1903; Arno Press Reprint, 1974).

American Distilling Company. The Wilson family founded this distillery in Pekin, Illinois, in 1892. In the 1920s the company merged with other companies in the Peoria area and Russell R. Brown became chief executive in this period. He remained as chairman until retirement in 1974. In 1940 the company bought the Guckenheimer brand. Over the years the firm added brands such as King James Scotch, Bourbon Supreme, El Toro Tequila, and a number of liqueurs and other spirits to its marketing line. Bernard Goldberg became president in 1974, and he was succeeded in 1977 by Marshall Berkowitz, who previously had been president at Glenmore (q.v.). In early 1980, company officials announced plans for sale of the major portion of its assets and brands to Standard Brands Incorporated.

SOURCES: Deborah Goeken, "The Spirits Move Him," *Journal Star*, Peoria, April 19, 1978; Stan Jones, *Jones' Complete Barguide* (Los Angeles, 1977); *Wall Street Journal*, January 17, 1980.

American Medicinal Spirits Company. Col. R. E. Wathen formed this combination of whiskey warehouses and distilleries in 1927. Federal authorities called for the concentration of warehouses, and Wathen responded by forming AMS, which was located in Jefferson County, Kentucky. Among the plants included were R. E. Wathen (*see* Wathen Distilleries), Kentucky Distilleries and Warehouse Company (q.v.), which included other firms, Daviess County (q.v.), Hill & Hill, E. H. Taylor (q.v.), and Sunny Brook (q.v.). National Distillers Products Company (q.v.) bought a majority of the stock in AMS soon after formation, and then dissolved American Medicinal Spirits in 1936 as the parent company assumed control of its operations.

SOURCES: "Kentucky Leviathan," *Spirits* (April 1935); "Whiskey," *Fortune* (November 1933).

American Society for the Promotion of Temperance. A temperance group established in Boston in 1826, this society used emotional techniques and educational arguments to convince the public of the evils of drinking alcoholic beverages. Local societies emerged in the next decade as the movement gained strength, especially in the northeast.

SOURCES: John A. Krout, *The Origins of Prohibition* (New York, 1925); Alice Felt Tyler, *Freedom's Ferment* (New York, 1962; 1st ed., 1944).

American Spirits Manufacturing Company. An outgrowth of the Distillers' and Cattle Feeders' Company (*see* Whiskey Trust), the company was centered in Peoria, Illinois. American Spirits was formed in 1896 after the Whiskey Trust went into receivership (q.v.). It was organized under the laws of the state of New York to take control of the main plants of the former company. The company owned the Great Western (q.v.), Monarch (q.v.), Manhattan, and Hanover distilleries of Peoria, although each operated under its own name. A number of additional plants operated, but many

were sold or dismantled. In the 1920s it was one of the organizations liquidated as National Distillers Products Company (q.v.) was being formed.

SOURCES: Victor S. Clark, *History of Manufactures in the U.S.*, vol. 3 (New
York, 1929); Distilleries File, Peoria Historical Society; Ernest E. East, "Distilling
Fires in Corning Plant," *Arrow Messenger* (March 1937); Jeremiah W. Jenks and
Walter E. Clark, *The Trust Problem* (New York, 1929).

Amylase. This enzyme (q.v.) is a by-product of the germination (q.v.) of
grain, usually barley, in the early stages of production of alcoholic beverages.
Amylase converts the starch in grains to glucose, which can then be attacked
by yeast to produce alcohol. Starch itself cannot be fermented by yeasts. In
the 1830s, just as the chemical processes were becoming more understood,
the enzyme was called diastase (q.v.), meaning separation. Distillers and
brewers continue to use the terms diastase and amylase interchangeably.

SOURCE: Harold Grossman, *Grossman's Guide to Wines, Beers, and Spirits*
(New York, 1977).

Anchor Brewing Company. Originally founded in 1894 by Charles H.
Kranam, the small San Francisco brewery was on the verge of liquidation
when President Fritz Maytag took it over in 1965. The distinctive product of
the company historically, and presently, has been "steam beer" (q.v.), and
the company is apparently the last brewery to produce this top-fermentation
(q.v.) brew of the West Coast.

SOURCES: Michael Jackson, ed., *The World Guide to Beer* (Englewood Cliffs,
N.J., 1977); *Newsweek* (September 4, 1978).

Anheuser, Eberhard (September 27, 1805-May 2, 1880). A successful St.
Louis businessman who had migrated from Germany, Anheuser was a
manufacturer of soap and candles but invested in the Hammer & Urban
brewery in the mid-1850s. In 1860, he purchased the minority interests of
this shaky operation and was joined by William D'Oench, who withdrew in
1864. In the meantime, Anheuser's daughter, Lilly, had married Adolphus
Busch (q.v.), who was in the brewers' supplies business. Because Anheuser
continued in the soap and candle trade, Busch gradually became the leader
of the Anheuser-Busch (q.v.) brewery, and Anheuser retired in 1877.

SOURCES: Roland Krebs and Percy J. Orthwein, *Making Friends Is Our Business* (St. Louis, Mo., 1953); Ronald Jan Plavchan, "A History of Anheuser-Busch,
1852-1933," unpub. Ph. D. dissertation, St. Louis University, 1969.

Anheuser-Busch, Inc. By the late 1970s this famous St. Louis-based brewing company could boast decisively that it was still No. 1 in what has been
called the "Beer Wars" and the "Battle of the Beers." In 1978, Anheuser-
Busch marketed 41 million barrels of beer compared with Miller's (q.v.)
No. 2 production of more than 30 million barrels. The original company

was built in 1852 by Georg Schneider, who was soon succeeded by Hammer and Urban and then by Eberhard Anheuser (q.v.) in 1860. Anheuser, a German immigrant, was a successful soap manufacturer who had invested in the brewery and then took it over. In 1865 his son-in-law Adolphus Busch (q.v.) joined the company, first as a salesman; but he eventually became president. The brewery was incorporated as the E. Anheuser Company's Brewing Association in 1875 and then became the Anheuser-Busch Brewing Association in April 1879. Upon the retirement of Anheuser in 1877, Busch assumed sole leadership, and the energetic and aggressive entrepreneur propelled the brewery into national marketing. From thirty-second in production (44,961 barrels) in 1877, Anheuser-Busch surged to second place in 1895 among American breweries, with output of nearly 800,000 barrels of beer. Pabst (q.v.) was first, with nearly 1 million barrels in output; in 1901 Anheuser-Busch also broke the 1 million mark. To accomplish the transition to the status of national brewer (q.v.), Busch established distribution agencies (q.v.) across the nation and incorporated innovative advertising and technological procedures. Anheuser-Busch was apparently the first American brewery to utilize pasteurization (q.v.) in the bottling process and very early, around 1877, invested in refrigerated freight railroad cars to transport its beer to its agencies. A subsidiary, Manufacturer's Railway Company, was founded in February 1887 and is still operating. Two examples of successful advertising were the adoption of its brand name "Budweiser" and distribution of the painting *Custer's Last Fight*. The Budweiser name was first used by C. Conrad & Company in 1876 but was brewed for Conrad by Anheuser-Busch. When Conrad went bankrupt in 1883, Anheuser-Busch acquired the rights to the name and proceeded to bottle and market Budweiser as the company's primary beer. Reproductions of the painting *Custer's Last Fight* were distributed for tavern display. In 1885 Busch contracted with artist F. Otto Becker of the Milwaukee Lithograph Company to reproduce the scene, from an original painting by Cassily Adams. In succeeding years, more than 1 million prints, carrying the Anheuser-Busch credentials at the bottom, were distributed to retailers across the U.S. Meanwhile August A. Busch, Sr. (q.v.), was becoming instrumental in company affairs, and he took over as president in 1913 upon his father's death. In 1909 the company underwent substantial business reorganization to accommodate expansion, and in 1919 the current name, Anheuser-Busch, Inc., was adopted. During Prohibition in the 1920s, Busch kept the company open by producing a near beer (q.v.) called Bevo, the New Budweiser, a cereal beverage, soft drinks, malt syrup, corn sugar, yeast, and ice cream. Busch even manufactured trucks and bus bodies, although the primary business was based on some form of grain conversion. Upon the repeal of Prohibition in 1933, the company resumed beer production. In 1934 Adolphus Busch III (q.v.) became president, and he was succeeded by brother August A. Busch, Jr. (q.v.), in 1946. The latter served as chief executive until 1975 when August A. Busch III (q.v.) assumed that position. The company has introduced various new beers—popular-priced Busch in 1955, in addition to the traditional premium Michelob of 1896, then classic dark beers and Natural Light in 1977. Plant expansions included new breweries in Newark (1951), Los Angeles (1954), Tampa (1959), Houston (1966), Columbus, Ohio (1968), Jacksonville, Florida (1969), Merrimack, New Hampshire (1970), Williamsburg, Virginia (1972), and Fairfield, California (1976). Diversification has included the manufacture of malt products, baker's yeast, brewer's yeast, and other similar products; ownership of the St. Louis Baseball Cardinals since 1953; and tourist attractions in Florida, Missouri, Virginia, and California. Large-scale advertising has included the promotion of activities such as the Clydesdales, power boat racing, auto racing, hot air ballooning, and a variety of sports events. By 1979, Anheuser-Busch was being challenged by other nationals, especially Miller, but President August Busch had resolved to win the beer battle. In a 1978 article, Busch complimented Miller but stated "we will remain No. 1."

SOURCES: Anheuser-Busch, Inc., "Fact Books" (1977, 1978); "How Anheuser-Busch Stays on Top," *Fortune* (January 15, 1979); Stanley Baron, *Brewed in America* (Boston, 1962); "The Battle of the Beers," *Newsweek* (September 4, 1978); "Here Comes the King—of the Beer Business," *Nation's Business* (November 1978); Roland Krebs and Percy J. Orthwein, *Making Friends Is Our Business* (St. Louis, Mo., 1953); Ronald Jan Plavchan, "A History of Anheuser-Busch, 1852-1933," unpub. Ph.D. dissertation, St. Louis University, 1969; *One Hundred Years of Brewing* (Chicago and New York, 1903; Arno Press Reprint, 1974).

Anti-Saloon League. In 1893 this organization was founded in Oberlin, Ohio, for the primary purpose of abolishing saloons. H. H. Russell, a Protestant minister and anti-saloon lobbyist, was the founder of the initial league, which functioned as a state organization until the holding of the first national convention in 1895. Westerville, Ohio, near Columbus, became the site of the national office. The league focused on local option (q.v.), then state laws to abolish saloons, and gradually became the driving force behind the prohibition of alcoholic beverages on the state and national levels. The organization consisted of a network of state boards or committees that appointed state superintendents. The national office maintained a national superintendent and numerous other legal and lobbyist positions to foster the educational, propagandist, and political programs of the league. At its base, the league received firm support from religious congregations and activist groups. Wayne B. Wheeler (q.v.) became the league's most noted and powerful leader during the crusade for liquor control, and he epitomized the tactics of pressure politics geared to achieve nationwide

Prohibition (q.v.). The Anti-Saloon League proved to be the most important factor in the passage of the Eighteenth Amendment (q.v.).

SOURCES: Ernest H. Cherrington, *Evolution of Prohibition in the United States* (Westerville, Ohio, 1920); Norman H. Clark, *Deliver Us from Evil* (New York, 1976); Peter Odegard, *Pressure Politics: The Story of the Anti-Saloon League* (New York, 1928).

Areometer. This was a type of bottle used by distillers in the late eighteenth and early nineteenth centuries to determine proof (q.v.), or percentage of alcohol in whiskey.

Arrow Distilleries, Inc. Robert Silberstein was president of this Peoria-based distilling firm, founded in 1933. It operated other plants in St. Louis, Chicago, and Claremont, Kentucky. The firm, which marketed many brands, but mainly Clark's Pure Rye & Bourbon, apparently ceased operation in 1943. The company published the *Arrow Messenger*, a trade paper, in the 1930s.

SOURCE: Distilleries File, Peoria Historical Society.

Arthur, Timothy Shay (1809-85). Author of several books and articles dealing with alcohol, Arthur achieved fame upon the publication of *Ten Nights in a Bar-Room* in 1854. The tract focused on liquor and its problems for humanity. Temperance and prohibitionist forces used his work in the drive against the liquor traffic.

SOURCES: J. C. Furnas, *The Life and Times of the Late Demon Rum* (New York, 1965); Andrew Sinclair, *Prohibition: The Era of Excess* (Boston, 1962).

Associated Brewing Company. A number of breweries organized this Detroit-based merger, initially in 1962. The original firms in the merger were Pfeiffer's (q.v.) and the E. and B. Brewing Company (q.v.). Eventually, they were joined by Drewry's (q.v.), Jacob Schmidt (q.v.), Sterling (q.v.), Hampden-Harvard (*see* Harvard Brewing Company), F. W. Cook (q.v.), and Piel Brothers (q.v.). After suffering sales losses beginning in 1969, Associated sold all but the Piel's plant to the G. Heileman Brewing Company (q.v.) in 1971.

Association Against the Prohibition Amendment. Founded in 1920, the AAPA organized to fight the Eighteenth Amendment (q.v.), using pressure politics similar to those of the Anti-Saloon League (q.v.). The AAPA was spearheaded by a group of wealthy Americans, among them John J. Raskob, the Du Ponts, and many brewers and distillers. They argued that Prohibition (q.v.) was not working and repeal would expand employment and purchasing power. Critics suggested that the wealthy proponents of

Repeal were primarily interested in easing their own tax burden by reestablishing two heavily taxed industries. The organization proved instrumental in the passage of the Twenty-first Amendment (q.v.), which repealed Prohibition in 1933.

SOURCES: Norman Clark, *Deliver Us from Evil* (New York, 1976); Andrew Sinclair, *Prohibition: The Era of Excess* (Boston, 1962).

Atherton, J. M., Distillery. John M. Atherton built this LaRue County, Kentucky, distillery in 1867. In 1899, the Athertons became part of the Kentucky Distilleries and Warehouse Company (q.v.) as they merged their three plants (Atherton, Mayfield, and Windsor), with the consolidation. Many of the KD&W Company's plants became part of American Medicinal Spirits (q.v.) in 1927, and then National Distillers Products Company (q.v.) in 1929, but the Atherton distilleries were taken over by Arthur Cummins, Jr. The plants were apparently closed or sold in the late 1930s or during the 1940s.

SOURCES: "Cummins on Famous Site," *Spirits* (April 1935); *Kentucky's Distilling Interests* (Lexington, Ky., 1893); Harry H. Kroll, *Bluegrass, Belles, and Bourbon* (New York, 1967).

Atlas Distilling Company. The Woolner brothers (*see* Woolner Distilling Company) operated this Peoria, Illinois, distillery from 1891 to 1898. They sold the plant to Standard Distilling and Distributing Company (q.v.), an extension of the Whiskey Trust (q.v.). It operated under the Atlas name until about 1905. The plant was bought later by the U.S. Industrial Alcohol Company (q.v.) and then by Century Distilling Company in 1933. Century operated it until 1943 when it was evidently bought by National Distillers Products Company (q.v.).

SOURCES: Distilleries file, Peoria Historical Society; Ernest E. East, "Distillery Fires in Corning Plant," *Arrow Messenger* (March 1937).

Attenuation. As fermentation (q.v.) proceeds in whiskey-making (q.v.), the liquor tends to turn, or lose density.

Austin, Nichols & Company, Inc. This distilling firm traces its 1855 origin to the grocery, food-importing, and distributing company established by Friend D. Fitts, David Martin, and Oscar H. Clough. Their business operated in New York City. In 1933, after Repeal, Thomas F. McCarthy led the move into the wine and liquor business as Austin, Nichols became an importer, rectifier, and wholesaler in New York. Liggett & Meyers, of the tobacco industry, purchased Austin, Nichols in 1969. The company's distilling operation is based in Lawrenceburg, Kentucky. The firm's primary and most famous brand has been Wild Turkey, a straight bourbon; other products are Wild Turkey Liqueur and Campari. Richard J. Newman, formerly of National Distillers, Heublein, and Seagram, has been president since the mid-1970s.

SOURCES: "The Austin, Nichols Story," *Associated Beverage Publications* (January 1978); Liggett Group, *The Companies of Your Pleasure* (ca. 1978).

Ayer Rubber Car. In the 1870s John Ayer developed a refrigerated railroad car used to transport beer. It was encased in rubber and impervious to heat and cold. Anheuser-Busch used the car for a time, mainly because of its lighter weight.

SOURCES: Stanley Baron, *Brewed in America* (Boston, 1962); *Western Brewer*, vol. 2 (June 15, 1876).

B

Bacon, Roger (ca. 1214-94). A philosopher and English Franciscan monk, Bacon conducted studies in optics and alchemy and was accused of dealing in black magic. He spent time in Europe and is sometimes credited with introducing the art of distilling to the British Isles.

SOURCES: Henry G. Crowgey, *Kentucky Bourbon* (Lexington, Ky., 1971); R. Vashon Rogers, *Drinks, Drinkers and Drinking, or the Law and History of Intoxicating Liquors* (Albany, N.Y., 1881).

Baeuerlein, C., Brewing Company. Established in 1845 by Adam Baeuerlein, this Pittsburgh concern became one of the city's more famous breweries. It was incorporated in 1888 as C. Baeuerlein Bro. & Co., Star Brewery, and then joined the 1899 merger known as the Pittsburgh Brewing Company (q.v.).

SOURCE: "Pittsburgh, History of Beer and a Market," *American Brewer* (June and July 1960).

Ballantine, Peter, & Sons (Brewery). Originally founded in 1805 by Gen. John N. Cumming, this Newark, New Jersey, brewery was leased to Peter Ballantine in 1840. Ballantine had moved from Albany, New York, where he had been operating a brewery since 1833. Known especially for the production of ale (q.v.), Ballantine also produced porter (q.v.) and lager beer (q.v.). By the 1870s it was the nation's fourth largest brewery and continued to operate as a successful regional brewery in the twentieth century. Carl and Otto Badenhausen bought the business after Repeal and ranked among the top ten leading brewers until into the 1960s. In 1972, Falstaff (q.v.) purchased the Ballantine brand names.

SOURCES: Stanley Baron, *Brewed in America* (Boston, 1962); *One Hundred Years of Brewing* (Chicago and New York, 1903; Arno Press Reprint, 1974).

Baltimore brewing industry. The earliest recorded breweries were those of Leonard and Daniel Barnetz in 1744 and James Sterret in 1761. Eventually, the Gottlieb-Bauernschmidt-Strauss (q.v.) brewery would occupy portions of the former company. The city, which had more than 500,000 people by 1900, had many breweries. In 1880 more than thirty firms were in operation, but the number declined thereafter; and after Repeal in 1933, approximately ten breweries reopened. During the 1970s, Carling National Breweries (q.v.) and F. & M. Schaefer (q.v.) were the only companies operating brewing plants. In 1899, the Maryland Brewing Company (q.v.) was the result of a merger movement and in 1901 Gottlieb-Bauernschmidt-Strauss took over the existing breweries in that company. Eventually, the National Brewing Company (q.v.) branch of the latter company would merge with Carling National Breweries, Inc. (q.v.).

SOURCES: Manfred Friedrich and Donald Bull, *The Register of U.S. Breweries* (Trumbull, Conn., 1976); William J. Kelley, *Brewing in Maryland* (Baltimore, 1965); *One Hundred Years of Brewing* (Chicago and New York, 1903; Arno Press Reprint, 1974).

Barley. A cereal grass or grain used in the brewing and distilling of alcoholic beverages, barley came to be used for two reasons. It was not very suitable for the making of bread, and in the Middle Ages in Europe many countries decreed that wheat and other grains could not be used in brewing because they were needed for food. As it turned out, barley proved to be a very suitable grain for alcoholic beverages, especially for beer.

SOURCE: *One Hundred Years of Brewing* (Chicago and New York, 1903; Arno Press Reprint, 1974).

Barleycorn, John. The name, a personification of alcoholic beverages, originated in England in the late Middle Ages.

Barrel, Beer. The primary packaging (q.v.) for draft beer (q.v.) is usually a thirty-one gallon container. Formerly, barrels were made primarily of wood and had to be pitched (coated with tar) in order to prevent beer from touching the wood. Since about 1950, stainless steel and aluminum barrels, which withstand higher pressure, have eliminated the necessity of pitching (q.v.), are lighter, and have replaced wooden barrels. Other sizes of barrels used by brewers have been half-barrels (15 gallons), quarters (7¾ gallons), sixths, and eighths (3.8 gallons called ''ponies''). The varieties were more common before bottling and canning.

SOURCES: Thomas C. Cochran, *The Pabst Brewing Company* (New York, 1948); Harold J. Grossman, *Grossman's Guide to Wines, Beers, and Spirits* (New York, 1977); Edward H. Vogel, Jr., et al., *The Practical Brewer* (St. Louis, Mo., 1946).

Barrel, Whiskey. Whiskies are aged in new or used charred oak barrels of about fifty gallons. Except for corn and light whiskey (q.v.), by federal regulation all new whiskey must be aged in new oak barrels that have been charred, or burned, on the inside. The whiskey most often associated with the charred barrels is bourbon (q.v.). During the aging (q.v.) in wood, the alcohol mellows, and in charred barrels the liquor, usually bourbon, takes on a unique flavor and deeper hue as it extracts and absorbs color and flavors from the wood. It also absorbs certain substances, such as tannic acid. The origin of aging in charred barrels is a matter of dispute. Various colorful stories about an accidential fire in a Jamaica rum warehouse, a careless cooper who burned some staves (q.v.) while heating and bending them, are probably fanciful. A recent scholarly account maintains that the practice apparently took hold in the early 1800s. Harrison Hall, an early nineteenth-century author who wrote about the distilling process, directed distillers to char their oak barrels in order to sterilize and purify the interior. Whatever the case, the method became more widely used, especially in the making of Kentucky bourbon, and federal regulations dating from the 1930s eventually stipulated that the charred barrels must be used in making certain kinds of whiskey. *See also*, Bourbon Whiskey, and Federal Liquor Regulations.

SOURCES: *Bourbon, the World's Favorite Whiskey* (New York, ca. 1970); Henry G. Crowgey, *Kentucky Bourbon* (Lexington, Ky., 1971); Harrison Hall, *The Distiller* (Philadelphia, 1818); John Ed Pearce, *Nothing Better in the Market* (Louisville, Ky., 1970); "Whiskey," *Spirits* (August 1937).

Barton Brands, Ltd. Thomas S. Moore, who was also involved in the Mattingly and Moore Distillery (q.v.) founded the Bardstown, Kentucky, distillery in 1889. Moore's plant was called the Tom Moore Distillery. In 1920, with the advent of Prohibition, the whiskey was removed and the plant dismantled. Moore rebuilt the plant in 1934, but died shortly afterward. Oscar Getz and Lester Abelson bought and rebuilt the company in the 1940s. The firm owns two distilleries in Scotland and markets House of Stewart and Highland Mist. Its main brands are Kentucky Gentleman, Tom Moore, and a new light whiskey, QT. Getz, who was president of the firm, established the Barton Museum of Whiskey History on the site of the distillery in 1957. The museum features a great volume of items such as books, catalogs, price lists, bottles, and so on, which make up an impressive collection of distilleria (q.v.).

SOURCES: H. W. Coyte, "Nelson County Distilleries," unpub. paper, ca. 1970; Sam Elliot, *Nelson County Record* (Bardstown, Ky., 1896); Harry H. Kroll, *Bluegrass, Belles, and Bourbon* (New York, 1967); *Spirits* (March 1950).

Beadleston & Woerz (Brewery). This New York City brewing company originated in 1846. The company was first called Nash, Beadleston & Company and had previously been an agent for the sale of Troy, New York's Nash ale brewing company. After a number of reorganizations, the firm was named Beadleston & Woerz in 1878. By then Ebenezer Beadleston had been replaced by his son, William, and E. G. Woerz had entered the business. The brewery occupied the old New York State Prison on West Tenth Street. The firm, known as the Empire Brewery, continued until Prohibition in the 1920s but did not reopen.

SOURCE: *One Hundred Years of Brewing* (Chicago and New York, 1903; Arno Press Reprint, 1974).

Beam, James B. (1864-1947). The noted Kentucky distiller joined his father's (David M. Beam) business in the early 1880s. In the 1890s, he moved the distillery, and located it near Bardstown in Nelson County, Kentucky, so it would be close to rail transport. He remained active in the James B. Beam Distilling Company (q.v.) well into the twentieth century.

Beam, James B., Distilling Company. This Clermont County, Kentucky, distillery traces its origins back to the 1780s. Jacob Beam, who arrived in the American colonies in 1752, lived in Pennsylvania and Maryland before moving on to what would later be Washington County, Kentucky, in 1788. Beam, one of the many farmer-distillers (q.v.) of the period, sold his first whiskey in 1795. His son, David, joined him in the distillery business and became manager of the plant upon Jacob's death around 1818. David Beam's son, David M., who was born in 1833, also became a distiller. He moved the plant to the Bardstown, Kentucky, area in the early 1850s. James B. Beam (q.v.), David M.'s son, joined the business in the early 1880s and succeeded his father as manager of the plant in 1888. In the 1890s, James B. Beam moved the distillery so that it would be closer to recently built railroad lines. The business operated as Beam and Hart, later as J. B. Beam, and was also known as the Clear Spring Distilling Company. In 1913, T. Jeremiah ("Jere") Beam, James's son, came into the business, which marketed its whiskies as Jim Beam, Pebble-Ford, Jefferson Club, and Old Tub. After repeal of Prohibition in 1933, the James B. Beam Distilling Company was organized as one element of the Philip Blum Company, a combine of several liquor companies. The Blum Company maintained corporate headquarters in Chicago. In 1947 that company was liquidated, and the current James B. Beam Distillery Company was reorganized as a separate entity by Harry Blum and M. H. Rieger, who were joined by T. Jeremiah Beam. Other members of the Beam family, Carl and his son, Baker, have also been involved in the business. The firm proved to be very successful in the 1930s and 1940s, and another plant was purchased in Churchill, Kentucky, in 1953. Booker Noe, grandson of James B. Beam, manages the plant's distilling operation. In 1967, American Tobacco Company (now known as American Brands) purchased the Beam company. James B. Beam died in 1947, and his son, T. Jeremiah, died in May 1977. Julian J. McShane has been president since May 1977. *See also*, Early Times Distillery Company (John H. Beam's plant).

SOURCES: "Beam and Bourbon," *Spirits* (April 1935); "Beam Distilling Company, Inc.," *Kentucky Beverage Journal* (May 1957); Company historical information; Sam Elliott, *Nelson County Record* (Bardstown, Ky., 1896); "The James B. Beam Story," *Spirits* (December 1949).

Beck, Magnus, Brewing Company. Joseph Friedman established this Buffalo, New York, firm around 1840. In 1855, he sold out to Beck & Baumgartner, but Magnus Beck became sole proprietor in 1860. Beck had left Germany in 1850. He died in 1883, and the company was incorporated a few years later, with the Beck family retaining control. The company survived Prohibition, had a capacity of about 100,000 barrels by the 1940s, but closed in 1954.

SOURCES: Manfred Friedrich and Donald Bull, *The Register of U.S. Breweries* (Trumbull, Conn., 1976); *One Hundred Years of Brewing* (Chicago and New York, 1903; Arno Press Reprint, 1974).

Beer. This beverage is derived from the brewing and fermenting of malted grain or cereal, usually barley (q.v.) and other cereals. The term "beer" is used generically to refer to any fermented drink made from malted cereal grains and comes from the Latin word *bibere*, meaning "to drink." The brew is flavored with hops, and the alcoholic content in contemporary beers in America is generally about 4 to 5 percent by volume. In the U.S., beer is normally taken to mean lager beer (q.v.), which is brewed in a bottom-fermentation (q.v.) technique. Other types are classed as ale (q.v.), porter (q.v.), stout (q.v.), malt liquor (q.v.), bock (q.v.), steam beer (q.v.), or sometimes according to region of origin such as Pilsener (q.v.), or Dortmunder (q.v.). The origins of beer and brewing can be traced to ancient Egypt, where barley was used as a brewing cereal. And during the Middle Ages in Europe beer was a common beverage. Until about 1840, however, virtually all beer was of the top-fermentation (q.v.) variety—ale, porter, stout, and what was called stong, or common beer, brewed by the common brewer (q.v.). Then in the 1830s a new yeast (q.v.) was discovered in Germany and introduced in America, probably in 1840. This yeast settled at the bottom of fermenting vats and resulted in a lighter, more effervescent brew, known as lager because it had to be stored for a few months after fermentation. Lager became very popular in German countries and in the U.S. Today about 90 percent of American beer is of the lager type. *See also,* Small Beer, and Strong Beer.

SOURCES: Stanley Baron, *Brewed in America* (Boston, 1962); Harold J. Grossman, *Grossman's Guide to Wines, Beers, and Spirits* (New York, 1977); *One Hundred Years of Brewing* (Chicago and New York, 1903; Arno Press Reprint, 1974).

Beer Riot (Chicago). Although often termed the "Beer Riot," the event was mainly a protest against discriminatory taxation of liquor. Even though distilled spirits would also be taxed, the brunt of the 1855 legislation was passed as a result of Chicago Mayor Levi Boone's agitation against the liquor trade. The problem was that most of the liquor establishments were run by German and Irish natives and the laws would be enforced by a watch of "native Americans" who were associated with the nativist Know-Nothing party of the 1850s. The result was that German and Irish protesters, led by brewer John A. Huck (*see* Huck, John A., Brewing Company), marched on the courthouse. After a scuffle with police, twenty-four protesters were indicated, but the incident's main result was that the Know-Nothings lost support.

SOURCE: Richard Wilson Renner, "In a Perfect Ferment: Chicago, the Know-Nothings and the Riot for Lager Beer," *Chicago History* (Fall 1976).

Bergdoll, Louis, Brewing Company. This Philadelphia brewery, established in 1849 by Louis Bergdoll, Sr., was conducted as a partnership until Bergdoll assumed sole ownership in 1876. In 1877 the company ranked twenty-first among the nation's brewers, with production of 57,000 barrels of beer. The company was incorporated in 1881, and Bergdoll's sons, Louis and Charles, and sons-in-law managed the business. Louis, Sr. died in 1894. The company continued to operate under the same name until 1934, when it went out of business.

SOURCES: Manfred Friedrich and Donald Bull, *The Register of U.S. Breweries* (Trumbull, Conn., 1976); *One Hundred Years of Brewing* (Chicago and New York, 1903; Arno Press Reprint, 1974).

Bergner & Engel Brewing Company. This famous brewery of Philadelphia traced its origins to the mid-1840s when Charles Wolf and Charles Engel built a brewery and a distillery in the city. Engel had learned the brewer's trade in Germany and France. The firm of Engel & Wolf operated until Wolf retired in 1870, and Engel entered into a new brewery association with Gustavus Bergner—thus the firm of Bergner & Engel. Charles Wolf is the source of the story that credits John Wagner (q.v.) with being America's first lager brewer. Apparently, Wolf submitted his version to the editors of the *Western Brewer* for inclusion in *One Hundred Years of Brewing*, which they published in 1903. At any rate, the brewery of Bergner & Engel became a very prominent company, ranking third in beer production in 1877 and fifteenth in 1895 with outputs of about 120,000 and 250,000 barrels respectively. The brewery, which closed during the Prohibition era, apparently made a brief reopening in the early 1930s but closed soon afterward.

SOURCES: Fortune (May 1932); *One Hundred Years of Brewing* (Chicago and New York, 1903; Arno Press Reprint, 1974).

Bernheim Distilling Company. The Bernheim brothers, Bernard and I. W. (Isaac Wolfe), founded this distilling business in the post-Civil War period.

The brothers entered the business about 1872 in Paducah, Kentucky, as wholesalers and rectifiers. They used direct mail advertising to market whiskies across the Midwest. They developed their own brand, I. W. Harper, named for Isaac Wolfe and one of their salesmen whose last name was Harper. In 1897, they built their first distillery; the plant was located in Louisville and the company was incorporated, with I. W. Bernheim as president. The plant was largely shut down during Prohibition; in 1933 Chicago whiskey broker Emil Schwarzhaupt, formerly of National Distillers Products Company (q.v.), bought the name and assets but not the plant because he had already purchased a distillery. In 1937, Schenley Distillers Company (q.v.) purchased the brand, assets, and distilleries from him.

SOURCES: Stan Jones, *Jones' Complete Barguide* (Los Angeles, 1977); "Whiskey," *Fortune* (November 1933).

Bernheimer & Schmid (Brewery). Emanuel Bernheimer, a German immigrant, founded the New York City firm. He and August Schmid opened a plant in 1850, parted in 1856, but then rejoined in 1862. They operated five breweries, with the primary one known as the Lion Brewery. Their sons and nephews assumed control in the late 1870s. By 1895 the firm was the nation's sixth largest brewery. After 1905, it was generally called the Lion Brewery, but also the Greater New York Brewery, Inc., just before going out of business about 1942.

SOURCES: Manfred Friedrich and Donald Bull, *The Register of U.S. Breweries* (Trumbull, Conn., 1976); Harlow McMillen, "Staten Island's Lager Beer Breweries, 1851-1962," *The Staten Island Historian* (July-September 1969); *One Hundred Years of Brewing* (Chicago and New York, 1903; Arno Press Reprint, 1974).

Best Brewing Company (Milwaukee). *See* Pabst Brewing Company.

Best Brewing Company of Chicago. The brewery, founded in 1885 as Klockgeter and Company became the Best Brewing Company in 1890. The Chicago firm was owned by Charles Hasterlik, who also purchased the Fairmount Brewing Company in Cincinnati in 1902. The Chicago brewery remained under Hasterlik management until closing in the early 1960s. The Cincinnati brewery was evidently a short-lived operation, bought by Hasterlik during a Cincinnati labor dispute. He operated it as a union plant, thus guaranteeing a lively market among striking workers who were boycotting nonunion beer.

SOURCES: William L. Downard, *The Cincinnati Brewing Industry* (Athens, Ohio, 1973); Richard J. La Susa, "Nevermore the Local Lagers," *Chicago Tribune Magazine* (April 24, 1977); *One Hundred Years of Brewing* (Chicago and New York, 1903; Arno Press Reprint, 1974).

Betz, John F., & Son, Inc. (Brewery). John F. Betz learned the brewers' trade at the Yuengling (q.v.) brewery in Pottsville, Pennsylvania. In 1853 he opened a brewery in New York and sold it to L. H. Roehmer in 1880. In addition, in 1867 he established a brewery in Philadelphia that was the third largest in output among the city's eighty-five breweries in 1878. He had bought the old Gaul (q.v.) brewery that Frederick Gaul had purchased from Reuben Haines in 1785. Upon the sale of his New York plant in 1880, Betz moved to a new site in Philadelphia and produced lager (q.v.), in addition to ale (q.v.) and porter (q.v.). In 1886 he took over the Germania brewery but sold it to Henry Hess around 1900. Then in 1897 Betz, and his son John, bought the David G. Yuengling Company brewery in New York and operated it until 1903. Philadelphia's John Betz & Son, Inc. continued in operation until 1939.

SOURCES: Will Anderson, *The Beer Book* (Princeton, N.J., 1973); John P. Arnold and Frank Penman, *History of the Brewing Industry and Brewing Science* (Chicago, 1933); Manfred Friedrich and Donald Bull, *The Register of U.S. Breweries* (Trumbull, Conn., 1976); *One Hundred Years of Brewing* (Chicago and New York, 1903; Arno Press Reprint, 1974).

Beverwyck Brewing Company. Michael Nolan founded his brewery in Albany as a lager beer plant sometime in the 1870s or 1880s. The firm was built as an addition to the ale brewery operated by Nolan and T. J. Quinn. The ale plant was built in 1845 by James Quinn, who became Nolan's father-in-law. The Beverwyck company, named after Albany's Dutch name, survived Prohibition but sold out to F. & M. Schaefer (q.v.) in 1950; the latter company operated the plant until 1974. The Quinn & Nolan Ale Brewing Company closed with the coming of Prohibition in 1920.

SOURCES: Manfred Friedrich and Donald Bull, *The Register of U.S. Breweries* (Trumbull, Conn., 1976); *One Hundred Years of Brewing* (Chicago and New York, 1903; Arno Press Reprint, 1974).

Birk Brothers Brewing Company. Jacob Birk and his sons, William and Edward, established their brewery in Chicago in 1891. Birk, a German immigrant, was first involved in the Wacker & Birk Brewing & Malting Company, which was sold to Chicago Breweries Ltd. (q.v.) in 1889. The Birk Brothers Company remained in operation and under family management until it was closed in 1950.

SOURCES: Richard J. La Susa, "Nevermore the Local Lagers," *Chicago Tribune Magazine* (April 24, 1977); *One Hundred Years of Brewing* (Chicago and New York, 1903; Arno Press Reprint, 1974).

Blatz, Valentine (October 1, 1826-May 26, 1894). A Bavarian-born Milwaukee brewer who migrated to the U.S. in the late 1840s, Blatz came from a brewing family and worked in John Braun's Milwaukee brewery before opening his own business in 1851. Braun died shortly afterward; Blatz subsequently married his widow and merged the two companies. He was a very successful brewer and entrepreneur who expanded his company to the limit of the local demand and expanded thereafter by branching out into bottled beer (q.v.). Blatz is considered the first Milwaukee brewer to capitalize on the large-scale marketing possibilities of bottled beer. Production increased from 52,000 barrels in 1874 to 125,000 by 1880. In 1891, three years before his death, Blatz sold control of his brewery to Milwaukee and Chicago Breweries, Ltd., an Anglo-American syndicate. The name was to be continued and the firm was to have a Blatz as president for ten years. *See also*, Blatz, Val., Brewing Company.

SOURCES: "Blatz Brewing Company's Centennial," *American Brewer* (April 1951); Wayne Kroll, *Badger Breweries* (Jefferson, Wis., 1976); *One Hundred Years of Brewing* (Chicago and New York, 1903; Arno Press Reprint, 1974).

Blatz, Val., Brewing Company. John Braun founded this Milwaukee brewery in 1846. Valentine Blatz (q.v.) who emigrated from Bavaria, worked at Braun's plant from 1848 to 1851. Braun died in 1851 and Blatz, who had already opened his own small plant, subsequently married Braun's widow and merged the two breweries. The business prospered, and Blatz was a pioneer in the bottling and exporting of beer. He began exporting his beer, establishing agencies (q.v.) and outlets in New York, Boston, Chicago, and other distant cities, during the mid-1870s. From twenty-ninth in production among the nation's brewers in 1877 with about 47,500 barrels in output, Blatz climbed to seventh in 1895 with more than 350,000 barrels produced. The firm was incorporated in 1889. In 1890, Blatz sold a share in his company to a British-American syndicate known as the Milwaukee and Chicago Breweries, Ltd., and he was named president. During the Prohibition era in the 1920s, however, the company was run by Edward Landsberg of the Chicago and Milwaukee group. Landsberg kept the company in operation by producing near beer (q.v.), and various carbonated beverages. He also kept the Blatz name before the public by wide-scale advertising. Upon Landsberg's death in 1941, Frank M. Gaber became president. In 1945, Schenley Industries, Inc. (*see* Schenley Distillers Company) purchased control of Blatz from Landsberg's heirs, and Gabel retired in 1946. Schenley named Frank C. Verbest as president, and he was noted for vigorous leadership and sales expansion and was ultimately succeeded by James C. Windham in the 1950s. Pabst (q.v.) bought Blatz in 1958, but federal intervention forced Pabst to divest itself of the Blatz brand—which it did to G. Heileman (q.v.) in 1969. Windham became president of Pabst in 1958.

SOURCES: "Blatz Brewing Company's Centennial," *American Brewer* (April 1951); Wayne Kroll, *Badger Breweries* (Jefferson, Wis., 1976); *One Hundred Years of Brewing* (Chicago and New York, 1903; Arno Press Reprint, 1974).

Blended straight whiskey. This is a mixture of two or more straight whiskies primarily to achieve a distinct type of whiskey (q.v.) as individual whiskies are chosen for flavor, body, and mellowness. The result is a character different from a single straight whiskey. This type accounts for a small portion of whiskey sales, although it does serve as the base for a number of blends.

SOURCES: *Alexis Lichine's New Encyclopedia of Wines and Spirits* (New York, 1974); Frank Haring, ed., *Practical Encyclopedia of Alcoholic Beverages* (New York, 1959).

Blended whiskey. One of the two major subdivisions of whiskey along with straight whiskey (q.v.), blended whiskey contains at least 20 percent straight whiskey, and the balance is neutral spirits (q.v.). Generally, blends consists of 30 to 40 percent straight whiskey and are bottled at about 86 proof (q.v.). In blending, several straight whiskies are mixed with flavorless neutral spirits (q.v.), resulting in a light whiskey. A small amount of sherry may be added. Today about 20 percent of marketable whiskey is blended. Historically, blended whiskey was called rectified whiskey. Rectification (q.v.), or blending, was made possible in the early nineteenth century largely because of the introduction of the patent, or continuous, still (q.v.), which permitted a greater quantity and variety of whiskies to be made. Consumer preference shifted over the years. Before 1830 or so, virtually all whiskey was straight (q.v.), then with the lighter, and less costly, blends the market increased considerably for that type. Prior to, and then during Prohibition era in the 1920s when only straight whiskey could be legally produced (for medicinal purposes), consumer tastes tended to be more refined and straight whiskey was in demand. Since 1933, blends have cut into the market, reflecting a demand for lighter whiskies. The issue of blends came up in relation to the Pure Food and Drug Act (q.v.) of 1906. Aimed at preventing adulteration of food products, the original interpretation of the act held that rectified whiskey was not genuine whiskey—and could not be labeled as such. But, in 1909, President William Howard Taft (q.v.) rendered the "Taft decision" (q.v.), holding that blends and straights were legal whiskies within the meaning of the 1906 law—although certain labeling restrictions were necessary.

SOURCES: *Alexis Lichine's New Encyclopedia of Wines & Spirits* (New York, 1974); Gerald Carson, *The Social History of Bourbon* (New York, 1963); Harold J. Grossman, *Grossman's Guide to Wines, Beers, and Spirits* (New York, 1977); Stan Jones, *Jones' Complete Barguide* (Los Angeles, 1977); U.S. Department of Justice, *Proceedings . . . Concerning the Meaning of the Term "Whisky"* (Washington, D.C., 1909).

Blind pig. The nineteenth-century counterpart of the speakeasy (q.v.), evidently this term came into use in Maine during the 1850s as saloon and storekeepers attempted to evade the prohibitory Maine Liquor Law (q.v.).

Some proprietors charged customers admission to view a "blind pig," which entitled them to a free drink, which could not be sold directly.

Blitz-Weinhard Company (Brewery). Henry Weinhard, a German immigrant, founded this Portland, Oregon, brewery in the mid-1860s. Weinhard had worked and been involved in other breweries before becoming sole owner of his own in 1866. In 1909, Arnold Blitz also purchased a Portland brewery, and in 1928 the Blitz and Weinhard concerns merged to form the Blitz-Weinhard Company. The company claims the distinction of being the oldest brewery west of the Mississippi in continuous operation and is, in addition, Oregon's sole brewing company. In 1979, the Pabst Brewing Company (q.v.) purchased Blitz-Weinhard and intended to operate it as a subsidiary.

SOURCES: Will Anderson, *The Beer Book* (Princeton, N.J., 1973); *One Hundred Years of Brewing* (Chicago and New York, 1903; Arno Press Reprint, 1974).

Bock beer. Brewed originally in Bavaria for the Easter celebration, it is dark brown in color because roasted malt is used, and it is richer than lager beer (q.v.). Traditionally, the beer was made available in the spring from the first brew drawn from the vats after lagering through the winter, but it could be produced anytime, and there is no legal definition. The origin of the term is disputed; one version is that it was named after *Einbecker Bier* of Einbeck, Germany, sometime around 1250. Bock is also the German word for male goat; thus the picture of a goat on most bock beer labels.

SOURCES: Frederic Birmingham, *Falstaff's Complete Beer Book* (New York, 1970); Harold J. Grossman, *Grossman's Guide to Wines, Beers, and Spirits* (New York, 1977); *One Hundred Years of Brewing* (Chicago and New York, 1903; Arno Press Reprint, 1974); Edward H. Vogel, Jr., et al., *The Practical Brewer* (St. Louis, Mo., 1946).

Bond & Lillard Distillery. The Hon. W. F. Bond founded a distillery in Anderson County, Kentucky, around 1870. He was later joined by Christopher Lillard. Their whiskey became popular in Chicago and other areas of the Old Northwest, largely because of the firm's marketing arrangement with James Levy Bro., a Cincinnati distribution company. Bond became sole owner in 1885. The distillery and brand were sold to Kentucky Distilleries & Warehouse Company (q.v.) in 1899 and were later administered by American Medicinal Spirits (q.v.), which in turn was purchased by National Distillers Products Company (q.v.) in 1927.

SOURCES: "Distilleries of Old Kentucky," *Spirits* (April 1935); "Great Names in Whiskey," *Spirits* (July 1937).

Bonded warehouse. The federal government licenses warehouses to protect itself against evasion of tax and duty payments. In the case of alcoholic beverages, stocks may be stored without paying the tax and are said to be "under bond."

Bonding period. This is the period of time whiskey (q.v.) may be stored in a warehouse before federal taxes must be paid. Thus a distiller was given some time to find a purchaser before having to pay the tax. In 1868, in connection with the revenue act that imposed a tax of $0.50 per gallon on whiskey, the bonding period was set at one year; in 1879 it was increased to three years and then to eight years in 1894. Hence after eight years distillers had to pay the federal tax even if they continued to age the whiskey in the warehouse. The 1894 revision from three to eight years was enacted because distillers, in unfavorable financial straits because of the national depression, had trouble meeting tax obligations. The bonding period was extended again in October 1958 by the passage of the Forand Act. At that time, a number of distillers, who had a large supply of aging whiskey, argued that the period should be abolished or at least extended. Anticipating wartime restrictions, many had overproduced "hedge" whiskey during the Korean war. Lewis S. Rosenstiel (q.v.) of Schenley Distillers (q.v.) was a major proponent, whereas others, such as Seagram (q.v.) and Brown-Forman (q.v.), who had lower warehouse stocks, were relatively unconcerned. They argued that those distillers who had overproduced earlier had possibly made unfavorable business decisions. The result was the Forand Bill permitting tax-free warehousing for up to twenty years. It was signed into law on September 2, 1958, and took effect July 1, 1959. The revision meant that distillers with larger stocks on hand would not be pressured by so-called forceout of whiskey from the warehouse, and consequent early tax payment.

SOURCES: Gerald Carson, *The Social History of Bourbon* (New York, 1963); "Forand Bill Creates Many Advantages," *Spirits* (September 1958); Stan Jones, *Jones' Complete Barguide* (Los Angeles, 1977); "The Seagram Saga," *Spirits* (February 15, 1966).

Bootlegging. The word derives from the practice of smugglers and Indian traders who hid liquor inside tall boots, and it refers to the selling or transporting of illegally produced alcoholic beverages. The term was used widely during the era of Prohibition (q.v.) from 1920 to 1933, although it has been commonly used locally and regionally in areas that prohibit the sale or manufacture of alcoholic beverages. During the period of national Prohibition, bootleg liquor probably totaled 100 million gallons per year. Illicit bootlegging organizations often controlled breweries and distilleries, and transported the product to retail speakeasies and outlets. The practice persists, but has declined considerably since Prohibition. *See also,* Moonshine.

SOURCES: Herbert Asbury, *The Great Illusion* (New York, 1950); *Dictionary of American History*, vol. 1 (New York, 1976); Oscar Getz, *Whiskey: An American Pictorial History* (New York, 1978).

Booze. This word for hard liquor was coined during the presidential "log cabin and hard cider" campaign of 1840 when Philadelphian Edmund C. Booze came out with a bottle shaped in the form of a log cabin. The "booze" bottle soon became interchangeable with the drink itself. Some sources indicate the term was used by the Dutch in the sixteenth century.

SOURCES: Gerald Carson, *The Social History of Bourbon* (New York, 1963); Norman Clark, *Deliver Us from Evil* (New York, 1976); Oscar Getz, *Whiskey: An American Pictorial History* (New York, 1978); William and Mary Morris, *Morris Dictionary of Word and Phrase Origins* (New York, 1971).

Boston Beer Company. This brewing corporation was founded in Boston, Massachusetts, in 1828. A group of proprietors invested in the firm, which was the nation's seventeenth largest in 1877. The company revived after Prohibition (q.v.) but closed in 1956.

Boston brewing industry. Boston had a few breweries up to the American Revolution, but the industry declined afterward. The city acted mainly as a distribution center for other beers in this period. Boston's immigrants were mainly of Irish and Italian descent, but still a number of German lager beer (q.v.) breweries were established in the mid-to-late nineteenth century. In 1890, for example, twenty-one breweries were in operation, although none would be classified as a national brewer (q.v.), nor was any among the largest brewers in output. Most notably, two mergers occurred, the New England Breweries, Ltd. (q.v.) in 1890 and Massachusetts Breweries Ltd. (q.v.) in 1901. British investors supported each consolidation. The former included Roessle's (q.v.), Haffenreffer & Company (q.v.), and Suffolk, and the latter had about ten breweries in the combine. By 1935 the number of firms had declined to three, and by 1973 no brewery operated in Boston. *See also*, Boston Beer Company, and Rueter & Alley.

SOURCES: Will Anderson, *The Beer Book* (Princeton, N.J., 1973); Stanley Baron, *Brewed in America* (Boston, 1962); Manfred Friedrich and Donald Bull, *The Register of U.S. Breweries* (Trumbull, Conn., 1976).

Bottled beer. This method of packaging dates to the eighteenth century, but was of increasing importance after 1870 or so. Initially the procedure was performed by hand as workers made use of a hose from a barrel to fill the bottles. After filling, a simple pressing device was used to insert a cork and then a wire was attached. Following pasteurization (q.v.), labels were glued on and the neck of the bottle covered with tinfoil. As the national market grew because of urbanization and rail transport, bottled beer increased in popularity, especially with the national brewers (q.v.). Bottle-washing and bottle-capping machines promoted cleanliness; and the pasteurization process, which killed off growing organisms, permitted beer stability and consistency, thus making bottled beer more practical on a wide scale. Beer bottling provided a ready market for bottle manufacturers, cork and label manufacturers, and makers of bottle washers, fillers, and similar machines. Stoppers for bottles presented a special problem until the introduction of William Painter's "Crown" stopper in 1892. The tin cover contained a thin cork which sealed the bottle and automatic stoppering devices speeded up the bottling process. Beer bottling was also given a boost when Michael J. Owens (q.v.) introduced a successful automatic bottle-making device in 1903. In 1915, 15 percent of all beer was bottled, and the figure rose to about 38 percent in 1937, and 65 percent in 1962. Canned beer (q.v.) became increasingly popular after 1940. *See also*, Packaging.

SOURCES: American Can Company, *A History of Packaged Beer and Its Market in the U.S.* (New York, 1969); Stanley Baron, *Brewed in America* (Boston, 1962); "The Beer Bottle, Its History," *American Brewer* (March 1963); Thomas C. Cochran, *The Pabst Brewing Company* (New York, 1948); Wayne Kroll, *Badger Breweries* (Jefferson, Wis., 1976); *One Hundred Years of Brewing* (Chicago and New York, 1903; Arno Press Reprint, 1974).

Bottled-in-Bond. The term refers to federal regulations certifying that certain whiskey has been bonded, ensuring that it has been stored in a bonded warehouse (q.v.) for at least four years, and has been bottled at one hundred proof (q.v.) under government supervision. Such bonding is not a guarantee of quality, but rather a guarantee that specified minimum standards have been met. The genesis of bonding dates to the late nineteenth century when two factors were instrumental in the move toward some sort of federal regulation. First, taxation and the Panic (Depression) of 1893 led to a change in the bonding period (q.v.). By the 1890s taxes had to be paid on whiskey after being in "bond," or locked in a warehouse, for three years, even if the whiskey had not been sold. The Panic of 1893 created a greater burden as distillers found it difficut to come up with tax payments. As a result of successful lobbying efforts in 1894, the bonded period was extended to eight years and a system of warehouse receipts (q.v.) was allowed whereby distillers could use their aging whiskey as collateral for tax payments. The other factor in encouraging bonded legislation came about as a result of the problem within the distilling business. After paying federal taxes on a barrel, distillers would usually sell whiskey in bulk form to retailers and rectifiers who in turn could water or otherwise change the nature of the product. To prevent such adulteration, and subsequent public distrust of whiskey in general, Col. Edmund Haynes Taylor, Jr. (q.v.), and other distillers, argued for federal regulation. Taylor, who was known for his "pure goods," joined with Secretary of Treasury John G. Carlisle (q.v.) to push for a bottled-in-bond bill. These efforts culminated in the Bottled-in-Bond Act of 1897, which was signed into law by President Grover Cleveland. The act specified that bonded whiskey had to be aged four years in a government-supervised bonded warehouse; the whiskey had to be made at one place and all at one time, bottled at 100 proof; and the name of the distiller had to be noted. A green stamp, bearing the portrait of Secretary Carlisle, was, and is, affixed to the bottle certifying that the provisions of the act had been followed. Among whiskies, only straight whiskey may be bonded, but other distillates may be so if they meet the requirements of the 1897 act. The legislation was very important at the turn of the century when quality distillers found it advantageous to assure the public that certain whiskies could be "counted on."

SOURCES: "The Bottled in Bond Act," American Wine and Liquor Journal (June 1938); Gerald Carson, The Social History of Bourbon (New York, 1963); Stan Jones, Jones' Complete Barguide (Los Angeles, 1977).

Bottom fermentation. This is both a particular strain of yeast (q.v.) and a fermentation process employed primarily in the brewing of lager beer (q.v.). The process was apparently introduced in Munich and Vienna in the 1830s by Anton Dreher (q.v.) and Gabriel Sedlmayr (q.v.). During bottom fermentation, the yeast settles in the bottom of the fermenting vat; the brew ferments at a lower temperature (about 45° to 60° Fahrenheit) than top-fermentation (q.v.) products, and fermentation takes approximately six to ten days. The resulting lager beer became popular, was noted for its lighter qualities, and was evidently introduced in the United States by John Wagner (q.v.) of Philadelphia in 1840.

SOURCES: Harold M. Broderick, ed., The Practical Brewer (Madison, Wis., 1977); Thomas C. Cochran, The Pabst Brewing Company (New York, 1948); One Hundred Years of Brewing (Chicago and New York, 1903; Arno Press Reprint, 1974).

Bourbon Institute, The. Leaders of the bourbon industry formed this trade organization in 1958 to further the interests of bourbon (q.v.), a distinctive American beverage. The agency was formed owing to the efforts of Schenley's (q.v.) Lewis Rosenstiel (q.v.). The primary objective was to promote the marketing of bourbon, especially for the international market. The Bourbon Institute joined with the Distilled Spirits Institute (q.v.) and the Licensed Beverage Industries (q.v.) in 1973 to form the Distilled Spirits Council of the U.S., Inc. (q.v.).

SOURCES: Frank Kane, Anatomy of the Whiskey Business (Manhasset, N.Y., 1965); Spirits (November 1958).

Bourbon whiskey. Current standards, dating mainly from federal liquor regulations (q.v.) of the 1930s, stipulate that bourbon, which consists mainly of corn and lesser amounts of rye and other grains, is whiskey produced from a fermented mash (q.v.) consisting of at least 51 percent corn, distilled at not more than 160 proof (q.v.), and aged in new charred oak barrels (q.v.). The origin and the history of bourbon are colorful and controversial. The traditionally accepted version of origin has it that Rev. Elijah Craig distilled the first bourbon at Georgetown, Kentucky, in 1789. Craig supposedly was one of the first to use corn as the main ingredient in his whiskey rather than the more common Pennsylvania practice of using primarily rye and barley. A recent scholarly account by Henry Crowgey discusses the "legend" and concludes that bourbon was probably first advertised in 1821, and the practice of using corn was a fairly general one, although first associated with Bourbon County, Kentucky, originally a very large portion of the state. Ironically, Craig's distillery was not in Bourbon County. Nevertheless, by the 1840s the term was used more widely as descriptive of a regional whiskey. During the early nineteenth century, in addition to the use of corn, another distinguishing characteristic in bourbon processing came into wider practice; namely, the aging (q.v.) of whiskey in charred, or burned, oak barrels. Such aging apparently gave the whiskey a reddish color and a distinctive taste. By the 1890s federal regulations were passed to define the product (*see* Bottled-in-Bond), and later laws in 1906 and 1909 set standards for whiskey and its various types. In the 1930s federal laws were written in substantially their current form. Bourbon over the years became known as a distinctly American whiskey, and in 1964 Senator Thruston Morton and Representative John C. Watts of Kentucky introduced resolutions, which were passed in Congress, declaring bourbon whiskey to be a distinctive product of the United States and stipulating that no imported whiskey could be designated as "bourbon whiskey." *See also*, Pure Food and Drug Act and Taft Decision.

SOURCES: Gerald Carson, *A Social History of Bourbon* (New York, 1963); Henry G. Crowgey, *Kentucky Bourbon* (Lexington, Ky., 1971);"Whiskey," *Spirits* (August 1937); H. F. Willkie, *Beverage Spirits in America: A Brief History* (New York, 1949).

Bowman, A. Smith, Distillery. A. Smith Bowman, Sr., founded the Sunset Hills, Virginia, distillery after the repeal of Prohibition in the early 1930s. Smith had been involved in distilling prior to the passage of the Eighteenth Amendment (q.v.), and moved to Fairfax County, Virginia, in 1927. He purchased 4,000 acres of farmland known as Sunset Hills. To supplement the farm and its corn production, Bowman built a distillery, which was opened in 1935. The white oak timber of the farm could be used in the making of cooperage for aging (q.v.) the whiskey, the primary brand being Virginia Gentleman. In 1947, the farm and distillery were merged in a partnership with the founder and his sons, E. DeLong and A. Smith, Jr., the partners. The same year, the firm purchased an additional farm. The firm was incorporated in 1949, and upon the death of A. Smith Bowman, Sr., in

1952, E. DeLong became president, a position he has held until the present (1979). A. Smith Bowman, Jr., has been chairman. In 1960 Sunset Hills Farm was sold and the town of Reston, Virginia, was built on the land. As a relatively small distilling operation, the company depends on the appeal of a traditional and consistent drink.

SOURCES: A. Smith Bowman, Jr., "A History of Sunset Hills Farm," *Historical Society of Fairfax County, Va. Yearbook*, vol. 6 (1958-59); Mary Bralove, "Bowmans Raise the 'Old South' Spirits," *Wall Street Journal*, October 14, 1975; Richard Brookhiser, "Americana: Virginia Gentleman," *National Review* (May 12, 1978).

Box malting. *See* Pneumatic Malting.

Brand, Michael, Brewing Company. Valentin Busch originally founded this Chicago brewery in 1851. Two years later he was joined by Michael Brand. In 1871 they dissolved the partnership and Busch took control of their plant in Blue Island. He died in 1872. Meanwhile, Brand's brewery was destroyed in the Chicago Fire of 1871; but he rebuilt the plant and operated it until selling out to the U.S. Brewing Company, a consolidation, in 1889. The U.S. Brewing Company continued to operate until 1955.

SOURCES: Manfred Friedrich and Donald Bull, *The Register of U.S. Breweries* (Trumbull, Conn., 1976); *One Hundred Years of Brewing* (Chicago and New York, 1903; Arno Press Reprint, 1974).

Brandy. This product is made from the distillation of a fermented mash (q.v.) of grapes. If other fruits are used, the product must be labeled peach brandy, cherry brandy, and so on. Brandy must be distilled at less than 190 proof and bottled at not less than 80 proof.

Brauer Gesellen Union. The first official brewery workers' union was formed in Cincinnati, Ohio, in December 1879. John Alexander was president of the union, which was organized in the aftermath of the nationwide railroad workers strike of 1877. The union joined the local Central Trades Assembly, and later affiliated for a short time with the Knights of Labor before joining Samuel Gompers's American Federation of Labor. The union called a strike and presented demands to local brewers in 1881 calling for a 10½-hour workday, $60 per month minimum wages, and worker freedom to board and room wherever he chose. Although a few weaker firms acceded, the union made little real headway, lost members, and remained largely inactive until 1886. Strikes followed in 1888, 1892, and 1902 centering on union recognition, better pay, hours, and working conditions. Recognition was achieved in 1892, along with other limited gains.

SOURCES: William L. Downard, *The Cincinnati Brewing Industry* (Athens, Ohio, 1973); Hermann Schlüter, *The Brewing Industry and Brewery Workers' Movement in America* (Cincinnati, 1910).

Breweriana. The term signifies any and all items related to beer and brewery packaging and advertising. According to Will Anderson, such items are "bottles, cans, trays, signs, ads, labels, glasses, coasters, taps, openers, bottle tops, mugs, etc." They are collected by enthusiasts.

SOURCES: Sonja and Will Anderson, *Beers, Brewers, and Breweriana*, and *The Beer Book* (Princeton, N.J., 1973); Wayne Kroll, *Badger Breweries* (Jefferson, Wis., 1976).

Brewers' schools. The first American brewing schools were founded in the 1860s. John E. Siebel (q.v.) established an early laboratory in 1868, later known as the Siebel Institute of Technology. Anton Swarz (q.v.) opened a practical brewing school in New York in 1876 and established the first scientific station for brewing, the U.S. Brewers Academy, in 1880. Subsequently it was known as Swarz Laboratories. Others were the Wahl-Henius Institute (q.v.) of Chicago (1886), the National Brewers' Academy and Consulting Bureau in New York (1887), Hantke's Brewers' School and Laboratories in Milwaukee (1896), Wallerstein Laboratories (q.v.) in New York (1902); the Scientific Station for Pure Products in New York (1904), and Carl Nowak's Chemical Laboratories in St. Louis (1919). The opening of the schools, laboratories, and stations coincided with, and supported, the late nineteenth-century advances in brewing. *See also*, Brewing Science and Technology.

SOURCES: John P. Arnold and Frank Penman, *History of the Brewing Industry and Brewing Science* (Chicago, 1933); Frederic Birmingham, *Falstaff's Complete Beer Book* (New York, 1970).

Brewery workers' movement. During the 1850s and 1860s brewers in a number of cities such as Cincinnati and St. Louis formed mutual aid societies that had an undertone of unionism. The first real union, however, was founded in Cincinnati in 1879 as the Brauer Gesellen Union (q.v.). In the 1880s, brewery workers in New York, Baltimore, Chicago, Newark, St. Louis, and other urban brewing centers followed the lead and formed local unions; and in 1886 delegates from five locals organized the National Union of United Brewery Workmen. The objectives were to (1) organize, (2) enlighten brewery workers, and (3) reduce working hours and increase wages. Strikes, boycotts, and often bitter struggles occurred in 1887-88 in the main brewing centers as unions struggled to gain recognition from brewers. The drive of the late 1880s proved unsuccessful, and the U.S. Brewers' Association (q.v.) encouraged opposition among its members. Between 1890 and 1910, however, the unions managed to gain most of their aims for recognition, better hours, wages, and the freedom for workers to lodge and board where they chose. Wages generally increased from $40-$55 per month in 1880 to $60-$72 in 1910; hours decreased from 14-18 hours per day to 9-10 hours per day during the same period. *See also*, National Union of United Brewery Workmen of America.

SOURCES: Stanley Baron, *Brewed in America* (Boston, 1962); Thomas C. Cochran, *The Pabst Brewing Company* (New York, 1948); William L. Downard, *The Cincinnati Brewing Industry* (Athens, Ohio, 1973); Hermann Schlüter, *The Brewing Industry and the Brewery Workers' Movement in America* (Cincinnati, 1910).

Brewery Workers' Union. *See* National Union of United Brewery Workmen of America.

Brewery Workmen's Union of New York and Vicinity. New York's first brewery union was formed in March 1881. The immediate cause was a fire at Peter Doelger's (q.v.) brewery in which four workers died, according to one report, because of lax management. Brewers fired the leaders of the new union, which in turn called for a boycott of beer in those breweries where the releases had occurred. The tactic worked, and the union then presented a list of demands for a twelve-hour day and higher pay. The owners refused, and the union called for a strike, which ended in failure five weeks later. The union died soon afterward and was not revived until 1884 as Brewers' Union No. 1. After another boycott against Doelger's, the union gained membership and strength, signing a favorable contract with the Brewers' Association in 1886.

SOURCES: Stanley Baron, *Brewed in America* (Boston, 1962); Herman Schlüter, *The Brewing Industry and Brewery Workers' Movement in America* (Cincinnati, 1910).

Brewing Industry Inc. The trade association was established in 1936 to promote brewing interests in a positive and direct manner through public relations efforts. The group was led mainly by western and midwestern brewers who believed the U.S. Brewers' Association (q.v.) was not giving sufficient energy to dealing with industry problems, especially with respect to prohibitionist forces. August A. Busch, Jr. (q.v.), was president, and Harris Perlstein, representing Pabst, was treasurer of the Chicago-based organization. They hired Bernard Lichtenberg of the Institute of Public Relations, and he drew up what was known as the Nebraska Plan (q.v.), based on self-regulatory measures. Brewing Industry Inc. settled the major differences with the U.S. Brewers' Association in 1938, and the two merged in January 1941.

SOURCES: Stanley Baron, *Brewed in America* (Boston, 1962); Thomas C. Cochran, *The Pabst Brewing Company* (New York, 1948); "The First Century: A History of the U.S.B.A.," *American Brewer* (January and February 1962).

Brewing process. Generally, the process of brewing consists of boiling grains and cereals, then inducing fermentation (q.v.), which converts the sugars into alcohol. Basically, beer is made from malted barley and various other cereals that are flavored with hops (q.v.). The process involves grinding malt, stirring or mashing (q.v.) it in hot water until the starch has been converted to malt sugar (maltose) by the malt enzymes, and then drawing off the wort (q.v.) which is boiled and infused with hops. Afterward, the wort is cooled and special yeast is added to begin fermentation. The beer is then stored (lagered), filtered, carbonated, and packaged. Carbon dioxide may be produced by kraeusening (q.v.), or some other procedure. The various steps in the process are: First, barley (q.v.) is the principal grain used in brewing and the first and distinct step is malting (q.v.) this grain. After separating out impurities and inferior grains, the best grain is steeped in water. In the early stages of American brewing, the wet grain was spread out on the floor of the malthouse where it germinated, or sprouted, but floor malting (q.v.) was gradually phased out in the late nineteenth and early twentieth centuries. During germination (q.v.), enzymes (q.v.), amylases (q.v.) or diastase (q.v.), are formed and convert starches of the barley into fermentable sugars. In its original state, starch is unfermentable. The germinated grain, known as green malt (q.v.), is then dried in a kiln (kilned), until light or dark malt is produced. After being ground into meal, the malt goes through a process known as mashing (q.v.). Second, in the mashing stage, the malt is put in a mash tun (q.v.), or tub, where it is mixed with hot water and other cereals known as adjuncts (q.v.). Historically, this was a laborious and time-consuming process in which some of the mash was drawn off, boiled, and put back in the mash tub. Third, the mash is then pumped into a lauter tun (q.v.) in which the solution is strained off; the resultant liquid is called wort (q.v.). The solids, or "spent" grains are rinsed, or sparged, with water in an effort to extract as much sugar as possible, and to dilute the wort. The water from this practice, known as sparging (q.v.), is added to the wort in the brew kettle; and hops (q.v.) are added at this point to flavor the beer. Fourth, the wort is boiled for 1 to 1½ hours and hops are added for flavor. The wort then passes through a hop straining device known as a hop jack (q.v.), and the boiled wort is then cooled and transferred to fermentation vats. Fifth, fermentation begins after yeast (q.v.) is added. For making lager beer (q.v.), a special yeast called bottom-fermentation yeast is used; it derives its name from the fact that it settles to the bottom of the vats. Conversely, ale (q.v.) is fermented with top-fermentation yeast (q.v.), which rises to the top of the vats. Also, lager beer is fermented at fairly low temperatures of between 45° and 60° Fahrenheit, whereas ale is fermented between 50° and 70° Fahrenheit. Prior to the introduction of ice and refrigeration devices, the production of lager beer could only take place during the months when cellar temperatures were conducive to fermentation. Overall, it normally takes six to ten days for lager fermentation, and five or six days for ale fermentation. Sixth, in the early stages of fermentation, a white froth accumulates on the surface of the tub and the beer is thus "in kraeusen," as it "works" and carbon dioxide is emitted. As fermentation ceases, the beer is drawn off, cooled, and put into storage tanks at just above freezing. Formerly this was generally called the "ruh" (q.v.), or rest, period of secondary fermentation and the beer was put in ruh casks for a period of some weeks depending on the brewer's policy and demand for the beer. The total storage, or lagering (q.v.), period takes from four to eight weeks. The seventh and last step is the carbonation stage, in which effervescence is added to the lager either by kraeusening or by direct injection of carbon dioxide. In the kraeusening procedure, some of the earlier "young beer" is added to the beer (one part new to four parts old beer), thus adding carbon dioxide in a natural manner, or modern mechanical techniques may be used to reinject CO_2 that had been collected during the fermentation stage. Finally, after the brewing process has been completed, the beer is ready for packaging (q.v.) in kegs (q.v.) or barrels (q.v.), bottles (q.v.), or cans (q.v.). The racking (q.v.), or filling, of beer in barrels and bottling is in pasteurized (q.v.) or unpasteurized form depending on the type of packaging. Unpasteurized beer, draft (q.v.), was formerly filled in barrels or, today, also in bottles. Until recently only pasteurized beer could be bottled or canned because the active yeast had been killed through pasteurization, thus preventing further CO_2 action which could destroy the product or the container. Today, because of sterile filtering procedures, unpasteurized beers may be packaged in bottles and cans. Federal regulations govern the conditions. Since the advent of pasteurization in the late nineteenth century, however, most bottled and canned beer has been, and continues to be, pasteurized, thereby killing any active yeast and permitting shipping, stability, and longer life for the beer.

SOURCES: John P. Arnold and Frank Penman, *History of the Brewing Industry and Brewing Science* (Chicago, 1933); Harold Broderick, ed., *The Practical Brewer* (Madison, Wis., 1977); Thomas C. Cochran, *The Pabst Brewing Company* (New York, 1948); Harold Grossman, *Grossman's Guide to Wines, Beers, and Spirits* (New York, 1977); *One Hundred Years of Brewing* (Chicago and New York, 1903; Arno Press Reprint, 1974).

Brewing science and technology. During the late nineteenth century, the introduction of new machinery and the growing emphasis on scientific knowledge combined to bring about substantial changes in the art of brewing. The malting (q.v.) process was transformed by the introduction of pneumatic malting (q.v.) systems that permitted greater control and efficiency in processing grains. The application of steam power and the use of hoists, pumps, keg scrubbers, and machines for mashing (q.v.) also increased the efficiency of production. One of the most important changes was the introduction of artificial refrigeration (*see* Refrigeration) devices by Ferdinand Carré, John C. De LaVergne (q.v.), and others. Previously cellars, caves, and ice had been necessary for "lagering" beer. Among the scientific advances were the introduction of pasteurization (q.v.) by Louis Pasteur and pure culture yeast by Emil Hansen (*see* Yeast) in the 1870s and 1880s. Their research contributed substantially to the expansion of bottled beer (q.v.), which could hold its stability for a longer period. And in 1892 William Painter's "Crown" stoppering devices encouraged further expansion. By 1900 the brewing industry had undergone important changes. After Repeal further automation and modern packaging (q.v.) characterized the industry, but the 1870-1900 period saw the transition to modern brewing.

SOURCES: John P. Arnold and Frank Penman, *History of the Brewing Industry and Brewing Science in America* (Chicago, 1933); Stanley Baron, *Brewed in America* (Boston, 1962); Thomas C. Cochran, *The Pabst Brewing Company* (New York, 1948).

Bronfman, Samuel (March 4, 1891-July 10, 1971). A Canadian-born distiller, Bronfman built the world's largest distillery organization by the mid-twentieth century. He began as a liquor distributor in Canada but built a distillery, Distillers Corporation Limited, in Montreal in 1924. Bronfman led the move for purchase of Ontario's Joseph E. Seagram and Sons, Ltd. (*see* Seagram, Jos. E., & Sons), in 1928 and then spearheaded acquisitions of a number of American distilleries and other businesses from 1933 to the late 1960s. His son, Edgar, assumed his position as chairman of Distillers Corporation-Seagram Limited, the parent company.

SOURCES: *Bev/Executive* (July 15, 1971); Samuel Bronfman, *From Little Acorns* (Montreal, 1970); Peter C. Newman, *King of the Castle, the Making of a Dynasty: Seagram's & the Bronfman Empire* (New York, 1979).

Brooklyn brewing industry. By 1898 nearly fifty breweries operated in the Brooklyn, New York, area. One especially noteworthy area was known as "Brewer's Row," a twelve-square-block section where about eleven breweries were centered in the late nineteenth century. Probably the most prominent of those companies was Samuel Liebmann's (q.v.) Rheingold brewery, although there were other well-known or colorful firms such as F. & M. Schaefer (q.v.), George Ehret's (q.v.), John F. Trommer's (q.v.), and Piels (q.v.). From forty-three breweries in 1879, the number diminished to three by 1973, and by 1977 no brewery operated in the Brooklyn area. Industry-wide factors of concentration, competition, and growth of national breweries, combined with the fact that Brooklyn plants were not modern enough to keep up with new plant economies and efficiency, contributed to the decline. *See also*, Consumer's Park Brewing Company, Peter Doelger

Brewing Company, Edelbrew, Nassau Brewing Company, and F. W. Witte.

SOURCES: Will Anderson, *The Beer Book* (Princeton, N.J., 1973), and *The Breweries of Brooklyn* (New York, 1976); *One Hundred Years of Brewing* (Chicago and New York, 1903; Arno Press Reprint, 1974).

Brown, George Garvin (1846-January 24, 1917). He and J. T. S. Brown founded the Brown-Forman Distillers Corporation (q.v.) in 1870. Brown came up with the brand name Old Forester and managed the Louisville distillery until his death in 1917—when he was succeeded by his son, Owsley Brown.

SOURCE: John Ed Pearce, *Nothing Better in the Market* (Louisville, Ky., 1970).

Brown, J. T. S., & Sons (Distilleries). John Thompson Street Brown entered the distillery business in Nelson County, Kentucky, and was associated for a time with his half-brother, George Garvin Brown (q.v.), in what became Brown-Forman Distillers Corporation (q.v.). He left the business in the 1870s and operated his own plant. Just after 1900 his five sons—Graham, Davis, Creel, Sr., J. T. S., Jr., and Hewitt—purchased the property and brand of the Old Prentice Company in Anderson County. The company was dormant during the Prohibition era, but Creel Brown, Jr., revived the firm in 1935 as he renovated the old Early Times (*see* Brown-Forman Distillers Corporation) plant near Bardstown, Kentucky. Later, in the 1950s, the company opened a plant in Lawrenceburg, Kentucky. In 1955, Creel Brown, Jr., sold the plant to Alvin A. Gould. The company continued as an independent under the J. T. S. Brown name; in the late 1970s Robert Gould was president of the firm. The original Old Prentice firm was renovated by Gratz Hawkins as the Old Joe Distillery (q.v.) in the 1930s and was purchased by Schenley in the mid-1970s.

SOURCES: Harry H. Kroll, *Bluegrass, Belles, and Bourbon* (New York, 1967); John Ed Pearce, *Nothing Better in the Market* (Louisville, Ky., 1970); *Spirits* (May 1936).

Brown, Owsley (February 29, 1879-October 31, 1952). The son of George Garvin Brown (q.v.), founder of the Brown-Forman (q.v.) distillery in 1870, Owsley Brown became president of the Louisville firm in 1917 and held the position until 1945 when he became chairman. Brown guided the company through the years of Prohibition in the 1920s and then involved himself more directly in the whiskey profession after Repeal. He was a founder and first president of the Distilled Spirits Institute (q.v.). His sons, W. L. Lyons and George Garvin II, gradually moved into management of the Brown-Forman company in the late 1930s and the 1940s.

SOURCES: John Ed Pearce, *Nothing Better in the Market* (Louisville, Ky., 1970); *Spirits* (November 1952).

Brown-Forman Distillers Corporation. This Louisville, Kentucky, distilling firm was founded initially in 1870 as J. T. S. Brown and Bro. in St. Mary's, Kentucky. The brother was George Garvin Brown (q.v.), half-brother of J. T. S. In 1873 Henry Chambers, a former employer, invested in the business and the name was changed to Brown, Chambers and Company. Soon after, J. T. S. left the partnership and when Chambers retired in 1881, the name was changed to Brown-Thompson and Company, because James Thompson, a salesman, bought into the company. In 1890 Thompson sold his interest and established Glenmore Distilleries (q.v.); he was replaced by George Forman, who had been a salesman since 1872. When Forman died in 1901, Brown bought his 10 percent share in the company from his widow and incorporated in 1902 as the Brown-Forman Distillery Company. The company's founding brand, Old Forester, dated from the mid-1870s, and was noted as ninety-proof, high-quality whiskey known for its consistency. Among its other brands were Old Tucker, Old Forman, Old Polk, and Gilded Age. George G. Brown remained president of the company until his death in 1917; his son, Owsley, then became president and held the position until 1945. Owsley managed to acquire one of the federal permits issued under the Volstead Act (q.v.) allowing storage of medicinal whiskey and transportation of it to druggists who could dispense it to consumers with a doctor's prescription. In 1923, because of the Liquor Concentration Act (q.v.) Brown moved his stock to Louisville and then purchased all of Early Times (q.v.) stock and labels from S. J. Guthrie. In 1930, federal authorities permitted limited distillation to replenish dwindling stocks of whiskey and Brown took advantage of the relaxation of the law to build up inventory—a factor that would prove beneficial upon the repeal of Prohibition. The distillery reopened after Repeal and Brown's sons, W. L. Lyons and George Garvin II, joined the company. Owsley was instrumental in the founding of the Distilled Spirits Institute (q.v.) in 1933 as a self-policing agency of the industry, and became its first president. Brown-Forman continued as a successful operation. By the mid-1930s, Brown-Forman was the nation's fifth largest distiller, behind Hiram Walker (q.v.), Seagram (q.v.), Schenley (q.v.), and National Distillers Products Company (q.v.). In 1940 the firm bought the Old Kentucky Distilling Company (q.v.) and the Labrot and Graham Distillery (q.v.). During World War II, the company produced industrial alcohol. W. L. Lyons became president in 1945, and Owsley was chairman of the board. Owsley retired from active directorship in 1951 and died the following year. Lyons became chairman, and George Garvin was president. They expanded the company in the mid-1950s with the acquisition of Jack Daniel (q.v.) and Jos. Garneau (q.v.) in 1956. The Jack Daniel purchase was accomplished in part because of the family-type management of each company and the fact that members of the Motlow and Brown families served on the boards of each company. Dan Street, a long-time employee, was the first non-Brown to serve as president of Brown-Forman. He held the post until 1969 when he was succeeded by William F. Lucas, who was subsequently succeeded by W. L. Lyons Brown, Jr. George Garvin II died in 1969 at the age of fifty-seven, and Lyons died a few years later in 1973. Other acquisitions were Quality Imports (Ambassador Scotch and Old Bushmill's Irish Whiskey) in 1967, and Pepe Lopez Tequila also in 1967. Then the company bought the rights to Martell Cognac, and the New York importer Fontana-Hollywood Corporation, in 1968. One short-lived purchase was Oertels Brewing Company (q.v.) in 1964, which did not do well and was sold in 1968. Brown-Forman maintains healthy growth as the fifth largest distiller in the U.S. In 1971 the firm purchased the Canadian Mist brand from Barton Distillers and acquired the Southern Comfort Corporation (q.v.) in March 1979.

SOURCES: "Distilleries of Old Kentucky," *Spirits* (April 1935); *Forty Years of Repeal* (New York, 1973); John Ed Pearce, *Nothing Better in the Market* (Louisville, Ky., 1970).

Buckeye Brewing Company. Julius Kohler founded this Toledo, Ohio, brewing company in 1838. The company was later known as Lehmann & Eckhardt Bros., then from 1877 to 1886 as Jacobi, Coghlin & Company. In 1886 the Buckeye name was adopted. The company survived Prohibition and was given a boost in the mid-1950s when noted athlete Richard "Red" Smith became general manager, and later president. In 1966 the company was acquired by the Peter Hand Brewing Company (q.v.) of Chicago; Buckeye then produced Meister Brau in addition to the Buckeye brand. The two breweries operated as Meister Brau, Inc., until the company was forced to liquidate in 1972. Miller Brewing Company (q.v.) purchased its Meister Brau and Lite brands.

SOURCES: *Brewers Digest* (November 1966); *One Hundred Years of Brewing* (Chicago and New York, 1903; Arno Press Reprint, 1974).

Budweiser Brewing Company. *See* Nassau Brewing Company.

Buffalo brewing industry. This western New York city was one of the late nineteenth-century urban brewing centers. By 1880, approximately thirty breweries operated in the city, which had a population of just over 150,000. Afterward the number of firms declined, as occurred nationally also, from twenty in 1890 to eight by 1935 to two in 1960. By 1973, no brewery operated in Buffalo. Two of the more famous and longest-running firms were the Magnus Beck Brewing Company (q.v.) and the William Simon Brewery (q.v.).

SOURCES: Will Anderson, *The Beer Book* (Princeton, N.J., 1973); *One Hundred Years of Brewing* (Chicago and New York, 1903; Arno Press Reprint, 1974).

Bulk whiskey. This refers to the sale of whiskey in barrel, or bulk, form. Prior to Prohibition, wholesalers and retailers purchased barrels from distillers and customers could have their bottles filled and refilled from barrels in a saloon or store. The Federal Alcohol Control Administration (q.v.) of 1933 banned such sales and limited bulk sales to distillers, rectifiers, wholesalers qualifying as rectifiers, and state liquor monopolies. Distillers often sell whiskey in bulk for buyers who order private labels, but the whiskey is bottled by the distiller.

SOURCES: Oscar Getz, *Whiskey: An American Pictorial History* (New York, 1978); "Of Railroads and Spirits," *Spirits* (October 1950).

Bunging. Bunging is the practice of stoppering beer storage casks during secondary fermentation. To retain effervescence by capturing carbonic acid in the beer in storage, a hole (bunghole) in the cask was bunged, or corked. A special type of cork, or bung, with vents was used in order to allow the cabonic acid to escape when the pressure reached a certain limit; otherwise the cask might break under pressure, or racking (q.v.) problems could occur. Bunging also refers to connecting a container to a pressure-regulating system.

SOURCE: *One Hundred Years of Brewing* (Chicago and New York, 1903; Arno Press Reprint, 1974).

Bureau of Alcohol, Tobacco, and Firearms. The BATF was established in 1972 as a reorganization and renaming of the Alcohol and Tobacco Tax Division. It remained a division of the Treasury Department. *See also*, Federal Liquor Regulations.

Burger Brewing Company. The Cincinnati brewery traced its origins to the Burger Brothers Malting Company of the late nineteenth century. In the early 1930s, the Burger Company, under the leadership of W. J. Huster, purchased the Lion Brewery, Inc., an organization that had acquired the Windisch-Muhlhauser (q.v.) brewery. Burger Brewing Company began operation in the 1940s, built a reputation by sponsoring radio broadcasts of the Cincinnati Reds baseball team until 1967, but sold out to the Hudepohl Brewing Company (q.v.) in 1973.

SOURCE: William L. Downard, *The Cincinnati Brewing Industry* (Athens, Ohio, 1973), and "When Gambrinus Was King," *Cincinnati Historical Society Bulletin* (Winter 1969).

Busch, Adolphus (July 10, 1839-October 10, 1913). A St. Louis brewer and German immigrant, Busch came to the U.S. in 1857. He went into the brewers' supply business, but after marrying Eberhard Anheuser's daughter, Lilly, in 1861, joined in management of his father-in-law's Bavarian Brewry in 1865. In 1873, he became a partner and the name was changed to the

Anheuser-Busch (q.v.) Brewing Association in 1879. Busch was responsible for establishing the brewery as a major national company. Under his entrepreneurial leadership, the company adopted up-to-date marketing and technological methods in the 1870s and 1880s as pasteurized (*see* Pasteurization) and bottled "Budweiser" was transported across the nation by refrigerated railroad cars to the company's many agencies (q.v.). In 1901, Anheuser-Busch surpassed the 1-million barrel mark, whereas the 1877 total had been about 50,000. Busch continued as president and was active in the business, even though he was a semi-invalid after 1906. Upon his death in 1913, his son August A. Busch, Sr. (q.v.), assumed control of the brewing company.

SOURCES: Stanley Baron, *Brewed in America* (Boston, 1962); Roland Krebs and Percy J. Orthwein, *Making Friends Is Our Business* (St. Louis, Mo., 1953); *The National Cyclopedia of American Biography*, vol. 12 (New York, 1904); Ronald Jan Plavchan, "A History of Anheuser-Busch, 1852-1933," unpub. Ph.D. dissertation, St. Louis University, 1969.

Busch, Adolphus, III (February 10, 1891-August 29, 1946). President of Anheuser-Busch, Inc. (q.v.), from 1934 until his death in 1946, Busch continued the family's successful entrepreneurial tradition. He guided the company as production went over the 3-million barrel figure in the early 1940, making the company the world's largest brewery in 1940.

SOURCE: Roland Krebs and Percy J. Orthwein, *Making Friends Is Our Business* (St. Louis, Mo., 1953).

Busch, August A., Sr. (December 29, 1865-February 13, 1934). Upon the death of his father, Adolphus Busch, in 1913, August became president of Anheuser-Busch (q.v.). He would lead the firm until 1933 when he relinquished active management. His notable accomplishment was to keep the company solvent and operating during the Prohibition era. Managing to protect jobs and the company, he initiated a number of innovative business measures as the company engaged not only in grain conversion but also manufactured bus and truck bodies.

SOURCES: Roland Krebs and Percy J. Orthwein, *Making Friends Is Our Business* (St. Louis, Mo., 1953); *The National Cyclopedia of American Biography*, vol. 38 (New York, 1953); Ronald Jay Plavchan, "A History of Anheuser-Busch, 1852-1933," unpub. Ph.D. dissertation, St. Louis University, 1969.

Busch, August A., Jr. (b. March 28, 1899). President of Anheuser-Busch, Inc. (q.v.), from 1946 to 1975, and then chairman until 1977, Busch took over from his brother, Adolphus III, and he expanded the company significantly during his tenure. Eight new plants were opened; sales increased to 34 million barrels by 1974; new beers were marketed; and the company branched out into a baseball franchise, family entertainment parks (Busch Gardens), beer containers, and real estate.

SOURCES: Anheuser-Busch, Inc., "Fact Books" (1977, 1978); Roland Krebs and Percy J. Orthwein, *Making Friends Is Our Business* (St. Louis, Mo., 1953).

Busch, August A., III (b. June 16, 1937). Sixth president and chief executive of Anheuser-Busch, Inc. (q.v.), Busch assumed company leadership in 1975 and has continued company trends of expansion and diversification. By the late 1970s he was facing challenges to Anheuser-Busch's No. 1 position in production and was determined to continue as the nation's largest brewer.

SOURCES: "The Battle of the Beers," *Newsweek* (September 4, 1978); "Beer: Big Battles Are Brewing," *Time* (February 20, 1978); "How Anheuser-Busch Stays on Top," *Fortune* (January 15, 1979).

Buse, R. L., Company. Ray L. Buse of Cincinnati established this whiskey brokerage firm in the 1930s. He contracted with distillers to sell their stock, all or in part. By 1937, Buse had control of the total stock of H. E. Pogue (q.v.), J. T. S. Brown & Sons (q.v.), and Old Lewis Hunter (q.v.). The Buse firm thus became one of the largest commission firms in the whiskey business as it used its financial and merchandising resources to market whiskey stock. The company continued to operate as a Cincinnati-based firm in the late 1970s.

SOURCES: "The Distilleries from Which Buse's Bourbon Comes," *Spirits* (May 1936); "Ray L. Buse," *Spirits* (May 1937).

C

California Brewing Company. (San Francisco). *See* Wunder Brewing Company.

Calvert Distillery. Jos. E. Seagram and Son (q.v.) purchased this Relay, Maryland, distillery in 1933 as part of the firm's American expansion program. The plant was initially known as Maryland Distilling Company of Baltimore and was part of the Fleischmann (q.v.) distilling operation.
   SOURCE: "Great Names in Whiskey," *Spirits* (May 1937).

Canadian Ace Brewing Company. Canadian was originally founded in 1893 in Chicago as the Manhattan Brewing Company. In 1919, mobster Johnny Torrio bought the company and it became known as Malt-Maid; later it was named Fort Dearborn Products Company before being renamed Manhattan in 1933 by manager and subsequent owner Alex Louis Greenburg. He had been made manager by Torrio, and assumed control in the late 1920s. The company produced bootleg beer during the Prohibition era, but Greenburg operated it as a legitimate business afterward. In 1947 he changed the name to Canadian Ace because of bad publicity surrounding the Manhattan name. He was shot and killed by unknown assailants in 1955. Company managers bought the Prima Brewing Company (q.v.) in the 1950s and Pilsen Brewing Company (q.v.) in 1963 before closing in 1968. The brand name was continued by the Eastern Brewing Corporation (q.v.).
   SOURCE: Richard J. La Susa, "Nevermore the *Local Lagers,*" *Chicago Tribune Magazine* (April 24, 1977).

Canadian whisky. This light-bodied blended whisky contains no distilled spirits less than three years old. Canadian law requires the use of cereal grain only, with rye, corn, wheat, and barley malt the most commonly used grains. The whisky must be aged for at least two years, but most is aged for six years, and blending is done either before or during the aging (q.v.) period. The whisky may be aged in used charred oak barrels, whereas bourbon must be aged in new charred oak barrels. Canadian light whisky evolved in the nineteenth century. One of the more popular brands, Canadian Club (*see* Walker, Hiram, Distillery), became an important competitor of American bourbon in the 1880s.

SOURCES: *Alexis Lichine's New Encyclopedia of Wines and Spirits* (New York, 1974); Harold J. Grossman, *Grossman's Guide to Wines, Beers, and Spirits* (New York, 1977).

Canned beer. Beer packaging in cans (q.v.) dates from 1934 when the American Can Company developed a suitable can for beer distribution. American Can came up with a container that could withstand the desired pressure and was lined with enamel to prevent beer from coming into contact with metal. Hence the can was called "keglined." The company entered into an agreement with the Gottfried Krueger Brewing Company (q.v.) of Newark, New Jersey. Krueger and American Can test-marketed the can in Richmond, Virginia, a low per capita consumption area, and the new package helped Krueger outsell the major brewers. Pabst and Schlitz came out with canned beer in 1935, and in the next few years promotional campaigns were launched to sell the new package to the public. Although only 187 of the 507 breweries in the U.S. used the can in 1941, and only 14 percent of beer was packaged in this form, it grew in popularity in the late 1940s and afterward. Flat-top cans predominated, although spout-tops were tried. A recent innovation was the introduction of the Alcoa Aluminum tab top in 1962 by the Pittsburgh Brewing Company (q.v.). Certain advantages accrued from can-type packaging: it was easier and less expensive to ship beer in the small, light-weight cans, thus giving an advantage to national brewers; labor costs for washing, collecting, and labeling bottles decreased; and cans appealed to the public because they are nonbreakable, nonreturnable, stackable, and easier to cool. Recently, however, the can has been criticized because of environmental and ecological problems. One by-product of beer in cans has been an important facet in American popular culture, namely, beer can collecting—one of the categories of breweriana (q.v.).

SOURCES: American Can Company, *A History of Packaged Beer and Its Market in the U.S.* (New York, 1969); Will Anderson, *The Beer Book* (Princeton, N.J., 1973); Stanley Baron, *Brewed in America* (Boston, 1962); Wayne Kroll, *Badger Breweries* (Jefferson, Wis., 1976).

Cannon, James, Jr. (November 13, 1864-September 6, 1944). A Methodist minister and bishop, Cannon held leadership positions in the Democratic party and Anti-Saloon League in Virginia. Upon Wayne Wheeler's (q.v.) death in 1927, Bishop Cannon became the leading figure in the Anti-Saloon League and turned on the Democratic Al Smith in the 1928 election campaign. Cannon, a virulent anti-Catholic, organized "Democrats for Hoover" and delivered the southern states for the Republican candidate, Herbert Hoover.

SOURCES: James Cannon, Jr., *Bishop Cannon's Own Story* (Durham, N.C., 1955); Virginius Dabney, *Dry Messiah: The Life of Bishop Cannon* (New York, 1949).

Carling National Breweries, Inc. In 1975 the Carling Brewing Company and National Brewing Company (q.v.) of Baltimore, Maryland, merged to form Carling National Breweries, Inc. Carling traces its origins to the brewery founded by Thomas Carling in London, Ontario, in 1840. Today the Carling O'Keefe brand of Canada continues that tradition. In 1933, Carling moved into the American market with the purchase of a plant in Cleveland, Ohio. That company was known as the Brewing Corporation of America until 1954 when the name was changed to Carling Brewing Company. In that year, Carling, led by Ian R. Dowrie, undertook a program of expansion to market its Black Label and Red Cap Ale brands. The strategy included purchasing existing plants and building new ones. Acquisitions included Griesedieck's Western Brewery (q.v.), with its Stag label, in Belleville, Illinois (1954), a plant in Frankenmuth, Michigan (1956), and the Heidelberg brewery in Tacoma, Washington (1958). New plant constructions occurred in Natick, Massachusetts (1956), Atlanta, Georgia (1958), and Baltimore, Maryland (1961). The expansion moved the company from sixty-second in production in 1949 to about tenth in 1955. In 1972, Carling contracted with Denmark's United Breweries, Ltd., to produce Tuborg in the U.S. Ranking twelfth in production in 1975, Carling merged with sixteenth-ranking National Brewing Company, and the merger moved Carling National Breweries up to eleventh place, with seven breweries and fifteen brands that included Colt 45, National Premium, Carlsberg, Heidelberg, and Altes. By early 1979, however, Carling National completed arrangements for sale of its company to G. Heileman (q.v.).

SOURCES: Stanley Baron, *Brewed in America* (Boston, 1962); "This Is Carling," and F. Donald Fenhagen, "Carling National Breweries, Inc." (brief company history).

Carlisle, John G. (September 5, 1835-July 31, 1910). A Kentucky lawyer and statesman, Carlisle left the U.S. Senate in 1893 to accept the position of secretary of treasury under President Grover Cleveland. Carlisle joined with Col. E. H. Taylor, Jr. (q.v.), to help argue for legislation that was passed as the Bottled-in-Bond (q.v.) Act of 1897. Carlisle's portrait is on the green stamp signifying bottled-in-bond. Carlisle also figured prominently in the 1909 hearings on the meaning of the term "whiskey." He sided with the producers of straight whiskey who claimed that rectified whiskey was not genuine whiskey. *See also*, Taft Decision.

SOURCES: Gerald Carson, *The Social History of Bourbon* (New York, 1963); *Dictionary of American Biography*, vol. 3; U.S. Department of Justice, *Proceedings . . . Concerning the Meaning of the Term "Whisky"* (Washington, D.C., 1909).

Central Consumers Company (Brewery). A 1901 consolidation of five Louisville, Kentucky, breweries, the companies in the merger were the Frank Fehr (q.v.), Nadorf, Phoenix, Schaefer-Meyer, and Senn & Ackerman breweries. The merger was characteristic of such movements at the turn of the century as brewers attempted to eliminate some of the unfavorable aspects of intense competition. *See also*, Consolidations, Brewery.

SOURCES: Manfred Friedrich and Donald Bull, *The Register of U.S. Breweries* (Trumbull, Conn., 1976); *One Hundred Years of Brewing* (Chicago and New York, 1903; Arno Press Reprint, 1974).

Century Distilling Company. *See* Atlas Distilling Company.

Champale, Inc. This Trenton, New Jersey, brewing company features a distinctive vinous-like beverage. The company traces its origins to the late 1890s when R. V. Kuser and Associates established the Peoples Brewing Company, also known as the Trenton Brewing Company. During the early twentieth century, Louis Hertzberg purchased the plant and the family figured in the expansion of brewery plants in the 1950s. The Hertzberg interests, headed in mid-century by Abraham and Benjamin, became known as the Metropolis brewery combine. The Champale trademark was registered in November 1939. In 1972, Iroquois Brands, Ltd., purchased the Champale company from the Hertzberg family. C. B. Tichenor of Iroquois Brands is chairman and president of Champale, Inc.

Chicago Breweries, Ltd. This British-organized syndicate bought out and merged the Wacker & Birk and McAvoy (q.v.) breweries in 1889. The company retained Charles Wacker (q.v.) as manager and then president until he resigned in 1901. The firm went out of business during the Prohibition era.

SOURCES: Manfred Friedrich and Donald Bull, *The Register of U.S. Breweries* (Trumbull, Conn., 1976); *One Hundred Years of Brewing* (Chicago and New York, 1903; Arno Press Reprint, 1974).

Chicago brewing industry. Chicago's first brewery was founded in 1833 by William Lill, and it later became known as Lill and Diversey (q.v.). One of the backers of the small brewery was Mayor William Ogden (q.v.). However, the first lager beer brewery was apparently the John A. Huck Brewery (q.v.), which opened in 1847. Most of the early breweries were built on the higher ground of the North Side, thereby permitting underground storage cellars to be built for lagering the beer. One event of note was the "Beer Riot" (q.v.) of 1855. By 1860, twenty-two breweries operated and among them were Busch and Brand (*see* Brand, Michael, Brewing Company) and M. Best (*see* Seipp, Conrad, Brewing Company). Catering to a growing local market, Chicago's breweries grew in a similar way to the many urban brewing industries, but received a setback with the Great Fire of 1871. Five of the breweries were destroyed, and their absence, combined with the lack of sanitary water, proved an advantage to the nearby Milwaukee brewing industry (q.v.). Schlitz (q.v.) and Pabst (q.v.) were especially aggressive in exporting their beer to Chicago, and Chicago brewers were hard-pressed to recover. By 1879, however, twenty firms were in operation and as many as fifty-four by 1910. In the aftermath of Prohibition the numbers declined from twenty-seven in 1935, to eighteen in 1950, to one in 1973, and by 1979 no brewery was extant in the great midwestern city. The Conrad Seipp brewery, one of the nation's largest brewers, ranked ninth in 1895, with 250,000 barrels produced, but none compared with the top three—Pabst, Anheuser-Busch (q.v.), and Schlitz. One of the more notable early brewers of Chicago was Charles Wacker (q.v.), Chairman of the Chicago Plan Commission. His firm and a number of others sold out to an English syndicate around 1890, Chicago Breweries Ltd. (q.v.), which along with United Breweries Ltd. bought out various firms. During the Prohibition era in the 1920s, a number of Chicago breweries came under the control of mobsters, the most well-known case being that of the Manhattan Brewing Company, a small firm dating from 1893. Johnny Torrio, nephew and successor to "Big Jim" Colosimo, bought the company in 1919, renamed it Malt-Maid, and managed it until 1924, when he was forced out by the Al Capone branch of the mob. Hymie Weiss and Dion O'Banion guided the flow of bootleg beer and changed the name to Fort Dearborn Products Company in 1925. The general manager, and eventual controller, however, was Alex Louis Greenburg, one of Torrio's men. In 1933, Greenburg changed the name back to Manhattan and marketed his Manhattan Premium in cans. The name of the firm was changed to coincide with its other brand, Canadian Ace (q.v.), in 1947. Other, perhaps less colorful, but successful breweries also operated in Chicago over the years. Among them were the Keeley Brewing Company (q.v.), the McAvoy Company (q.v.), the Best Brewing Company (q.v.) of Chicago, Chicago Breweries Ltd. (q.v.), U.S. Brewing Company (q.v.), Birk Bros. Brewing Company (q.v.), the Schoenhofen-Edelweiss (q.v.) company, Sieben's Brewery (q.v.), and the historic but recently closed Peter Hand (q.v.) brewery.

SOURCES: Will Anderson, *The Beer Book* (Princeton, N.J., 1973); Thomas C. Cochran, *The Pabst Brewing Company* (New York, 1948); Rudolph A. Hofmeister, *The Germans of Chicago* (Champaign, Ill., 1976); Richard J. La Susa, "Nevermore the Local Lagers," *Chicago Tribune Magazine* (April 24, 1977); *One Hundred Years of Brewing* (Chicago and New York, 1903; Arno Press Reprint, 1974); Bessie L. Pierce, *A History of Chicago*, vols. 2-3 (New York, 1957).

Cincinnati brewing industry. By 1840, of the 46,000 people living in the "Queen City," more than 10,000 were of German origin. Thus, in the 1840s and 1850s, the city's brewers tended more and more to be German in nature, and they brewed lager beer (q.v.). Previously the eight to ten breweries, the first dating to 1811, had been mainly English in nature and the products were ale, porter, and stout. After 1850 the city's population increased substantially and the brewing industry corresponded as the number of firms reached about twenty-five in the mid-1890s. The largest was the Christian Moerlein Brewing Company (q.v.), although many other substantial and successful breweries operated. Among them were the Windisch-Muhlhauser (q.v.), John Hauck (q.v.), Hudepohl (q.v.), Herancourt (one of the earliest in the 1840s), Lackman, Gerke, Kauffman, Sohn, and Foss-Schneider breweries. The many breweries had a very high total production, considering the population, and this was encouraged by high per capita consumption. Milwaukee however had a much higher output per capita, but a large portion of the "Cream City's" brew was being exported (*see* Milwaukee brewing industry). As in other cities, English investors attempted to buy brewery stock in Cincinnati in the 1890s. Only a few smaller firms joined the merger however. In 1919, on the eve of Prohibition, there were still more than twenty breweries operating, indicating stability in numbers, probably because of large local consumption. In 1935, eleven breweries were again in business, but the decline continued so that by the late 1970s only Hudepohl and Schoenling (q.v.), dating from 1935, still managed plants. The large late nineteenth-century firms, most notably Moerlein, sold out during Prohibition. *See also*, Red Top Brewing Company, Wiedemann Brewing Company, and Burger Brewing Company.

SOURCES: Will Anderson, *The Beer Book* (Princeton, N.J., 1973); William L. Downard, *The Cincinnati Brewing Industry* (Athens, Ohio, 1973), and "When Gambrinus Was King," *Cincinnati Historical Society Bulletin* (Winter 1969); *One Hundred Years of Brewing* (Chicago and New York, 1903; Arno Press Reprint, 1974).

Cistern room. This is a room in a distillery where whiskey (q.v.) is stored after distillation (q.v.). Distilled water is added to lower the proof (q.v.) from about 125 proof to 103 proof. From the tanks in this room, the whiskey is poured into fifty-gallon barrels for aging (q.v.).

Clarke Bros. & Company. Charles Clarke established this Peoria, Illinois, distillery around 1862. His brother, Sumner, joined the company later. The firm was part of the Whiskey Trust (q.v.) in the 1890s. William E. Hull (q.v.), who was later a U.S. congressman and sales manager for the Hiram Walker distillery, was involved in the firm. The company closed with Prohibition, was later purchased by U.S. Industrial Alcohol (q.v.), and the brand name that was evidently purchased by Arrow Distilleries, Inc. (q.v.) became that company's most prominent product.

SOURCES: Ernest E. East, "Romance of Peoria Industry," *Peoria Journal Transcript*, April 28, 1940; "Whiskey," *Fortune* (November 1933).

Clausen, H., & Son (Brewery). Henry Clausen, Sr., founded his brewery in New York City in 1855. His son, Henry, Jr., became very important in the business and was noteworthy as a founder and subsequent president of the U.S. Brewers' Association (q.v.). Clausen & Son merged with Flanagan, Nay & Company (q.v.) in 1888 as the New York Breweries Company, and a short time later the company was purchased by an English syndicate. In 1877, the company was the nation's sixth largest brewery, producing about 90,000 barrels. Henry Clausen, Jr. (q.v.), died in 1893.

SOURCE: One Hundred Years of Brewing (Chicago and New York, 1903; Arno Press Reprint, 1974).

Clausen, Henry, Jr. (1838-December 28, 1893). President of the U.S. Brewers' Association (q.v.) from 1866 to 1875, Clausen worked in the brewery, H. Clausen & Son (q.v.), founded by his father in 1855.

SOURCE: One Hundred Years of Brewing (Chicago and New York, 1903; Arno Press Reprint, 1974).

Cleveland & Sandusky Brewing Company. Initially founded as the Schmidt and Hoffman brewery in 1852, in 1898 the Cleveland, Ohio, company consolidated nine breweries in Cleveland and Sandusky. Among those included were the Gehring, Sar and Baehr, and Bohemian plants. The firm reopened after repeal of Prohibition but closed in 1962.

Cleveland brewing industry. The city was founded in 1796, and the first commercial breweries date from the 1820s or 1830s. One of the earliest breweries was the Cleveland Brewery, first built in 1832 by Joseph and Richard Hawley. Afterward, it changed hands a number of times, and its history is obscure. Another early plant, known for its "Hughes Ale," was founded by John M. Hughes. That brewery closed in 1895. One of the first lager beer breweries was the Schmidt and Hoffman brewery, later known as the Cleveland & Sandusky Brewing Company (q.v.), which was a consolidation of nine breweries. The city's population of 380,000 in 1900 supported more than twenty-five breweries, but fewer than ten reopened after Repeal in 1933; and by the mid-1970s only C. Schmidt (q.v.) of Philadelphia operated a plant in Cleveland. Schmidt had bought the brewery from Carling (q.v.) in 1971.

SOURCES: Stanley Baron, *Brewed in America* (Boston, 1962); *One Hundred Years of Brewing* (Chicago and New York, 1903; Arno Press Reprint, 1974).

Coffey-still. *See* Still.

Cold Spring Brewing Company. Michael Sargel founded this regional brewery in 1874 in Cold Spring, Minnesota. Over the years the brewery was known as Jacob Haeman, Haeman & Oster, Oster and Hilt, and incorporated as the Cold Spring Brewing Company in 1900. In the 1920s the brewery marketed near beer (q.v.) and soft drinks. Myron C. Johnson, chairman, bought control in 1942, and in the late 1970s the brewery had an annual production of 275,000 barrels.

SOURCES: Brewers Digest (September 1972); James D. Robertson, *The Great American Beer Book* (Ottawa, Ill., 1978).

Columbia Brewing Company. The St. Louis plant, in 1892 with Charles Koehler as president, became part of the Independent Breweries Company (q.v.) in 1907, was continued after repeal of Prohibition, and was acquired by Falstaff (q.v.) in 1948.

Commission merchant. A middleman in the whiskey business, the commission merchant operated in ways similar to a broker but normally handled the goods, completed the transaction, and returned the proceeds from the sales, minus commission, to the seller. The commission merchant usually advanced capital to the distiller and held warehouse receipts (q.v.) giving him title to whiskey stock. Cincinnati, Ohio, was a very important center for commission merchants in the nineteenth and well into the twentieth century.

Commission on Law Enforcement and Observance. *See* Wickersham Commission.

Common beer. This top-fermentation (q.v.) brew required a short fermentation period. Similar to English beers, this type of beer was the predominant product of American brewers, who were generally non-German, until the introduction of lager (q.v.) in the mid-nineteenth century.

Common brewer. The term common brewer referred to the commercial brewer in the colonial period as opposed to a home brewer of small beer (q.v.). The common brewer produced a commercial, or standard, product called strong beer (q.v.). It was top-fermentation (q.v.) beer normally higher in alcoholic content than homebrew. Robert Sedgwick of Massachusetts Bay was one of the first common brewers and received a license from the colony in the 1630s.

SOURCE: Stanley Baron, *Brewed in America* (Boston, 1962).

Compartment malting. *See* Pneumatic Malting.

Condenser. *See* Worm.

Congeners. Congeners are traces of fusel oils (q.v.), acids, and other non-alcohol by-products of distillation that are vaporized with the alcohol and impart flavor, aroma, and character to the distillate. If the spirits (q.v.) are distilled at lower proof (q.v.), the congeneric content will be higher. Thus bourbon (q.v.), which is distilled at below 160 proof, will contain more congeners, and have more body, than vodka (q.v.), which is distilled at above 190 proof. The question of whether congeners improve whiskey surfaced in the debate over the Pure Food and Drug Act (q.v.) of 1906, which led to the "Taft decision" (q.v.) of 1909. During the hearings on the interpretation of the act, the whiskey blenders and rectifiers pointed out that blended whiskey contained fewer congeners and fusel oils, and thus was in a sense purer than straight whiskey (q.v.). It was generally assumed at the time that although congeners added flavor to the drink, they also contributed to headaches for drinkers.

SOURCE: U.S. Department of Justice, *Proceedings . . . Concerning the Meaning of the Term "Whisky"* (Washington, D.C., 1909).

Consolidations, brewery. Increasing competition among brewers led to numerous mergers during the 1880s and 1890s. Price wars and price cutting especially hurt small brewers and encouraged many firms to consider some sort of consolidation as a means of promoting cost efficiencies, especially in purchasing raw materials. In some cities local concerns combined as a result of the pressures, but in many urban areas, British investors provided the structure and capital for brewing syndicates. Often, when English-oriented mergers did occur, nonsyndicate firms formed local consolidations of their own. British investors did buy into breweries in many areas but were unable to buy out any of the large national companies. An 1889 offer to buy out Schlitz (q.v.), Pabst (q.v.), and Blatz (q.v.) for $16.5 million was turned down, as were offers for Anheuser-Busch (q.v.) and Moerlein (q.v.). The big brewers apparently preferred to continue managing their own breweries. Mergers, both local and external, continued to occur or were attempted up until Prohibition in 1920.

SOURCES: Stanley Baron, *Brewed in America* (Boston, 1962); Thomas C. Cochran, *The Pabst Brewing Company* (New York, 1948); William L. Downard, *The Cincinnati Brewing Industry* (Athens, Ohio, 1973); *One Hundred Years of Brewing* (Chicago and New York, 1903; Arno Press Reprint, 1974).

Consumers Park Brewing Company. A large group of hotel and saloon-keepers established this Brooklyn brewery in 1897. The brewery featured a recreation-like decor that included a hotel, a beer garden, and concert facilities. The company sold out during the 1920s. The primary organizer and first president was Herman Raub. After a dispute with the directors, he returned to the hotel business in 1907, and died in 1915 at the age of forty-six.

SOURCES: Will Anderson, *The Breweries of Brooklyn* (New York, 1976); *One Hundred Years of Brewing* (Chicago and New York, 1903; Arno Press Reprint, 1974).

Consumption of alcoholic beverages. *See* Prohibition, and Appendixes I and II.

Cook, F. W., Brewing Company. Originally established in Evansville, Indiana, in 1853 as Cook and Rice, the firm was incorporated as F. W. Cook in 1885. In 1902 an English syndicate bought the company but continued the name of Cook. The brewery reopened after repeal of Prohibition and continued as Evansville's Sterling (q.v.) Breweries stiffest competitor until each was merged with Associated Brewing Company (q.v.) in the early 1960s. G. Heileman (q.v.) purchased control in 1971 and continued to market the brew in the late 1970s.

SOURCES: *One Hundred Years of Brewing* (Chicago and New York, 1903; Arno Press Reprint, 1974); James D. Robertson, *The Great American Beer Book* (Ottawa, Ill., 1978).

Cooperage. Coopers constructed barrels necessary for the production of alcoholic beverages, today especially in the aging (q.v.) of whiskey. Brewers used the wooden barrels widely in the nineteenth century and then gradually replaced this means of packaging (q.v.) with aluminum and stainless-steel barrels. Until the advent of whiskey bottling in the late nineteenth century, distillers generally marketed their products in barrels. Therefore, there was a great demand for cooperage, both for aging and for distribution. Sometimes brewers and distillers made their own barrels and staves (q.v.), but many independent firms also supplied cooperage. In the past, barrels were mostly handmade. Trees were cut in the winter when the sap was down. Then the timber was split with a frow (q.v.) into staves that were dried in the open air for nearly a year. After kiln-drying to eliminate all the sap, staves were shaped and put together with a hand joiner. *See also*, Barrel, Beer, and Barrel, Whiskey.

SOURCES: Gerald Carson, *The Social History of Bourbon* (New York, 1963); George Ehret, *Twenty-five Years of Brewing* (New York, 1891); Darrell Sifford, "Bourbon Whiskey: Kentucky's All-American Drink," *Louisville Courier-Journal Magazine* (March 27, 1966); Charles E. Thomason, unpub. paper, distributed by Willett Distilling Company, Bardstown, Ky.

Coors, Adolph, Brewing Company. One of the most well-known and interesting breweries in the U.S., Coors was established in 1873 by Adolph

Coors (q.v.) and Jacob Schueler. The brewery was, and is, located in Golden, Colorado, a short distance from Denver. In 1880 Schueler sold his interest to Coors. Known as the Golden Brewery, the company competed successfully with the seven Denver breweries. Coors and Schueler apparently selected Golden, Colorado, for their brewery because it was a point on the Colorado Central railroad that acted as a gateway to western mining towns and was the site of several underground springs. The company incorporated in 1913 with Adolph Coors as president, Adolph, Jr., as vice-president and treasurer, and Grover Coors as general manager of the plant. During the years of Prohibition in the late 1920s, the brewery produced near beer, malted milk, and butter. The company had to make the transition sooner than others becouse Colorado enacted a prohibition law in 1916. The company, fifth largest in the U.S. by the mid-1970s, remained under the control of the Coors family although shares of stock were offered to the public for the first time in 1975. Part of the tradition of the brewery has been emphasis on the free enterprise system in America and consequent activities on political and social issues such as environmental responsibility —as exemplified by the use of aluminum recyclable cans and additional environmental programs. Another part of the traditional appeal has been limited availability (especially in the East) of the beer, which is sterile-filtered rather than pasteurized (q.v.). In the late 1960s and early 1970s, Coors enjoyed tremendous popularity while investing little in advertising. But competition from other brewers, coupled with a costly strike in 1977, has encouraged a change to a more aggressive market posture. In 1978 William K. Coors was chairman, Joseph Coors, president, Peter Coors, senior vice-president of marketing and sales, and Jeff Coors, senior vice-president of technical operations.

SOURCES: *Brewers Digest* (March and April 1973); Michael Jackson, ed., *The World Guide to Beer* (Englewood Cliffs, N.J., 1977); William Kostka, Sr., *The Pre-Prohibition History of Adolph Coors Company, 1873-1933* (n.d., ca. 1970); *Newsweek* (September 4, 1978); *Wall Street Journal*, January 19, 1979.

Coors, Adolph Herman Joseph (1847-1929). In 1868, at the age of twenty-one, Coors left Germany for the U.S. He had been orphaned at the age of fifteen, then worked at various jobs, one in brewing. Eventually making his way to Chicago, where he worked on the Illinois-Michigan Canal and then in a Naperville brewery, Coors left for Denver in 1872. He entered the bottling business at first, then sold out and entered into the brewing business in 1873 with Jacob Schueler, who sold his interest in 1880. His Golden Brewery, just west of Denver, managed to prosper, and his three sons eventually continued the business. Coors set the style of independent self-help and emphasis on free enterprise that has characterized the company. During the "dry" years, which began in 1916 in Colorado, the company produced near beer (q.v.), cream, butter, and malted milk, in time becoming the nation's third largest producer of the latter. *See also*, Coors, Adolph, Brewing Company.

SOURCES: *Adolph Coors Company Profile* (November 1977); *Brewers Digest* (March and April 1973); William Kostka, Sr., *The Pre-Prohibition History of Adolph Coors Company, 1873-1933* (n.d., ca. 1970).

Cordial. This distilled beverage is flavored by the addition of syrup for sweetening. It was available in the late eighteenth century although it was not as common as rum or whiskey. *See also*, Liqueurs.

SOURCE: Henry G. Crowgey, *Kentucky Bourbon* (Lexington, Ky., 1971).

Corn whiskey. Made from a mash (q.v.) of at least 80 percent corn, this whiskey type is usually aged in uncharred oak barrels. It is normally aged for a short time and is light-colored and fairly harsh. Bourbon (q.v.) and other American whiskies, conversely, are aged in new charred oak barrels.

Corning and Company Distillery. Franklin T. Corning founded this Peoria, Illinois, distillery around 1880. The major brand name, issued in 1897 as a 100 proof (q.v.), bottled-in-bond (q.v.) whiskey, was Old Quaker. Evidently, the firm did not join the Peoria-centered Whiskey Trust (q.v.). Sources indicate the plant ceased operation in 1920, but that the brand name, Old Quaker, was subsequently acquired by Schenley Distillers Corporation (q.v.). Schenley built a plant in Lawrenceburg, Indiana, in 1933 and named it Old Quaker.

SOURCES: Distilleries file, Peoria Historical Society; "Great Names in Whiskey," *Spirits* (May 1937); Carl J. Kiefer, "Schenley," *Spirits* (December 1933).

Couching. *See* Floor-Malting.

Cream City Brewing Company. Named after Milwaukee's title of the "Cream City" because of the city's production of cream-colored bricks, the company was organized in 1879. It had earlier operated under various names. Jacob Veidt and William Gerlach were the 1879 organizers of the company, which was managed by various groups until it was closed in 1937.

SOURCE: Wayne Kroll, *Badger Breweries* (Jefferson, Wis., 1976).

Crow, James (1789-1856). Crow, a Scottish-born physician, was credited by many sources with discovering the importance of limestone water (q.v.) in whiskey-making. A man of letters as well as medicine, Crow came to Kentucky in the early nineteenth century and became involved in the whiskey business at the urging of Col. Willis Field of Woodford County. Field knew of Crow's chemical ability and persuaded him to take over his distillery. The chemist applied a scientific process to his distillery and, according to some accounts, introduced the sour mash (q.v.) method. Old Crow became a popular brand; the name was continued by W. A. Gaines and was acquired by National Distillers Products Company (q.v.) in 1929.

SOURCES: Gerald Carson, *The Social History of Bourbon* (New York, 1963); "Jim Crow's Formula," *Spirits* (April 1935).

Cullen Act. Federal legislation to modify the Volstead Act (q.v.) was passed in March 1933 and became effective on April 7. The act permitted the production and sale of light wines and beer not exceeding 3.2 percent alcohol by volume. Thus it encouraged resumption of the brewing industry before ratification of the Twenty-first Amendment (q.v.), which repealed Prohibition (*see* Eighteenth Amendment) in December 1933. The act was also known as the Cullen-Harrison Act and the Beer-Wine Revenue Act.

D _____

Daniel, Jack (September 5, 1846-October 9, 1911). Jasper Newton "Jack" Daniel was the last of ten children born to Calaway Daniel and his wife. Jack apparently felt left out, a "runt," and left home at an early age to live with a neighbor, Felix Waggoner. A short time later, he went to live and work on the farm of Dan Call, a young farmer-distiller who had inherited a farm. Daniel later bought Call's still, sold whiskey during the Civil War, and in 1866 bought a tract of land in the Lynchburg, Tennessee, area to build his distillery. He located at Cave Spring about four miles from Lynchburg in "the Hollow," known for ideal pure limestone water (q.v.). The distillery proved very successful. Daniel was a shrewd businessman and cultivated an image for the distillery that was based in part on his personality. He wore a planter's hat, a knee-length frock coat, and grew a mustache and goatee. Evidently, he wore the outfit even when doing manual labor at the distillery. During the 1880s, Daniel's nephew Lem Motlow began to work in the distillery and took over when Daniel retired in 1907. Jack Daniel died in 1911 apparently in part from complications owing to a 1905 toe injury, from angrily kicking a safe that refused to open. After the toe problem, Daniel had to have his leg amputated.

SOURCES: Ben A. Green, *Jack Daniel's Legacy* (Shelbyville, Tenn., 1967); *Bev/Executive* (July 15, 1966); Jeanne Ridgway Bigger, "Jack Daniel Distillery and Lynchburg," *Tennessee Historical Quarterly* (Spring 1972).

Daniel, Jack, Distillery. This famous and successful distillery was founded in 1866 by Jack Daniel (q.v.) in Lynchburg, Tennessee. Daniel learned the distiller's trade on Dan Call's farm, where he worked in the 1850s. Eventually, Daniel bought Call's still and sold his whiskey during the Civil War. After the war, Daniel formed a short-lived partnership with Col. John Hughes. In 1866 he bought some land and established his distillery at Cave Spring in a place known as "the Hollow," a short distance from Lynchburg. The limestone water (q.v.) of the spring was alleged to be free of iron and reputed to be at an almost constant temperature of 56° Fahrenheit— ideal qualities for making whiskey. Soon after he had begun operation, Daniel was informed of federal regulations that had been passed in 1862 and had been in abeyance during the war. Deciding to concentrate on production instead of litigation, Daniel promptly registered his business, which became known as the oldest registered distillery in the country—thus the name, Jack Daniel Distillery No. 1. The distillery proved very successful and became more so when Daniel adopted the trade name, Old Time No. 7. He had been marketing brands known as Belle of Lincoln and Old Fashioned but apparently got the idea for No. 7 in 1887 when, during a trip to Tullahoma, he visited a friend who was operating a chain of seven stores. Whatever the origin, the name became popular and the distillery became known for producing its "Tennessee sippin' whiskey" by the "Lincoln County Process" (Lynchburg was initially in Lincoln County, which became part of Moore County in 1879). The process was based on mellowing the liquor and leaching, or filtering, it through charcoal. Daniel remained a bachelor, but his sister, Finetta Motlow, had seven sons, some of whom worked in the business. The eldest, Lem Motlow (q.v.), began working in the distillery in the 1880s and encouraged "Uncle Jack" to market his whiskey in bottles, as well as in bulk in barrels. He did so in square distinctive bottles, and again the practice was very successful. Daniel retired in 1907 and deeded his distillery to Lem and a cousin, Dick Daniel. Motlow bought Daniel's interest. When Tennessee went "dry" (q.v.) in 1910, Motlow opened a plant in St. Louis and another in Alabama before the advent of nationwide Prohibition (q.v.) in 1920. During the 1920s, Motlow ran his farms in Tennessee setting up a resort and wildlife reserve. With Repeal he was eager to return to distilling but first had to convince legislative and legal agencies to permit distilling in Tennessee and his home county. After a successful local election in 1938, he returned to whiskey production. By the time he died in 1947, Motlow had restored the Jack Daniel Distillery to its former prominence. His four sons, led by Reagor Motlow, who became president, took over the business. Reagor was instrumental in the passage of federal regulations recognizing "Tennessee whiskey" (q.v.) as a distinctive product. The need for liquid capital to pay taxes on stored whiskies, plus concerns about potential inheritance taxes on estate settlements, encouraged the Motlows to consider selling the distillery. In 1956 an agreement was reached with Brown-Forman (q.v.) distillers, who would pay a reported $18 million for the business, which would continue to be run locally by the Motlow family. Thus the two family-oriented businesses merged in a relationship that has proved beneficial to each. An important factor in Jack Daniel's success was apparently the business acumen of Winton Smith, who became president in 1968. He was succeeded by Martin S. Brown.

SOURCES:Bev/Executive (July 15, 1966); Jeanne Ridgway Bigger, "Jack Daniel Distillery and Lynchburg," *Tennessee Historical Quarterly* (Spring 1972); Ben A. Green, *Jack Daniel's Legacy* (Shelbyville, Tenn., 1967); Stan Jones, *Jones' Complete Barguide* (Los Angeles, 1977); "Rare Jack Daniel's," *Fortune* (July 1951).

Dant, J. B., Distillery. Joseph Bernard Dant, one of the seven sons of J. W. Dant (*see* Dant, J. W., Distillery), built the Cold Spring Distillery at Gethsemane, Kentucky, in 1865. Dant contracted with the Louisville sales firm of Taylor & Williams. J.B., who was known as the "Grand Old Man," had six Yellowstone name was first used in the 1870s at the suggestion of Charles Townsend, a salesman who visited Yellowstone Park, was impressed, and convinced his associates that it would be a good name for a whiskey. Dant later assumed control of the firm and changed the name of the company to Taylor & Williams. J.B., who was known as the "Grand Old Man," had six sons, each of whom joined the Taylor & Williams firm; he retired in 1935 and died in December 1939 at the age of eighty-nine. In 1944, the Dants sold their plant and Yellowstone brand to Glenmore Distilleries (q.v.).

SOURCES: "J. B. Dant Backs Taylor & Williams," *Spirits* (April 1935); *Spirits* (December 1939); "The Yellowstone Formula," *Spirits* (April 1952).

Dant, J. W., Distillery. Joseph Washington Dant built his small still at Dant, Kentucky, in Marion County in 1836. His first still was a hollowed-out log, cut in half, with a copper pipe inside. The process of using this early still was called "on a log," or "running it on a log" (*see* Still). He was known for producing sour mash (q.v.) whiskey. Dant had seven sons, including J. B., who was known as a first-rate and careful distiller noted for introducing the Yellowstone brand and formula, which was eventually purchased by Glenmore Distilleries Company (q.v.). Another son was George W. Dant, who became head of the newly incorporated J. W. Dant Company in 1897. J. B. Dant took a position with the Taylor & Williams Distillery, and his six sons joined him in the 1930s. The Dant family permeated the Kentucky bourbon industry, as various distilleries have had the Dant name. The J. W. Dant brand was purchased by Schenley Distillers Corporation (q.v.) as part of its expansion program after the repeal of Prohibition.

SOURCES: "Dant's Handmade 'On a Log,'" *Spirits* (April 1935); "Great Names in Whiskey," *Spirits* (July 1937); Stan Jones, *Jones' Complete Barguide* (Los Angeles, 1977); "Kentucky's Sons," *Spirits* (May 1936).

Daviess County Distilling Company. This Owensboro, Kentucky, distillery was first organized in 1873. R. Monarch, a noted Daviess County distiller, operated the plant for a time, and in 1901 George E. Medley purchased an interest in the firm. In 1904 Medley joined with Dietrich ("Dick") Meschendorf (q.v.) of the Old Kentucky Distillery (q.v.) to purchase full ownership of the Daviess County distillery. Medley's six sons came into the business, and Thomas A. became president in 1910 upon George E.'s death. The sons ran the company and were sole owners of the partnership until it was sold to Fleischmann (q.v.) in 1940. During Prohibition (q.v.), the brothers continued under the name and sold its whiskey stock to American Medicinal

Spirits (*see* Kentucky Distilleries and Warehouse Company) in 1927. *See also*, Medley Distilling Company.

SOURCES: "The Medley Family Incorporates," *Spirits* (July 1946); *Spirits* (April 1935, May 1936).

De LaVergne, John C. (active, 1850-1896). LaVergne invented a refrigerating machine for breweries. His ammonia-compression machine became the most popular and widely adopted machine during the 1880s and 1890s. He organized the De LaVergne Refrigerating Machine Company in New York City in 1881. Upon De LaVergne's death in 1896, Jacob Ruppert (q.v.) was elected president of the company. *See also*, Refrigeration.

SOURCES: Stanley Baron, *Brewed in America* (Boston, 1962); George Ehret, *Twenty-five Years of Brewing* (New York, 1891); *One Hundred Years of Brewing* (Chicago and New York, 1903; Arno Press Reprint, 1974).

Desert Springs, Inc. The parent company of this Orange, California, company was John Peace Enterprises, founded in 1977 in Hawaii as a distiller, rectifier, wholesaler, and importer of alcoholic beverages. The company's major brands, distributed mainly as Hawaiian Distillers Products, are Diamond Head Rum and Servok Vodka. The firm, headed by President John Peace, is building a distillery for the production of Hawaiian rum.

Detroit Brewing Company. Frank and John Martz originally established this firm in 1868, and in 1886 it was incorporated as the Detroit Brewing Company. The company survived Prohibition and closed in 1949.

Detroit brewing industry. Settled in 1701, Detroit did not become a truly American center until the 1790s because the French and then the British occupied the area until then. There were undoubtedly some brewers of ale and porter in the period, but the industry got its "advertised" beginning in the 1830s. One of the first companies was Emerson, Davis, and Moore, but soon, in the 1840s and 1850s, the trend was to German brewing—and thus lager beer (q.v.). One of the early firms was Stroh (q.v.), which was established by Bernhard Stroh in 1850. He was probably the city's first lager brewer. Joining him in the mid-nineteenth century were Philip Kling (q.v.), the Columbia Brewing Company, E. W. Voight (q.v.), Kaiser and Schmidt, and the Detroit Brewing Company (q.v.). Later in the century, Tivoli Brewing Company (q.v.), Goebel (q.v.), Pfeiffer (q.v.), E. & B. (q.v.), and Koppitz-Melchers (q.v.) would be among the many breweries opened. By 1890, thirty-three breweries operated in Detroit; the number declined to nineteen by 1910, fifteen by 1935, and in the late 1970s, only Stroh (which bought Goebel in the mid-1960s) was in operation. Detroit was able to support the large number of firms largely because of the number of German settlers, but the city had no national brewery in the period, and competition from the large nationals tended to hurt local brewers after 1890. The trend, of course, occurred nationwide.

SOURCES: Will Anderson, *The Beer Book* (Princeton, N.J., 1973); Stanley Baron, *Brewed in America* (Boston, 1962); David T. Glick, "The Beverage of Moderation: Brief History of the Michigan Brewing Industry," *Chronicle* (Summer 1977).

Dextrin. This soluble gummy sugar, along with maltose (q.v.), is formed by the action of an enzyme (q.v.) during the germination of barley. The sugar is fermentable, whereas the starch in the grain from which it was converted is not.

Diastase. The name of this enzyme that converts starch into dextrin and sugars originated in the 1830s and is derived from the Greek word meaning "separation." It is a by-product of the germination (q.v.) of barley, which occurs early in the malting (q.v.) process. Diastase is used interchangeably by brewers and distillers with the word amylase (q.v.).

SOURCE: Harold J. Grossman, *Grossman's Guide to Wines, Beers, and Spirits* (New York, 1977).

Dickel, George A., Distillery. George Dickel settled in Nashville, Tennessee, in the 1850s, went into whiskey wholesaling and sales, and then opened a store in 1866. The store handled liquor, and Dickel rectified (blended) bulk whiskey and bottled it before buying his own distillery in 1870. He died in 1894, but the company continued on until Tennessee went "dry" (q.v.) in 1910. The business was relocated in Kentucky until nationwide Prohibition (q.v.) led to its closing. Schenley Distillers Corp. (q.v.) bought the rights to the company in the early 1950s, and relocated at Tullahoma, Tennessee, producing a "Tennessee whiskey" (q.v.) to compete with Jack Daniel (q.v.).

SOURCE: Stan Jones, *Jones' Complete Barguide* (Los Angeles, 1977).

Distillation. *See* Distilling.

Distilled Spirits Council of the United States, Inc. (DISCUS). The merger of three distilling industry trade associations—Licensed Beverage Industries (q.v.), Distilled Spirits Institute (q.v.), and the Bourbon Institute (q.v.)— DISCUS was formed in 1973. It established its offices in Washington, D.C., on the premises of the Distilled Spirits Institute in the Pennsylvania Building. The new association would prevent duplication of efforts by the three and enabled consolidation of time and economic resources. It represents the producers of 95 percent of the distilled spirits manufactured in the U.S. The objectives of the agency are to foster the position of the industry by education, response to taxing regulations, promotion of American spirits in international trade, monitoring of alcohol laws, dissemination of information on the industry, and encouragement of studies to curb alcohol abuse.

SOURCE: Discus Facts Book, 1977, and Distilled Spirits Council of the U.S., "This Is Discus" (n.d.).

Distilled Spirits Institute (DSI). Distilling industry leaders organized this national trade association in 1933 to cooperate with government authorities in the formation of regulatory industry laws, maintain ethical standards, and in general to promote a sound public position for the industry in the aftermath of the repeal of Prohibition (q.v.). The agency maintained offices in Washington, D.C., and encouraged full compliance within the industry with all legal requirements at the various governmental levels. It also acted as an educational agency, formulating statistical, legal, and general information pertaining to the alcoholic beverage industry. Owsley Brown (q.v.) of Brown-Forman Distillers Corporation was instrumental in the establishment of the institute and became its first president. DSI merged with Licensed Beverage Industries (q.v.) and the Bourbon Institute (q.v.) in 1973 in the formation of the Distilled Spirits Council of the U.S., Inc. (q.v.).

SOURCES: Frank Kane, *Anatomy of the Whiskey Business* (Manhasset, N.Y., 1965); *Red Book, Encyclopedic Directory of the Wine and Liquor Industries, 1955-56.*

Distilleria. The term refers to items connected with the history of distilling. Books, catalogs, price lists, bottles, labels, tools, warehouse receipts, documents, and advertising signs are common items for collectors, but virtually any item connected with the industry has interest for collectors. The Barton Museum of Whiskey History in Bardstown, Kentucky, at the Barton (q.v.) distillery has an impressive display.

Distillers' & Cattle Feeders' Trust. *See* Whiskey Trust.

Distillers' Securities Corporation. *See* National Distillers Products Company, and Whiskey Trust.

Distillery, Rectifying and Wine Workers International Union of America. Organized in the late 1930s after the organization of a national council of federal labor unions in the industry, the union was chartered as a member of the American Federation of Labor in December 1940. The union maintained offices in Washington, D.C., and increased its membership of 10,000 in 1941 to 34,000 in 1962.

SOURCES: American Federation of Labor, *History Encyclopedia Reference Book*, vol. 3, pt. 1 (1955); Florence Peterson, *Handbook of Labor Unions* (Washington, D.C., 1944) and *American Labor Unions* (New York, 1963); Philip Taft, *Organized Labor in American History* (New York, 1964).

Distilling. Basically, this is the very important stage in the whiskey-making process (q.v.) whereby alcohol is separated from fermented mash by vaporization and condensation into a liquid. Alcohol boils at 173° Fahrenheit, whereas water must be heated to 212° Fahrenheit. Therefore, the alcohol can be boiled off or vaporized in a relatively simple procedure. The distilling is done in a pot-still (*see* Still) or continuous still, which was formerly called a patent-still (*see* Still). The science of distilling probably dates to the ancient Egyptians and Chaldeans, and the Chinese and Indians quite possibly engaged in some kind of distillation. Later, the Arabs or Saracens, sometime after 700 A.D., were known for distilling and contributed the words "alcohol" and "alembic" ("still") to the English language. However, one source maintains that the Celts of Ireland and Scotland distilled spirits before the Arabs. Whiskey (q.v.) derives from a Gaelic word, "uisgebeatha" or "usquebaugh," meaning "water of life." Other accounts maintain that distilling was introduced in Europe in the twelfth century and into the British Isles in the thirteenth century by the Franciscan friar Roger Bacon (q.v.). Early American colonists distilled fruit and grain, and rum (q.v.) became a very popular distilled beverage in the colonial period. Toward the end of the eighteenth century, farmer-distillers (q.v.) began to move west and especially into Kentucky. Spirits proved generally acceptable and popular among Americans overall. Gen. George Washington (q.v.) believed that distilled drinks were good for his soldiers, and he apparently enjoyed them also. During the nineteenth century, whiskey, and especially bourbon (q.v.), grew in popularity, was centered in Kentucky and southern Indiana, and became a very important industry.

SOURCES: Gerald Carson, *The Social History of Bourbon* (New York, 1963); Henry G. Crowgey, *Kentucky Bourbon* (Lexington, Ky., 1971); H. F. Willkie, *Beverage Spirits in America* (New York, 1949).

Distilling Company of America. Centered in Peoria, Illinois, the company was an outgrowth of the Whiskey Trust (q.v.) of the late 1890s. It was a consolidation of a number of the combines that had been organized in the wake of the trust's legal and financial problems. It consisted of American Spirits Manufacturing Company (q.v.), Kentucky Distilleries and Warehouse Company (q.v.), and Standard Distilling and Distributing Company (q.v.), each of which controlled numerous distilleries. It was apparently dissolved by 1902 and gave way to the Distillers' Securities Corporation. *See also*, National Distillers Products Company.

SOURCES: Victor S. Clark, *History of Manufactures in the U.S.*, vol. 3 (New York, 1929); Ernest E. East, "Distilling Fires in Corning Plant," *Arrow Messenger* (March 1937); Jeremiah W. Jenks and Walter E. Clark, *The Trust Problem* (New York, 1929).

Distilling process. *See* Whiskey-Making Process, and Distilling.

Diversey, Michael (ca. 1816-December 12, 1869). A Chicago brewer who came to the United States in 1836 from Germany, Diversey moved to Chicago in 1838 and bought William Ogden's (q.v.) interest in the Lill and Diversey (q.v.) brewery in 1840. Diversey was a philanthropist and civic leader who served as an alderman and donated ground for St. Michael's Church in 1852. His brewery was destroyed in the Great Fire of 1871.

SOURCE: Paul Angle, "Michael Diversey & Beer in Chicago," *Chicago History* (Spring 1969).

Dixie Brewing Company. This pre-Prohibition New Orleans brewery has marketed its beers primarily in the local area. By 1978 it was the only independent brewery remaining in the Crescent City.

Dobler Brewing Company. Darius Wood built his brewery in Albany, New York, in the early 1860s. John Dobler bought the plant about 1875, then sold out to Theodore Amsdell and George C. Hawley in the mid-1880s. A few years later, they sold the firm to A. S. Dobler. In 1892 it was incorporated as the Dobler Brewing Company; the firm survived Prohibition and continued in operation until 1959. Early in the twentieth century, the company was brought by Newark's Christian Feigenspan, Inc. (q.v.). Piels (q.v.) eventually bought the Dobler brand name.

SOURCES: Manfred Friedrich and Donald Bull, *The Register of U.S. Breweries* (Trumbull, Conn., 1976); James Robertson, *The Great American Beer Book* (Ottawa, Ill., 1978).

Doelger, Peter, Brewing Corporation. Peter Doelger migrated to America from Bavaria in 1850. Doelger, whose brother Joseph had opened a brewery in 1846, opened a small brewery in New York City in 1859, then moved to a new place, where he operated a very successful brewery (eleventh largest in the U.S. in 1895). During the 1880s, Doelger was involved in a number of labor disputes as workers were forming unions. In one incident four men died in an accident at his plant. Afterward, workers engaged in a successful boycott and strike. Doelger died in 1912 at the age of eighty. The family, led by his son, Peter, moved the business in the 1920s and finally settled in Harrison, New Jersey, at the former Peter Hauck brewery. The new brewery went out of business in 1947.

SOURCES: Will Anderson, *The Breweries of Brooklyn* (New York, 1976); Stanley Baron, *Brewed in America* (Boston, 1962); *One Hundred Years of Brewing* (Chicago and New York, 1903; Arno Press Reprint, 1974); Hermann Schlüter, *The Brewing Industry and Brewery Workers' Movement* (Cincinnati, 1910).

Doing Business As (DBA). The term is commonly used in the whiskey industry to indicate that a firm or person may be operating multiple distilleries under different names. For example, in 1949 Brown-Forman Distilleries Corporation (q.v.) was listed as "Doing Business As" Labrot & Graham (q.v.) and Kentucky Dew Distilling Company. One advantage is that one company might thus utilize several brand names. Also, the company maintains the image of a traditional, appealing, and independent name for its products.

Dona. This small mash (q.v.) of barley malt is used in the sweet mash (q.v.) process. A jug of yeast culture is added to the mash, "dona," after twenty-four hours and it ferments until ready to be added to the larger tub mash. Sometimes the dona is referred to as the dona tub. *See also,* Whiskey-Making Process.

Dortmunder. Receiving its name from the town of Dortmund in Germany, this beer type is fairly pale and is similar to Pilsener (q.v.). Many American brewers used the term in naming some of their products, especially before Prohibition.
   SOURCE: Frederic Birmingham, *Falstaff's Complete Beer Book* (New York, 1970).

Doubler. Formerly a pot-still in which low wines (q.v.), or singlings, are distilled a second time, the doubler apparently got its name in the late eighteenth century. Thus paired stills came into use, and distillers found the system preferable to a single distilling that produced an unpalatable whiskey.
   SOURCES: Henry G. Crowgey, *Kentucky Bourbon* (Lexington, Ky., 1971); James Boone Wilson, *The Spirit of Old Kentucky* (Louisville, Ky., 1945).

Dow, Neal (March 20, 1804-October 2, 1897). A famous temperance advocate, Dow supported the "Maine Liquor Law" (q.v.) of 1851, which banned the manufacture and sale of liquor in the state. He helped found the Maine Temperance Union in 1838. An initial law, which proved inadequate, was passed in 1846, and Dow, who was selected mayor of Portland in 1851, campaigned for tougher legislation. The law was repealed a few years later but was reenacted in 1857.
   SOURCES: Frank L. Byrne, *Prophet of Prohibition: Neal Dow and His Crusade* (Madison, Wis., 1961); *Dictionary of American Biography*, vol. 5.

Draft beer. This is an unpasteurized beer normally packaged in kegs (q.v.) and barrels (q.v.). Beer in this form is perishable and must be stored at low temperatures to prevent spoiling. Until the advent of pasteurization (q.v.), most beer was packaged in this form; afterward bottled and canned beer was pasteurized to enhance stability. Draft beer is fresher. Because of recent developments in sterile filtering processes, draft beer may be canned or bottled.

Draught beer. *See* Draft Beer.

Dreher, Anton (active, 1830s). A German brewer, Dreher was noted for scientific research and introduction of the bottom-fermentation process (q.v.) to Vienna in 1840.

Drewry's Ltd., U.S.A. (Brewery). Originally established in St. Paul, Minnesota, in the 1860s, the firm later operated plants in South Bend, Indiana, Chicago, and Willmansett, Massachusetts (*see* Harvard Brewing Company). The Drewry family also operated a plant in Winnipeg, Manitoba, Canada. During the early 1960s, Drewry's became part of the Associated Brewing Company (q.v.), which was later purchased by G. Heileman (q.v.).

   SOURCES: One Hundred Years of Brewing (Chicago and New York, 1903; Arno Press Reprint, 1974); James Robertson, *The Great American Beer Book* (Ottawa, Ill., 1978).

Drum malting. *See* Pneumatic Malting.

Dry. The term, dry, is commonly used in reference to a state, county, or local area that bans the liquor trade. Public officials and politicians who supported Prohibition (q.v.) were also referred to as "dry," especially during the struggle leading up to passage of Eighteenth Amendment (q.v.), and during the 1920s when the Prohibition Amendment was in force. And, of course, temperance and prohibition advocates became known as "drys."

Dubuque Star Brewing Company. *See* Pickett, Joseph S., & Sons, Inc.

Dukehart Manufacturing Company. (Brewery). Jacob Medtart established his Baltimore, Maryland, brewery in 1844. Known as the Saratoga Brewery, the company was comparatively small and was managed by the Dukehart family until it was closed in 1913.

   SOURCE: William J. Kelley, *Brewing in Maryland* (Baltimore, 1965).

Duncan Brewing Company. This small Florida brewery was organized by L. N. Duncan in 1973. The company markets a number of different brands in the area. Duncan is a subsidiary of Todhunter International, Inc., a privately owned firm that also owns Florida Distillers Company (q.v.).

Duquesne Brewing Company. In March 1899 five Pittsburgh businessmen formed this brewing company. John Benz was the first president. The company proved successful and in 1901 became noted for its Silver Top beer, which was developed and promoted by brewmaster Charles Weiland, who became notable for wearing ten-gallon hats. In an effort to compete with

the Pittsburgh Brewing Company (q.v.), a consolidation of numerous breweries, Duquesne organized a merger of fifteen other Pittsburgh breweries
into the Independent Brewing Company. During Prohibition (q.v.), all but
Duquesne were liquidated. Reorganized in 1933, the company continued in
operation, but in the 1960s and 1970s was beset by strikes, management
problems, and tough competition. In 1972 the company was bought by C.
Schmidt's (q.v.) of Philadelphia.

SOURCES: Stanley Baron, *Brewed in America* (Boston, 1962); Steven M. Fine,
"The King of Suds," *The Pittsburgher* (October 1977); *One Hundred Years of
Brewing* (Chicago and New York; 1903; Arno Press Reprint, 1974).

E

E. & B. Brewing Company. E. & B., a Detroit brewing company, was founded originally as Eckhardt and Becker in 1883. The firm reopened after repeal of Prohibition as Eckhardt and Becker Brewing Company, Inc. Then, in 1943, it became known as E. & B. Brewing Company, until it merged with Pfeiffer (q.v.) in the Associated Brewing Company (q.v.) in 1962.

Early Times Distillery Company. John H. Beam founded the distillery about 1853 near Bardstown, Kentucky. John (Jack) was one of three sons of David Beam. His brothers, David, Jr., and Joseph were also distillers. The Early Times plant was four miles south of the Jim Beam distillery (*see* Beam, James B., Distilling Company). For a time in the 1880s and 1890s, B. H. Hurt was president and Beam was vice-president and distiller. In 1910 or so, John Shaunty took over and was succeeded by S. J. Guthrie, who became sole owner in 1920. The Early Times plant was sold to J. T. S. Brown (q.v.) and the brand name to Brown-Forman (q.v.) in 1923.

SOURCES: James B. Beam Company historical information; Sam Elliot, *Nelson County Record* (Bardstown, Ky., 1896); *Kentucky's Distilling Interests* (Lexington, Ky., 1893); Harry H. Kroll, *Bluegrass, Belles, and Bourbon* (New York, 1967).

Eastern Brewing Corporation. This small brewery in Hammonton, New Jersey, was organized in the post-Prohibition period. A main feature of the company is the varied number of brands marketed. Among these are ABC Premium, Canadian Ace, Dawson, and Foxhead. The brand names have been purchased from defunct breweries.

SOURCE: James D. Robertson, *The Great American Beer Book* (Ottawa, Ill., 1978).

Eberhardt & Ober (Brewery). C. Eberhardt established this Pittsburgh brewing concern in 1848. In 1870 it became Eberhardt & Ober and in 1883 bought out the J. N. Straub Brewing Company. This company was part of the group that consolidated as the Pittsburgh Brewing Company (q.v.) in 1899. Although most of the plants were shut down, Eberhardt & Ober remained open as part of the Pittsburgh Brewing Company until 1952.

SOURCES: One Hundred Years of Brewing (Chicago and New York, 1903; Arno Press Reprint, 1974); "Pittsburgh, History of Beer and a Market," *American Brewer* (June and July 1960).

Edelbrew Brewery, Inc. A German immigrant, Otto Huber, Sr., who had worked for other breweries in Brooklyn, established his own plant in the late 1860s. He purchased the Joerger Brewery in 1866 and built the new plant, which was one of the largest and most productive breweries in Brooklyn. After his death in 1889, his sons, Otto, Jr., Joseph, Charles, and Max managed the company and it rcmained a family enterprise until the 1920s when it was sold to Edward Hittleman, who renamed the brewery after himself. Hittleman produced near beer (q.v.) until repeal of Prohibition, and in 1934 he changed the name of the company to Hittleman-Goldenrod Brewery. Goldenrod was a traditional brand name dating to the Huber brewery. After being renamed in 1940 as Edelbrau after a popular beer, it was finally changed to Edelbrew in 1946. Not long after Hittleman's death in 1951 at age sixty-eight, the brewery closed.

SOURCES: Will Anderson, *The Breweries of Brooklyn* (New York, 1976); *One Hundred Years of Brewing* (Chicago and New York, 1903; Arno Press Reprint, 1974).

Ehret, George (April 6, 1835-1927). A New York brewer who migrated to the U.S. from Germany in 1857, Ehret joined his father, who had made the transition a few years earlier. Ehret had a knowledge of brewing and worked for the Hupfel brewery as an employee and foreman before establishing the Ehret (q.v.) brewery in 1866. Known as the Hell Gate brewery, it became one of the nation's leading concerns in the 1870s and 1880s. Ehret directed his brewery and was active in promoting the interests of his industry as an officer in the U.S. Brewers' Association (q.v.). Following his death in 1927, the company was directed by his son, Louis Ehret.

SOURCES: Will Anderson, *The Breweries of Brooklyn* (New York, 1976); George Ehret, *Twenty-five Years of Brewing* (New York, 1891); *One Hundred Years of Brewing* (Chicago and New York, 1903; Arno Press Reprint, 1974).

Ehret's, George, Hell Gate Brewery. Ehret's was a prominent New York City brewing company founded in 1866 by George Ehret (q.v.), an 1857 German immigrant. The brewery was situated across from a precarious passage on the East River known as Hell Gate. Ehret chose the name for his brewery. After a fire in September 1870 destroyed much of the original plant, Ehret rebuilt and took advantage of the loss by installing more modern equipment and expanding facilities. For example, he added a De LaVergne refrigeration (q.v.) system to his plant. By 1877, the Hell Gate Brewery was the largest producer in the U.S. although Ehret's marketing area continued to be geared primarily to New York. His ranking as a large brewer dropped to fourth place in 1895, behind Pabst (q.v.), Anheuser-Busch (q.v.), and Schlitz (q.v.), but the brewery continued successfully into the 1920s. When Ehret died in 1927, his estate was estimated at $40 million. The heirs kept the plant open for a few more years but sold out to Col. Jacob Ruppert (q.v.) in April 1935. But the Ehrets reentered the brewing business later the same year with the purchase of Brooklyn's Interboro Beverage Company, which had been the Leonard Eppig brewery until 1920. Louis Ehret headed the new enterprise. In 1949 the company sold its Brooklyn plant to Schlitz, that company's first venture in opening a non-Milwaukee plant. Meanwhile, Ehret's moved to Union City, New Jersey, but closed in 1951.

SOURCES: Will Anderson, *The Breweries of Brooklyn* (New York, 1976); George Ehret, *Twenty-five Years of Brewing* (New York, 1891); *One Hundred Years of Brewing* (Chicago and New York, 1903; Arno Press Reprint, 1974).

Eighteenth Amendment. Known also as the Prohibition Amendment, this constitutional amendment prohibited the manufacture, sale, transportation, import, or export of intoxicating liquor for use as beverages. The Congress and the states were authorized to enforce the legislation. The proposed amendment came before the Congress in 1914, largely as a result of the efforts of the Anti-Saloon League (q.v.). In 1917, the amendment passed Congress and was then submitted to the states, which completed the ratification process on January 16, 1919. The enforcement provision, the Volstead Act (q.v.), was passed in October 1919. The amendment became effective January 16, 1920, and remained in effect until repeal by the Twenty-first Amendment (q.v.) in December 1933. *See also*, Prohibition.

Enzyme. This biological catalyst occurs naturally and induces changes in other substances. In brewing and distilling the enzymes of malt, known as diastase (q.v.) or amylase (q.v.), convert the starches in grain to sugars, maltose (q.v.), and dextrin (q.v.).

Erie Brewing Company. The Erie, Pennsylvania, brewery was established by Charles Koehler in 1862. Frederick, his eldest son, assumed control in 1869 upon Charles's death. Another son, Jackson, was involved in the brewery known as Fred Koehler & Company until 1883 when he built his own plant. However, the two merged with the Cascade Brewery, which was built in 1893, and formed the Erie Brewing Company in 1899. Jackson Koehler's family continued to operate the firm in the twentieth century and produced a number of brews under the Koehler brand name. C. Schmidt's (q.v.) purchased the company in February 1978.

SOURCES: James D. Robertson, *The Great American Beer Book* (Ottawa, Ill., 1978); *One Hundred Years of Brewing* (Chicago and New York, 1903; Arno Press Reprint, 1974).

Esslinger Brewing Company. Founded by George Esslinger in 1868, this Philadelphia brewery continued to operate successfully well into the twentieth century. The firm managed two plants between 1937 and 1953 but closed in 1954. The brand name was sold to C. Schmidt's (q.v.), which in turn sold the name to Lion, Inc. (q.v.) of Wilkes-Barre, Pennsylvania.

SOURCES: Will Anderson, *The Beer Book* (Princeton, N.J., 1973); *One Hundred Years of Brewing* (Chicago and New York, 1903; Arno Press Reprint, 1974).

Evans, C. H., & Sons (Brewery). This Hudson, New York, company was established first by Benjamin Faulkins in 1786. He produced the noted Hudson Ale. Robert W. Evans bought the plant in the 1850s; the name was changed to C. H. Evans in 1878, and the company stayed in business until Prohibition.

SOURCES: John P. Arnold and Frank Penman, *History of the Brewing Industry and Brewing Science* (Chicago, 1933); *One Hundred Years of Brewing* (Chicago and New York, 1903; Arno Press Reprint, 1974).

Everard, James, Brewing Company. In 1885 James Everard, an Irish immigrant, founded his New York City ale, porter, and lager beer brewery. He had been involved in the Shook & Everard brewery before building his plant. In 1891, the two breweries were combined under the name James Everard's Breweries. In 1895, his breweries ranked thirteenth in beer production among U.S. brewers. The firm went out of business during Prohibition in the 1920s.

SOURCES: Manfred Friedrich and Donald Bull, *The Register of U.S. Breweries* (Trumbull, Conn., 1976); *One Hundred Years of Brewing* (Chicago and New York, 1903; Arno Press Reprint, 1974).

Excise Act, 1791. Passed on March 3, 1791, this act levied duties on all domestic distilled spirits. It went into effect on July 1 and was passed partly as a revenue measure and partly as a deterrent to strong drink. The tax varied from $.09 to $.25 per gallon, depending on the percentage of proof (q.v.), on stills in any city, town, or village. The law stipulated that an annual tax of $.60 per gallon of still (q.v.) capacity would be due on country stills, but the operator could pay $.09 per gallon on actual output instead of potential output. Because of early opposition to the tax, the law was modified in 1792 by reductions on the classes of proof from $.02 to $.07 cents a gallon. Also, taxes on country stills were lowered. The change was made largely to conciliate western distillers who operated smaller stills. Nevertheless, the tax eventually culminated in the Whiskey Rebellion (q.v.) in western Pennsylvania.

SOURCES: Gerald Carson, *The Social History of Bourbon* (New York, 1963); Henry G. Crowgey, *Kentucky Bourbon* (Lexington, Ky., 1971); U.S., *American State Papers*, Finance, 1:110-11.

F

Falls City Brewing Company. A Louisville, Kentucky, brewery founded in 1905, Falls City was one of the many "consumers" breweries across the nation. It was organized by local citizens and tavern owners. The firm survived Prohibition in the 1920s by producing near beer and soft drinks. In the early 1970s, the Drummond Bros. brand was marketed, and Falls City was also a producer of short-lived Billy Beer, named after President Jimmy Carter's brother.

SOURCE: James D. Robertson, *The Great American Beer Book* (Ottawa, Ill., 1978).

Falstaff Brewing Corporation. Originally based solely in St. Louis, Falstaff was founded in 1917 by Joseph ("Papa Joe") Griesedieck, who bought the Forest Park Brewing Company, possibly to provide a position in the business for his son, Alvin. The Griesediecks had been in the brewing business since the late 1870s when Joseph's father, Anton, a German immigrant, bought the Phoenix (q.v.) brewery in St. Louis. After operating other plants, Anton sold out to a British syndicate in 1889 known as the St. Louis Brewing Association (q.v.). Joseph and two brothers, Henry and Bernard, first built the National Brewery in 1891, but then joined a merger known as Independent Breweries Company (q.v.) to compete with other consolidations. The company encountered financial problems, prompting Henry and his sons to organize an independent company. They incorporated the Griesedieck Brothers Brewery in the early twentieth century. In the meantime the Griesediecks also bought the Belleville, Illinois, Western Brewery (Stag) (q.v.) in 1912 and then Joseph bought the Forest Park plant in 1917. Thus, on the eve of Prohibition, the Griesediecks essentially operated three different plants that were intertwined at some level. The Forest Park company, however, initially called the Griesedieck Beverage Company, became the Falstaff Brewing Corporation by 1933. The firm bought the Falstaff name, after Shakespeare's character, from the William J. Lemp Brewing Company (q.v.) in the 1920s. During the Prohibition period, the company marketed near beer (q.v.), soft drinks, and nonbeer products such as hams and bacon. With the repeal of the Eighteenth Amendment (q.v.), Falstaff, with Alvin Griesedieck directing the company, began to expand. Credited with being one of the first "chain" brewers, Griesedieck bought Omaha's Fred Krug Brewery in 1935 and the National Brewery of New Orleans in 1937. Other acquisitions were the Berghoff Brewing Company plant in Ft. Wayne, Indiana, the Narragansett Brewing Company (q.v.) of Rhode Island in 1966, and the Ballantine (q.v.) brands in 1972. By the late 1970s, Falstaff operated about five plants and was the nation's eleventh largest brewer in 1977.

SOURCES: Alvin Griesedieck, *The Falstaff Story* (1952); *One Hundred Years of Brewing* (Chicago and New York, 1903; Arno Press Reprint, 1974); James D. Robertson, *The Great American Beer Book* (Ottawa, Ill., 1978).

Farmer-distiller. The term describes many late eighteenth- and early nineteenth-century distillers who were primarily farmers. Conversion of corn into whiskey was attractive for a number of reasons. It avoided corn spoilage, could be more easily and economically transported overland, acted as a medium of exchange in many areas, and could be used for home consumption. Farmer-distillers included the whiskey "rebels" of western Pennsylvania who refused to pay the 1791 excise tax, the Rev. Elijah Craig (q.v.), reputed to be the "first distiller" of Kentucky, Elijah Pepper (*see* Pepper, James, Distillery), and George Washington (q.v.), a planter-distiller. *See also*, Whiskey Rebellion.

SOURCES: Gerald Carson, *The Social History of Bourbon* (New York, 1963); Henry G. Crowgey, *Kentucky Bourbon* (Lexington, Ky., 1971); Howard T. Walden, *Native Inheritance* (New York, 1966).

Federal Alcohol Administration. Successor to the Federal Alcohol Control Administration (q.v.), the FAA administered federal liquor regulations until 1940, when it was replaced by the Alcohol Tax Unit (q.v.) of the Department of the Treasury. The Federal Alcohol Administration Act, passed in 1936, set forth the most detailed classifications of liquors since the "Taft decision" (q.v.) of 1909. Definitions were spelled out for the manufacture and aging of the various whiskey types—among them straight whiskey, straight bourbon whiskey, blended whiskey, and blended rye whiskey.

SOURCES: Gerald Carson, *The Social History of Bourbon* (New York, 1936); Harold J. Grossman, *Grossman's Guide to Wines, Beers, and Spirits* (New York, 1977); Morris V. Rosenbloom, *The Liquor Industry* (Braddock, Pa., 1937).

Federal Alcohol Control Administration. President Franklin Roosevelt established this agency by an executive order on December 4, 1933, under the authority of the National Industrial Recovery Act. Roosevelt created the FACA to approve codes of fair competition in the industry, but also as a control agency to prevent the social and political problems of the pre-Prohibition liquor trade. Thus a system of liquor control regulations was established. Six codes—the Distillers' Code, the Wine Code, the Rectifiers' Code, the Wholesale Liquor Dealers' Code, the Brewers' Code, and the Importers' Marketing Agreement—were formulated. Consumer protection and protection of state liquor laws would be objectives, as well as trade and price controls as a means of combating the Depression. One of the most important regulations for the brewing industry made it illegal for brewers to own retail outlets. Standards of identity (q.v.) and classification were drawn up, going beyond the definitions of the "Taft decision" (q.v.) of 1909. After the Supreme Court invalidated the NIRA in 1935, the Federal Alcohol Administration (q.v.) succeeded the FACA. *See also*, Federal Liquor Regulations.

SOURCES: *Red Book, 1961-62; Encyclopedic Directory of the Wine and Liquor Industries* (New York, 1961); Morris Victor Rosenbloom, *The Liquor Industry* (Braddock, Pa., 1937).

Federal liquor regulations. Although state and local government regulations and licensing of the sale of alcoholic beverages date from the colonial period, federal laws date mainly from 1890s. The Wilson Act (q.v.) of 1890 and the Webb-Kenyon Act (q.v.) of 1913, which removed intoxicating beverages from the protection of the interstate commerce clause, reflected the early nature of federal legislation. Another form of federal involvement, not necessarily control, was the Bottled-in-Bond Act (q.v.) of 1897, which set minimum standards for specified whiskey. The Pure Food and Drug Act (q.v.) of 1906 likewise included certain whiskies among its list of adulterated beverages. In 1909 President William Howard Taft (q.v.) further defined such beverages in the "Taft decision" (q.v.), which established definitions for various types of whiskey. Malt liquors have been much less regulated but were under the Department of Agriculture in the 1890s and subject to requirements under the Pure Food and Drug Act. Definitions for malt liquors have been spelled out by the federal laws governing such beverages. The Eighteenth Amendment (q.v.) mandating nationwide Prohibition (q.v.) marked the modern extensive federal regulation of the liquor trade. The Prohibition Bureau (q.v.) attempted to enforce the amendment but found many obstacles especially as the 1920s ended. Upon repeal of Prohibition by the Twenty-first Amendment (q.v.) in 1933, President Franklin Roosevelt created the Federal Alcohol Control Administration (q.v.) as the regulatory agency for alcoholic beverages. The FACA, operating under the authority of the National Industrial Recovery Act, drew up codes of fair trade and expanded the standards of identity (q.v.) begun earlier. When the Supreme Court ruled against the NIRA in 1935, the Federal Alcohol Administration (q.v.) succeeded the FACA. The Federal Alcohol Administration Act of 1936 spelled out precise classifications of whiskies and established the modern definitions. A succession of reorganizations and name changes followed over the years. The Alcohol Tax Unit (q.v.) of the Treasury Department governed from 1940 to 1952, when the Alcohol and Tobacco Tax Division (q.v.) of the Treasury Department took over. That unit was changed in 1968 to the Alcohol, Tobacco, and Firearms Division (q.v.) until the latest reorganization in 1972 as the Bureau of Alcohol, Tobacco, and Firearms (q.v.), still under the Treasury Department. The BATF is responsible for public protection, trade practices, revenue collection, and enforcement of federal laws and regulations. The various agencies have operated under the Internal Revenue Service, which comes under the Treasury Department. The liquors under federal control include distilled spirits, wine, beer, and alcoholic compounds. *See also*, Standards of Identity.

SOURCES: Stanley Baron, *Brewed in America* (Boston, 1962); Jack S. Blocker, Jr., *Alcohol, Reform and Society* (Westport, Conn., 1979); Gerald Carson, *The Social History of Bourbon* (New York, 1963); Harold J. Grossman, *Grossman's Guide to Wines, Beers, and Spirits* (New York, 1977); *Red Book, 1961-62; Encyclopedic Directory of the Wine and Liquor Industries* (New York, 1963); Gilman G. Udell, *Liquor Laws* (Washington, D.C., 1978).

Fehr, Frank, Brewing Company. This Louisville, Kentucky, brewery was established by the German immigrant Frank Fehr in the 1870s. He had managed other breweries before taking over the Otto brewery in 1872. He became sole owner in 1876, and prospered to the point of buying another plant in New Orleans in 1884. That plant was later sold to the New Orleans Brewing Company, a syndicate, and his Louisville plant eventually became part of the Central Consumers Company (q.v.). Frank Fehr died in 1891. The Frank Fehr branch of Central Consumers reopened with the repeal of Prohibition and continued to operate until 1963.

SOURCES: Manfred Friedrich and Donald Bull, *The Register of U.S. Breweries* (Trumbull, Conn., 1976); *One Hundred Years of Brewing* (Chicago and New York, 1903; Arno Press Reprint, 1974).

Feigenspan, Christian, Inc. (Brewery). Originally founded in 1866 by Charles Kolb, Christian Feigenspan took over the Newark, New Jersey, brewery in 1870. The company gained control of the Dobler Brewing Company (q.v.) of Albany, New York, and the Yale Brewery of New Haven, Connecticut. The latter did not reopen after the repeal of Prohibition, but the Dobler plant continued until 1959. In 1944, Feigenspan sold out to P. Ballantine (q.v.), which revived the Feigenspan name in the 1960s and sold the Dobler brand to Piels (q.v.).

SOURCE: James D. Robertson, *The Great American Beer Book* (Ottawa, Ill., 1978).

Fermentation. Fermentation is the natural action of yeast (q.v.) in wort (q.v.) or a batch of grain, in which the agent (yeast) of change converts fermentable sugars in the wort, or mash (q.v.), to alcohol and carbon dioxide. The gas is released into the air, and alcohol remains. Enzymes of yeast are the primary agents responsible for the conversion. In the making of whiskey, fermentation procedures vary depending on whether sour mash (q.v.) or sweet mash (q.v.) is being produced. In the former, about one-fourth of the previous day's fermented mash is added to the present day's batch; in the latter, fresh mash and fresh yeast are used. Sweet mash requires two or three days for fermentation, and sour mash three to four days. Fermentation occurs at fairly high temperatures in both cases, but is higher for sour mash (about 80° Fahrenheit). The resulting liquid is called "distillers beer" (q.v.). For brewing, the fermentation is different mainly because of the two types of yeast processes, top fermentation (q.v.) and bottom fermentation (q.v.). Top-fermentation yeast floats on the top of the fermenting vats and is used in brewing ale (q.v.), porter (q.v.), and stout (q.v.). Bottom-fermentation yeast, which was introduced in the early nineteenth century in Germany, is used for brewing lager beer (q.v.) and its varieties.

SOURCES: Jean De Clerck, *A Textbook of Brewing*, vol. 1 (London, 1957); Harold J. Grossman, *Grossman's Guide to Wines, Beers and Spirits* (New York, 1977); Frank Haring, ed., *Encyclopedia of Alcoholic Beverages* (New York, 1959).

Finch, Jos. B., Distillery. Joseph Finch founded his Schenley, Pennsylvania, plant near Pittsburgh in the mid-1850s. The most famous brand was Golden Wedding. Other owners managed the plant under the Finch name in the early twentieth century. Schenley Distillers Corporation (q.v.) bought the distillery, brands, and stock in 1924.

SOURCES: "Great Names in Whiskey," *Spirits* (May 1937); "Whiskey," *Fortune* (November 1933).

Fining. In the final stages of fermentation, beer was clarified or filtered by the use of shavings or chips, usually of beech or maple wood. Beer was drawn from ruh (q.v.) casks and put in chip casks in which the chips attracted and then attached to solid particles of yeast and other impurities in the beer. Another method of clarifying was the insertion of isinglass (q.v.) into the beer at this stage. Both methods of fining were very popular in the U.S. prior to the introduction of commercial filtering mechanisms such as Stockheim or Enzinger filters in the late 1880s.

SOURCES: John P. Arnold and Frank Penman, *History of the Brewing Industry and Brewing Science* (Chicago, 1933); Thomas C. Cochran, *The Pabst Brewing Company* (New York, 1948); *One Hundred Years of Brewing* (Chicago and New York, 1903; Arno Press Reprint, 1974).

First bourbon distiller. *See* "First Distiller of Kentucky."

"First Distiller of Kentucky." The designation of one person as Kentucky's first distiller occurred with frequency in late nineteenth-century histories and has continued to be considered one of the necessary points to be made in any number of modern publications—whether in journalistic articles on the industry or in brief commercial histories sponsored by distilling concerns. In an 1892 account, Reuben Durrett suggested that Evan Williams was one of the earliest distillers in the state in 1783—and possibly the earliest. In his recent scholarly study of the industry, Henry Crowgey properly indicates the problems involved in making a firm designation of the "first distiller." In an era of many farmer-distillers (q.v.) a definite conclusion would be impossible. Sources indicate that Jacob Myers probably preceded Williams in any case. Among other early distillers were William Calk and Isaac Shelby, Kentucky's first governor. Another question, that of who distilled the first bourbon, is equally elusive. The Rev. Elijah Craig, a Baptist minister, is often given the credit for making the first bourbon in 1789, but the distinction appears unwarranted. In 1874 Richard Collins, in his *History of Kentucky*, was evidently the first source to refer to Craig and the evidence is shaky. Moreover, the drink in question, bourbon, was clearly a different product from that of the late nineteenth century. The general practice of aging whiskey in charred barrels did not occur until long after Craig had made his whiskey. Thus bourbon as known by a contemporary of the 1870s and 1880s was probably unknown before 1850. In sum, questions as to who was the "first distiller" and "first bourbon distiller" are academic, as many names have surfaced for answering each question.

SOURCES: Gerald Carson, *The Social History of Bourbon* (New York, 1963); Henry G. Crowgey, *Kentucky Bourbon* (Lexington, Ky., 1971); Willard Rouse Jillson, *Early Kentucky Distillers* (Louisville, Ky., 1940).

Flakestand. In the distilling (q.v.) process, this was the barrel or drum of cold water in which the condenser, or worm (q.v.), was immersed to vaporize the alcohol. Modern methods of cooling have largely replaced this method, especially since the repeal of Prohibition in 1933.

SOURCES: Carl J. Kiefer, "Planning a Modern Distillery," *Spirits* (October 1933); David W. Maurer, *Kentucky Moonshine* (Lexington, Ky., 1974).

Flanagan, Nay & Company (Brewery). The nation's seventh largest brewer in 1877, this New York City company was originally founded in the 1850s as F. W. Wallace & Company. Later it became Flanagan & Wallace, and in 1881 Flanagan, Nay & Company. It merged with H. Clausen (q.v.) in 1888 as the New York Breweries Company. In 1903 it was reorganized as the Flanagan Branch of the Clausen-Flanagan Brewery and from Prohibition in the 1920s to 1937, when it closed, as the Flanagan-Nay Brewing Company.

SOURCES: Manfred Friedrich and Donald Bull, *The Register of U.S. Breweries* (Trumbull, Conn., 1976); *One Hundred Years of Brewing* (Chicago and New York, 1903; Arno Press Reprint, 1974).

Fleischmann Distilling Company. The company was founded in 1868 by Charles and Maxmillian Fleischmann and James Graff of Cincinnati. The firm maintained two plants at Riverside, Ohio. The company's distilling operations were closed during Prohibition. Toward the end of the 1920s Standard Brands, Inc., purchased the firm's assets and developed various food-processing operations. In 1940, Fleischmann's (operating under that name) built up whiskey inventories by purchasing the Daviess County Distillery (q.v.) in Owensboro, Kentucky, and has continued to base its distilled spirits business at that location. Fleischmann's, reputed to be America's first distiller of gin (q.v.) in 1870, is noted for its Preferred Blended Whiskey, distilled Dry Gin, and Royal Vodka. Leo Begleiter became president of the firm in 1976. Present production facilities include locations in Dayton, New Jersey, Plainfield, Illinois, Clinton, Iowa, and Owensboro, Kentucky.

SOURCES: *Bev* (May 1, 1964); "Great Names in Whiskey," *Spirits* (May 1937); Stan Jones, *Jones' Complete Barguide* (Los Angeles, 1977).

Floor-malting. Until the introduction of mechanical devices in the 1870s and 1880s, floor-malting was the most common method of malting (q.v.). Wet barley that had been steeped, or soaked in hot water, was spread out evenly about 24 inches deep over a concrete or stone floor and the mixture would be turned a number of times by hand. Later the barley was spread out to a depth of about 6 inches. Then it was turned, or shoveled, a number of times, before being ready for kilning (q.v.). Gradually, after 1880, this laborious procedure was replaced as pneumatic malting (q.v.) devices became available. Nevertheless, some maltsters continued to use floor-malting well into the twentieth century.

SOURCES: John P. Arnold and Frank Penman, *History of the Brewing Industry and Brewing Science* (Chicago, 1933); Thomas C. Cochran, *The Pabst Brewing Company* (New York, 1948); *One Hundred Years of Brewing* (Chicago and New York, 1903; Arno Press Reprint, 1974).

Florida Distillers Company. This distilling company operates as a wholly owned subsidiary of Todhunter International, Inc. Florida Fruit Distillers, Inc., the predecessor to Florida Distillers, was organized in 1943. Al S. Elfenbein was the principal owner. Florida Distillers, which operates in Lake Alfred, Florida, produces grain alcohol, cane alcohol, rum, and brandy and sells in bulk to other distillers and rectifiers. The company itself does not bottle any products. A. Kenneth Pincourt, Jr., and Leonard G. Rogers are the main stockholders of Todhunter International, a privately owned company.

Flower City Brewing Company. Frederick Miller founded his Rochester, New York, brewery in the mid-1860s. From 1883 to 1902 it was known as the Miller Brewing Company. After 1902 it was known as the Flower City Brewing Company and after repeal of Prohibition in 1933 was reorganized as the Standard Brewing Company (*see* Standard Rochester Brewing Company, Inc.).

SOURCES: Manfred Friedrich and Donald Bull, *The Register of U.S. Breweries* (Trumbull, Conn., 1976).

Foreshots. Also called heads or first shots, these are the first run of spirits that vaporize from the still. The substance is usually redistilled, and the term is used in both the processing of low wines (q.v.) and high wines (q.v.).

Ft. Pitt Brewing Company. This Sharpsburg, Pennsylvania, brewery was organized in 1906 to compete with Pittsburgh's two brewery consolidates, Pittsburgh Brewing Company (q.v.) and Duquesne (q.v.). Ft. Pitt managed to survive Prohibition, operated into the mid-1950s, then sold out in 1957 to Gunther Brewing Company of Baltimore, which in turn sold out to Hamm (q.v.) in 1959.

SOURCE: Steven M. Fine, "King of Suds," *The Pittsburgher* (October 1977).

Fox, Hugh F. (active ca. 1880-1933). Secretary of the U.S. Brewers' Association (q.v.) from 1908 to 1933, Fox also compiled the *Yearbook* of the association during the period.

SOURCE: John P. Arnold and Frank Penman, *History of the Brewing Industry and Brewing Science in America* (Chicago, 1933).

Frankfort Distilleries, Inc. Paul Jones, a whiskey salesman from Tennessee, moved to Kentucky with his son in 1886. He obtained the rights to Four Roses, the brand of the Rose family (then living in Tennessee), and built a strong reputation for the brand. In 1902 several distilleries were joined as the Frankfort Distillery, Inc. During the 1920s, the company received a permit for medicinal whiskey and produced 25 percent of the nation's supply. Lawrence Jones, Jr., headed the firm, which was reorganized as Frankfort Distilleries, Inc., in 1933. Jos. E. Seagram (q.v.) purchased Frankfort, which also owned Mattingly and Moore (q.v.), in the 1940s.

SOURCES: Stan Jones, *Jones' Complete Barguide* (Los Angeles, 1977); Morris V. Rosenbloom, *The Liquor Industry* (Braddock, 1937); *Spirits* (May 1952).

Fromm and Sichel, Inc. Founded as a wine distributor by Franz W. Sichel and Alfred Fromm in 1944, the company has distributed only Christian Brothers Wine, Champagnes, and Brandy since 1945. In 1950, Samuel Bronfman (q.v.), who had met Sichel in Germany in the 1930s, was instrumental in his firm's (Seagram, [q.v.]) purchase of the controlling interest in

Fromm and Sichel. Sichel, who died in 1967, was president from 1944 to 1965 and was succeeded by Fromm, who later became chairman.

SOURCE: Samuel Bronfman, *From Little Acorns* (Montreal, 1970).

Frow. Early coopers used this tool to make whiskey barrels (q.v.). The frow was used to split the timber for making staves.

Fusel oil. This is one of the congeners (q.v.), or impurities, in whiskey (q.v.) after distillation. During aging (q.v.), the oily liquid apparently is transformed and adds character to the whiskey.

G

Galland, Nicholas (active, 1870-80s). A French maltster and brewer, Galland invented and patented a pneumatic malting (q.v.) device in the 1870s. First he produced box, or compartment, systems, then went over to the drum system in 1885. Improvements were made on his system, which became known as the Galland-Henning drum. Henning was director of a company in Berlin that had adopted Galland's drum in 1885. A Milwaukee malting firm adopted the device in 1889, and a few years later, company officials organized the Galland-Henning Pneumatic Malting Drum Company of Milwaukee. *See also*, Malting.

    SOURCE: One Hundred Years of Brewing (Chicago and New York, 1903; Arno Press Reprint, 1974).

Gambrinus, King. The legendary king of beer is often credited with having originated the science of brewing. The statue or picture of this mythological god of beer has been used by many breweries in advertising, and many have used the name as a designation of their breweries or beer. Jan Primus (Johann the First), Duke of Brabant in the late twelfth century, was made an honorary member of the brewers' guild of Brussels. Apparently, the name Gambrinus is derived from him.

    SOURCES: Stanley Baron, *Brewed in America* (Boston, 1962); Frederic Birmingham, *Falstaff's Complete Beer Book* (New York, 1970); George Ehret, *Twenty-five Years of Brewing* (New York, 1891).

Garneau, Jos., and Company. The company was originally an importer of French wine and was founded in 1859 as Schmidt and Peters. Joseph Garneau joined the firm soon after its inception and proved to be an aggressive salesman. In 1913 he became sole owner and acted as an agent for Clicquot champagne and a number of other French wine makers. Upon Garneau's death in 1917, he was succeeded by nephew Joseph Garneau Ringwalt. During the Prohibition era, Ringwalt imported wine, under permit, for medicinal purposes. In 1946, Garneau obtained distribution rights for Usher's Scotch. The company was purchased by Brown-Forman Distillers Corporation (q.v.) in 1956. Brown-Forman, which had just purchased the Jack Daniel Distillery (q.v.), was expanding and in the market for an importer of Scotch (q.v.). Mason L. Tush, of Brown-Forman, was president of the company in the late 1970s.

SOURCES: "The House of Garneau," Spirits (October 1935); John Ed Pearce, Nothing Better in the Market (Louisville, Ky., 1970); Art Williams, "Brown-Forman Bids for Big Five Position," Spirits (September 1956).

Gaul Brewery. Frederick Gaul and Casper Morris operated this Philadelphia brewing business in 1804. It was subsequently known as the Gaul Brewery until closing in 1841. Reuben Haines, who had occasionally supplied President George Washington with beer, established the original brewery in 1785. In 1867, John F. Betz (see Betz, John F., and Sons, Inc.) opened a brewery on the site.

SOURCES: Stanley Baron, Brewed in America (Boston, 1962); One Hundred Years of Brewing (Chicago and New York, 1903; Arno Press Reprint, 1974).

General Brewing Company. The San Francisco, California, and Vancouver, Washington, brewing concern evolved from the Lucky Lager Brewing Company. Lucky Lager was organized in the early twentieth century by Canadian Lucky Lager Breweries, Ltd. Alternately known as the General Brewing Corporation, Lucky Lager Brewing Company, and Lucky Breweries, Inc., the company assumed the General Brewing Company name in 1963. For a time, from 1958 to 1971, the company was controlled by Labatt Breweries of Canada. Many brands have been marketed, and Falstaff (q.v.) and Walter Brewing Company (q.v.) of Pueblo, Colorado, have produced Lucky Lager for various local markets. The Lucky Lager plant of Azusa, California, which was part of the general organization, was sold to Miller Brewing Company (q.v.) in the mid-1960s.

SOURCES: James D. Robertson, The Great American Beer Book (Ottawa, Ill., 1978); Manfred Friedrich and Donald Bull, The Register of U.S. Breweries (Trumbull, Conn., 1976).

Genesee Brewing Company. Louis A. Wehle reorganized the Rochester, New York, company in 1932. The Genesee Brewing Company was originally founded in 1878 and marketed its Liebotschaner brand in western New York. In 1889 the Bartholomay Brewing Company, which consisted of two breweries and two malting companies, took over the Genesee brewery, which continued under the same name. Wehle worked in the brewery, ultimately became brewmaster, and then entered the grocery and bakery business during the Prohibition era of the 1920s. In 1932, however, he organized a new Genesee brewery as he bought the old plant in anticipation of Repeal, and was ready to market his beer in April 1933. John L. Wehle currently is chairman of Genesee, which continues as a successful regional brewery marketing its full-bodied and krausened beers and ales in fourteen northeastern states. In 1978 the company was twelfth largest in the U.S., with more than 3 million barrels produced.

SOURCE: Will Anderson, *The Beer Book* (Princeton, N.J., 1973); Company historical information.

Germination. Barley grains sprout during the malting (q.v.) process. After soaking, barley is put through a growth, or germination, process. Until the introduction of pneumatic malting (q.v.) devices in the 1870s and 1880s, the wet barley was spread out on concrete or stone floors in a procedure known as flooring, floor-malting (q.v.), or couching. When, after a few weeks, the sprouts, or acrospires (q.v.), grow to about the size of the barley kernels (about three-fourths of an inch), the grain is ready for kilning (q.v.).

SOURCE: One Hundred Years of Brewing (Chicago and New York, 1903; Arno Press Reprint, 1974).

Gettelman, Adam, Brewing Company. This Milwaukee brewing company was originally founded in the 1850s by Stroh & Reitzenstein. They died soon after in a cholera epidemic, and the plant was purchased by George Schweickhart in 1855. His son-in-law, Adam Gettelman, bought a share in the brewery in 1871 and then purchased control of the business in 1876. He incorporated the company in 1887 as the Adam Gettelman Brewing Company. The company was noted for its "$1,000 Natural Process," beer which was copyrighted in 1890 as the firm offered $1,000 to anyone who could disprove that the beer was made with pure malt and hops. The brewery, which marketed its beer mainly in the Wisconsin and northern Illinois areas, produced near beer (q.v.) during the 1920s and was reopened as a brewery in 1933. Frederick Gettelman ran the company successfully until 1961 when he sold the company to the Miller Brewing Company (q.v.). Miller closed the plant in 1971, but continued to market Gettelman beer.

SOURCES: "The A. Gettelman Brewing Company," *Brewers Digest* (September 1954); Will Anderson, *The Beer Book* (Princeton, N.J., 1973); Wayne Kroll, *Badger Breweries* (Jefferson, Wis., 1976); "Milwaukee Beer—It Made a City 'Famous,'" *Wisconsin Then and Now* (February 1968).

Geyer Bros. Brewing Company. Founded in 1862, originally as the Cass River Brewery, John George Geyer acquired the Frankenmuth, Michigan, brewery in 1874. It continued under his name until about 1905 when the company became Geyer Bros. The small company maintained a tavern before Prohibition and much of its beer was sold on the premises. Over the years the Geyer family has exercised some form of control over the brewery, which brews Frankenmuth Light and Dark.

SOURCE: David T. Glick, "The Beverage of Moderation; Brief History of Michigan Brewing Industry," *Chronicle* (Summer 1977).

Gin. Gin is an alcoholic beverage made from a base of neutral spirits (q.v.) that are redistilled and flavored with juniper berries and other agents. The still (q.v.) is fitted with a special gin head, which is packed with trays of berries, herbs, and other botanical products, and fitted in the top of the still. As the vapors rise from the still, they pass through the trays of agents, are flavored, and then condensed. Some gins, which have a strawlike color, are aged, but aging may not be noted in advertising. Francis de La Boe, professor of medicine at Leyden University in Holland in the seventeenth century, is credited with developing the first gin. He used the French name, *jenievre* (Genevre), because juniper berries made up the primary ingredients among the botanicals he used. The name was shortened to gin by the British.

SOURCES: Frank Haring, ed., *Practical Encyclopedia of Alcoholic Beverages* (New York, 1959); George Packowski, "Beverage Spirits, Distilled," *Kirk-Othmer Encyclopedia of Chemical Technology*, 3rd ed., vol. 3 (New York, 1978).

Glencoe Distillery Company. The Stitzel Brothers established the Louisville, Kentucky, distillery in the 1870s. In 1901, "Phil" Hollenbach purchased the plant and brand name and operated it until 1919. His son, Louis, built a new plant, which opened in 1935. National Distillers Products Company (q.v.) bought the plant about 1940.

SOURCE: "Glencoe Expands on Eighteen Acres," *Spirits* (April 1935).

Glenmore Distilleries Company. An Irish immigrant James Thompson founded this Owensboro, Kentucky, distillery in 1871. Thompson entered the whiskey business first as a broker, or commission merchant (q.v.), selling whiskey to wholesalers and retailers. Thompson joined George Garvin Brown (*see* Brown-Forman Distillers) for a time in the 1880s but withdrew in 1890. He named his own plant Glenmore after the castle in Ireland that was near his home. In 1901 Thompson purchased the R. Monarch plant in Owensboro. When he died in 1924 his sons, Col. Frank B. and James P. Thompson, assumed leadership, with Frank becoming chairman and president. Joseph A. Englehard served as president during the 1940s and 1950s. He was succeeded by Frank B. Thompson, Jr., from 1964 to 1974. The Thompson family continued to control the company into the 1970s, with James Thompson, Frank's son, currently serving as chairman and chief executive officer. Glenmore proved a successful and durable company, its main brand being Kentucky Tavern. In 1944 the firm purchased the Yellowstone brand from the Taylor & Williams Distillery (q.v.) of Louisville. Glenmore has followed the lead of the large firms and markets imported whiskies and cordials through its subsidiaries, Mr. Boston, Foreign Vintages, and Viking Distillery.

SOURCES: "The Glenmore Story," *Spirits* (July 1951); Dorothy L. Korell, "Bourbon Capital of the World," *Louisville* (October 20, 1965); Harry H. Kroll, *Bluegrass, Belles, and Bourbon* (New York, 1967); "The Yellowstone Formula," *Spirits* (April 1952).

Goebel Brewing Company. This Detroit brewery was established in 1873 by August Goebel and Theodore Gorenflo as A. Goebel & Company. Goebel, born in 1839, was a German immigrant who came to Detroit in the 1850s. He managed the brewery and was instrumental in working out the details for English investors to consolidate four Detroit breweries in the late 1890s. The merger of the Bavarian, Endriss, Jacob Mann, and Goebel breweries was known as Goebel Brewing Company, Ltd. When Goebel died in 1905, his son, August, Jr., took over the company. The consolidation dissolved during Prohibition in the 1920s and Goebel closed. But it was reorganized in the early 1930s, primarily by Walter Haas, who served as president until his death in 1941. Goebel bought the Koppitz-Melchers (q.v.) plant in 1947, but closed it in 1958. Stroh (q.v.), Detroit's largest brewery, acquired Goebel in 1964 and continued to market beer under the Goebel brand name.

SOURCE: "The Story of Goebel," *Brewers Journal* (June 15, 1941).

Gottlieb-Bauernschmidt-Strauss Brewing Company. Tracing its origins to the brewery established by Leonard and Daniel Barnetz in 1744, the Baltimore, Maryland, brewery has been owned by a variety of firms. One of the most notable events in the brewery's history was its involvement in the Maryland "beer trust" in 1899. The Gottlieb-Bauernschmidt-Strauss Brewing Company emerged from this merger of seventeen companies in 1901 and continued in business until 1914.

SOURCES: John P. Arnold and Frank Penman, *History of the Brewing Industry and Brewing Science* (Chicago, 1933); William J. Kelley, *Brewing in Maryland* (Baltimore, 1965); *One Hundred Years of Brewing* (Chicago and New York, 1903; Arno Press Reprint, 1974).

Gough, John B. (August 22, 1817-February 18, 1886). A reformed drinker who lectured in New York, Boston, and Baltimore against the evils of liquor, Gough was a member of the "Washingtonian Movement" of the 1830s and 1840s, which consisted of reformed drunkards. Gough became one of the best-known temperance speakers during the mid-nineteenth century.

SOURCES: *Dictionary of American Biography*, vol. 7; J. C. Furnas, *The Life and Times of the Late Demon Rum* (New York, 1965).

Grain Belt Breweries, Inc. The Minneapolis, Minnesota, brewing concern was organized under the Grain Belt name in 1967. The firm originated in 1890 as the Minneapolis Brewing and Malting Company, a consolidation of the John Orth Brewing Company, founded in 1850, the Heinrich Brewing Company, established in 1860, the Noerenberg brewery, founded in 1870, and the Germania Brewing Association, founded in 1884. The Orth firm became the main plant. In 1893, the firm was renamed the Minneapolis Brewing Company and retained that title until the adoption of the Grain

Belt name in 1967. The company was the nation's eighteenth largest firm in 1973 with 1 million barrels produced. G. Heileman (q.v.) purchased the company in 1976.

SOURCES: Manfred Friedrich and Donald Bull, *The Register of U.S. Breweries* (Trumbull, Conn., 1976); *One Hundred Years of Brewing* (Chicago and New York, 1903; Arno Press Reprint, 1974).

Grain neutral spirits. These are spirits (q.v.) distilled at 190 proof (q.v.) or higher, from a mash of grain. The product is nearly tasteless and odorless.

Grant. *See* Underback.

Great Eastern Distillery. One of the Peoria firms in the Whiskey Trust (q.v.) of the 1890s, the company was incorporated in 1886, with Edward Spelman and Peter Coffey among the major stockholders. The company went out of business about 1905.

SOURCES: Ernest E. East, "Distillery Fires in Corning Plant," *Arrow Messenger* (March 1937), and "Joseph B. Greenhut and the Whiskey Trust," *Arrow Messenger* (April 1937).

Great Western Distillery. Established in 1881, the Peoria, Illinois, distillery was reputed to be the world's largest such company during much of its operation. Joseph B. Greenhut (q.v.), who was the first president of the Distillers' and Cattle Feeders' Trust (*see* Whiskey Trust), John H. Francis, Peoria distiller, and Nelson Morris, a Chicago meat packer, were among the organizers of the company. Great Western became an important plant in the trust in 1887 and continued to operate under the auspices of the American Spirits Manufacturing Company (q.v.) from the late 1890s until 1921 when it closed. Greenhut sold his interest in 1898.

SOURCES: Ernest E. East, *Arrow Messenger*, various articles, (March, April, May 1937), and "Romance of Peoria Industry," *Peoria Journal-Transcript* (April 28, 1940).

Green malt. Essentially, this is germinated barley. After being soaked in hot water, the wet barley was formerly spread out on the floor of the malthouse and allowed to germinate, or sprout. During this period, lasting a few days to a few weeks, an enzyme (q.v.) was produced.

Greenhut, Joseph B. (February 28, 1843-November 17, 1918). A prominent distiller and president of the Whiskey Trust (q.v.), Greenhut came to the U.S. from Austria. He served in the Union army in the Civil War. Greenhut lived in Chicago, came to know Nelson Morris, a prominent meat packer, and in 1878 was hired by Morris to manage the latter's cattle-feeding business in Peoria. Greenhut had been involved in distilling, and he and Morris helped establish the Great Western Distillery (q.v.) in 1881. In 1887 Greenhut was elected president of the trust and held the position until 1895, when the organization, after legal and financial problems, went into receivership. Greenhut continued his involvement in distilleries and remained in the Peoria area until 1905, when he and his wife retired to live in New York City. Allegedly, he came to Peoria with $50 and left with $10 million.

SOURCES: Ernest E. East, "The Distillers' and Cattle Feeders' Trust, 1882-1895," *Journal of the Illinois Historical Society* 45 (Summer 1952), and "Romance of Peoria Industry," *Peoria Journal-Transcript* (April 28, 1940).

Greenway Brewing Company. The Syracuse, New York, brewery dates from the early 1850s when John and George Greenway, who were English in origin, entered the ale brewing business. In 1858, they took over the business and built the city's largest brewery. It was reopened after the repeal of Prohibition but was a comparatively small enterprise and closed in 1952. *See also*, Syracuse Brewing Industry.

Grinding. In this step in the malting (q.v.) process, prepared barley malt that has been germinated and kilned is ground into grist, or meal, in specially designed mills. The malt kernels are partially ground up, but care is taken not to shatter the husks which later act as a filter for the wort (q.v.). Ground malt (q.v.) and adjuncts (q.v.) are then ready for mashing (q.v.). Grinding of the grain is also part of the whiskey-making (q.v.) process of preparing grains for whiskey-making.

Grosscurth Distilleries, Inc. C. A. Grosscurth assumed control of the former Waterfill and Frazier plant at Anchorage, Kentucky, in 1948 and produced the brand Supreme Bourbon. The company apparently was short-lived, and the distillery subsequently was dismantled.

Growler. A quart bucket to hold beer was called a growler. Often the beer was from the bottom of the barrel and sold at a lower than regular price. Because the beer foamed easily, customers supposedly complained, or growled, about the lower quality of the beer. "Rushing the growler" was the practice of going to the saloon or tavern to obtain a growler full of beer to serve a number of people. The practice was common in the prebottling and saloon era of the late nineteenth century but continued as a tradition in many urban brewing centers well into the 1900s.

H

Haberle Brewing Company. This Syracuse, New York, brewery was founded by Benedict Haberle in 1857. Although the plant reopened after the repeal of Prohibition, it was closed in the early 1960s—the last Syracuse brewery. *See also*, Syracuse Brewing Industry.

Haffenreffer & Company (Brewery). Founded around 1880, this Boston brewery was merged with the John Roessle Brewery (q.v.) and Suffolk Brewing Company in 1890 to form the New England Breweries, Ltd. That company ended with Prohibition, but in an apparent reorganization, Haffenreffer & Company, Inc., continued to operate three plants after Repeal (q.v.) in 1933. One closed in 1934, another in 1951, and the third in 1964. Narragansett Brewing Company (q.v.) purchased the brand name, and then Falstaff (q.v.) purchased both breweries' labels in 1966.

    SOURCES: Manfred Friedrich and Donald Bull, *The Register of U.S. Breweries* (Trumbull, Conn., 1976); *One Hundred Years of Brewing* (Chicago and New York, 1903; Arno Press Reprint, 1974).

Hamm, Theodore, Brewing Company. The St. Paul, Minnesota, brewery was built in 1864 and was purchased by Theodore Hamm in 1865. Hamm came to America from Baden, Germany, in 1854 at the age of nineteen. After working in Buffalo and Chicago, he moved to St. Paul in 1856, where he operated a boardinghouse and saloon. The company was incorporated in 1896 and continued as a regional plant in San Francisco. The Hamm Company bought Gunther of Baltimore in 1959 and then sold that plant to F. and M. Schaefer in 1962. In 1975, Olympia Brewing Company (q.v.) purchased the Hamm Company.

    SOURCES: Stanley Baron, *Brewed in America* (Boston, 1962); *One Hundred Years of Brewing* (Chicago and New York, 1903; Arno Press Reprint, 1974).

Hand, Peter, Brewing Company. Peter Hand, a Prussian immigrant, initially established this recently reorganized Chicago company, in 1891. Hand had worked in the Conrad Seipp Brewing Company (q.v.) before going into business for himself. The company continued under the same

name until 1967 when it took on the name of its most popular beer, Meister
Brau. In 1965, an investment business group led by James W. Howard
took over the company, but nonbrewery reversals forced Meister Brau's
bankruptcy in 1972. In 1966 the Buckeye Brewing Company (q.v.) of
Toledo had been acquired and helped produce Meister Brau. The Meister
Brau and Lite brands were purchased by Miller Brewing Company (q.v.) in
1972. The plant was purchased by Fred Huber of Wisconsin's Huber Brewing Company (q.v.) and the old name, Peter Hand, was revived. New
brands were Old Chicago and Van Merritt. But Hand's, Chicago's sole
brewery by 1977, was forced to shut down also and began liquidation in
September 1978.

SOURCES: *Brewers Digest* (November 1966 and June 1973); *Chicago Tribune*,
February 27, 1979; Richard J. La Susa, "Nevermore the Local Lagers," *Chicago
Tribune Magazine* (April 24, 1977); *One Hundred Years of Brewing* (Chicago and
New York, 1903; Arno Press Reprint, 1974).

Harvard Brewing Company. Organized in 1898, the Lowell, Massachusetts,
brewery reopened after the repeal of Prohibition in 1933 and remained an
independent brewery until 1957 when it merged with the Hampden Brewing
Company of Willmansett. Hampden-Harvard closed the Lowell plant and
subsequently merged with the Associated Brewing Company (q.v.) in 1962.

Hauck, John, Brewing Company. John Hauck, a German immigrant of
1852, and John U. Windisch established the Cincinnati brewery in 1863.
Hauck bought the Windisch shares upon the latter's death in 1879. It was
called the Dayton Street Brewery and became one of the larger breweries in
the city—and its beer was one of the most popular. Louis Hauck assumed
management of the company when his father, John, died in the mid-1890s.
The company produced near beer (q.v.) for a time during Prohibition in the
1920s, but competition from bootleg beer and home brew forced the management to close the plant in 1927. The Red Top Malting Company (*see* Red
Top Brewing Company) purchased the company.

SOURCES: William L. Downard, *The Cincinnati Brewing Industry* (Athens,
Ohio, 1973), and "When Gambrinus Was King," *Cincinnati Historical Society
Bulletin* (Winter 1969); *One Hundred Years of Brewing* (Chicago and New York,
1903; Arno Press Reprint, 1974).

Heaven Hill Distilleries, Inc. In 1935 the Shapira family founded a distillery
in Bardstown, Kentucky. Gary, Mose, George, Edward, and David Shapira
established the distillery and named it Heaven Hill after William Heavenhill
(1783-1870), who had operated a farm on the site in the nineteenth century.
The company markets a large percentage of its whiskey in bulk and bottled
form to meet the requirements of distributors and customers. The bulk-
sales approach, a traditional method of distribution, was utilized by few

distillers in the 1970s, but Heaven Hill accepts the method as a sound business approach. The company's main brands are Heaven Hill and Evan Williams (q.v.), the latter a brand that was reactivated in 1957. Named after one of Kentucky's first distillers, it is a premium brand. George Shapira is president and Max Shapira, Edward's son, has moved into the business as a second-generation family distiller.

SOURCES: Harry H. Kroll, *Bluegrass, Belles, and Bourbon* (New York, 1967); "Spotlight on Heaven Hill Distilleries," *Beverage Analyst*, ca. 1975.

Hedrick Brewing Company. This Albany, New York, brewery, established by John F. Hedrick in 1852, survived Prohibition and continued to operate until 1966.

Heileman, G., Brewing Company, Inc. The LaCrosse, Wisconsin, company has become widely known since the late 1960s for its aggressive expansion by acquisitions of regional breweries. Gottlieb Heileman joined John Gund in 1858 as a partner in the City Brewery in LaCrosse. Gund left the company in 1872 to establish the Empire Brewing Company, later known as the John Gund Brewing Company. His company prospered but closed during Prohibition. Meanwhile Heileman continued to operate the City Brewery until his death in 1878. His widow, Johanna, headed the business afterward (with the assistance of E. T. Mueller) until her death in 1917. In 1902, Old Style Lager was copyrighted, and in 1911 R. A. Albrecht aided in management of the company. He guided the business through the Prohibition era by producing near beer, and in 1933 Harry Dahl became president as the company was reorganized under the direction of Paul H. David & Company of Chicago. Albert J. Bates succeeded Dahl in 1936 and continued as president until 1944. After several interim presidents, Ralph T. Johansen took over from 1951 to 1956. Company treasurer Roy E. Kumm became president in 1956, a position he held until 1970. During his tenure, the company began its acquisition program. Since 1959 the company has acquired thirteen regional breweries at favorable prices. Among the acquisitions have been Kingsbury of Sheboygan, Wisconsin, Wiedemann (q.v.) of Newport, Kentucky, Blatz (q.v.) of Milwaukee, Jacob Schmidt (q.v.) of St. Paul, Sterling (q.v.) of Evansville, Indiana, and Rainier (q.v.) of Seattle. Other breweries and brands, Drewry's (q.v.), Pfeiffer (q.v.), Weber, Mickey's Malt Liquor, Grain Belt (q.v.), and Special Export, have also been established or acquired. A number of the breweries had been part of the Associated Brewing Company (q.v.) of Detroit. Heileman, currently led by President Russell G. Cleary, has climbed from thirty-ninth to sixth place in production among the nation's brewers since 1960. In 1979, Heileman also purchased Carling National Breweries, Inc. (q.v.), increasing its production from 7 million barrels to more than 10.5 million barrels. The company operates brewing plants in LaCrosse, Wisconsin; Newport, Kentucky; St. Paul, Minnesota; Frankenmuth, Michigan; Seattle, Washington; Baltimore, Maryland; Evansville, Indiana; and Phoenix, Arizona.

SOURCES: *Fortune* (June 18, 1979); Wayne Kroll, *Badger Breweries* (Jefferson, Wis., 1976); *One Hundred Years of Brewing* (Chicago and New York, 1903; Arno Press Reprint, 1974); *Value Line*, June 15, 1979.

Hell Gate Brewery. *See* Ehrets, George.

Heublein, Inc. Gilbert and Louis Heublein established the Farmington, Connecticut, firm in 1875 as an importer and distributor of foods and beverages. Their father, Andrew, had operated a small hotel and restaurant on the site of their business in Hartford. In 1892 they produced their first prepared cocktails and incorporated as G. F. Heublein & Bro. in 1899. They produced their first gin, Milshire, in 1901. In 1906 the company became a distributor of A.1 Sauce and received American producing rights in 1918. Expansion of the A.1 business aided the firm during Prohibition in the 1920s. In the 1930s, they reentered the gin and cocktail business and obtained U.S. production and marketing rights to Smirnoff Vodka in 1939. In 1955 the name was changed to Heublein, Inc. Over the years the company made many acquisitions and purchases of distribution rights in the wine, spirits, and food areas. Among them were: Harvey's Sherries and Ports (1957), Arrow Liqueurs (1964), International Vintage Wines and its Lancers brand (1965), Coastal Valley Canning Company (1966), United Vintners, Inc., and Beaulieu Vineyard (1969), Kentucky Fried Chicken (1971), and the Drury-Fasano Group, Brazil's major liquor producer (1973). John G. Martin, grandson of the founders, was president and responsible for the Smirnoff purchase in 1939. Martin continued as retired chairman and consultant in the late 1970s as Stuart Watson served as chairman and Hicks B. Waldron as president. Liquor plants currently operate in Hartford, Connecticut, Allen Park, Michigan, Menlo Park, California, and Paducah, Kentucky.

SOURCES: "Genievre According to Heublein," *Spirits* (October 1933); *Heublein at 100* (Farmington, Conn., 1975); "Profile of Heublein, Inc.," (brief company history, February 1978).

High wine. After the first run, or low wine (q.v.), of fermented mash in whiskey-making has been redistilled, the product is known as high wine, or finished whiskey, and is ready for aging. Thus high wine is whiskey that has gone through two distillings.

Hiram Walker (Distillery). *See* Walker, Hiram (Distillery).

Hirsch, L., & Company. Louis Hirsch founded this wholesale liquor dealership in 1912. The El Segundo, California, company has been under the control of the Hirsch family throughout its history, and Gene and Donald Hirsch ran the company as partners in the late 1970s.

Hoffman Distilling Company. Isaac Hoffman and S. O. Hackley established the original distillery sometime after 1850. Old Hoffman became a popular brand and was revived by Ezra and Robert Ripy in 1934. The Hoffman distillery was evidently associated with the Old Spring Distilling Company of the Wertheimer (q.v.) firm of Cincinnati. Prior to 1960 the major brands were Old Hoffman and Old Spring, but about 1960 the company came out with Ezra Brooks. In the late 1970s, Edward Wertheimer was president of Hoffman Distilling Company. *See also*, Ripy, T. B., Distillery.

SOURCES: "Great Names in Whiskey," *Spirits* (July 1937); "Hoffman Distillery a Year-Round Plant," *Spirits* (April 1935); Art Williams, "Kentucky Roundup," *Spirits* (August-September, 1963).

Hope Distillery. Although this Louisville company was organized in New England, it was incorporated in Kentucky. The plant opened in 1817 and utilized the steam process, instead of direct fire, to heat the mash. It was the largest such plant in Kentucky, producing more than 1,200 gallons of whiskey per day. Nevertheless, the ambitious project apparently was unprofitable, because the organizers closed the plant by 1850.

SOURCE: Henry G. Crowgey, *Kentucky Bourbon* (Lexington, Ky., 1971).

Hop-jack. A straining device in brewing, the hop-jack is a hop-strainer. Boiled wort (q.v.) that has been flavored with hops (q.v.) is passed through a hop-jack as the hops are strained off and the brew is ready for fermentation (q.v.). Until the late nineteenth century, a straw-lined basket or vessel with a perforated bottom was used.

Hop-strainer. *See* Hop-jack.

Hops. The flowers of the vine *Humulus lupus* are used in brewing to impart character, flavor, and a pleasant aroma to the beer. The dried blossoms of the female hop plant are used exclusively. Hops, which are added to the wort (q.v.) in the brew kettle, were first generally used in brewing around the thirteenth century. Although partly added for flavor, hops were very important historically for protecting beer against spoilage, as the use of hops inhibited bacterial growth. In the past few decades, the hopping rate has been reduced because of the popularity of lighter, milder beers.

SOURCES: Harold M. Broderick, ed., *The Practical Brewer* (Madison, Wis., 1977); John P. Arnold and Frank Penman, *History of the Brewing Industry and Brewing Science* (Chicago, 1933); *One Hundred Years of Brewing* (Chicago and New York, 1903; Arno Press Reprint, 1974).

Horlacher Brewing Company. Initially established in 1897 as the Allentown Brewing Company, the name of the Pennsylvania brewery was changed to Horlacher in 1902. Fred and George Horlacher were the principal officers. The brewery produced Purox soft drinks and distilled water during Prohibition, and after an abortive reopening in 1933, was successfully reorganized and reincorporated in 1935 by Fred Franks, Jr. In 1969 Letzgro Enterprises purchased the company and then sold it to another group. In 1976, W. J. Ramey, formerly of Anheuser-Busch (q.v.), became president. The company markets its Brew II and Perfection brands primarily to a local market.

SOURCES: Brewers Digest (March 1976); *One Hundred Years of Brewing* (Chicago and New York, 1903; Arno Press Reprint, 1974); James D. Robertson, *The Great American Beer Book* (Ottawa, Ill., 1978).

Huber, Jos., Brewing Company. The Monroe, Wisconsin, brewery traces its origins to 1840. It was operated by John Kinpschilt for a time, then by Jacob Hefty. In 1891 Adam Blumer took over, and the Blumer family operated it as the Blumer Brewing Company until the early 1940s when the corporation was dissolved. Joseph Huber had held various positions in the company, and he emerged as president of a newly organized company in 1946. Thus, since 1946, Huber has been president of the Jos. Huber Brewing Company. Vice-president Fred Huber became an important force in a variety of innovations in the 1970s. He was involved in the attempted revival of the Peter Hand (q.v.) company and led the move to acquire a large number of brand names (Rhinelander, Regal Brau, Bavarian Club, and so on) for the company.

SOURCES: Brewers Digest (February 1976); Wayne Kroll, *Badger Breweries* (Jefferson, Wis., 1976); James D. Robertson, *The Great American Beer Book* (Ottawa, Ill., 1978).

Huck, John A., Brewery. Credited with being Chicago's first lager beer (q.v.) brewery, this plant was founded in 1847 by John A. Huck and John Schneider. The latter sold out two years later, and Huck's business was destroyed in the Chicago Fire of 1871. Huck died in 1878 while making plans for a new brewery. His son, Louis C. Huck, established a malting (q.v.) business. *See also*, Huck, L. C., Malting Company.

SOURCE: One Hundred Years of Brewing (Chicago and New York, 1903; Arno Press Reprint, 1974).

Huck, L. C., Malting Company. In 1871 Louis C. Huck founded this malting company in Chicago. Huck had been with the John Huck Brewing Company (q.v.). The malting company was incorporated in 1878 and was noted for introducing the first Saladin pneumatic malting system in the U.S. The company was sold to the Chicago Consolidated Brewing and Malting Company in 1890, which later was bought out by another company. The firm apparently closed during Prohibition. *See also*, Pneumatic Malting.
    SOURCE: *One Hundred Years of Brewing* (Chicago and New York, 1903; Arno Press Reprint, 1974).

Hudepohl Brewing Company. The Cincinnati brewery was established in 1885 by Cincinnati-born Louis Hudepohl and George Kotte, who acquired the Koehler brewery, which was also known as the Buckeye Brewery. In 1900, Hudepohl became the sole owner and incorporated the brewery as Hudepohl Brewing Company. In the 1920s, during the era of Prohibition, production of near beer (q.v.) and soft drinks kept the company in operation. In 1934, the Lackman plant, also a local company, was acquired and Hudepohl moved its operation to that plant in 1958. In 1973 the company bought another local plant, Burger Brewing Company (q.v.), and marketed Hudepohl, Hofbrau, Burger, and Hudy Delight. The tradition as a limited regional (primarily Ohio, Indiana, and Kentucky) brewery has been continued. When Louis Hudepohl died in 1902, his widow, Mary Elizabeth, managed the brewery with the assistance of son-in-law William A. Pohl. Upon her death in 1923, daughter Celia Hesselbrock became president and she held the position, assisted by general manager and husband, John, until her death in 1959. Their son, John A. Hesselbrock, then assumed the presidency until Thomas A. Zins, great-grandson of Louis Hudepohl took over in August 1978.
    SOURCES: William L. Downard, *The Cincinnati Brewing Industry* (Athens, Ohio, 1973); "The Hudepohl Brewing Co.," *Brewers Digest* (July 1971); "Hudepohl Scores with Hudy Delight," *Brewers Digest* (February 1979); *One Hundred Years of Brewing* (Chicago and New York, 1903; Arno Press Reprint, 1974).

Hull, William E. (January 13, 1866-May 30, 1942). A Republican Congressman (1923-33) from Peoria, Illinois, Hull was part owner of the Clarke Bros. and Company Distillery and had fought for bottled-in-bond (q.v.) legislation. In the early 1930s, he was instrumental in convincing Harry Hatch of Hiram Walker (q.v.) to build a plant in Peoria; he was also hired by Hatch to become sales manager for Hiram Walker in the U.S.
    SOURCES: *Biographical Directory of the American Congress, 1774-1949* (Washington, D.C., 1950); "Whiskey," *Fortune* (November 1933).

Hull Brewing Company. Founded in 1870 in New Haven, Connecticut, as William Hull & Son, the name of the small brewing firm was changed during the Prohibition era and over the years the company has been noted for the production of ale (q.v.).

SOURCE: *One Hundred Years of Brewing* (Chicago and New York, 1903; Arno Press Reprint, 1974).

Hyde Park Brewing Association (St. Louis). *See* St. Louis Brewing Association.

Hydrometer. Used in brewing and distilling to determine the specific gravity or density of liquids, the instrument normally is a hollow glass or metal device weighted at one end so it will float upright. According to some sources, the first brewer to use a hydrometer was James Baverstock, an Englishman who used the device in the family's brewery in England in the 1770s. In distilling the hydrometer came into general use in the late eighteenth century and was especially important for determining the proof (q.v.), or percentage of alcohol, in whiskey. The Excise Act of 1791 (q.v.) specified various proofs for spirits distilled in the U.S. and the official standard of measurement was designated as Dicas's hydrometer. Thus the instrument came to be widely used in the late eighteenth century and afterward.

SOURCES: Henry G. Crowgey, *Kentucky Bourbon* (Lexington, Ky., 1971); *One Hundred Years of Brewing* (Chicago and New York, 1903; Arno Press Reprint, 1974).

Independent Breweries Company. A St. Louis organization, the company consisted of approximately six breweries that merged to compete with the St. Louis Brewing Association (q.v.). The group, which dated from about 1907, counted among its members the Columbia Brewing Company (q.v.), Gast Brewing Company, the American Brewing Company (*see* Falstaff Brewing Corporation), and the Home Brewing Company. The Independent Breweries Company closed during the Prohibition era, although some of the companies reopened independently.

SOURCES: Don Crinklaw, "The Battle of the Breweries," *St. Louis Post-Dispatch*, June 9, 1974; Manfred Friedrich and Donald Bull, *The Register of U.S. Breweries* (Trumbull, Conn., 1976).

Internal Revenue Act, 1862. Effective September 1, 1862, the federal act placed a tax of $1 per barrel on all beer sold, plus a special license fee for individual brewers. Passed to raise revenue for the Civil War effort, the legislation led to the formation of the U.S. Brewers' Association (q.v.), which would attempt to define and protect brewers' interests. The tax itself was continued after the war although the rate was changed to coincide with necessary revenues. The act also placed a tax of $0.20 per gallon on distilled spirits and was generally raised thereafter. *See also*, Taxation of Malt Liquor, Federal, and Taxation of Distilled Spirits, Federal.

SOURCES: Stanley Baron, *Brewed in America* (Boston, 1962); Gerald Carson, *The Social History of Bourbon* (New York, 1963); Thomas C. Cochran, *The Pabst Brewing Company* (New York, 1948); Harry E. Smith, *The United States Federal Internal Tax History from 1861-1871* (Boston, 1914).

International Union of United Brewery, Flour, Cereal, Soft Drink and Distillery Workers of America. *See* National Union of United Brewery Workmen of America.

Irish Whiskey. The name applies to whiskies made exclusively in Ireland. One, a blend of malt whiskies (q.v.) and grain whiskey, is made in northern Ireland, whereas the other, a blend of similar whiskies, is produced in the

Republic of Ireland. The making of whiskey (q.v.) in Ireland dates from at least 1400 A.D., but probably had its origin sometime earlier. The whiskey is made primarily in pot-stills from a mash (q.v.) of malted barley, corn, rye, wheat, and oats. Whereas Scotch whisky (q.v.) is distilled only twice, Irish whiskey is distilled 3 times. Also, the mash is dried in a kiln, whereas Scotch is dried directly over peat, giving it a "smokey" or "peaty" flavor. If Irish whiskey is distilled in column, or continuous stills, the grain whiskey is blended with pot-still whiskey to produce a beverage of lighter body and character. The whiskey must be aged for at least four years, but is normally stored from seven to twelve years. The popular name for illegally produced Irish whiskey is poteen, which means "little pot."

SOURCES: *Alexis Lichine's New Encyclopedia of Wines and Spirits* (New York, 1974); Harold J. Grossman, *Grossman's Guide to Wines, Beers, and Spirits* (New York, 1977); Esther Kellner, *Moonshine, Its History and Folklore* (Indianapolis, Ind., 1971).

Isinglass. A gelatinous substance, isinglass is derived from the air bladders of certain fish, especially sturgeon, cod, ling, and carp. Until the late nineteenth century, this substance was a common method of fining (q.v.) or clarifying beer in the final stages of fermentation. The isinglass was dissolved and treated and acted as a filter, attracting various impurities in beer before drawing them to the bottom of the fining casks.

SOURCES: *One Hundred Years of Brewing* (Chicago and New York, 1903; Arno Press Reprint, 1974); Edward H. Vogel, Jr., et al., *The Practical Brewer* (St. Louis, Mo., 1946).

Jack Daniel Distillery. *See* Daniel, Jack, Distillery.

Jackson Brewing Company. This New Orleans brewery was founded in 1890. Lawrence Fabacher was a major stockholder and in 1895 became president. The Fabacher family continued to manage the business until the mid-1970s when the plant was closed. The company's main brand, Jax beer, dating from 1919, was purchased by the Pearl Brewing Company (q.v.) of San Antonio.

SOURCES: *Brewers Digest* (October 1970); James D. Robertson, *The Great American Beer Book* (Ottawa, Ill., 1978).

Jefferson, Thomas (April 1743-July 4, 1826). America's third president (1801-9) was also known as a "gentleman-brewer." Jefferson, aided by Capt. Joseph Miller, engaged in brewing at Monticello from 1813 to his death in 1826. He read numerous books on the art of brewing and pursued the activity more as an agricultural-scientific endeavor than as a means of providing himself with malt liquor for beverage purposes.

SOURCE: Stanley Baron, *Brewed in America* (Boston, 1962).

Jones, Frank, Brewing Company. John Swindels founded this Portsmouth, New Hampshire, ale and porter brewery in 1854. Frank Jones entered the business in 1856 and assumed control in 1860. Jones remained chairman until his death in 1902. He was also a member of the Forty-fourth and Forty-fifth U.S. Congresses (1875-79). The firm was the nation's fourteenth largest in 1877, with 71,471 barrels produced, and tenth in 1895, with a production of more than 250,000 barrels. After Repeal (q.v.) in 1933, the company was known as the Eldredge Brewing Company, Inc., and later as the Frank Jones Brewing Company, Inc. The company closed in 1950.

SOURCES: *Biographical Directory of the American Congress, 1774-1961* (Washington, D.C., 1961); *One Hundred Years of Brewing* (Chicago and New York, 1903; Arno Press Reprint, 1974); Manfred Friedrich and Donald Bull, *The Register of U.S. Breweries* (Trumbull, Conn., 1976).

Jones Brewing Company. The Smithton, Pennsylvania, brewery was founded in 1907 by William B. ("Stoney") Jones, Sr., an 1885 immigrant from Wales. The company's original name, Eureka Brewing Company, gave way to the present title in 1933. During Prohibition in the 1920s, Jones produced ice and near beer (q.v.) as the company operated as the Pure Aqua Products and Ice Company. Jones ran the company until his death in 1936. William Jones, Jr., then took over and led the brewery as chairman until 1965. In the meantime, Hugh H. Jones and Paul Jones served as presidents from 1936 to 1953 and 1953 to 1959, respectively. Paul Jones, who died in 1959, was the father of Shirley Jones, well-known actress and entertainer. William B. Jones III assumed leadership of the company in 1965 and continues to hold the position. The company's beer, Stoney's, is marketed primarily within a fifty-mile radius of Smithton, which is just south of Pittsburgh. Basing its appeal on service and the local trade, the company sells more than 30 percent of its beer in draft form to taverns. In addition to Stoney's and Esquire brands, the company markets Old Shay's Ale, a brand acquired from the American Brewing Company in 1965.

SOURCE: "A Local Brewer Makes Good," *Brewers Digest* (May 1978).

Jungenfeld, E., & Company. This was a late nineteenth-century St. Louis brewery architectural firm. Established by Edmund von Jungenfeld, the firm planned many of the Anheuser-Busch (q.v.) buildings in the 1860s and 1870s.

SOURCE: Ronald Jan Plavchan, "A History of Anheuser-Busch, 1852-1933," unpub. Ph.D. dissertation, St. Louis University, 1969.

K

Kasser Distillers Products Corporation. The Philadelphia distillery dates from 1934, the year after repeal of Prohibition (q.v.). Samuel Kasser founded the company; his son, Raymond H., became president in 1957 and continued in the position in the late 1970s. The company markets its own whiskey, but also distributes wine and other national brands, mainly in New Jersey and other East Coast states.

Katzenmayer, John (ca. 1810-66). A New York brewer who worked for A. Schmid & Company, in the early 1860s Katzenmayer called for brewers to organize a national association to promote their common interests. His appeal proved an important plea in the formation of the U.S. Brewers' Association (q.v.). Katzenmayer served as the association's first secretary from 1862 until his death in 1866.

SOURCE: One Hundred Years of Brewing (Chicago and New York, 1903; Arno Press Reprint, 1974).

Katzenmayer, Richard (April 1839-October 3, 1898). Secretary of the U.S. Brewers' Association (q.v.) from 1866 to 1898, Katzenmayer succeeded his father in the position.

SOURCE: One Hundred Years of Brewing (Chicago and New York, 1903; Arno Press Reprint, 1974).

Keeley Brewing Company. Michael Keeley established this Chicago brewery in 1876 after being involved in bottling and liquor businesses. He was one of the few Irish immigrants to enter the brewing industry. The company reopened after Prohibition (q.v.) and survived until 1952.

*SOURCES: Will Anderson, *The Beer Book* (Princeton, N.J., 1973); *One Hundred Years of Brewing* (Chicago and New York, 1903; Arno Press Reprint, 1974).

Keg. Usually having a capacity of eight gallons or less, the keg is also known as a quarter-barrel. Kegs, which make up one form of packaging (q.v.) for beer, may be made of wood, stainless steel, or aluminum. Since the mid-1950s wood barrels, which had to be "pitched," or coated, with a tree resin, have been largely replaced by aluminum and stainless steel kegs. *See also*, Pitching.

SOURCES: Harold M. Broderick, ed., *The Practical Brewer* (Madison, Wis., 1977); Edward H. Vogel, Jr., et al., *The Practical Brewer* (St. Louis, Mo., 1946).

Kentucky Distilleries and Warehouse Company. The Kentucky "Whiskey Trust" was formed in 1899 and was apparently related to the earlier trust (*see* Whiskey Trust) that had been organized in Peoria, Illinois. The Kentucky group, consisting of approximately fifty-nine distilleries, evolved from an analysis of the industry by Thomas H. Sherley (q.v.) of the New Hope Distillery (q.v.). He—and later on, a number of other entrepreneurs—believed that greater profits could be made from the many Kentucky distilleries if their numbers could be reduced, overproduction curtailed, and efficiencies applied. The Kentucky Distilleries and Warehouse Company (KD & WHC) was thus organized in 1899; it was incorporated in New Jersey because of the state's lenient trust laws, with Julius Kessler (q.v.) as president. Standard Distilling and Distributing Company (q.v.), a subsidiary of the Peoria "Trust," was represented on the board of directors. Between 1899 and 1916 Kessler purchased many distilleries, shutting down some, combining others, and producing the more popular brands at the larger plants. A number of the plants operated as Julius Kessler & Company, but were distinct from the Kessler Distilling Company (*see* Seagram, Jos. E., and Sons) of the post-Prohibition period. Those closed were the outmoded firms or those too distant from railroad terminals. In all, Kessler evidently ran the operation efficiently; and, of course, many of the smaller companies lost their independence. During Prohibition (q.v.) in the 1920s KD & WHC was essentially inoperative. Kessler left the organization and U.S. Food Products (*see* National Distillers Products Company) in the early 1920s. In 1927 R. E. Wathen formed the American Medicinal Spirits Company (q.v.), which included many of the KD & WHC companies. Later, National Distillers Products Company bought American Medicinal Spirits. Among the notable plants in KD & WHC and American Medicinal Spirits were: R. E. Wathen & Company (q.v.), Bond & Lillard (q.v.), J. M. Atherton & Company (q.v.), T. B. Ripy (q.v.), and New Hope (q.v.). *See* Appendix VIII for a more complete list of companies in the Kentucky Distilleries and Warehouse Company.

SOURCES: Gerald Carson, *The Social History of Bourbon* (New York, 1963); Victor S. Clark, *History of Manufactures in the U.S.*, vol. 3 (New York, 1929); H. W. Coyte, "The Whiskey Trust," unpub. paper, 1977; A. C. Stagg, "Report of Distilled Spirits, 1914-25," unpub. list, Frankfort, Kentucky State Historical Society, 1950; "The Trust," and "Kentucky Leviathan," *Spirits* (April 1935).

Kentucky distilling industry. Settlers, mainly from Virginia, Pennsylvania, and Maryland, began moving into the Kentucky region in the 1770s and

1780s. Many of them were farmer-distillers (q.v.) who produced various grains and fruits and turned a portion of their yield into a variety of alcoholic beverages. Cider, peach brandy, and whiskey, probably made mainly from rye at first, were made primarily for home consumption, and secondarily for commercial purposes. Much has been made of the "first distiller of Kentucky" (q.v.). The two people most often credited with being "first" are Evan Williams (1783) and Elijah Craig. Because the latter did not arrive in the area until 1786, it is doubtful that he deserves the distinction. As Henry Crowgey notes in his recent scholarly account, *Kentucky Bourbon*, the "first distiller should be considered purely academic since the position and production of distilled spirits was so common among a people for whom liquor was viewed as one of the necessities of life." The "first distiller" debate aside, Kentucky proved to be a very favorable area for producing distilled spirits. Kentucky had abundant limestone water (q.v.) from springs; corn and other grains could be readily grown; and the climate proved favorable for the production of spirits. Whiskey production expanded toward the end of the eighteenth century, and tavern rates were passed to indicate differences in quality among liquors available. The beverage was being used as a medium of exchange in frontier areas, as well as for medicinal purposes; and it served as pay and a source of recreation among the military. All in all, distilled liquor was an important commodity in America, especially on the frontier, and whiskey was replacing rum, which suffered in the post-Revolutionary era. Rum was made from molasses and the cost of that commodity increased substantially after 1790 because the British imposed restrictions on the West Indies trade; in addition, the Jefferson administration's abolition of the slave trade in 1808 interrupted the triangular trade system. Whiskey, made from abundant grain, proved cheaper, and it was popular enough that Secretary of the Treasury Alexander Hamilton convinced Congress to pass the Excise Tax of 1791 (q.v.), levying a high tax on domestic distilled spirits. The tax led to the Whiskey Rebellion (q.v.) in western Pennsylvania. Although dissatisfaction with the tax did not result in armed rebellion in Kentucky, Thomas Marshall, the first collector, frequently complained of tax evasion and evidence suggests that the state's distillers generally avoided payment. The "hateful tax" notwithstanding, Kentucky proved to be in a favorable position to offer the nation a new national beverage, "bourbon" (q.v.). The drink, which is made mainly from corn plus a small amount of rye, was named after the Kentucky county of its apparent origin. Bourbon County was named after the French royal family and was one of the many regions named in honor of the French who had joined the American colonies in the American Revolution. In 1786, when the county was designated, it included thirty-four of today's counties; thus it made up most of the eastern part of the eventual state of Kentucky. Products from the area often became identified as 'unique and took on the name. In the case of whiskey, the mixture of corn and rye became identified with Bourbon County, apparently in the 1830s and 1840s, although other regions produced whiskey from the same ingredients. In contrast to modern requirements specifying the use of charred barrels in aging, early bourbon was simply whiskey made from a mixture of corn and rye. However, references to "Old Bourbon" and "old whiskey" indicate that many distillers believed aging (q.v.) resulted in a better drink. Dr. James Crow (q.v.), a Scottish physician, is often credited with introducing a number of quality innovations for the production of bourbon. By the mid-nineteenth century, Kentucky had gained a reputation for quality whiskey, and much of the drink was being exported from Louisville. One factor in the expansion of the industry was the generally widespread adoption of up-to-date distilling methods by local distillers. Still (q.v.) construction improved; the second still, or doubler (q.v.) came into wider use; and steam gradually replaced the direct-fire method of heating the mash (q.v.), thus eliminating many fires and preventing spoilage of the drink. In 1817 the Hope Distillery (q.v.) in Louisville was one of the largest steam-based distilleries in the state. The counties most often associated with distilling were Nelson, Jefferson, Daviess, Woodford, and Franklin; and Louisville was the main city connected with the industry. Small towns, such as Bardstown, also boasted of having a number of companies. By 1890, Kentucky's distilleries produced more than 180,000 gallons of spirits, second only to the state of Illinois, where Peoria was a major center noted for large-capacity distilleries (*see* Peoria Distilling Industry). Citation of the number of firms in Kentucky varies according to sources and interpretation. One statement in 1891 lists Kentucky as having 172 distilleries, whereas other sources put the number at 200 to 250. Another list, by A. C. Stagg, puts the count at about 570. One reason for the discrepancy is that many owners had interests in multiple enterprises (*see* Doing Business As). The existence of so many small distilleries in Kentucky did create problems, however, notably in price competition and overproduction. Consolidation was one remedy, and in the late 1890s, the Kentucky Distilleries and Warehouse Company (q.v.), a combine of nearly sixty firms, was organized as a subsidiary of the Whiskey Trust (q.v.). Julius Kessler (q.v.) headed the Kentucky branch for a time and applied various cost-cutting efficiencies. On the eve of Prohibition (q.v.) some attrition in the industry had occurred, owing partly to consolidations and also to the fact that temperance (q.v.) forces made it increasingly difficult for many plants to operate as various counties went "dry." In 1908 much of Kentucky was legally "dry." Even so, a large number of companies continued to operate. Naturally, many went out of business during the 1920s as nationwide Prohibition seriously altered the industry. A few, such as Brown-Forman (q.v.), received licenses to distribute whiskey for medicinal purposes, but most went under, and stocks were concentrated in specified concentrated warehouses under federal requirements in the 1920s. In 1927, R. E. Wathen formed the American Medicinal Spirits Company (q.v.), which included many of the companies formerly in the Kentucky Distilleries and Warehouse Company. When Prohibition ended in 1933, however, there were only four plants operating—Brown-Forman, Stagg (q.v.), Glenmore (q.v.), and Stitzel-Weller (q.v.). As Repeal (q.v.) seemed imminent, however, Schenley (q.v.), National Distillers Products Company (q.v.), and Seagram (q.v.) moved into Kentucky and began buying up whiskey stocks and brand names—and would occasionally purchase plants. Some new plants were also built, a number of them in Louisville and Lawrenceburg. During the 1930s, a number of the older plants reopened, but usually outside capital played an important role. Production increased, and by the mid-1960s the twenty-four companies operating the state's forty-five distilleries produced more than 70 percent of the nation's bourbon. After Repeal the industry reflected the national trend toward consolidation and mergers. The large corporations were able to invest necessary capital in reconversion, research, and equipment. A few smaller companies, however, such as the Willett Distilling Company (q,.v.) and Maker's Mark (q.v.), illustrate that small family-operated distilleries can still be run profitably. Prior to Prohibition, among the notable distilling families and firms were: E. H. Taylor (q.v.), the Wathen family (q.v.), the Medleys (q.v.), the Wertheimers (q.v.), Beam Distilling Company (q.v.), Glenmore (q.v.), James E. Pepper Company (q.v.), Brown-Forman (q.v.), Bernheim Distilling Company (q.v.), J. W. Dant (q.v.), Hoffman Distilling Company (q.v.), T. B. Ripy Distilleries (q.v.), and J. M. Atherton Distillery (q.v.). Many of the companies and brand names were revived after the repeal of Prohibition.

SOURCES: Gerald Carson, *The Social History of Bourbon* (New York, 1963); Steven A. Channing, *Kentucky* (New York, 1977); Henry G. Crowgey, *Kentucky Bourbon* (Lexington, Ky., 1971); Woodward Kirkpatrick, "Kentucky Saga," *Spirits* (January 1934); Dorothy L. Korell, "Bourbon Capitol of the World," *Louisville* (October 20, 1965); Darrell Sifford, "Bourbon Whiskey; Kentucky's All-American Drink," Louisville *Courier-Journal Magazine* (March 27, 1966); A. C. Stagg, "Report of Distilled Spirits, 1882-1884," unpub. paper, 1950, Frankfort, Kentucky State Historical Society; George Washburne, "Statement of Distillers in 1891," *Wine and Spirits Bulletin* (February 3, 1891).

Kessler, Julius (1855-December 10, 1940). The noted distiller and business executive migrated from Budapest, Hungary, in the 1870s. He worked as a journalist first in Omaha in the 1870s and then in Denver before going into whiskey sales. Around 1900 he bought two distilleries in Kentucky, Old Lewis Hunter (q.v.) and Crab Orchard. Kessler's success was mainly as a distributor, and he sold his product directly to retailers, instead of commission merchants. He was later hired by the Whiskey Trust (q.v.) to sell its supplies of whiskey. In 1913, Kessler became president of Distillers Securities Company (the Trust) and sold pent-up stocks to competitors who feared he would "dump" the whiskey at low prices. Kessler resigned as president of Distillers Securities Trust (which was then known as U.S. Food Products) in 1921 and toured Europe. Upon his return in the early 1930s, Samuel Bronfman (q.v.) approached him with an offer to head a distillery that would be a subsidiary of Seagram (q.v.). Kessler thus became president of the Kessler Distilling Company.

SOURCES: "Whiskey," Fortune (November 1933); Fortune (February 1934).

Kieft, William (active, 1630s-40s). Director of the Dutch colony of New Netherland, Kieft took office in 1638 and was responsible for a number of actions affecting brewing and distilling. In 1642 he ordered that a tavern be built to serve as an official source of entertainment for visitors and traders in New Amsterdam. He also administered the regulations of taverns and levied an excise tax on liquors. Kieft is also credited with setting up the first still in North America in 1640. He made gin and brandy.

SOURCES: Stanley Baron, Brewed in America (Boston, 1962); Gerald Carson, The Social History of Bourbon (New York, 1963); Oscar Getz, Whiskey: An American Pictorial History (New York, 1978).

Kilning. Barley (q.v.) is dried by heating in the last stage of the malting (q.v.) process. Germination (q.v.) of wet barley, called green malt (q.v.), is halted in this step as hot air circulates under a perforated iron floor above a malt kiln (q.v.). The drying of the green malt usually takes two to three days. The temperature and length of drying, or roasting, of the malt are primary factors in the flavor and color of the final brew. The heating of malt continues until light or dark, or some variation of, malt is derived.

SOURCES: Harold J. Grossman, Grossman's Guide to Wines, Beers, and Spirits (New York, 1977); One Hundred Years of Brewing (Chicago and New York, 1903; Arno Press Reprint, 1974); Edward H. Vogel, Jr., et al., The Practical Brewer (St. Louis, Mo., 1946).

Kinsey Distilling Corporation. This Linfield, Pennsylvania, distillery was established by Jacob G. Kinsey in 1892. He sold the plant in 1904 and worked for various distilling businesses until 1933 when he reentered the industry as an owner and organized a new Kinsey distillery, once again at Linfield. The company, which produced rye whiskey, was later acquired by Publicker Distillers (q.v.).

SOURCE: Spirits (July 1936 and April 1951).

Kling, Philip, Brewing Company. In 1856 Philip Kling founded the Detroit brewing concern. One of the city's early lager breweries, it closed during Prohibition but reopened in 1936 before being bought by Pfeiffer (q.v.) in 1947. The plant was closed in 1958.

Koch, Fred, Brewery, Inc. The Dunkirk, New York, brewery was founded in 1888 by Fred Koch and Frank Werle. Known originally as the Lake City Brewery, the plant was destroyed by fire in 1896. Afterward Koch bought out Werle, rebuilt the brewery, and incorporated in 1911. Upon his death a few years later, Koch's three sons assumed control of the company. The firm coped with Prohibition (q.v.) by producing soft drinks, a near beer (q.v.) known as Kobru, and malt syrup. After Repeal (q.v.), the brewery resumed operation and remains in the hands of the Koch family.

SOURCES: *Brewers Digest* (April 1966); James D. Robertson, *The Great American Beer Book* (Ottawa, Ill., 1978).

Koppitz-Melchers Brewing Company. Founded in 1891 by Konrad Koppitz and Arthur Melchers, the Detroit brewery survived Prohibition (q.v.) and was sold to Goebel Brewing Company (q.v.) in 1947. Goebel closed the plant in 1958.

Kraeusening. In brewing, a small amount (about 15-20 percent) of wort that is still fermenting (thus young beer) may be added to beer that has been brewed and fermented and is in storage. To kraeusen, therefore, means to add carbon dioxide to stored beer to give it effervescence and zest. It is one method of reintroducing carbon dioxide, which was released during fermentation, into the brew. Carbon dioxide may also be infused directly. In this more recent method, brewers collect gases from early fermentation, store them, and then inject them later.

SOURCES: Harold M. Broderick, ed., *The Practical Brewer* (Madison, Wis., 1977); Harold J. Grossman, *Grossman's Guide to Wines, Beers, and Spirits* (New York, 1977).

Krausening. *See* Kraeusening.

Krueger, Gottfried, Brewing Company. This Newark, New Jersey, brewery was founded originally as Braun & Laible in 1852. By 1865 it had become Hill & Krueger, and when Gottlieb Hill retired in 1875, Gottfried Krueger took over. The family ran the brewery, but in 1889 the firm became part of the U.S. Brewing Company, Ltd., of New York, one of the many consolidates formed by British capitalists in the period. Krueger continued under the same name and reopened as Gottfried Krueger Brewing Company, Inc., with repeal of Prohibition (q.v.) in 1933. Krueger was one of the first breweries to package its beer in cans (*see* Canned Beer). The firm closed in 1960, but the Krueger brand name was purchased by the Narragansett Brewing Company (q.v.) of Rhode Island, which was later bought by Falstaff (q.v.).

SOURCES: Manfred Friedrich and Donald Bull, *The Register of U.S. Breweries* (Trumbull, Conn., 1976); *One Hundred Years of Brewing* (Chicago and New York, 1903; Arno Press Reprint, 1974).

L

Labrot and Graham Distillery. Originally, Oscar Pepper built this distilling plant near Frankfort, Kentucky, in 1838. James E. Pepper, his son, inherited the distillery, but it was later taken over by Col. E. H. Taylor (q.v.), who sold it to George T. Stagg in 1878. Soon after, Stagg sold the plant to James Graham and Leopold Labrot. The Labrots continued to operate the business until 1940, when they sold out to Brown-Forman (q.v.).

SOURCES: "Distilleries of Old Kentucky," *Spirits* (April 1935); "Kentucky's Sons," *Spirits* (May 1936); John Ed Pearce, *Nothing Better in the Market* (Louisville, Ky., 1970).

Lager beer. An effervescent malt beverage, lager is brewed by using the bottom-fermentation (q.v.) process, in which a special yeast settles as residue at the bottom of the brewing vats. The distinctly German beer was popular in German countries in the early nineteenth century, and was introduced in the U.S. probably in the 1840s by John Wagner (q.v.). Because the process for making this light, sparkling brew involved storage while fermentation (q.v.) occurred, it was termed "lager," which is derived from the German verb *lagern*, meaning to stock or store.

SOURCES: Stanley Baron, *Brewed in America* (Boston, 1962); Frederic Birmingham, *Falstaff's Complete Beer Book* (New York, 1970); *One Hundred Years of Brewing* (Chicago and New York, 1903; Arno Press Reprint, 1974).

Lagering. After fermentation, beer has been traditionally stored in casks for several weeks in an effort to enhance the flavor. The word "lager" is derived from the German word for storehouse or "to store." The German brewing influence and tradition were felt in America with the introduction of lager beer (q.v.) during the early nineteenth century as German breweries in America brewed a beer using the bottom-fermentation (q.v.) process and lagering. Although such storage (lagering) is not necessary for beer production, responding to consumer preference, American brewing has incorporated this process almost exclusively. English beers, in contrast, are normally bottled or kegged without being stored or lagered.

SOURCES: Stanley Baron, *Brewed in America* (Boston, 1962); *One Hundred Years of Brewing* (Chicago and New York, 1903; Arno Press Reprint, 1974).

Latrobe Brewing Company. The James B. Tito family established the company in 1933. The small brewery in Latrobe, Pennsylvania, markets Rolling Rock beer. Two other breweries, one founded by the Benedictine Society in 1844, and another in Pittsburgh that joined the merger known as the Pittsburgh Brewing Company (q.v.), have also been referred to as the Latrobe Brewery. *See also*, St. Vincent Abbey, Brewery of.

SOURCE: American Brewer (December 1950); Stanley Baron, *Brewed in America* (Boston, 1962).

Lauer, Frederick (October 14, 1810-September 5, 1883). First president of the U.S. Brewers' Association (q.v.) in 1862, Lauer migrated to the U.S. from Germany in 1822 and settled in Reading, Pennsylvania. He became a successful brewer and served in various offices of the U.S. Brewers' Association from 1862 to his death in 1882.

SOURCE: One Hundred Years of Brewing (Chicago and New York, 1903; Arno Press Reprint, 1974).

Lauter tun. The tun is a tub or vessel used in brewing that contains a false perforated bottom and movable rakes. The solids settle on the false bottom and form a natural filter bed. The liquid that flows through is called wort (q.v.), and this passes to the brew kettle. Prior to the development of mechanical innovations, such as the false bottom and pumps, during the nineteenth century, the tun was simply the mash tub with a hole in the center plugged with a shaft called a tap-tree (q.v.). For lautering (q.v.) the shaft was pulled out and the liquid would run out through the hole in a small stream. The tub rested on a platform, and thus the liquid drained down into another tub known as an underback (q.v.), or grant.

SOURCES: John P. Arnold and Frank Penman, *History of the Brewing Industry and Brewing Science* (Chicago, 1933); *One Hundred Years of Brewing* (Chicago and New York, 1903; Arno Press Reprint, 1974).

Lautering. In the lautering process, wort (q.v.) is strained or removed from solid and "spent" grains. A lauter tun (q.v.), or tub, today made of copper or stainless steel, is used to permit the solids to settle out.

SOURCE: One Hundred Years of Brewing (Chicago and New York, 1903; Arno Press Reprint, 1974).

Leaching. Liquor is filtered through charcoal before the distilled whiskey is poured into barrels for aging (q.v.). Today most distillers have eliminated this step, although it was formerly practiced fairly generally.

Leinenkugel, Jacob, Brewing Company. The Chippewa Falls, Wisconsin, brewery was established in 1867 by Jacob Leinenkugel and John Miller as the Spring Brewery. Jacob was three years old when the family of Matthias Leinenkugel migrated from Germany to the U.S. in 1845. Matthias opened a brewery in Sauk City, Wisconsin, and Jacob moved to Chippewa Falls in the mid-1860s. Miller sold his interest in 1883, and the brewery was incorporated as the Jacob Leinenkugel Brewing Company in 1898. Upon Jacob's death in 1899, his son Matthias and sons-in-law Henry Casper and John Mayer managed the business. Matthias died in 1927 and Susan Leinenkugel, daughter of the founder, managed the brewery until her son, Raymond Mayer, took over in 1929, a position he held until 1964. During Prohibition (q.v.), the company produced near beer (q.v.) and soda water. William Casper succeeded Mayer as president in 1965 and has been chairman since 1971 when J. William Leinenkugel, great grandson of Jacob, became president. The small brewery, which markets most of its 75,000 barrels per year within a hundred miles, stresses the importance of pure water, which is supplied by the Big Eddy Springs.

SOURCES: *Brewers Digest* (April 1967 and February 1978); Wayne Kroll, *Badger Breweries* (Jefferson, Wis., 1976); *Newsweek* (September 4, 1978).

Lemp, William J., Brewing Company. This early St. Louis brewery was founded in 1842 by J. Adam Lemp, a German immigrant, who brewed the city's first lager beer (q.v.). Lemp died in 1862 and his son, J. William, assumed management of the business. In 1877 the brewery ranked nineteenth in production among the nation's brewers, with 61,000 barrels, and was the city's largest brewer. By 1895 Lemp was eighth among the nation's brewers, but Anheuser-Busch (q.v.) had surged to second nationally and first in St. Louis. Still Lemp was considered a "national brewer" (q.v.) as it maintained an elaborate system of agencies (q.v.) and branches. Some sources claim it was the first national brewery. In 1896, the company began using the Falstaff (q.v.) trademark, registered the name in 1903, and later during the 1920s sold it to the Griesedieck brewing interests. The Lemp brewery closed as a result of Prohibition (q.v.) and did not reopen. There is evidence that the great brewery was on the brink of trouble anyway as its equipment was becoming outmoded and sales were dropping.

SOURCES: Stanley Baron, *Brewed in America* (Boston, 1962); Don Crinklaw, "A Saga: The Lemps of St. Louis," *St. Louis Post-Dispatch* (December 2, 1973); James Lindhurst, "History of the Brewing Industry in St. Louis, 1804-1860," unpub. M.A. thesis, Washington University, 1939; *One Hundred Years of Brewing* (Chicago and New York, 1903; Arno Press Reprint, 1974).

Lever Food and Fuel Control Act. As a war conservation measure, legislation was passed in August 1917 prohibiting the use of foodstuffs in the manufacture of distilled liquors. Thus the distilling industry was virtually shut down. The president was also given the authority to initiate other measures to conserve and control food and fuel production.

Licensed Beverage Industries. Founded in 1946, the New York-based organization was the result of a merger of the Allied Beverage Industries and

Allied Liquors Industry. Licensed Beverage Industries (LBI), with Munson Shaw (*see* Shaw, Alex D., Company) as chairman and Thomas McCarthy of Austin, Nichols and Company (q.v.) as president, was to act as a national public relations organization representing all branches of the distilling industry. The agency distributed information on taxation, social problems, liquor use, alcohol education, and the economic importance of the industry. In 1973, LBI merged with the Bourbon Institute (q.v.) and the Distilled Spirits Institute (q.v.), forming the Distilled Spirits Council of the U.S., Inc. (q.v.).

SOURCES: Frank Kane, *Anatomy of the Whiskey Business* (Manhasset, N.Y., 1965); *Red Book, Encyclopedic Directory of the Wine and Liquor Industry, 1955-56*; *Spirits* (May and June 1946).

Liebert & Obert (Brewery). P. P. Liebert and Herman Obert built a lager beer brewery in Philadelphia in 1873. It remained a successful but relatively small brewery (28,000 barrels ca. 1900 and 150,000 ca. 1945). The plant became Cooper Brewing Company, Inc., in 1945 but that company closed in 1948.

SOURCES: Manfred Friedrich and Donald Bull, *The Register of U.S. Breweries* (Trumbull, Conn., 1976); *One Hundred Years of Brewing* (Chicago and New York, 1903; Arno Press Reprint, 1974).

Liebmann, S., Brewing Company. *See* Rheingold Breweries, Inc.

Light whiskey. Whiskey (q.v.) in the U.S. that is distilled between 160 and 190 proof (q.v.) and aged in either used charred barrels or new uncharred barrels is classified as light whiskey. Federal regulations were changed in 1968 to permit U.S. distillers to produce light whiskies that might compete with popular Scotch (q.v.) and Canadian (q.v.) whiskies. American whiskies had to be distilled at 160 proof or lower. The lower the percent of alcohol, the more flavor a whiskey has; thus a light whiskey could only be made if distilled at a proof higher than 160. As proof rises toward 200, or 100 percent grain alcohol, the liquid is tasteless, as in the case of vodka (q.v.). Thus the law was changed on January 26, 1968, and became effective July 1, 1972.

SOURCES: Alexis Lichine's New Encyclopedia of Wines and Spirits (New York, 1974); U.S., Department of Treasury, Bureau of Alcohol, Tobacco, and Firearms, *Code of Federal Regulations*, Title 27, Standards of Identity for Distilled Spirits.

Lill and Diversey (Brewery). The origins of this Chicago brewery date from 1833 when William Lill and William Haas built their plant on Chicago's West Side. It was that city's first brewery, and a financial backer, albeit a silent partner, was Mayor William B. Ogden (q.v.). In 1840, Michael Diversey (q.v.) came into the business and replaced Ogden and Haas. The brewery was successful and noted for Lill's Cream Ale, but was destroyed in the Chicago Fire of 1871 and did not reopen.

SOURCES: Paul Angle, "Michael Diversey and Beer in Chicago," *Chicago History*, vol. 8 (Spring 1969); Richard J. La Susa, "Nevermore the Local Lagers," *Chicago Tribune Magazine* (April 24, 1977); *One Hundred Years of Brewing* (Chicago and New York, 1903; Arno Press Reprint, 1974).

Limestone water. During the late eighteenth and early nineteenth centuries, because of various pressures many eastern farmer-distillers (q.v.) moved to Kentucky and southern Indiana. A mantle of limestone cuts across southern Indiana and into Kentucky, and the water that filters through the layers of rock was, and is, considered excellent for making whiskey. Apparently, the calcium in the water, the purity of it, and the absence of iron salts work very well with yeast. Until later developments in water technology and processing, the location of distilleries was largely governed by the availability of suitable water. The necessities of nature, in any event, have proved a great benefit to Kentucky historically and economically (*see* Kentucky Distilling Industry). Another area noted for limestone water, and a center of American whiskey production, was Peoria, Illinois (*see* Peoria Distilling Industry).

SOURCES: Gerald Carson, *The Social History of Bourbon* (New York, 1963); Harold J. Grossman, *Grossman's Guide to Wines, Beers, and Spirits* (New York, 1977).

Lion, Inc. (Brewery). The Wilkes-Barre, Pennsylvania, company was first founded about 1905 as the Luzerne County Brewing Company. About 1910, after being in receivership (q.v.), the company apparently was called the Lion Brewing Company. After Repeal (q.v.) in 1933 the firm was also called the Gibbons brewery and continued into the 1970s with William Smulowitz as president. In 1967, Lion acquired the Bartels brand and in 1974 the Stegmaier (q.v.) brand.

SOURCES: Will Anderson, *The Beer Book* (Princeton, N.J., 1973); James D. Robertson, *The Great American Beer Book* (Ottawa, Ill., 1978).

Liqueurs. Also referred to as cordials, these distilled beverages are flavored by the addition of syrup for sweetening. The flavoring material is either infused or distilled. Liqueurs must contain 2½ percent sugar by volume. Some types are Triple Sec, Benedictine, sloe gin, Chartreuse, and Cointreau.

Liquor Concentration Act. Legislation enacted by Congress in 1922 required that all whiskey stocks be placed in designated federal warehouses for closer supervision. Many distillers had whiskey inventories that had been distilled before January 16, 1920, the effective date of the Eighteenth Amendment (q.v.). To prevent illegal use of such stocks, all whiskey in certain areas had to be transported and stored in the large concentration warehouses.

SOURCES: Gerald Carson, *The Social History of Bourbon* (New York, 1963); John Ed Pearce, *Nothing Better in the Market* (Louisville, Ky., 1970); "Schenley," *Fortune* (May 1936).

Local Option. The term describes local regulatory liquor laws, which are normally prohibitory in nature. Maine and Connecticut pioneered such laws in the 1830s. The statutes permitted a town, city, or county to regulate the liquor traffic by prohibition or by licensing of saloons. Most states first had to permit such laws through an enabling act. Ohio became a model of the local option drive in the 1880s, and by 1900, thirty-seven states had passed enabling acts. Supporters stressed the "Jeffersonian doctrine" of localism, and the local option law has remained in operation in many states through the twentieth century. Since repeal of Prohibition, (q.v.), forty-one states have permitted local option.

SOURCE: Norman Clark, *Deliver Us from Evil* (New York, 1976).

Lone Star Brewing Company. A group of businessmen established the San Antonio, Texas, brewery in 1883. Adolphus Busch (q.v.), the sole nonresident, headed the stock company and was president, thus representing an early thrust of the St. Louis brewery into an expansionist program. Busch was also investing in other concerns at that time. The company continued into the twentieth century, and the plant was purchased by Olympia (q.v.) in 1977—although it continued under the Lone Star name.

SOURCES: Stanley Baron, *Brewed in America* (Boston, 1962); *One Hundred Years of Brewing* (Chicago and New York, 1903; Arno Press Reprint, 1974).

Louisville brewing industry. The "Falls City," located on the Ohio River, was founded in 1780 and as one of the western river cities grew rapidly in the nineteenth century. By 1900, the population was 204,000 with about 12,000 of the city's populace being of German nativity. The city became one of the nation's brewing centers, although not on the scale of Milwaukee or Cincinnati. Nevertheless, the twenty or so breweries in operation did encourage a local merger as five joined as the Central Consumers Brewing Company (q.v.) in 1901. Frank Fehr (q.v.) was in the group, although two other long-lived firms, Falls City (q.v.) and John F. Oertel (q.v.), remained independent.

Low wine. This is the first run of fermented mash through distillation (q.v.). Also known as "singlings," the spirit is low in alcoholic content and relatively unpalatable. During the late eighteenth century, the process of doubling, or second distillation, was introduced to produce a better product. *See also*, Doubler.

M

McAvoy Brewing Company. The Chicago brewery originated in the 1860s. It was known as Downer, Bemis & Company from 1860 to 1882 when it was changed to Bemis & Company and then to McAvoy Brewing Company in 1887. John H. McAvoy came into the business in 1865. In 1877 the brewery installed a Boyle refrigerating machine, the first such usage of the machine. The McAvoy company was bought out by Chicago Breweries Ltd. (q.v.) in 1889; the firm of Wacker & Birk was also included. The company closed during the Prohibition (q.v.) era. *See also*, Wacker, Charles, and Refrigeration.

SOURCE: One Hundred Years of Brewing (Chicago and New York, 1903; Arno Press Reprint, 1974).

McBrayer's Cedar Brook Distillery. The Anderson County, Kentucky, distillery was operated in the late nineteenth century by Judge W. H. McBrayer. After his death in 1887, the estate went to his grandchildren, and their father, D. L. Moore, ran the distillery. The Kentucky Distilleries and Warehouse Company (q.v.) bought the plant about 1900 and continued to market "McBrayer's Cedar Brook Whiskey" until the advent of Prohibition (q.v.).

SOURCES: Gerald Carson, *The Social History of Bourbon* (New York, 1963); H. W. Coyte, "Anderson County Distilleries," unpub. paper, ca. 1970; *Kentucky's Distilling Interests* (Lexington, Ky., 1893).

McCormick Distilling Company. In 1856 David Holladay established this Weston, Missouri, distillery. He received financial backing from his brother Ben, an enterprising businessman who would build a stagecoach line and the Oregon Central Railroad before experiencing financial ruin in the Panic of 1873. In 1890, George Shawhan bought the distillery. E. R. McCormick was a local distilling competitor. After the repeal of Prohibition (q.v.) in 1933, Isadore Singer bought the Shawhan plant and McCormick name and changed the name of this distillery from Old Weston to McCormick. In 1947, United Distilleries acquired the plant in a move mainly to gain control of the whiskey stock, rather than to operate the distillery. In 1950, Cloud L.

Cray, Sr., president of Midwest Solvents, a nearby Kansas company, purchased the firm. Midwest then supplied McCormick with grain neutral spirits used for blended whiskey, gin, vodka, and alcohol. The Cray family continued as managers of the distillery in the late 1970s, with Richard B. Cray as president.

SOURCES: *The McCormick Gazette*, company newspaper; "A Missouri Heritage," *Spirits* (April 1959).

McKenna, Henry, Distillery. This was one of the many distilleries of Nelson County, Kentucky. It was founded by Irish immigrant Henry McKenna in the 1850s. Upon his death in 1892, his three sons carried on the business. The distillery and brand were brought by Seagram (q.v.) in the 1940s as part of its post-Prohibition American expansion program. In 1976 the property was sold to private parties and dismantled.

SOURCES: Sam Elliott, *Nelson County Record* (Bardstown, Ky., 1896); Henry Kroll, *Bluegrass, Belles, and Bourbon* (New York, 1967).

Mail order business (packaged liquor). The shipment of packaged liquor by mail began in the late nineteenth century as the Prohibition (q.v.) movement gained momentum. Mail order dealers shipped whiskey into all areas but did a lively business in the "dry" areas. One of the largest shippers was the Hayner Distillery Company of Dayton, Ohio. Express companies often gave special rates to large dealers. Hayner paid a special rate and paid a minimum of $0.35 per package. In 1911, one estimate claimed that 20 million gallons of liquor was being shipped to consumers. Prohibition ended the practice.

SOURCE: "Of Railroads and Spirits," *Spirits* (October 1950).

Maine Liquor Law. The first of the state prohibition laws was passed in Maine in 1846. In 1851, a second law, supported by Neal Dow (q.v.), revised and put strength in the prohibition statute banning the manufacture and sale of intoxicating liquors. The primary objective was to abolish public drunkenness. Twelve other states followed the example of Maine, but most had repealed their laws by the mid-1860s. Constitutional and political problems countered the effectiveness of the laws. Maine repealed its law temporarily but reenacted it in 1857, and the law remained in effect until 1934.

SOURCES: Norman H. Clark, *Deliver Us from Evil* (New York, 1976); J. C. Furnas, *The Life and Times of the Late Demon Rum* (New York, 1965); Ian R. Tyrell, *Sobering Up: From Temperance to Prohibition in Antebellum America* (Westport, Conn., 1979).

Majestic Distilling Company. Zeli Cohen founded his distillery in Lansdowne, Maryland, in 1951. Originally a distiller of Maryland rye whiskey, the firm's main brands are Old Setter Bourbon, Zelko and Rikaloff Vodka,

Travelers Club, and Old Boston Bourbon. Sidney Cohen is the current president.

Maker's Mark Distillery, Inc. The distillery was founded in 1953 by T. William Samuels, a member of the sixth generation of a family that traces its whiskey-making roots to 1779 and the American Revolution. Samuels serves his company today as chairman and chief executive officer. His son, T. W. Samuels, Jr., joined the firm in 1967 and in 1975 became its president. The family's whiskey-making heritage, begun by Robert Samuels (1758-1823) while an officer in the Pennsylvania militia, continues today in Loretto, Kentucky. Migrating to Kentucky in 1784, Robert continued as a farmer-distiller (q.v.), later to be joined by his son, William (1779-1836). William's son, Taylor William (1820-98), recognized the commercial opportunities of the fledgling industry in Kentucky and established the family's first full-time distillery in Deatsville in 1844. This distillery was later operated by Taylor's son, William Isaac, until his death in 1898; and afterward by William's son, Leslie, until the advent of Prohibition (q.v.) in 1920. Upon Repeal (q.v.) in 1933 Leslie Samuels reorganized the company and built a new plant in Deatsville, which he managed until his death in 1936. Leslie's son, the present T. William Samuels, assumed management of the company until 1943 when he decided to leave the industry. Reentering the distilling industry in 1953, Samuels purchased a small, defunct distillery on the outskirts of Loretto, which has subsequently been restored. Known also as the Star Hill distillery after the farm on which it is located, the firm uses the name of its whiskey, Maker's Mark, as the official designation of the business. The distillery was recently designated a *National Historic Landmark*. The small, successful, family-owned firm bases its appeal on a premium product available on a limited basis.

   SOURCES: Sam Elliott, *Nelson County Record* (Bardstown, Ky., 1896); T. W. Samuels, Jr., "The Samuels: A Family of Distillers Since 1779," unpub. paper, 1975; *Spirits* (September 1958).

Malt. Grain, often barley, is soaked in hot water; after it germinates, or sprouts, it is kilned or dried. The resulting product, or malt, contains less moisture than in the original form, is mellower, and is better able to undergo the chemical changes necessary for the brewing process (q.v.) and whiskey-making (q.v.).

Malt kiln. Wet barley, or green malt (q.v.), is dried during the malting process in a furnace or stovelike tower or building. At the beginning of the nineteenth century most kilning (q.v.) was done in smoke-drying kilns, but these were gradually replaced by air dryers. During the 1880s and 1890s, a number of different dumping kiln floors were introduced in the U.S. Briefly, malt was dumped from one perforated steel-wire floor to the next, with perhaps as many as four levels, thereby aerating the malt and eliminating hand shoveling. Among the firms producing the dumping kiln floors were W. Toeper & Sons of Milwaukee, and Goetz Flodin of Chicago.

SOURCES: Thomas C. Cochran, The Pabst Brewing Company (New York, 1948); One Hundred Years of Brewing (Chicago and New York, 1903; Arno Press Reprint, 1974).

Malt liquor. Although brewed like lager beer (q.v.) in a bottom-fermentation (q.v.) process, malt liquor is brewed from wort (q.v.), which contains a higher degree of fermentable sugars than in the case of lager. This brew has a higher alcoholic content than regular beer and is of paler color. The taste is more aromatic and is slightly malty. The beverage has been brewed and marketed recently in an effort to compete with sweet wines.

SOURCES: Frederic Birmingham, Falstaff's Complete Beer Book (New York, 1970); "New Brands, Malt Liquors Abrewing," Bev, vol. 2 (February 15, 1964).

Malt whiskey. A full-bodied distillate, almost exclusively Scotch whisky (q.v.), malt whiskey is made from malted barley (q.v.), distilled in pot-stills (see Still), and contains no grain whiskey. In the U.S. malt whiskies were fairly popular prior to Prohibition (q.v.).

Malting. In the initial stage of grain preparation prior to brewing and distilling, grain, usually barley, is sieved as the best grains are used. This grain is then steeped in water, allowed to sprout, and then dried or kilned. During malting, enzymes (q.v.) are produced that will convert the starches in grain to sugars, maltose (q.v.) and dextrin (q.v.). In brewing, well into the twentieth century, the three types of malting were floor-malting (q.v.), compartment malting, and drum malting. The latter two are forms of pneumatic malting (q.v.) and have been adopted by most maltsters since the turn of the century. The production of malt has been done primarily by independent malting companies. At the turn of the century there were more than 150 malting establishments catering to the brewing industry; today, 15 to 20 firms supply brewers with malt.

SOURCES: John P. Arnold and Frank Penman, History of the Brewing Industry and Brewing Science (Chicago, 1933); One Hundred Years of Brewing (Chicago and New York, 1903; Arno Press Reprint, 1974); Edward H. Vogel, Jr., et al., The Practical Brewer (St. Louis, Mo., 1946).

Maltose. A sugar results from the action of an enzyme (q.v.), amylase (q.v.), which is produced during the germination (q.v.) of barley. The enzyme converts the starch in the grain into a sugar, maltose, which is fermentable.

Maryland Brewing Company. This Baltimore consolidation of sixteen breweries was reorganized as the Gottlieb-Bauernschmidt-Strauss Brewing Company (q.v.) in 1902.

SOURCE: William J. Kelley, *Brewing in Maryland* (Baltimore, 1965).

Mash. A mixture of ground grains and water that is cooked or steeped, mash is a fermentable starchy material from which alcoholic beverages are made. In the brewing process (q.v.), the mash, called wort (q.v.) after straining, is fermented and then normally stored for a time, while in the whiskey-making process (q.v.), the mash is distilled after being fermented.

SOURCES: Harold M. Broderick, ed., *The Practical Brewer* (Madison, Wis., 1977); Frank Haring, ed., *Practical Encyclopedia of Alcoholic Beverages* (New York, 1959); *One Hundred Years of Brewing* (Chicago and New York, 1903; Arno Press Reprint, 1974).

Mash-tub. *See* Mash-tun.

Mash-tun. This is a cylindrical vessel known as a tun or tub. Mash (q.v.) is placed in the tun and heated and stirred. The transition from hand mashing, or stirring, with rakes or paddles to mechanical means, and from wooden to copper and stainless steel tuns occurred during the nineteenth and early twentieth centuries.

SOURCE: One Hundred Years of Brewing (Chicago and New York, 1903; Arno Press Reprint, 1974).

Mashing. The mashing process consists of mixing grain or malt (q.v.) with water in a mash tub, or tun, thus converting "dry" materials and starches of the grain into sugar and dextrin (q.v.). In the brewing process (q.v.) the resultant substance is termed "wort" (q.v.), whereas in the distilling process (q.v.) the term maltose (q.v.) is often used. In brewing, the mashing process underwent considerable change in the nineteenth century. Mechanical stirring devices, false bottoms for the mash tun (q.v.), admission of water from below in the tun by a pfaff (q.v.), and perforated metal plates instead of false bottoms were among the innovations of the 1870s and 1880s.

SOURCES: Harold Broderick, ed., *The Practical Brewer* (Madison, Wis., 1977); *In Olde Kentucke* (Frankfort, ca., 1970); *One Hundred Years of Brewing* (Chicago and New York, 1903; Arno Press Reprint, 1974); John Willett, "Design of a Distillery," unpub. B.A. paper, University of Louisville, 1938.

Massachusetts Breweries Company, Ltd. This Boston-based merger of approximately ten breweries was organized in 1901, evidently to compete against the New England Breweries, Ltd. (q.v.). In the group were American Brewing Company, Franklin Brewing Company, Continental Brewing

Company, Alley Brewery, William Smith & Sons, Habich & Company, Hanley & Casey, H. & J. Pfaff, and Robinson Brewing Company.

SOURCES: Will Anderson, *The Beer Book* (Princeton, N.J., 1973); Manfred Friedrich and Donald Bull, *The Register of U.S. Breweries* (Trumbull, Conn., 1976).

Massey, William, & Company (Brewery). William Massey, an English immigrant, founded his Philadelphia ale (q.v.) brewery in 1849. The firm operated under a variety of names because Massey had a number of partners before becoming sole proprietor about 1870. In 1877, the brewery ranked as the nation's eleventh largest, but closed in 1894, a few years after Massey's death in February 1891.

SOURCES: Manfred Friedrich and Donald Bull, *The Register of U.S. Breweries* (Trumbull, Conn., 1976); *One Hundred Years of Brewing* (Chicago and New York, 1903; Arno Press Reprint, 1974).

Master Brewers' Association. Organized in Chicago on March 21, 1887, and also known as the Brewmasters' Association, the group was formed to promote the interests of brewing, brewing education, and technical discussion.

SOURCES: John P. Arnold and Frank Penman, *History of the Brewing Industry and Brewing Science* (Chicago, 1933).

Mattingly and Moore Distillery Company. The distilling company near Bardstown, Kentucky, dates from 1876 when Thomas S. Moore and Ben F. Mattingly formed a partnership. They bought the Willett Franche and Company plant, which had been built in the late 1860s. R. H. Edelen and John Simms entered the business in 1881, and Mattingly withdrew. Tom Moore left the business in 1889 to build his own distillery. In 1921 Frankfort Distilling Company (q.v.) purchased the Mattingly and Moore name. Seagram (q.v.) bought the brands in the 1940s.

SOURCES: Sam Elliott, *Nelson County Record* (Bardstown, Ky., 1896); "Great Names in Whiskey," *Spirits* (July 1937).

Medley Distilling Company. The Medley family founded this Owensboro, Kentucky, distilling firm in 1940. The involvement of the Medleys in Kentucky distilling dates from about 1800. Thomas Medley built a distillery near Lebanon in the very early 1800s. His son, William, and grandson, George E., who was born in 1850, continued the tradition. George became an owner of the Daviess County Distilling Company (q.v.) in 1904 and his sons continued the business until they sold it to Fleischmann in 1940. Thomas A., Ben F., John A., Wathen, George E., II, and Edwin W. Medley organized a new business in that year. They bought the Kentucky Sour Mash Distillery Company, which had been built in 1937. In 1946 they reorganized the partnership into a corporation. In the late 1970s the Medley family continued to be principal operators of the firm and also operated the Double Springs Distillery of Bardstown, Kentucky. In 1901, Thomas A. Medley married Florence Wathen (*see* Wathen Distilleries) of the prominent Kentucky distilling family.

SOURCES: "The Medley Family Incorporates," *Spirits* (July 1946); *Spirits* (April 1935 and May 1936).

Megibben, T. J., distilleries. Thomas Jefferson Megibben ran a number of distilleries in Cynthiana, Kentucky, in the post-Civil War era. He produced Excelsior, Edgewater, and Old Lewis Hunter whiskies. Upon his death in 1891, G. R. Sharpe purchased the brands, which were sold to Julius Kessler & Company in 1902. *See also*, Old Lewis Hunter (Distillery).

SOURCES: Gerald Carson, *The Social History of Bourbon* (New York, 1963); H. W. Coyte, "Kentucky Distilleries," unpub. paper, ca. 1970; *Kentucky's Distilling Interests* (Lexington, Ky., 1893).

Meister Brau, Inc. *See* Hand, Peter, Brewing Company, and Buckeye Brewing Company.

Meschendorf, Dietrich W. (1858-1911). A Kentucky distiller who owned the Old Kentucky Distillery from 1892 to 1911, Meschendorf had interests in the Old Times Distillery, Pleasure Ridge Distillery, and Daviess County Distilling Company (q.v.). Meschendorf was considered an authority on whiskey and was consulted by President Theodore Roosevelt concerning standards for straight whiskey when the Pure Food and Drug Act (q.v.) was being considered. He also testified on the meaning of "whiskey" during the hearing that culminated in the "Taft decision" (q.v.) of 1909.

SOURCES: *Kentucky's Distilling Interests* (Lexington, Ky., 1893); *Spirits* (April 1935); U.S. Department of Justice, *Proceedings . . . Concerning the Meaning of the Term "Whisky"* (Washington, D.C., 1909).

Michter's Distillery, Inc. Claiming the distinction of making whiskey at the nation's oldest operating distillery site, the current company traces the origins of the site as a distillery to 1753. John Shenk, and his brother, Michael, Swiss Mennonite farmer-distillers, began operating their distillery on Snitzel Creek in 1753. The distillery was enlarged in the 1780s, and Rudolph Meyer, Michael's son-in-law, directed the operation. He produced rye whiskey (q.v.) for the Philadelphia market. In 1827, Elizabeth Shenk Kratzer, a granddaughter, inherited the business and her husband, John, managed it until 1860. She sold the plant to Abe Bomberger, a Shenk Descendant, in 1861; the Bombergers managed the distillery until the advent of Prohibition in 1920. During their ownership, it was known as the Bomberger

Distillery, the most common historical designation of the plant. After 1933 it came under the control of various distillers and was utilized primarily as a producer of bulk whiskey (q.v.) for other distilleries. Lebanon Valley, Schenley (q.v.), and Pennso were among the owners. It was reorganized under the present Michter auspices in 1975. Louis Forman is president and Charles Romito general manager. The company bases its appeal largely on the historic nature of the firm; its use of the pot-still (*see* Still) method and connection with the Amish and Dutch grain farmers of the area who supply the grains for whiskey-making support the tradition.

SOURCES: Michter's Distillery, Inc., *Michter's: The Whiskey That Warmed the Revolution* (Schaefferstown, Pa., n.d.); Michter's Distillery Newspaper Clipping Files; "National Register Inventory Form for Bomberger's Distillery," 1975.

Miles, E. L., Distillery Company. *See* New Hope Distillery Company.

Miller, Frederick (November 24, 1824-June 11, 1888). Founder of the Miller Brewing Company, Miller migrated to the U.S. from Germany around 1850. He had worked in the Royal Brewery at Sigmaringen, Hohenzollern. After working in Rochester, New York, he settled on Milwaukee as a promising site for his planned brewing business. Miller bought the Plank Road Brewery from Charles Lorenz Best in 1855 and successfully ran the business until his death in 1888. He kept up with modernization and increased the capacity from 300 to 80,000 barrels production. Upon his death, his sons assumed management of the brewery.

SOURCES: *Dictionary of Wisconsin Biography* (Madison, Wis., 1960); "History of the Miller Brewing Company" (brief company history, 1979).

Miller, Frederick C. (February 26, 1906-December 17, 1954). Miller was the grandson of Frederick Miller, founder of the Miller Brewing Company (q.v.). A standout football player at Notre Dame as a tackle in the late 1920s, Miller returned to Milwaukee after graduation and worked in his father's lumber, real estate, and mortgage business. In 1936 he became vice-president of the Miller Brewing Company and then president in 1947. His leadership in building and advertising was largely responsible for the company's expansion in the period. In December 1954 Miller and his son, Fred, Jr., died in a tragic airplane crash in Milwaukee.

SOURCES: *Dictionary of Wisconsin Biography* (Madison, Wis., 1960); "History and Current Operation of the Miller Brewing Company" (brief company history, 1979).

Miller Brewing Company. The Milwaukee brewery was originally built by Jacob Best, Sr., in 1850. Best's sons, Lorenz and Charles, took over the business soon afterward, but they sold the Plank Road Brewery to Frederick

Miller (q.v.) in 1855. During the next three decades, Miller expanded production from 300 to about 80,000 barrels per year. In 1888, the same year of the founder's death, the company was incorporated as the Frederick Miller Brewing Company. Upon Miller's death, his sons, Ernest, Fred A., and Emil, along with son-in-law, Carl Miller, assumed management of the company. By 1919, production had increased to 500,000 barrels. During the Prohibition (q.v.) era, the firm produced cereal beverages, soft drinks, and malt-related products. In the meantime, Frederick A. Miller succeeded his brother, Ernest, as president upon the latter's death in 1922. Frederick A. Miller remained chief executive until 1947 when he was succeeded by nephew, Frederick C. Miller (q.v.), who died in a plane crash in 1954. Over the years the company's main brand, Miller High Life, had proved to be popular, and the operation was modernized in the post-Prohibition period. By 1954 the company was ninth in production among the nation's brewers. After Frederick C. Miller's untimely death in that year, Norman Klug, an officer of the company since 1947, became president. An expansion program, begun under Miller, was continued by Klug as Miller purchased the A. Gettelman Company (q.v.) of Milwaukee in 1961 and General Brewing Corporation of Azusa, California, in 1966, the first non-Milwaukee Miller plant. The expansion program continued as a Carling plant was purchased in Ft. Worth in late 1966. Just before Klug's death in October 1966, Miller had completed arrangements for the W. R. Grace Company to purchase 53 percent of the brewing company's stock. Klug was succeeded by Charles Miller (not related to the Miller family), who held the position of president until 1969 when Philip Morris Incorporated purchased the Grace stock for $130 million. In 1970, Philip Morris bought the remaining 47 percent of Miller stock from the De Rance Foundation of Milwaukee. In 1971, John A. Murphy, a Philip Morris executive, was named chief executive and in 1972 president. Again, expansion continued with the acquisition of the brand names Meister Brau, Buckeye, and Lite from Meister Brau, Inc. (*see* Hand, Peter, Brewing Company). After test marketing, Miller began to distribute Lite on a wider scale, and this brand proved to be instrumental in Miller's success during the late 1970s. The firm also arranged to produce Lowenbrau in the U.S. When Philip Morris took over in 1970, sales totaled about 5 million barrels but had climbed to nearly 25 million barrels in 1977, establishing the firm as the nation's second largest brewery (from seventh in 1972) behind Anheuser-Busch (q.v.). In 1978, the brewery produced more than 31 million barrels. Other plant expansions have been initiated with the building of new facilities in Fulton, New York (1976), Eden, North Carolina (1979), Irwindale, California (1980), and Albany, Georgia (1980). By the late 1970s Miller was challenging Anheuser-Busch's position as No. 1 —and the two companies' competitive statures involved a variety of tactics, including advertising and legal strategies.

SOURCES: Stanley Baron, *Brewed in America* (Boston, 1962); Thomas C. Cochran, *The Pabst Brewing Company* (New York, 1948); "History and Current Operation of the Miller Brewing Company" (brief company history, 1979); *Newsweek* (September 1978); *One Hundred Years of Brewing* (Chicago and New York, 1903; Arno Press Reprint, 1974).

Milwaukee brewing industry. The famous Wisconsin "beer city" entered its period of commercial growth during the 1830s and 1840s, and between 1840 and 1850 grew from about 1,700 in population to just over 20,000. As in the case of most other American brewing centers, a number of factors converged to encourage the establishment of brewing as a viable industry. German immigrants made up more than one-third of the population by 1850, and natural resources and harbor facilities were very promising, thus creating favorable conditions for the brewing of the recently introduced lager beer (q.v.). The light, bottom-fermented brew was very popular among Germans, and Milwaukee's first breweries were founded in the 1840s. During the 1850s, about fifteen such breweries were in operation; among them were Jacob Best (*see* Pabst Brewing Company), August Krug, which was to become Schlitz (q.v.), Blatz (q.v.), Miller (q.v.), and Gettelman (q.v.). A portion of the beer was already being exported in the 1850s, possibly an early indication of the inclinations of Milwaukee's brewers. After leveling off in the late 1850s and 1860s because of depression, Civil War, and taxation, the industry began to expand again during the late 1860s. Then between 1870 and 1900, Milwaukee established itself as a major brewing city, even though its population of 285,000 was considerably lower than that of New York City, Philadelphia, or Chicago. The reasons for the prominence of Milwaukee and its large brewers, Pabst, Schlitz, and Blatz, which were first, third, and seventh, respectively, in production in 1895, are interesting. The cool climate helped in refrigeration for lagering (q.v.), and this was a distinct advantage until the widespread use of artificial refrigeration (q.v.) devices after 1900. Relatively inexpensive wood, or cooperage (q.v.), for barrels also helped, but apparently a very important factor was the limited local market that acted as a prod for brewers to develop national marketing in order to suceed. Illustrating, and perhaps initiating this trend, was Chicago's Great Fire of 1871. Some of Chicago's breweries were destroyed, but safe drinking water was scarce, and the city's populace eagerly bought up Milwaukee beer. In 1872 sales increased by 44 percent for the Wisconsin city's beer. During the latter part of the century, the brewers also invested heavily in advertising and promotion and often identified their product with Milwaukee. Schlitz adopted the slogan, "Schlitz, the Beer That Made Milwaukee Famous," in this period, and in 1900 Pabst, Schlitz, and Blatz combined in a lawsuit against New York brewers who were advertising their brew as "Milwaukee beer." Brewers also sponsored beer halls and gardens, hotels, and theaters, and all of these activities helped label the city as a *gemutlich* society, with beer as a main ingredient socially and economically. Although the large companies remained open during Prohibition (q.v.) in the 1920s, producing near beer (q.v.), syrups, and other products, the smaller breweries generally went out of business. From about twelve companies in 1910, the figure declined in the 1920s, then rose to eleven by 1935, only to fall to six by 1960, and three by the late 1970s. Among the city's smaller breweries were Banner Brewing Company, Capitol Brewing Company, Cream City Brewing Company (q.v.), Independent Milwaukee Brewery, C. T. Melms, and Richard G. Owens.

SOURCES: Thomas C. Cochran, *The Pabst Brewing Company* (New York, 1948); Richard N. Current, *Wisconsin* (New York, 1977); "Milwaukee Beer—It Made a City 'Famous,'" *Wisconsin Then and Now* (February 1968); Bayrd Still, *Milwaukee: The History of a City* (Madison, Wis., 1948).

Moerlein, Christian (May 13, 1818-May 14, 1897). The noted Bavaria-born brewer settled in Cincinnati in 1842. After working in various minor occupations, Moerlein, who had a knowledge of brewing techniques from his German background, entered the brewing trade in 1853 with a partner, Adam Dillman. Following a subsequent partnership with Conrad Windisch (*see* Windisch-Muhlhauser Company), another successful Cincinnati brewer, Moerlein expanded his own company (*see* Moerlein, Christian, Brewing Company) in the late nineteenth century until it became one of the nation's largest breweries. Moerlein was one of a number of very successful brewers who came to the U.S. in search of economic opportunity, and who took advantage of the growing market of German immigrants who preferred lager-type beers as opposed to ale, porter, and stout.

SOURCES: *Cincinnati Enquirer* (May 15, 1897); William L. Downard, *The Cincinnati Brewing Industry* (Athens, Ohio, 1973).

Moerlein, Christian, Brewing Company. The Cincinnati brewery was founded in 1853 by Christian Moerlein (q.v.) and Adam Dillman. When Dillman died soon afterward, Conrad Windisch (*see* Windisch-Muhlhauser Company) joined Moerlein—but withdrew in 1866. The Moerlein firm expanded in the 1870s and 1880s, and a main factor was the vigorous leadership of George Moerlein, the founder's son, who became general manager in 1872 at the age of twenty. By 1877, the company ranked thirteenth among the nation's brewers, with an output of 72,000 barrels. But the next year, sales jumped to almost 100,000 barrels. By 1895, Moerlein was Ohio's largest brewery and the nation's fourteenth largest, with an output of more than 250,000 barrels. Pabst was first, with nearly 1 million barrels produced. The brewery was incorporated in 1881, and was a national brewery because it distributed its beer across the U.S. George Moerlein died in 1891 at the age of thirty-nine, and when Christian died in 1897, John Moerlein, another son, became president. After trying a near beer (q.v.) called Chrismo at the onset of the Prohibition (q.v.) period, Moerlein directors dissolved the business beginning in 1919. The large real estate investment, family involvement, and distant location of the firm from rail facilities prompted the decision to liquidate. A brief attempt to redevelop occurred in the early 1930s but was not successful.

SOURCES: William L. Downard, *The Cincinnati Brewing Industry* (Athens, Ohio, 1973); *One Hundred Years of Brewing* (Chicago and New York, 1903; Arno Press Reprint, 1974).

Molasses Act, 1733. By means of this act, the British Parliament placed a 6-pence per gallon tax on molasses imported into the American colonies. The intent was to restrict such imports from the Spanish and French West Indies, by means of the high tax, thereby forcing trade with the British West Indies. Molasses was an important commodity because of its use in making rum (q.v.). The act was one of a number of the Acts of Trade and Navigation aimed at implementing mercantilism.

Monarch distilleries (Kentucky). M. V. Monarch entered the distillery business near Owensboro in Daviess County, Kentucky, in 1867. By the 1890s he was a prominent Kentucky distiller. Richard Monarch, his brother, distilled whiskey under the Glenmore label, and James Thompson (*see* Glenmore Distilleries Company) purchased his plant in 1901.

SOURCES: Gerald Carson, *The Social History of Bourbon* (New York, 1963); *Kentucky's Distilling Interests* (Lexington, Ky., 1893).

Monarch Distilling Company (Peoria). John Kidd and John H. Francis founded Monarch in 1879. It became part of the Distillers' and Cattle Feeders' Trust (*see* Whiskey Trust) and later a firm in American Spirits Manufacturing Company (q.v.), a branch of the trust. The plant was apparently closed about 1905.

SOURCES: Distilleries file, Peoria Historical Society; Ernest E. East, "Distillery Fires in Corning Plant," *Arrow Messenger* (March 1937).

Moonshine. The term apparently originated in Scotland and Ireland in the late eighteenth century. It was applied to smuggled liquor, which had become fairly common since the first English whiskey revenue tax had been imposed by Parliament in the seventeenth century. In America, in the nineteenth century, moonshine was considered as illegally or illicitly produced whiskey, and moonshining was the act of distilling it (often by moonlight). Many Scots-Irish migrated to America, and when the Excise Act of 1791 (q.v.) had been passed, they were among the disgruntled farmer-distillers (q.v.) of the western region. Resentment led to the Whiskey Rebellion (q.v.) of 1794, and in part to increased westward migration. The production of moonshine moved into the Kentucky area in the 1790s as many farmer-distillers found conditions favorable for the production of both grain and whiskey. Rum had declined after the Revolution, and wine was in short supply, giving added impetus to the expansion of the whiskey trade. Federal excise taxes (*see* Taxation of Distilled Spirits, Federal) and regulatory laws directly affected the moonshine business. As taxes were imposed, raised, lowered, or abolished, moonshine rose or declined in popularity. As regional temperance and prohibition forces became successful, and during the era of national Prohibition (q.v.), moonshine increased in production, demand, and profit. During the "dry decade" of the 1920s, moonshine took on larger significance and some new characteristics. The practice, which had been largely regional and southern in nature, became nationwide in the Prohibition era. Kentucky, which had long been a center of moonshine production, at least became known for production of good whiskey. Another factor was that, with increased demand, producers became involved in a chain of production and marketing that went from the moonshiner (q.v.) to a transporter, to a wholesaler who bottled the drink, to the retailers or bootleggers who sold it to the public. Aging (q.v.) was all but eliminated; blending and watering became common, artificial coloring was often added, and the practice was largely influenced by racketeers and syndicate figures who made fortunes during the 1920s. After repeal of Prohibition, moonshine did not quite return to the calmer, more rustic, days before 1920. The more elaborate system of production and marketing persists to the present. The 1950s marked a high point for moonshine, but since then the trade has tapered off, partly because of more affluence, different attitudes, the decline of old-time producers, and decline in quality. The product itself is interesting. Moonshine generally had more "kick" than legal drink and is sometimes referred to as "fighting whiskey" as opposed to legal liquors, called "courting whiskey." The former apparently breaks down inhibitions more quickly.

SOURCES: Jess Carr, *The Second Oldest Profession* (Englewood Cliffs, N.J., 1972); Gerald Carson, *The Social History of Bourbon* (New York, 1963); Esther Kellner, *Moonshine, Its History and Folklore* (Indianapolis, Ind., 1971); David Maurer, *Kentucky Moonshine* (Lexington, Ky., 1974).

Moonshiner. Technically, this is any producer of illegal whiskey, but the more general application refers to those who produce such drink for marketing—at times in the moonlight. The intent is, of course, to escape taxation and other regulation and thus dispose of the product at a very competitive, but profitable price. *See also*, Moonshine.

Morris, Anthony, II (1654-1721). A famous Philadelphia maltster and brewer, Moris came to the colony of William Penn in the 1680s and became a very prominent member of the community, both in business and civic affairs. His beer, ale (q.v.), and stout (q.v.) were popular. Upon his death in 1721, Anthony III, his son, took over the company. Morris's will, which was indicative of the period, read in part: "To my son, Anthony Morris, my bank and water lot in Philadelphia, with brewhouse, malthouse, brewing utensils, negroes, horses and cattle (except one cow, which I intend for my wife)." Later the firm became known as Francis Perot's Sons (q.v.).

SOURCES: Stanley Baron, *Brewed in America* (Boston, 1962); Madelein Blitzstein, "The History of Francis Perot's Sons," *Modern Brewery* (December 15, 1933); *One Hundred Years of Brewing* (Chicago and New York, 1903; Arno Press Reprint, 1974).

Motlow, Lem (1869-September 1, 1947). The nephew of Jack Daniel (q.v.), Motlow began working in his uncle's famous Tennessee distillery in the 1880s. He was a capable and innovative businessman-distiller; in 1907 Daniel deeded the business to Motlow and Dick Daniel, Jack's cousin. Motlow soon bought Daniel's interest and managed the company until his death in 1947. He came out with the famous Black Label brand in 1911, as a memorial to "Uncle Jack," but it proved so successful that it was continued as the five-year-old whiskey; Green Label was four years old. During the Prohibition (q.v.) period, Motlow successfully raised mules and champion walking horses on his farm, but in the 1930s was ready to resume distilling. However, Tennessee continued statewide prohibition. Motlow was elected to the legislature and was instrumental in relegalization of liquor production in 1938. When he died in 1947, the business passed on to his four sons. *See also*, Daniel, Jack, Distillery.

SOURCES: Jeanne Ridgway Bigger, "Jack Daniel Distillery and Lynchburg," *Tennessee Historical Quarterly* (Spring 1972); Ben A. Green, *Jack Daniel's Legacy* (Shelbyville, Tenn., 1967); *Bev/Executive* (July 15, 1966); "Rare Jack Daniel's," *Fortune* (July 1951).

N

Narragansett Brewing Company. Established in 1890, the Cranston, Rhode Island brewery survived Prohibition (q.v.) and in 1964 purchased the Haffenreffer Brewing Company (q.v.) brand name. In 1966, however, Falstaff (q.v.) purchased Narragansett and marketed both the Narragansett and Haffenreffer brands.

SOURCES: Will and Sonja Anderson, *Beers, Breweries & Breweriana* (New York, 1969); James D. Robertson, *The Great American Beer Book* (Ottawa, Ill., 1978).

Nassau Brewing Company. Nassau was the final name of a fairly successful brewing company in Brooklyn, New York. Founded originally in 1849 as Limberger and Walter, it changed hands in 1866 as Christian Goetz bought the brewery, calling it the Bedford Brewery. He operated it successfully until 1884 when William Brown and a group of businessmen bought the plant. Brown renamed the brewery Budweiser Brewing Company in reference to the quality beer of Budweis, Bohemia. Inevitably, Anheuser-Busch (q.v.) brought suit against Brown for copying their name, which had been trademarked in 1878. Brown gave in, changed the name to Nassau Brewing Company, and directed the company from 1898 to 1914 when it closed.

SOURCE: Will Anderson, *The Breweries of Brooklyn* (New York, 1976).

Nation, Carry A. (November 25, 1846-June 9, 1911). A flamboyant crusader for temperance and prohibition, Nation was known for smashing saloons with a hatchet. She left her first husband because of his alcoholism and thereafter she campaigned against the liquor traffic. In December 1900 she made her first hatchet attack on the Carey Hotel in Wichita, Kansas, and was arrested on many occasions because of her repeated use of the tactic. Receipts from the sale of souvenir hatchets helped pay her legal expenses and fines. Nation was a prominent member of the Women's Christian Temperance Union (q.v.).

SOURCES: Herbert Asbury, *Carry Nation* (New York, 1929); Carry Nation, *The Use and Need of the Life of Carry A. Nation* (Kansas City, 1908); Robert Lewis Taylor, *Vessel of Wrath* (New York, 1966).

National brewer. During the 1870s, a number of successful local and regional firms made decisions to "go national," meaning that the company would market its beer nationally. The transition required establishment of distribution agencies (q.v.) in the desired market areas, and technical improvements made the move possible. Refrigerated railcars aided the movement, as did the pasteurization (q.v.) and bottled beer (q.v.) processes. Advertising (q.v.) became a necessity, and brewers began to use labels, trade names, and symbols to identify their beers. Clearly, the decision to market nationally involved a large capital outlay. The national brewers competed with one another but also provided stiff competition for the local beers, resulting in concentration within the industry. Among the more noted "nationals" were Anheuser-Busch (q.v.), Pabst (q.v.), Schlitz (q.v.), Miller (q.v.), Lemp (q.v.), and Moerlein (q.v.). One goal was to reach the 1-million-barrel mark, a figure that only the largest surpassed in the period around 1900.

SOURCES: Stanley Baron, *Brewed in America* (Boston, 1962); Thomas C. Cochran, *The Pabst Brewing Company* (New York, 1948); William L. Downard, *The Cincinnati Brewing Industry* (Athens, Ohio, 1973).

National Brewers' and Distillers Association. In 1879, representatives of 300 distillers, rectifiers, importers, and wholesalers met in Cincinnati to discuss topics of mutual interest. Their main concern was how to combat the growing strength of prohibitionist and temperance groups. Three years later, in 1882, distillers and liquor dealers called another meeting and were joined in Chicago by representatives of many brewers in May of that year. They formed the National Brewers' and Distillers Association and organized the National Protective Association as the political arm of the association. At a subsequent meeting in Milwaukee in October 1882, the name of the latter subgroup was changed to the Personal Liberty League of the U.S. The organization, which changed names several times over the year, functioned during the 1880s as an information agency attempting to counter the spread of prohibitionist sentiment and laws, particularly the Sunday saloon closing laws which were being passed. In the early 1890s, however, the association declined as "dry" forces gained momentum and brewers and distillers often found themselves at odds over how to oppose the growth of antisaloon and temperance sentiment. Another problem was that brewers began to dissociate themselves from distillers as malt liquor more and more came to be billed as the "beverage of moderation."

SOURCE: Herbert Asbury, *The Great Illusion* (Garden City, N.Y., 1950).

National Brewing Company. (San Francisco). The steam beer (q.v.) brewery was founded in 1861 by John F. Glueck, a German immigrant. His partner, Charles Hansen, managed the firm after Glueck died in 1877. The company became part of the California Brewing Association in 1916, and was conducted as the Cereal Products Refining Corporation from the early years of Prohibition (q.v.) in the 1920s until closing in 1935.

National Brewing Company, Inc. Organized initially in 1885 as the National Brewing Company, the Baltimore, Maryland, brewery closed during Prohibition (q.v.) in the 1920s but was rebuilt, reorganized, and expanded in 1933. Jerold Hoffberger and family took over the brewery and marketed National Premium and National Bohemian. By the 1950s and 1960s, new brands were added, Colt 45 and Altes (*see* Tivoli Brewing Company), the latter resulting from acquisition of that Detroit brewery. Other plants were acquired in Miami, Florida, and Phoenix, Arizona. In 1975, National merged with Carling to form Carling National Breweries, Inc. (q.v.).

SOURCES: Stanley Baron, *Brewed in America* (Boston, 1962); Donald Fenhagen, "Carling National Breweries, Inc." (brief company history, ca. 1978); William J. Kelley, *Brewing in Maryland* (Baltimore, 1965).

National Distillers Products Company. National Distillers was formed in the 1920s. The company was an outgrowth of the Whiskey Trust (q.v.) of the 1880s and 1890s, which was formally known as the Distillers' Securities Corporation after 1902. As Prohibition (q.v.) became a reality in the early 1920s, the name of Distillers' Securities was changed to U.S. Food Products Corporation, a company based on the production of yeast, vinegar, and cereal products. The company went into receivership (q.v.) in 1921, however, and the financiers in charge of the company eventually hired Seton Porter (q.v.) of the Sanderson & Porter engineering firm to manage U.S. Foods. Porter reorganized the company and formed a new company, National Distillers Products Corporation, in April 1924. The company and its subsidiaries produced industrial alcohols, some medicinal alcohol, and yeast, but the latter branch was sold to Fleischmann (q.v.) soon afterward for $4 million. Thereafter, the Porter-directed company began building up whiskey stocks and became the largest stockholder in American Medicinal Spirits Company (q.v.) in 1927. The latter company, consisting of some fifty-nine companies, was successor to the Kentucky Distilleries and Warehouse Company (q.v.), a subsidiary of the Whiskey Trust. Thus when Prohibition ended in 1933, National Distillers commanded possibly 50 percent of the nation's whiskey inventory. Among the companies and brands included under the National umbrella were Old Sunny Brook, Old Overholt, Old Taylor, Bond & Lillard (q.v.), and Old Crow. Some of the firms in American Medicinal Spirits, which was dissolved in 1936, were Hill & Hill, E. H. Taylor & Sons (*see* Taylor, Edmund, H., Jr.), R. E. Wathen, and W. A. Gaines with its Old Crow brand. In all, nearly 140 brands came under National's control. National Distillers, under Porter's leadership, was also working on other projects geared to enhance its share of the anticipated whiskey market. Penn-Maryland Company was formed as a subsidiary owned by National Distillers and U.S. Industrial Alcohol (q.v.), which would be a supplier of alcohol. The arrangement was for Penn-Maryland to produce blended whiskey (q.v.), while National Distillers would sell only straight whiskey (q.v.). In another move, National arranged to market Fleischmann's gin through Penn-Maryland; Fleischmann (q.v.) was owned by Standard Brands by this time. National also bought a controlling share in the wine importing firm, Alex D. Shaw Company (q.v.). One of the major acquisitions was that of the Overholt (q.v.) distillery in Pennsylvania. The company had a large amount of whiskey stock and would provide a base of inventory for the market after repeal of Prohibition. Porter's moves proved successful on balance, and in the mid-1930s, National made agreements with deKuyper & Zoon of Holland and W. A. Gilbey, Ltd., of Great Britain to produce cordials and gin. In 1936, two of National's subsidiaries, American Medicinal Spirits and Penn-Maryland, were dissolved as National assumed operations of all distilleries. Another of the many acquisitions was K. Taylor Distilling Company (q.v.) in 1940. Glencoe Distillery Company (q.v.) was also purchased around 1940. In 1957 National reorganized as National Distillers and Chemical Corporation, and established two divisions, one in liquor and one in chemicals. National continued its diversification with the purchase of Bridgeport Brass in 1961. Thus it has evolved as a broadly based corporation with interests in chemicals (U.S. Industrial Chemicals, apparently a reorganization of U.S. Industrial Alcohol), metal (Bridgeport Brass), and textiles (Beacon Manufacturing). In the mid-1970s, National was marketing Old Grand Dad, Old Taylor, Old Crow, Windsor Canadian, Gilbey's, and many other brands. In the 1960s, the company had added Holland House and Almaden Vineyards to its acquisitions.

SOURCES: "Distilling Industry," *Forbes* (April 1, 1965); "Seton Porter," *Spirits* (March 1953); "Whiskey," *Fortune* (November 1933); *Forty Years of Repeal* (New York, 1973).

National Prohibition Act. *See* Volstead Act.

National Union of United Brewery Workmen of the U.S. The national union was founded in August 1886 in Baltimore, Maryland. The name first adopted was the National Union of the Brewers of the U.S., but that was changed at the next convention in Detroit in September 1887. The name was changed to include brewery engineers, firemen, maltsters, and drivers. In 1886 the union established a newspaper, the *Brauer-Zeitung (Brewers' Journal)*. Some 6,000 workers were counted among the membership by the time of the 1887 Detroit convention. A decision was made at that meeting to sever local union ties with the Knights of Labor because of that union's stand in favor of Prohibition (q.v.). The brewery union affiliated with the American Federation of Labor (AFL), which had also been founded in 1886. The relationship proved stormy at times because of jurisdictional disputes over whether engineers and firemen could form their own unions, or whether the Brewery Workers had jurisdiction to organize all workers in breweries. Difficulties such as occurred in the Cincinnati strike of 1902 prompted the AFL to revoke the Brewery Workers' charter in 1907. Although it was restored a year later, the problem continued, and in 1941 the Brewery Workers were again suspended for refusing to permit the Teamsters to organize certain members. In 1946, the Brewery Workers joined the Congress of Industrial Organizations (C10) and continued as an affiliate of the AFL-CIO when the two merged in 1955. In 1957 the Teamsters were expelled for corrupt leadership, the same year that Brewery Worker President Karl Feller was named a vice-president of the AFL-CIO; but he was expelled from the executive council in 1973 for holding merger meetings with the International Brotherhood of Teamsters, Chauffeurs, Warehousemen, and Helpers. The Brewery Workers' Union changed names over the years as additional groups have been organized. From National Union of United Brewery Workmen, it became the International Union of United Brewery, Flour, Cereal, Soft Drink and Distillery Workers of America as a portion of distillery workers joined.

SOURCES: Stanley Baron, *Brewed in America* (Boston, 1962); Gary M. Fink, ed., *Biographical Dictionary of American Labor Leaders* (Westport, Conn., 1974), and *Labor Unions* (Westport, Conn., 1977); Mauer, Fleisher & Associates, *Union with a Heart: International Union of United Brewery, Flour, Cereal, Soft Drink, and Distillery Workers of America: 75 Years of a Great Union, 1886-1961* (Washington, D.C., 1961); Herman Schlüter, *The Brewing Industry and the Brewery Workers' Movement in America* (Cincinnati, 1910).

Near beer. This cereal beverage is made using the bottom-fermentation (q.v.) process but has most of the alcoholic content removed (less than 0.5 percent alcohol). Brewers either made real beer and de-alcoholized it, or used a procedure in which fermentation was checked. After 1917 many brewers turned to this beverage as a way of dealing with the threat and then reality of nationwide Prohibition (q.v.). A few of the brands produced were PABLO by Pabst (q.v.), FAMO by Schlitz (q.v.), VIVO by Miller (q.v.), LUX-O by Stroh (q.v.), and QUIZZ by Wiedemann (q.v.). At first, brewers were encouraged by sales, but as the 1920s wore on, more and more Americans turned to bootleg beer and whiskey.

SOURCE: Stanley Baron, *Brewed in America* (Boston, 1962).

Nebraska Plan. Bernard Lichtenberg of the Institute of Public Relations drew up the Nebraska Plan, geared to implement a strategy of "Action in

Place of Propaganda.'' He was retained by Brewing Industry, Inc. (q.v.), in 1937 to map out ways in which brewers could most effectively counter prohibitionist activity. Lichtenberg's plan, tested in Nebraska during the summer of 1938, stressed that brewing interests should engage in self-regulation by organizing state and regional committees to investigate and police offending tavern owners, bootleggers, and other retailers. The plan was presented to the various brewing trade associations and helped heal differences among the factions. *See also,* U.S. Brewers' Association.

SOURCES: Stanley Baron, *Brewed in America* (Boston, 1962); ''The First Century: A History of the U.S.B.A.,'' *American Brewer* (January and February 1962).

Neutral spirits. A distilled product from any material, such as grain, molasses, or cane, the distillate is run at 190 proof (q.v.) or higher, and is used in making gin (q.v.), vodka (q.v.), cordials (q.v.) and blended whiskey (q.v.). *See also,* Grain Neutral Spirits.

New Albion Brewing Company. A small and recently established brewery, John R. McAuliffe founded the firm in October 1976. McAuliffe was a ''home-brewer'' who decided to establish his own company. Suzanne P. Stern and Jane H. Zimmerman joined him in organizing and designing the Sonoma, California, brewery. Marketing of the 350 barrels annual production is generally limited to the San Francisco area, and New Albion claims to be the only traditional ale (q.v.) brewery in the U.S.

New England Breweries, Ltd. New England Breweries was a consolidation of at least three Boston breweries by a British syndicate in 1890. Roessle (q.v.), Haffenreffer & Company (q.v.), and Suffolk Brewing Company were involved in the merger, which reflected British investment in this period. New England Breweries went out of business during the Prohibition (q.v.) era, but Haffenreffer continued to operate.

SOURCES: Manfred Friedrich and Donald Bull, *The Register of U.S. Breweries* (Trumbull, Conn., 1976); *One Hundred Years of Brewing* (Chicago and New York, 1903; Arno Press Reprint, 1974).

New England Distilling Company. This large Covington, Kentucky, rum distillery was founded in 1885. Schenley Distillers Corporation (q.v.) bought the plant in 1935 at a time when the plant was known as the largest international producer of industrial rum used for tobacco, confectionery, and bakery products; it was apparently closed in the late 1960s.

New Hope Distillery Company. The Nelson County, Kentucky, distillery was built in 1875. Thomas H. Sherley (q.v.), distiller and commission merchant (q.v.), was involved in the firm. It was connected with the E. L. Miles Distillery, which dated from Henry Miles's small distillery operation of 1796. Both became part of the Kentucky Distilleries and Warehouse Company (q.v.) about 1900.

SOURCES: Sam Elliot, *Nelson County Record* (Bardstown, Ky., 1896); *Spirits* (April 1935).

New York City brewing industry. By the time of the American Revolution in the 1770s, New York, had, with Philadelphia, established itself as a leading brewing center among the states. More than twenty brewers and maltsters operated in the city between 1695 and 1786. Under Dutch rule before 1664, a number of breweries had also been established. Prior to the 1840s the brews were of the top-fermentation variety, often ale (q.v.) and porter (q.v.), and the brewers mainly Dutch and English. Among the pre-lager beer (q.v.) breweries founded around 1800 were the Milbank brewery, John Henry's brewery, the "Old Brewery" (Coulter's) founded in 1972, the Miles's Croton brewery in 1823, and Beadleston & Woerz (q.v.). During the 1840s, a number of brewers made the transition to the brewing of lager beer. George Gillig, a Bavarian immigrant brewed the beer in 1844, and Frederick and Maximilian Schaefer established their first brewery in 1842. One drawback New York faced was the problem of poor quality water. In the 1840s water from upstate was imported and that factor, combined with the introduction of lager, encouraged the growth of the city's brewing industry. By 1879 there were seventy-eight breweries in existence, but by 1910 the number had declined to thirty-nine and by the mid-1970s no brewery operated in the city. The most prominent New York breweries over the years were Ehret (q.v.), H. Clausen & Son (q.v.), Flanagan, Nay & Company (q.v.), Ruppert (q.v.), Beadleston & Woerz, F. & M. Schaefer (q.v.), Clausen & Price, Bernehimer & Schmid (q.v.), Conrad Stein, Tracey & Russell, Elias & Betz, Peter Doelger (q.v.), and James Everard (q.v.). The brewing industry was characterized by a large number of brewers catering to a very large population (nearly 2 million by 1880), but the number of breweries began to decline as national breweries, especially from Milwaukee and St. Louis, made inroads into the local market. Locational advantages, the availability of natural resources, and the lack of a large local market seemed to aid the western brewers in their quest for national trade. New York brewers, conversely, remained primarily local and regional—even the gigantic Ruppert. Thus by the mid-twentieth century the New York breweries (only five in 1950) found it more and more difficult to compete with national marketing and advertising trends and the building of newer, more modern plants by the nationals. Also, a three-month strike against the city's fourteen breweries in 1949 proved costly. *See also*, Brooklyn Brewing Industry.

SOURCES: Will Anderson, *The Beer Book* (Princeton, N.J., 1973) and *Breweries of Brooklyn* (Croton Falls, N.Y., 1976); Stanley Baron, *Brewed in America* (Boston,

1962); Thomas C. Cochran, *The Pabst Brewing Company* (New York, 1948); Harlow McMillen, "Staten Island's Lager Beer Breweries, 1851-1962," *The Staten Island Historian* (July-September 1969); *One Hundred Years of Brewing* (Chicago and New York, 1903; Arno Press Reprint, 1974); "A Rheingold with a Pepsi Chaser?" *Bev for Executives* (March 1964).

Newark brewing industry. A number of ale and porter breweries in the English tradition operated in the Newark, New Jersey, area in the eighteenth and early nineteenth centuries, but most of these concerns gave way to the lager beer (q.v.) brewers in the 1840s and 1850s. One of the earliest, and most notable of the city's brewers, was Ballantine (q.v.), founded in 1840 by Peter Ballantine. Two of the more durable Newark breweries were C. Feigenspan (q.v.) and Gottfried Krueger (q.v.), although each was closed by 1960. Newark, a city of about 250,000 people by 1900, had approximately 30 breweries in the later nineteenth century. Prohibition led to the closing of most of the plants during the 1920s.

SOURCES: Manfred Friedrich and Donald Bull, *The Register of U.S. Breweries* (Trumbull, Conn., 1976), *One Hundred Years of Brewing* (Chicago and New York, 1903; Arno Press Reprint, 1974).

O

Obert, Louis, Brewing Company. Louis Obert, a German immigrant, became a partner in the St. Louis brewery of Weiss & Obert about 1866, and he bought Weiss's share in 1881. Obert was an independent brewer, who along with Anheuser-Busch (q.v.), refused to merge in either of the St. Louis mergers, St. Louis Brewing Association (q.v.) or Independent Breweries Company (q.v.). He died in 1916 at age sixty-nine, and the Obert family continued to operate the brewery until Prohibition (q.v.). Then Louis's three sons began to dispose of real estate and closed the brewery. An attempt to reopen in 1933 failed for lack of sufficient financing.

SOURCE: Don Crinklaw, "The Battle of the Breweries," *St. Louis Post-Dispatch*, June 9, 1974.

Oertel, John F. (Brewery). Charles Hartmetz established the Louisville brewery about 1880. Oertel entered the brewery in the mid-1880s, and in 1892 it became known as John F. Oertel and was noted for Oertel's 92 beer. The company survived Prohibition (q.v.) and continued to operate until 1968. From 1964 to 1968 it was owned by Brown-Forman Distillers (q.v.).

SOURCE: Manfred Friedrich and Donald Bull, *The Register of U.S. Breweries* (Trumbull, Conn., 1976).

Ogden, William B. (June 15, 1805-August 3, 1877). The first mayor of Chicago in 1837, after his term Ogden served on the city council for many years. He engaged in land speculation and a number of business ventures, mainly in railroad construction, eventually amassing a fortune. One of Ogden's enterprises was investment as a silent partner in Chicago's first brewery, Lill and Diversey (q.v.). Ogden was apparently involved with the firm from 1839 to 1841.

SOURCES: Dictionary of American Biography, vol. 13; *One Hundred Years of Brewing* (Chicago and New York, 1903; Arno Press Reprint, 1974).

Old Boone Distillery Company. In the early 1930s Jacob B. Dant and Marvin Padgett established this Meadowlawn, Kentucky, distillery. The

Buse (q.v.) firm of Cincinnati subsequently bought the plant, which bottles many labels for non-Kentucky distribution.

SOURCE: Dorothy Korell, "Bourbon Capital of the World," *Louisville*, (October 20, 1965).

Old Joe Distillery Company. The Lawerenceburg, Kentucky, distillery was first built by Joe Peyton about 1818 near Gilbert's Creek in Anderson County. G. B. Hawkins and other investors bought the plant and brand name Old Joe in 1912. The Hawkins family reactivated the name in the early 1930s—using the adjacent Old Prentice works. The original Old Joe property was rebuilt as Bonds Mill and later operated as Bond & Johnson, J. T. S. Brown, J. W. Dant, and others. Agnes F. Brown, widow of Davis Brown, president of the previous organization, became vice-president, and her son, Wilgus Naugher, also held a position in the Old Joe. National Distillers Products Company (q.v.) acquired the firm in the late 1930s or early 1940s, and the brand name was evidently phased out in the late 1950s. *See also*, J. T. S. Brown.

SOURCES: H. W. Coyte, "Anderson County Distilleries," unpub. paper, ca. 1970; "Old Joe Steeped in Tradition," *Spirits* (April 1935); "Ten Years of Progress: Distillers," *Spirits* (November 1943).

Old Kentucky Distillery, Inc. Located just south of Louisville, the Jefferson County, Kentucky, distillery was incorporated in 1901 by Dietrich Meschendorf (q.v.). The plant itself dates from around 1880, and the firm's major brand name, Kentucky Dew, evidently originated with the Wallwork & Harris distilling business in 1881. Meschendorf managed the firm until his death in 1911. O. H. Irvine then took over the business and brands, but the business later was purchased by Col. Joseph J. Sass, who erected a modern plant in the early 1930s. In 1940, Brown-Forman Distillers Corporation (q.v.) purchased the company from the Sass family.

SOURCES: "Great Names in Whiskey," *Spirits* (July 1937); "The Old Kentucky," *Spirits* (April 1935); A. C. Stagg, "Report of Distilled Spirits 1882-1884," unpub. list, Lexington, 1950.

Old Lewis Hunter (Distillery). The firm operated in the post-Prohibition period but traces its Cynthiana, Kentucky, origins to the 1850s. The company operated Megibben, Bramble & Co., T. J. Megibben & Bro., and G. R. Sharpe until Julius Kessler (q.v.) purchased it in 1902. Kessler then introduced the Old Lewis Hunter brand and was challenged by the makers of the well-known Hunter Rye brand in Baltimore, Maryland. Kessler claimed the name belonged to an early settler who made whiskey nearby. No proof of such a person was ever produced; however, Kessler continued to use the name. From 1920 to the 1930s the property deteriorated until the Old Lewis

Hunter Distillery Company was organized with Samuel B. Walton as president. The R. L. Buse Company (q.v.) marketed its products in the 1930s. This company continued operations until about 1950 when it was sold to Seagram (q.v.), which continues to operate it on occasion. It has not produced since 1976.

SOURCES: H. W. Coyte, "Kentucky Distilleries," unpub. paper, ca. 1970; "Distilleries of Old Kentucky," *Spirits* (April 1935); "Great Names in Whiskey," *Spirits* (May 1937); Woodward Kirkpatrick, "Kentucky Saga," *Spirits* (January 1934).

Olympia Brewing Company. Founded by Leopold F. Schmidt (q.v.) in 1896, the brewery was originally called the Capital Brewing Company, but the name was changed to Olympia Brewing Company in 1902. Schmidt, who had operated a Montana brewery, located his plant in Tumwater, just outside Olympia, Washington. He was successful and opened other plants in Washington, and one in San Francisco. Prohibition (q.v.), which began in 1916 in Washington, eventually led to the closing of all of the breweries. In 1933, a new plant was built at Tumwater, and it remained the lone Olympia brewery until 1975 when the company purchased the St. Paul, Minnesota, brewery of Theodore Hamm Company (q.v.)—plus the Hamm label. The company then purchased the Lone Star Brewing Company (q.v.) of San Antonio, Texas, in 1976, which made Olympia the nation's sixth largest brewer in 1978. Over the years the Schmidt family has remained in control of the brewery, which is noted for its "clean-tasting" brew. The presidents after Leopold F. Schmidt have been Peter G., Adolph D., Jr., Robert A., and Leopold F. ("Rick") Schmidt, who became chief executive officer in April 1977.

SOURCES: Will Anderson, *The Beer Book* (Princeton, N.J., 1973); Stanley Baron, *Brewed in America* (Boston, 1962); *One Hundred Years of Brewing* (Chicago and New York, 1903; Arno Press Reprint, 1974).

Open rick warehouse. Made of wood and sheathed in galvanized iron, this type of whiskey warehouse is unheated and is designed as it is on the belief that whiskey should age in barrels stored where the air can circulate and natural variations in weather aid the aging (q.v.) process. Many windows permit the air flow. Usually, the newest barrels of whiskey are put on the first floor, which is cooler and where soakage of whiskey into the wood is slower. As maturing continues, the barrels are moved up to higher floors, where the temperature is higher. Recently, most larger distilleries have built more economical brick and concrete warehouses in which temperatures and moisture levels are controlled.

SOURCES: Dorothy L. Korell, "Bourbon Capital of the World," *Louisville* (October 20, 1965). James Boone Wilson, *The Spirit of Old Kentucky* (Louisville, Ky., 1945).

Ortlieb, Henry F., Brewing Company. Ortlieb was founded by August Kuehl in the early 1860s. The Philadelphia brewery changed hands in 1869 and 1885 and was ultimately purchased by Henry Ortlieb in 1893. The Ortlieb family has remained in control of the company. The firm acquired the Kaier brand in 1966, the Neuweiler brand in 1974, and also markets McSorley's Ale, which had been produced by Rheingold (q.v.). By the late 1970s the firm was making news as President Joseph Ortlieb demonstrated his pluck in attempting to compete with the large national brewers. Appearing on television to support "Joe's Beer," Ortlieb symbolized the struggle of the small local brewer in the era of large-scale advertising and intense competition from the national firms.

SOURCES: "Beer in America," MacNeil/Lehrer Report (Transcript, EBC show, May 24, 1978). *Newsweek* (September 4, 1978); *Wall Street Journal* (July 10, 1978).

Outage. During aging (q.v.), whiskey (q.v.) loses a percentage (about 20 percent) of volume in the barrel as water evaporates. For example, after aging 4 years, a barrel of 50 gallons (25 gallons of alcohol and 25 gallons of water) loses about 10 gallons of liquid. Because the loss results from water evaporation, the alcoholic content, proof (q.v.), of the whiskey increases. The loss of the liquid is the outage. In 1880, at the urging of Representative John G. Carlisle (q.v.) of Kentucky, Congress passed a law excusing distillers from paying taxes on liquor that had dissipated. The act became known as the "Carlisle allowance."

SOURCE: Gerald Carson, *The Social History of Bourbon* (New York, 1963).

Overholt, A., & Company. The western Pennsylvania rye whiskey distillery dates from Abraham Overholt's small plant in 1810. During the nineteenth century, his son, Jacob, and a cousin, Henry, expanded their operations, which after 1860 were centered at Broad Ford, Pennsylvania. The company eventually became part of National Distillers Products Company (q.v.) but experienced an interesting and colorful history before that transaction. In the 1890s, Henry Clay Frick's mother, an Overholt, held shares in the company, which went to her son upon her death. Thereafter Frick acquired full ownership of the firm but sold a third interest to Andrew Mellon of the Pittsburgh financial family. When Frick died in 1919, Mellon received another one-third interest. As secretary of the treasury in the 1920s, Mellon was primarily responsible for the enforcement of Prohibition (q.v.) and he tried to dispose of his interest in Overholt. After some difficulty and embarrassment, Mellon sold the firm to National Distillers in the mid-1920s. Old Overholt, a National product, continues as one of the few rye whiskies marketed on a national scale.

SOURCES: Stan Jones, *Jones' Complete Barguide* (Los Angeles, 1977); "Whiskey," *Fortune* (November 1933).

Owens, Michael Joseph (active, 1900). An inventor and glass manufacturer, Owens introduced the first successful automatic glass-making machine for bottles in 1903. In 1903, Kentucky distillers bottled 400,000 gallons of bourbon, and the figure rose to 9 million gallons by 1913. Brewers also benifited and produced substantially more bottled beer. *See also*, Bottled Beer, and Packaging.

SOURCES: "The Beer Bottle, Its History," *American Brewer* (March 1963); Gerald Carson, *The Social History of Bourbon* (New York, 1963).

P

Pabst, Frederick (March 28, 1836-January 1, 1904). Leader of Milwaukee's Pabst Brewing Company (q.v.) during the late nineteenth century, Pabst started out as a cabin boy, navigator, and captain of steamers in the Goodrich Line on Lake Michigan. In 1862 he married Maria Best. The next year Captain Pabst became an equal partner in his father-in-law's Philip Best Brewing Company. Fred Pabst quickly moved the brewery into a leading position in Milwaukee and the U.S. as he expanded sales and output and pushed the operation into national marketing.

SOURCE: Thomas C. Cochran, *The Pabst Brewing Company* (New York, 1948).

Pabst Brewing Company. Founded in 1844 as the Best Brewing Company, the Milwaukee brewery became the nation's largest in the 1890s and maintained a position in the top three until the mid-1970s. Jacob Best, Sr., a German immigrant of 1844, established his company in the promising Milwaukee area. A successful businessman, Best sold his German wine and beer business to enter the seemingly more lucrative American market. He was joined by his four sons, Jacob, Jr., Charles, Phillip, and Lorenz. Jacob, Sr., retired in 1853, and eventually Phillip became the sole owner of the business. Called the Empire Brewery, the plant grew gradually. In 1862, Capt. Fred Pabst (q.v.), a steamer captain, married Maria, Phillip's daughter, and in 1865 he became a partner. A few years later, Phillip sold out to Pabst and another son-in-law, Emil Schandein. They incorporated the brewery in 1873 as the Phillip Best Brewing Company and in 1889, a year after Schandein's death, the name was changed to the Pabst Brewing Company. From the nation's second largest brewer in 1877 (about 120,000 barrels), just behind Ehret (q.v.), Pabst moved into first position by the late 1880s and reached the 1-million-barrel mark by 1892, the first brewer to do so. Capt. Fred Pabst expanded the brewery from a regional to a national brewery as agencies (q.v.) were established, bottling and rail transportation were emphasized, and, just as important, new scientific brewing techniques and successful advertising apparently paid off. J. F. Theurer, the captain's brewmaster, was instrumental in employing up-to-date brewing methods and utilizing modern pneumatic malting (q.v.) and refrigeration (q.v.)

devices. The brand name, Blue Ribbon, became widely used after 1892 and symbolized the "award" trend as breweries competed at expositions and fairs in the late nineteenth century. A controversy exemplifying the nature and intensity of this period's advertising arose at the Chicago World's Columbian Exposition in 1893 as Pabst and Anheuser-Busch were involved in a hotly disputed contest over the highest award. After complaints of unfairness from both sides, Pabst won, with just over ninety-five points to Anheuser-Busch's ninety-four-plus points. Upon the captain's death in 1904, his son Gustav Pabst became president and held the position until 1921 when he resigned to direct affairs of the newly created Pabst Realty Company. Fred Pabst, Jr., his brother, who had left the company earlier for work in scientific agriculture, now returned to direct the brewery operation. Near beer (q.v.), malt syrup, tonic, cheese, and other products were manufactured during the 1920s as the company struggled to cope with Prohibition (q.v.). As Repeal (q.v.) seemed imminent in 1932, Pabst merged with Premier Malt Products Company (q.v.) of Peoria, Illinois. Premier, an outgrowth of the Decatur Brewing Company, supplied capital, labor, and a sales force, while Pabst had the brewery and a national reputation. Premier's president, Harris Perlstein, became chairman. In 1938, the name was changed to Pabst Brewing Company. Perlstein and Pabst ran the company and boosted sales with plant expansions in Peoria in 1934, Newark in 1945, and Los Angeles in 1948. In 1958, Pabst bought the Blatz Brewing Company (q.v.) from Schenley (q.v.). James C. Windham, chief executive at Blatz, became president of Pabst. Perlstein continued as chairman, a position he had taken in 1954, until 1972. Windham pushed the company forward notably in 1971 with the building of a plant in what would be named Pabst, Georgia, near Macon. Blatz was sold in 1969 to G. Heileman (q.v.) because of alleged violation of antitrust laws, but in 1975 Pabst bought the brand names of Burgermeister and Burgie from the Theodore Hamm (q.v.) company. Frank DeGuire became president of the company in 1973, and by the late 1970s Pabst was the nation's fourth largest brewer.

SOURCES: Thomas C. Cochran, *The Pabst Brewing Company* (New York, 1948); Wayne Kroll, *Badger Breweries* (Jefferson, Wis., 1976); *Milwaukee Journal*, May 21, 1978; *One Hundred Years of Brewing* (Chicago and New York, 1903; Arno Press Reprint, 1974).

Packaging. Beer is packaged in three forms, kegs (q.v.) or barrels (q.v.), bottles, and cans. Old wooden barrels that were lined with pitch have been replaced by stainless steel and aluminum containers for draft beer (q.v.). The newer containers are able to withstand greater pressure. Racking (q.v.) of beer in barrels takes place under counterpressure to prevent the escape of gas. Kegs and barrels are filled with unpasteurized beer that is kept at low temperatures to enhance preservation. Since the late nineteenth century, with pasteurization (q.v.), bottled beer (q.v.) has become commonplace, and since the 1930s canned beer (q.v.) has been an important form of packaging. The latter were especially important in the drive, after Repeal (q.v.), to emphasize the respectability of beer drinking by stressing consumption in the home. Packaging of distilled spirits was first in barrels, or bulk, and then in jugs or bottles of some variety; because such drink is "still" or noneffervescent, the problems of packaging have been minimal. With the introduction of the Coffey, or patent-still (*see* Still) in the 1830s, the use of glass bottles became more common because the blending of Scotches was widely practiced. In the U.S. in the 1890s the increasing use of brand names for whiskey encouraged bottling, rather than distribution in bulk form to distributors. Also, the passage of the Bottled-in-Bond Act (q.v.) in 1897, and later federal regulations to discourage adulteration of whiskey, led to the expansion of bottling. As early as 1870, however, George Garvin Brown (q.v.) had begun bottling Old Forester so that the public would know that the drink would have a consistent, regulated quality.

SOURCES: Stanley Baron, *Brewed in America* (Boston, 1962); Gerald Carson, *The Social History of Bourbon* (New York, 1963); Harold J. Grossman, *Grossman's Guide to Wines, Beers, and Spirits* (New York, 1977); John Ed Pearce, *Nothing Better in the Market* (Louisville, Ky., 1970).

Pasteurization. Louis Pasteur discovered the process of sterilization in the 1860s and 1870s. Pasteur, who wished to help improve the French brewing industry, found that bacteria caused the "diseases" of fermented liquids. He wrote *Etudes sur la Biere* in the 1870s. Bacteria-free yeast resulted in disease-free fermentation. By heating, or "pasteurizing," beer, or other products, to a temperature just below boiling, harmful bacteria and micro-organisms could be killed. Thus further fermentation or spoilage could be prevented. The process encouraged expansion of beer bottling for shipment because it enhanced the quality and stability of beer. *See also*, Bottled Beer, and Yeast.

SOURCES: Stanley Baron, *Brewed in America* (Boston, 1962); *One Hundred Years of Brewing* (Chicago and New York, 1903; Arno Press Reprint, 1974).

Patent-still. *See* Still.

Pearl Brewing Company. Founded as the San Antonio Brewing Association, the company changed the name to Pearl Brewing Company in 1952. A group of San Antonio citizens formed the company and bought an existing brewery in 1886. President Otto Koehler bought the Pearl name for its beer from the Kaiser-Beck brewery of Bremen, Germany. The firm did very well, was known as the City Brewery, and managed to survive Prohibition, albeit with much difficulty, as Alamo Industries and Alamo Foods Company. The company reentered the brewing business in 1933 and grew during the next decades. In 1961, the firm acquired the Goetz Brewing Company of Missouri (which was subsequently closed); and the Jax brand was purchased from New Orleans' Jackson Brewing Company (q.v.) in the early 1970s.

SOURCES: Will Anderson, *The Beer Book* (Princeton, N.J., 1973); Stanley Baron, *Brewed in America* (Boston, 1962); James L. Nelson, "Business History of San Antonio Brewing Association," unpub. M.A. thesis, Trinity University, 1976; *One Hundred Years of Brewing* (Chicago and New York, 1903; Arno Press Reprint, 1974).

Penn, William (October 14, 1644-July 30, 1718). Penn was proprietor of the colony of Pennsylvania. Soon after founding the colony in 1682, he built a brewhouse on the site of his mansion at Pennsbury.

SOURCES: Stanley Baron, *Brewed in America* (Boston, 1962); *One Hundred Years of Brewing* (Chicago and New York, 1903; Arno Press Reprint, 1974).

Peoria distilling industry. Almiran Smith Cole built the first distillery in Peoria, Illinois, in 1844. He sold that plant a few years later and built a larger one, which he sold in the 1860s. In 1865, 15 distilleries operated in the city, and by 1880 Peoria was considered the distilling center of the world. Kentucky's production in 1880 was 15,011,279 gallons compared with Peoria's production of 18,475,565 gallons. In that year Kentucky had more than 200 distilleries and Peoria had only about 10 firms. The large output of the city's distilleries resulted from favorable historical and locational factors. The industry grew as an offshoot of the flour milling industry. As an important grain market for the area's corn and wheat, Peoria's mills needed an outlet for surplus grain. "Soft" corn, a result of an early frost, was difficult to prevent from spoiling and was therefore an ideal source of grain for distilleries. In addition to surplus grain, Peoria was noted for its cool limestone water (q.v.), at an almost constant 53° Fahrenheit, that could be found about 60 feet underground. The city also boasted of favorable river and rail transportation, available coal supplies, and as a cattle and livestock center, offered a market for the residue of sour mash grain (slop) as feed. Among the city's firms were the Great Western (q.v.), Woolner (q.v.), Monarch (q.v.), Great Eastern (q.v.), Atlas (q.v.), Clarke Bros. (q.v.), and Corning (q.v.) distilleries. Peoria was the center of the Whiskey Trust (q.v.), which was formed in 1887 as a means of controlling production and prices, and inducing cost economies by combining more than sixty-five midwestern distilleries. Earlier efforts at pooling gave way to the trust. After 1890, the trust and its activities dominated Peoria's history as a distilling center as most of the local companies were absorbed either by the main branch (Distillers' and Cattle Feeders' Trust) or its subsequent subsidiaries. Between 1910 and the advent of Prohibition (q.v.) in 1920, the city's seven distilleries continued to produce a great volume of spirits. After Repeal (q.v.) in 1933, a number of firms reorganized. Arrow Distilleries (q.v.), Century (*see* Atlas Distilling Company), Penn-Maryland Corporation, a division of National Distillers Products Company (q.v.), and American Distilling Company (q.v.) of Pekin, Illinois, began operations. The most notable Peoria distillery, however, would be the Hiram Walker (q.v.) plant, which was built on the site of the Great Western. Walker would continue to operate long after Arrow and Century had closed but in 1979 announced plans to shut down the plant in the early 1980s.

SOURCES: Gerald Carson, *The Social History of Bourbon* (New York, 1963); Victor S. Clark, *History of Manufactures in the U.S.*, vols. 1-2 (New York, 1929); Distilleries file, Peoria Historical Society; Ernest E. East, "Peoria Whiskey Plants Grew to Seven in 1860," *Arrow Messenger* (January 1937); and "Romance of Peoria Industry," *Peoria Journal-Transcript*, April 28, 1940.

Pepper distilleries. This Lexington, Kentucky, area distillery was established originally by farmer-distiller (q.v.) Elijah Pepper around 1780. Pepper was descended from the Culpeppers of Virginia but left for the Kentucky area in 1776. He settled in Lexington, and as many others, was mainly a farmer, but turned to distilling whiskey as an economic necessity. Corn could be grown in abundance and transport costs for distilled grain were much lower than for the raw product. Itinerant peddlers from the East passed through with their packhorses, and Pepper traded in whiskey for his family's needed products. The slogan for Pepper's whiskey, "Born with the Republic," was kept alive by his son Oscar, and grandson, James, who formed James E. Pepper and Company in 1879. The Pepper distilling interests benefited from the knowledge of Dr. James Crow (q.v.), who was associated with Oscar Pepper about 1850. The Peppers marketed an Old Crow at one point. The company, which marketed Old Henry Clay and James E. Pepper, was bought by Chicago investors about 1908. Schenley Distillers Corporation (q.v.) purchased the firm in the early 1930s; the brand was apparently phased out around 1960. Schenley used the property for warehouse purposes until selling it in 1977.

SOURCES: Gerald Carson, *The Social History of Bourbon* (New York, 1963); H. W. Coyte, "Kentucky Bourbon," unpub. paper, Frankfort, Ky., 1940, and "Fayette County Distilleries," ca. 1970; "Distilleries of Old Kentucky," *Spirits* (April 1935).

Perot's Sons, Francis (Malting Company). The famous Philadelphia malting company could trace its origin to the Morris family's brewing business of the late seventeenth century. Anthony Morris II (q.v.) came to America from London in 1682 at the age of twenty-eight and founded a malthouse and brewery in Philadelphia in 1687. His son, Anthony III, succeeded him in 1721, and his son, Anthony IV, came into the business in the 1740s; the Morris family continued to manage the business until Francis Perot took over in the 1820s. Perot, who had worked in the Morris brewery, married Thomas Morris's daughter, Elizabeth, in 1823. He ran the Morris brewery and was joined by his brother as they renamed it Francis & Wm. S. Perot. In 1850 it became a malting firm exclusively and was incorporated in 1887 as the Francis Perot's Sons Malting Company. The firm continued to operate into the twentieth century but apparently went out of business in the 1960s or 1970s.

SOURCES: Stanley Baron, *Brewed in America* (Boston, 1962); Madelein Blitzstein, "The History of Francis Perot's Sons," *Modern Brewery* (December 15, 1933); *One Hundred Years of Brewing* (Chicago and New York, 1903; Arno Press Reprint, 1974).

Pfaff. The term applies to the tube or pipe used in the mashing (q.v.) process. Brewers adopted this device in the nineteenth century to infuse water into the mash tun (q.v.) from the bottom, permitting more uniform control of the mash (q.v.).

Pfeiffer Brewing Company. Conrad Pfeiffer founded the Detroit brewery around 1890. The company was revived after repeal of Prohibition (q.v.) and joined with the E. & B. Brewing Company (q.v.) in one of the first mergers of the Associated Brewing Company (q.v.) in 1962. Pfeiffer bought the Philip Kling (q.v.) company in 1947 but closed it in 1958.

SOURCES: Manfred Friedrich and Donald Bull, *The Register of U.S. Breweries* (Trumbull, Conn., 1976); *One Hundred Years of Brewing* (Chicago and New York, 1903; Arno Press Reprint, 1974).

Philadelphia brewing industry. The first brewers in Philadelphia date from the 1680s. William Penn (q.v.) evidently built a brewhouse in Pennsbury, and he mentioned the construction of William Framton's brewery in 1685 in one of his letters. In 1687, Anthony Morris founded the family's first Morris brewery (*see* Perot's Sons, Francis), and their involvement continued until 1838. In the meantime, the Perot family became involved with the Morris family and the brewery was continued by Francis Perot, who married the daughter of Thomas Morris. By 1850 the company that would become known as Francis Perot & Sons had switched to malting as its exclusive business. Philadelphia brewing continued to grow in the eighteenth century as brewers such as Thomas Paschall, George Emlen, Valentine Standley, and George Campion entered the business. Colonial regulations in Pennsylvania were passed to encourage home manufactures, and especially malt liquors; wine, rum, brandy, and other spirits were taxed but not beer. By the 1790s, Philadelphia had nearly thirty-five taverns and a street named Brewers Alley. In addition to the Morris brewers, Robert Hare, Reuben Haines, and Robert Smith Ale Brewing Company (q.v.) figured as prominent brewers at the turn of the century. Then, in the 1840s, the transition to lager beer (q.v.) and the identification of beer with German-Americans slowly changed the industry. Apparently, the first lager in America was brewed by John Wagner (q.v.) in Philadelphia in the early 1840s. By 1879, Philadelphia had ninety-four breweries; in 1910 the figure had declined to forty-six, and then from fifteen in 1935 the number dropped to eight in 1950 and to two in the 1970s. As in the case of many cities with large German populations, consumers could support many local breweries—especially before the adoption of pasteurization (q.v.) and shipment by the national brewers in the 1880s and 1890s. In 1900, Philadelphia, the nation's third largest city, had a population of about 1.3 million, of whom 71,319 were of German nationality. But by 1900, the city's many brewers were receiving stiff competition from Milwaukee's national brewers (Pabst, Schlitz, Miller, and Blatz) and other national firms such as Anheuser-Busch (q.v.) of St. Louis. During the late nineteenth century, Philadelphia's most prominent breweries were Bergner & Engel (q.v.), Wm. Massey & Company (q.v.), and Louis Bergdoll (q.v.), and they were joined by smaller but successful companies such as Liebert & Obert (q.v.), F. A. Poth & Sons (q.v.), John F. Betz & Son (q.v.), and Esslinger (q.v.). Only two Philadelphia breweries continued to operate by the late 1970s, Ortlieb (q.v.) and C. Schmidt (q.v.), but they could trace their origins to the mid-nineteenth century.

SOURCES: Will Anderson, *The Beer Book* (Princeton, N.J., 1973); Stanley Baron, *Brewed in America* (Boston, 1962); *One Hundred Years of Brewing* (Chicago and New York, 1903; Arno Press Reprint, 1974).

Phoenix Brewery (St. Louis). Founded initially by Christian Staehlin about 1860, Anton Griesedieck bought this St. Louis firm in 1880. The label was retired in favor of Pearl beer, until Griesedieck sold out to the St. Louis Brewing Association (q.v.) in 1889. That company reviewed the Phoenix brand name, but the plant was closed about 1912.

SOURCE: Don Crinklaw, "The Battle of the Breweries," *St. Louis Post-Dispatch,* June 9, 1974.

Phoenix Brewing Company. This Pittsburgh brewery was incorporated in 1891. It was an outgrowth of the Woods & Hughes brewery, which had opened in 1845. The president of the company was F. W. Mueller. In 1899 this company merged with other breweries to form the Pittsburgh Brewing Company (q.v.), and Mueller was the first president.

SOURCES: One Hundred Years of Brewing (Chicago and New York, 1903; Arno Press Reprint, 1974); "Pittsburgh, History of Beer and a Market," *American Brewer* (June and July 1960).

Pickett, Joseph S., & Sons, Inc. (Brewery). Established originally in 1898 as the Dubuque Star Brewing Company in Dubuque, Iowa, the company was bought by Joseph Pickett in 1971. J. H. Rhomberg established the plant, and the Rhomberg family continued its involvement until the sale of Pickett in 1971. Pickett, who was brewmaster for Chicago's Schoenhofen-Edelweis (q.v.) and Drewry's (q.v.), updated the plant and bought the Edelweis and Champagne Velvet brands. Other brands were Dubuque Star, Vat 7, and Weber.

SOURCES: "Dubuque Star Brewing Co.," *Brewers Digest* (August 1971); *One Hundred Years of Brewing* (Chicago and New York, 1903; Arno Press Reprint, 1974); James D. Robertson, *The Great American Beer Book* (Ottawa, Ill., 1978).

Piel Brothers (Brewery). Gottfried, Michael, and Wilhelm Piel migrated to the U.S. from Dusseldorf, Germany, in the early 1880s. They bought a small brewery in 1883 in Brooklyn and built a small beer garden to market a large portion of their beer. The garden was closed in 1911 to permit plant expansion. The company produced near beer (q.v.) during the 1920s and managed to survive Prohibition (q.v.). Gottfried, who was president, died in 1935 at the age of eighty-two, and his nephew, William, guided the business. William expanded the business in the 1940s and 1950s and bought out Trommer's (q.v.) in 1951. Upon William's death on April 6, 1953, Henry J. Muessen became president. Piel Brothers bought out a Staten Island brewery, Rubsam and Horrmann, in 1953 but sold it in 1963. The same year, the company sold out to Detroit's Associated Brewing Company (q.v.) which included Sterling (q.v.) of Evansville, Indiana, Drewry's (q.v.) of South Bend, Indiana, and Chicago and Hampden-Harvard (*see* Harvard Brewing Company) of Massachusetts. In 1971 Associated, after suffering sales losses for two years, sold all but its Piel plants to G. Heileman Brewing Company (q.v.) of La Crosse, Wisconsin. In 1973 the Piel name was sold to Schaefer (q.v.).

SOURCES: Will Anderson, *The Breweries of Brooklyn* (New York, 1976); "A Rheingold with a Pepsi Chaser?" *Bev for Executives* (March 1964).

Pilsen Brewing Company. This Chicago brewery was founded around 1907 and purchased by the Canadian Ace (q.v.) company in 1963.

Pilsener. Named after the town, Pilsen, in Bohemia, where it originated, Pilsener is a popular type of beer. Historically, the beer has been known for its relatively light and hoppy character. It was one of the most prominent Bohemian, or Austrian, beers, all of which were known for similar qualities. Since the 1840s, American lager beers (q.v.) have been similar to the Pilsener type.

SOURCES: Frederick Birmingham, *Falstaff's Complete Beer Book* (New York, 1970); Jean De Clerck, *Textbook of Brewing*, vol. 1 (London, 1957); *One Hundred Years of Brewing* (Chicago and New York, 1903; Arno Press Reprint, 1974).

Pitching. The term is used to describe two processes in brewing. One is the process of lining wooden kegs and barrels with pitch, a resin from trees, to prevent the beer from coming in contact with wood and taking on a "woody" flavor. Pitching methods progressed dramatically in the nineteenth and twentieth centuries. Until the 1860s the pitch was applied by a direct fire process; then a Chicago brewer, Matheus Gottfried, came up with a hot-air process, which was later replaced by spraying. After 1950, the increased use of aluminum and stainless steel containers eliminated the necessity of pitching. The other process of pitching is when yeast (q.v.) is added to wort (q.v.) to initiate fermentation.

SOURCES: John P. Arnold and Frank Penman, *History of the Brewing Industry and Brewing Science* (Chicago, 1933); *One Hundred Years of Brewing* (Chicago and New York, 1903; Arno Press Reprint, 1974); Edward H. Vogel, Jr., et al., *The Practical Brewer* (St. Louis, Mo., 1946).

Pittsburgh Brewing Company. Originally founded in 1861 as Frauenheim, Miller & Company, this Pittsburgh company was established by German immigrants Edward Frauenheim and August Hoevler. It was known as the Iron City Brewery, and the designation continues as the principal brand name for its beer. The company grew in the 1860s and 1870s, and during this period the name was changed to Frauenheim and Vilsack as Leopold Vilsack bought Hoevler's interest. The brewery was apparently one of the most aggressive in the area, and showed interest in market expansion beyond the immediate area. Thus Iron City was the core brewery for a consolidation (*see* Consolidations, Brewery) that took place in February 1899. Reflecting a nationwide trend toward mergers, twenty-one breweries joined as the Pittsburgh Brewing Company. Some of the other firms—Wainwright (q.v.), Eberhardt & Ober (q.v.), Winter Bros. (q.v.), Phoenix (q.v.), and Straub (q.v.)—were fairly large concerns, but most members were small breweries. The new company thus became the nation's third largest plant, with capacity of more than 1 million barrels and continued through the 1920s producing near beer (q.v.), ice cream, and soft drinks as Tech Food Products. The firm survived difficult times in the 1940s when union troubles led to what was called the "Beer Wars," and a boycott by whites in the early 1970s because the company had worked out an employment settlement with the National Association for the Advancement of Colored People (NAACP). Over the years the company has been managed by John Hubbard, Carl Vilsack, William Heckman, and in the 1940s, 1950s, and 1960s by Milton G. Hulme and S. E. Cowell. From 1965 to 1977, Louis J. Slais was president; in 1975 William F. Smith, Jr., former company official who went with Miller (q.v.), rejoined Pittsburgh Brewing and was named president in 1978. The company cultivated the image of producing a working-class beer but has branched out with new brands such as Robin Hood Cream Ale, Olde Frothingslosh, and in the 1960s a lime-flavored beer,

Hop'n'Gator, to attract a broad range of consumers. The 1970s brought further diversification with Iron City Light, a low-calorie product, and Rose Ale, a champagne-tasting malt liquor (q.v.).

SOURCES: Stanley Baron, *Brewed in America* (Boston, 1962); Steven M. Fine, "The King of Suds," *The Pittsburgher* (October 1977); "Iron City Beer's 100 Year History and Annual Report" (Pittsburgh, ca. 1961); *One Hundred Years of Brewing* (Chicago and New York, 1903; Arno Press Reprint, 1974); "Pittsburgh, History of Beer and a Market," *American Brewer* (June and July 1960).

Pittsburgh brewing industry. The city's first commercial brewery was founded in 1795 by George Shiras on the Point, the famous triangle of land where the confluence of the Allegheny and Monongahela Rivers forms the Ohio. Although many of the city's 8,000 residents in 1815 preferred whiskey, four breweries were in operation and a street near the Point became known as Brewhouse Alley. They produced ale (q.v.) and porter (q.v.), and, as in the case of the American brewing industry generally, the transition to the lighter lager beer (q.v.) occurred in the 1840s and 1850s, especially as more German immigrants settled in the area. By 1890 the city and surrounding area had more than thirty breweries. Naturally competition was intense, and this encouraged consolidation. In February 1899, twenty-one companies joined in the Pittsburgh Brewing Company (q.v.). A few years later, in 1905, Duquesne Brewing Company (q.v.) led another merger, known as the Independent Brewing Company. After Prohibition (q.v.) the Pittsburgh Brewing Company and Duquesne, which was the lone survivor of its merger, continued as the major breweries but found some competition from Ft. Pitt (q.v.) of Sharpsburg. Among the city's breweries were Philip Lauer, C. Baeuerlein (q.v.), Straub Brewery (q.v.), Nusser, Hauch, F. L. Ober, Darlington & Company. The larger companies forming the Pittsburgh Brewing Company were Iron City (*see* Pittsburgh Brewing Company), Z. Wainwright (q.v.), Eberhardt & Ober (q.v.), Winter Bros. (q.v.), Phoenix (q.v.), and Straub.

SOURCES: Stanley Baron, *Brewed in America* (Boston, 1962); Steven M. Fine, "The King of Suds," *Pittsburgher* (October 1977); *One Hundred Years of Brewing* (Chicago and New York, 1903; Arno Press Reprint, 1974); "Pittsburgh, History of Beer and a Market," *American Brewer* (June and July 1960).

Plamondon, Ambrose (active, 1870s-1896). The Chicago maltster bought the rights to the Saladin Pneumatic Malting device in 1887. Plamondon organized the Saladin Pneumatic Malting Construction Company and remained president until his death in 1896. Various improvements were made on the system by the company engineer, W. H. Prinz.

SOURCE: *One Hundred Years of Brewing* (Chicago and New York, 1903; Arno Press Reprint, 1974).

Pneumatic malting. This is a system, in brewing technology, of pressuring air through wet barley that is in the germination (q.v.) stage. The process could thus be better controlled with respect to temperature, and the need for hand-turning the malt (q.v.) would be minimized. Nicholas Galland (q.v.) of France was one of the first to patent such a device, but his box-malting system of the 1870s gave way to improved systems in the 1880s. The more successful device was invented by Frenchman Jules Alphonse Saladin (q.v.) and made available in the 1880s. The Louis C. Huck Malting Company (q.v.) of Chicago was the first to install the machine, which combined the pressured air-drying feature with machinery for stirring and turning the malt. Ambrose Plamondon (q.v.) secured the American rights to the Saladin machine in 1887. Plamondon's Saladin Pneumatic Malting Company of Chicago became the major supplier of the machines, and improvements were made on it, most notably by engineer W. H. Prinz of the Saladin Company. The Saladin process continues to be used today. The Saladin method, also known as the box or compartment method, found competition from variations on the drum-malting system by which malt was put into cylindrical drums that were turned, first by hand, and later mechanically. Some of the other drum-malting devices were the Galland-Henning, J. A. Tilden, and the J. F. Dornfield systems. Overall, three systems of malting (q.v.) have been utilized: floor-malting, box or compartment malting, and drum-malting. The latter two have been used almost exclusively in the twentieth century.

SOURCES: Harold M. Broderick, ed., *The Practical Brewer* (Madison, Wis., 1977). *One Hundred Years of Brewing* (Chicago and New York, 1903; Arno Press Reprint, 1974); Edward H. Vogel, Jr., et al., *The Practical Brewer* (St. Louis, Mo., 1946).

Pogue, H. E., Distillery. The Maysville, Kentucky, distillery was founded around 1870 by Henry E. Pogue and John N. Thomas. Its main product was Old Time. In the 1930s the R. L. Buse Company (q.v.), a whiskey brokerage firm, marketed its products. The company apparently ceased operations in the 1940s.

SOURCES: "The Distilleries from Which Buse's Bourbon Comes," *Spirits* (May 1936); "Great Names in Whiskey," *Spirits* (May 1937).

Porter. A predecessor to stout (q.v.), porter is a malt beverage in which top fermentation yeast is used. Porter is heavier and darker than ale (q.v.) but a bit sweeter in taste; it is not as heavy as stout and does not have as strong a hop (q.v.) taste. Porter ranges between ale and stout with respect to color, and malt and hop flavor. The term is used very seldom today. One explanation for the derivation of the term is that it was popular among English porters.

SOURCES: Frederic Birmingham, *Falstaff's Complete Beer Book* (New York, 1970); Jean De Clerck, *A Textbook of Brewing*, vol. 1 (London, 1957); Edward H. Vogel, Jr., et al., *The Practical Brewer* (St. Louis, Mo., 1946).

Porter, Seton (1882-February 6, 1953). Organizer and chairman of National Distillers Products Company (q.v.), Porter was a partner in the engineering firm of Sanderson & Porter. He became manager of U.S. Food Products, an outgrowth of Distillers' Securities Company (*see* Whiskey Trust) in 1922. In 1924 he reorganized the business as National Distillers and began building up sales for industrial and medicinal alcohol while preparing for the possible repeal of Prohibition (q.v.). Porter was mainly responsible for the firm's emergence as one of the nation's two largest distilling corporations as he bought up a multitude of brands and companies.

SOURCES: "Seton Porter," *Spirits* (March 1953); "Whiskey," *Fortune* (November 1933).

Pot-still. *See* Still.

Poth, F. A., & Sons, Inc. (Brewery). Founded by Fred A. Poth in 1865, the Philadelphia company was incorporated as F. A. Poth in 1887 and changed to F. A. Poth & Sons in 1898. It was a very successful brewery, continuing under that name until 1934. From 1934 to 1936 it operated as Class & Nachod Brewing Company and then as Poth Brewing Company, Inc., from 1936 to 1940 when it closed.

SOURCES: Manfred Friedrich and Donald Bull, *The Register of U.S. Breweries* (Trumbull, Conn., 1976); *One Hundred Years of Brewing* (Chicago and New York, 1903; Arno Press Reprint, 1974).

Premier Malt Products Company (Peoria). Premier was first established as the Decatur Illinois Brewing Company in 1855 and became a distributing agent for the Pabst Brewing Company (q.v.) in 1912. Decatur shifted to the manufacture of malt syrup as prohibition sentiment increased, and the name Premier Malt Products Company was being used by 1918. By 1925, Harris Perlstein, of Singer-Perlstein chemical consultants, had come into the business and a plant was built at Peoria. Perlstein was also president of the National Malt Products Manufacturers Association and became acquainted with fellow director Frederick Pabst. Their association culminated in the merger of Pabst and Premier in 1932. Thus a major malt products firm and the nation's once largest brewer combined as the Premier-Pabst Corporation, with Harris Perlstein as president and Frederick Pabst as vice-president. The name was changed to the Pabst Brewing Company in 1938.

SOURCE: Thomas C. Cochran, *The Pabst Brewing Company* (New York, 1948).

Prima Brewing Company. Opened in 1933, the Chicago firm merged with the Bismarck Company in 1941. It closed in 1952, but the plant was subsequently purchased by Canadian Ace (q.v.).

Prinz Brau Alaska, Inc. A recently founded brewery in Anchorage, it is owned by the Dr. August Oetker Company of West Germany. The brewery, which opened in 1976, competes for the Alaskan market primarily with Anheuser-Busch, Olympia, and Schlitz. Peter Bading is the brewery's president.

SOURCES: *Brewers Digest* (December 1976); James D. Robertson, *The Great American Beer Book* (Ottawa, Ill., 1978).

Prohibition. The ratification of the Eighteenth Amendment (q.v.) to the Constitution on January 29, 1919, and passage of the enforcement law, the Volstead Act (q.v.), were the end results of a century-long struggle to outlaw the liquor traffic in the U.S. American interest in temperance (q.v.) dated from the colonial period but was based primarily on moral rather than legal sanctions until well into the nineteenth century. Both Secretary of Treasury Alexander Hamilon and, later, President Thomas Jefferson came to view alcoholic beverages as a danger to society. Consumption of ardent spirits in particular reached high levels in the early 1800s. In a recent study, Norman H. Clark concluded that per capita consumption of absolute alcohol among eligible drinkers in New York City could be estimated at 10 gallons in 1810. W. J. Rorabaugh, in *The Alcoholic Republic*, indicates that the national per capita consumption of distilled spirits increased after 1800, exceeding 5 gallons annually by 1830. Compared with consumption of 2.10 gallons of distilled spirits in 1850 and 2.61 in 1970, the period would have to be considered one of the heaviest drinking ages in American history. Temperance forces reacted to the high rate of consumption by turning to legislative means to deal with the liquor problem. In 1846, owing largely to the efforts of Neal Dow (q.v.), Maine passed a prohibition law, and by 1855 twelve other states had followed its lead. These laws, patterned after the Maine Liquor Law (q.v.), generally banned the manufacture and sale of "spiritous or intoxicating liquors" but were aimed primarily at abolishing public intoxication. There was little notable opposition to the laws, and after passage, enforcement was moderate because there existed a general belief that the "good sense" of the laws would result in voluntary cooperation. Because of constitutional problems and political upheaval over slavery and its expansion in the 1850s, the laws in nine states had been repealed or declared unconstitutional by 1865. In the late 1860s, however, a second prohibition movement gathered momentum. The Prohibition party (q.v.) was formed in 1869, the Woman's Christian Temperance Union (q.v.) in 1874, and then the powerful and successful Anti-Saloon League (q.v.) in 1893. The direct thrust of the movement was to outlaw the saloon, which was connected with drunkenness, prostitution, crime, and corrupt politics. The drive against saloons enlisted many middle-class supporters who saw the nation's nearly 300,000 saloons in 1900 as unfortunate by-products of an urban-industrial society. Although the ultimate aim of the temperance groups was to ban drinking, the saloon connection gave the movement wider support. Through the use of bureaucratic and political pressure tactics, reformers, most notably the Anti-Saloon League, first stressed state laws to permit local option (q.v.) on the saloon and drinking issues. The next stages in the evolutionary process were state prohibition laws and, of course, eventually nationwide prohibition. By 1905 many local option laws had been passed, and Kansas, Maine, Nebraska, and North Dakota were prohibition states. In 1917, just prior to American entry into World War I, thirteen states were considered "bone dry" and a total of twenty-six had passed some kind of prohibitory law. After 1913 the Anti-Saloon League, led by chief counsel and legislative superintendent Wayne B. Wheeler (q.v.), focused its efforts on the passage of a constitutional amendment. The method would be to support politicians for national office who were either "dry" (q.v.) in belief or who recognized the social or political advantage in supporting legal national prohibition. The Congress of 1916, which was considered "dry," and the spirit of sacrifice that accompanied U.S. entry into World War I, combined to help pass a resolution for a constitutional amendment in December 1917. Senator Morris Sheppard of Texas proposed the original version, which would prohibit the "manufacture, sale, or transportation" of intoxicating liquors "for drink or beverage use." By January 16, 1919, three-fourths of the states had ratified the Eighteenth Amendment, which would take effect one year later in January 1920. Meanwhile, the Volstead Act was passed over President Woodrow Wilson's veto in October 1919. The act would continue wartime restrictions on the manufacture of alcoholic beverages and would go into effect in January 1920. Thus the Volstead Act became the enforcement legislation for the Eighteenth Amendment and defined alcoholic beverages of more than ½ of 1 percent as intoxicating. Actually, the effective date was academic because "wartime" prohibition had begun in distilling with the Lever Act (q.v.) of 1917 and an amendment to the Food Stimulation Act in September 1918. The era of Prohibition in the 1920s proved to be very controversial in that sources then and since have argued as to whether the law ushered in a decade of speakeasies, evasion of the law, wide-scale racketeering, and economic problems; or rather, considerably reduced drinking overall, resulted in higher worker productivity, increased bank deposits, and was largely responsible for the prosperity of the 1920s. Predictably, the enactment of the Prohibition amendment dealt a devastating blow to the brewing and distilling industries. Some brewers turned to the production of a variety of malt products such as near beer (q.v.), and some branched out into new areas, but a great many decided to sell their property because of family or business pressures, or because the prospect for resumption of brewing looked bleak in the years immediately following the enactment of the Prohibition law. Although a few distillers managed to profit from the production of legal medicinal and industrial spirits, most turned to other areas of endeavor. As the decade of legislated nondrinking wore on, however, it became increasingly apparent that the law was virtually unenforceable. Even though it is true that net drinking probably declined considerably, the bootlegging (q.v.) and illegal trade accompanying Prohibition proved very damaging. The Prohibition Bureau (q.v.) found it very difficult to enforce the law. A movement against Prohibition began with the formation of the Association Against the Prohibition Amendment (q.v.) in 1920. The group helped gather momentum for a new constitutional amendment to repeal the Eighteenth Amendment. By 1932, the notorious activities of organized crime, the doldrums of the Depression, and the general feeling that the law was a failure combined to help make Repeal (q.v.) a genuine possibility. Historian Norman Clark cites another factor. Ironically, the Eighteenth Amendment had effectively destroyed the "saloon," thus enabling growing support for the repeal of Prohibition. The Democratic National Convention of 1932 went on record for Repeal, and the congressional proposal passed in February 1933. By December the Twenty-first Amendment (q.v.) had been ratified. It repealed the Eighteenth Amendment, thereby giving the states the brunt of the responsibility for the "liquor traffic." Before ratification, however, the Cullen Act (q.v.) of March 1933 had modified the Volstead Act by permitting the manufacture and sale of light wines and beer of up to 3.2 percent of alcohol by volume. The end of the "Noble Experiment" led to a revival of the brewing and distilling industries, but each would be different. Self-policing, decline of the saloon image, emphasis on responsible and respectable drinking, and business concentration would be earmarks of the post-Repeal industries.

SOURCES: Jack S. Blocker, Jr., *Alcohol, Reform and Society* (Westport, Conn., 1979); Ernest H. Cherrington, *Evolution of Prohibition in the United States of America* (Westerville, Ohio, 1920); Norman H. Clark, *Deliver Us from Evil* (New York, 1976); Larry Engelmann, *Intemperance: The Lost War Against Liquor* (New York, 1979); John Kobler, *Ardent Spirits* (New York, 1973); John Krout, *The Origins of Prohibition* (New York, 1925); Charles Merz, *The Dry Decade* (New York, 1931); Peter Odegard, *Pressure Politics: The Story of the Anti-Saloon League* (New York, 1928); W. J. Rorabaugh, *The Alcoholic Republic* (New York, 1979); Andrew Sinclair, *Prohibition: The Era of Excess* (Boston, 1962); James H. Timberlake, *Prohibition and the Progressive Movement, 1900-1920* (Cambridge, Mass., 1963); Ian R. Tyrrell, *Sobering Up: From Temperance to Prohibition in Antebellum America, 1800-1860* (Westport, Conn., 1979).

Prohibition Bureau. Established in 1920, the agency was to enforce national Prohibition (q.v.). John F. Kramer, the first prohibition commissioner, held the position for a year and a half. Roy A. Haynes succeeded him and was replaced by Lincoln A. Andrews in the mid-1920s. Other changes followed. The bureau operated under the Internal Revenue Department until 1930 when President Herbert Hoover, with congressional approval, transferred authority to the Department of Justice. The agency encountered problems from the outset. Agents were paid low salaries; charges of corruption occurred regularly; and financing proved inadequate. Appropriations rose from $6 million in 1921 to $16 million by 1932, but even that outlay was not sufficient to eliminate widespread bootlegging, moonshine, speakeasies, smuggling from Canada and Mexico, and racketeering.

   SOURCES: Norman H. Clark, *Deliver Us from Evil* (New York, 1976); Andrew Sinclair, *Prohibition: The Era of Excess* (Boston, 1962).

Prohibition Party. Organized in Chicago on September 1, 1869, the party nominated James Black of Pennsylvania as its first presidential candidate in 1872. Its national convention was held in Columbus in that year, with nine states sending representatives. New York and Ohio were the early strongholds of the party, which reached the height of its strength in 1892, when the presidential candidate received 271,000 votes. The party found itself at odds with the Anti-Saloon League (q.v.), which had formed in 1893. The league, believing third-party politics ineffective, chose to support any politician who voted "dry," whereas Prohibition party faithfuls regarded this tactic as lacking in principle. The party continued to nominate candidates in presidential elections but also exerted influence for more effective governmental policies toward alcoholic beverages.

   SOURCES: Norman H. Clark, *Deliver Us from Evil* (New York, 1976); D. Leigh Colvin, *Prohibition in the United States* (New York, 1926); Roger C. Storms, *Partisan Prophets: A History of the Prohibition Party* (Denver, Colo., 1972); E. J. Wheeler, *Prohibition: The Principle, the Policy and the Party* (New York, 1889).

Proof. The term applies to the amount, or percentage of alcohol in spirits (q.v.). The proof is twice the percentage of alcohol; therefore, 100 proof whiskey is 50 percent alcohol. The character of the distillate is determined by the proof at which the liquor is distilled. Neutral spirits (q.v.) are distilled at above 190 proof, and whiskies between 160 and 100 proof or so. The beverage will be bottled at usually between 60 and 110 proof, and is watered to lower the proof. Until the late eighteenth century, crude but colorful methods were employed to determine proof. One method was to mix equal amounts of the spirit and gunpowder, put a flame to it, and if the spirit did not burn it was too weak. If it burned, it was considered above proof and thus had been "proved." This, and other such techniques, gave way to more scientific means with the introduction, after 1780, of hydrometers (q.v.) and areometers (q.v.).

   SOURCES: Gerald Carson, *The Social History of Bourbon* (New York, 1963); Henry G. Crowgey, *Kentucky Bourbon* (Lexington, Ky., 1971).

Publicker Distillers Products, Inc., Harry Publicker founded the Philadelphia company in 1913 as an industrial alcohol firm. Simon Neuman, Publicker's son-in-law, became president in the late 1920s and the firm hoped to take advantage of the post-Prohibition whiskey demand by producing a whiskey through an artificial (and brief) aging (q.v.) process. Publicker organized Continental Distilling Corporation as a subsidiary in 1933. Later, the firm acquired the Kinsey Distilling Corporation (q.v.) and W. A. Haller. Over the years, the company produced industrial alcohol in addition to Old Hickory, Governor's Club, Skol gin and vodka, Inver House, Haller's, and Pinwiddie. Harry Publicker died in 1951. The firm operates plants in Philadelphia, Lemont, Illinois, and Airdrie, Scotland. The Neuman family has been involved with the company, and John P. Welch was president in the late 1970s.

SOURCES: "Harry Publicker," *Spirits* (April 1951); *Value Line*, December 1978; "Whiskey," *Fortune* (November 1933).

Pure Food and Drug Act, 1906. The act was the culmination of nearly thirty years of agitation for national legislation to prevent the adulteration of food and drugs. In 1905 President Theodore Roosevelt requested that a law be passed to regulate the interstate shipment and trade of misbranded and adulterated foods and drugs. He signed the law on June 30, 1906, and it would become effective on January 1, 1907. It would prevent the "manufacture, sale, or transportation of adulterated or misbranded or poisonous or deleterious foods, drugs, medicines, and liquors." The act applied to goods involved in interstate or foreign commerce. The question of liquor, and its position with reference to the legislation, had created considerable controversy during congressional debate. The main problem centered on the definition of whiskey. Producers of straight bourbon whiskey, mostly from Kentucky, argued that their product was pure and the only genuine whiskey, whereas the whiskey blenders and rectifiers claimed that their beverage was milder and more palatable. Because blended whiskey made up over 70 percent of the alcoholic spirits being consumed, the struggle between the two was hard-fought. The result, largely owing to the power and pressure of Dr. Harvey W. Wiley (q.v.), head of the Department of Agriculture's Bureau of Chemistry, was that blended or rectified whiskey had to be labeled "compound whiskey," "imitation whiskey," or "blended whiskey." Wiley's interpretation of adulteration held up until the "Taft decision" (q.v.) of 1909, which put both blended and straight whiskey in the category of whiskey. The act also specified standards for malt liquors, and the question of adjuncts (q.v.) in beer proved a problem. The U.S. Brewers' Association (USBA) argued against an interpretation that held that adjuncts were "adulterations." The "Taft decision" agreed with the USBA's interpretation.

SOURCES: Oscar E. Anderson, Jr., *The Health of a Nation: Harvey W. Wiley and the Fight for Pure Food* (Chicago, 1958); John P. Arnold and Frank Penman, *History of the Brewing Industry and Brewing Science* (Chicago, 1933); Gerald Carson, *The Social History of Bourbon* (New York, 1963).

R

Racking. This is the process of transferring beer from storage to barrels. Thus the beer is racked, or poured, into kegs (q.v.) or barrels (q.v.). Innovations in the filling process date from the 1870s when at least one brewing technician, John E. Siebel (q.v.), came up with a device for relatively efficient racking. Other improvements followed but continued to be based on the principle that the container to be filled should be put under counter-pressure so that carbonic acids in the beer in storage would not be lost; otherwise, the carbonic acid would expand without resistance, create foaming, and cause a loss of effervescence in the beer.

SOURCES: One Hundred Years of Brewing (Chicago and New York, 1903; Arno Press Reprint, 1974); Edward Vogel, Jr., et al., *The Practical Brewer* (St. Louis, Mo., 1946).

Radeke, F. D., Brewing Company. Jacob Hanley built the Kankakee, Illinois, brewery in 1860. It was subsequently known as the Beckman & Meyer, and then Beckman & Schneider Brewery. F. D. Radeke puchased the company in 1872 and incorporated as F. D. Radeke Brewing Company in 1877. The company closed during the Prohibition (q.v.) era.

SOURCE: One Hundred Years of Brewing (Chicago and New York, 1903; Arno Press Reprint, 1974).

Rainier Brewing Company. Andrew Hemrich, a German immigrant and brewer, established the Seattle Brewing and Malting Company in 1878 in Seattle, Washington. His premium beer was called Rainier, and the business remained in operation until Prohibition (q.v.). Two Canadian brewers, Fritz Sick and his son, Emil, purchased the old Hemrich works in 1933, and rebuilt it. By the 1930s they were able to brew Rainier beer because they had successfully repurchased the name from a California concern that had earlier acquired the brand name. The company's name was changed from Sick's Century Brewing Company and eventually became the Rainier Companies, in which Molson of Canada held a substantial interest. In 1977, the G. Heileman Brewing Company (q.v.) bought the brewery from the parent company. Emil Sick had died in 1964, and his adopted son, Alan B. Ferguson, headed the company until Edwin S. Coombs, Jr., became president in the late 1970s.

SOURCES: Stanley Baron, *Brewed in America* (Boston, 1962); "Rainier Beer: The First Hundred Years" (brief company history, 1977).

Receivership. In this court-arranged status a person or party is given the responsibility of administering property or funds that are disputed. The receiver takes possession of the property, but does not gain title to it, and may receive profit and other benefits. Often a bankrupt company will be put into receivership, and the creditors might be satisfied by a reorganization of the business by the court-appointed receiver. National Distillers Products Company (q.v.) is a well-known case in point. U.S. Food Products went into receivership, and the banks that were the main creditors authorized the reorganization of the company by Seton Porter (q.v.). He then organized National Distillers in the mid-1920s.

Rectification. In the process of blending spirits (q.v.), straight whiskey is rectified by mixing with grain neutral spirits (q.v.) and flavoring elements. Such elements are used in the making of cordials (q.v.) and liqueurs (q.v.). *See also*, Blended Whiskey.

Red Top Brewing Company. The Cincinnati brewery was organized in 1933. Its precursor, the Red Top Malting Company, bought the John Hauck Brewing Company (q.v.) works in 1927. The malting firm had been founded in 1904 by Louis Ullman and Edgar Mack, Sr. The families continued to direct the brewery in the post-Prohibition period, but by the 1950s the company was sold to nonbrewing investors.

SOURCE: William L. Downard, *The Cincinnati Brewing Industry* (Athens, Ohio, 1973).

Refrigeration. Cooling is very important at various stages of the brewing process. Wort (q.v.) must be cooled, and low temperatures are necessary for fermentation (q.v.), and the storage of beer (q.v.) and hops (q.v.); racking (q.v.) and bottling also require controlled temperatures. Thus the introduction of artificial refrigeration mechanisms during the late nineteenth century was welcomed by brewers who formerly had to depend upon the vagaries of climate and temperature, and the availability and price of ice. In Germany, brewers were limited by law to brewing in cool months because beer brewed in warm months was considered a health hazard. In the U.S., brewers stored ice in cellars and above-ground icehouses, one of which was patented by David W. Davis of Detroit. The breakthrough came in October 1860 with the patenting of the Carré ice machine by Frenchman Ferdinand Carré; but the first machine in an American brewery was that of Charles

Tellier, also of France. A New Orleans brewer installed this machine in 1869. During the 1870s and 1880s, a number of refrigerating machines were patented; they were either ice machines, or a bit later, air-cooling machines. Each was based on the compression principle, often using liquid ammonia. Some of the names associated with the innovations were Samuel D. Lount, P. H. Van der Weyde, Daniel Holden, David Boyle, A. T. Ballantine, and John Enright (Arctic Machine Company) of the U.S., and Franz Wind-hausen of Germany. One of the most widely adopted machines was that of John C. De LaVergne (q.v.) of New York. Cooling played a smaller but still important part in distilling and is necessary primarily in cooling the mash (q.v.) before fermentation (q.v.) and cooling the worm (q.v.). Before refrigeration devices were adopted, spring water, or natural cooling, pre-dominated. During the twentieth century—mostly after 1933—there has been a movement toward mechanical and vacuum refrigeration.

SOURCES: Stanley Baron, *Brewed in America* (Boston, 1962); William L. Dow-nard, *The Cincinnati Brewing Industry* (Athens, Ohio, 1973); George Ehret, *Twenty-five Years of Brewing* (New York, 1891); Carl J. Kiefer, "Planning a Modern Distillery," *Spirits* (October 1933); *One Hundred Years of Brewing* (Chicago and New York, 1903; Arno Press Reprint, 1974); Harry A. Tuer, "Vacuum Refrigeration for the Distillery," *Spirits* (December 1936).

Regional brewer. This type of brewery markets its beer to a local or regional market exclusively. Most breweries were limited to the smaller area until after 1850 when transportation, pasteurization (q.v.), and bottling tech-niques permitted wider distribution. The bulk of the nation's brewers con-tinued on this basis, but a few, such as Pabst, Anheuser-Busch, and Schlitz, began to "go national" in the 1870s and 1880s. Beer output among the nationals usually surpassed that among the regionals, but a few local and regional firms, notably Ehret (q.v.) and Ruppert (q.v.) in New York, con-tinued to rank among the nation's largest brewers by relying on the New York market. The regional brewers in the Midwest often marketed in two or three states but again on a limited basis. *See also*, National Brewer.

Regulation of liquor, Federal. *See* Federal Liquor Regulations.

Regulation of liquor, State. *See* State Liquor Regulations.

Repeal. The movement against the Eighteenth Amendment (q.v.) to the Constitution culminated in the passage of the Twenty-first Amendment (q.v.) in December 1933. The term "Repeal" became synonymous with the movement against nationwide prohibition, with the passage of the Twenty-first Amendment, and with the era following the end of Prohibition (q.v.).

Rheingold Breweries, Inc. Samuel Liebmann (q.v.) founded this famous and long-lived Brooklyn, New York, brewery in 1855. Born in 1799, he left Wurtemberg, Germany, in 1854, partially for political reasons. Liebmann and his sons, Joseph, Henry, and Charles, built a large brewery. The sons carried on the business after Samuel died in 1872, but changed the name to S. Liebmann's Sons. In 1905, on the fiftieth anniversary of the company, the three sons retired and their six sons took over. In 1878 the John P. Schoenwald brewery was purchased, Claus-Lyssius in 1902, and Obermeyer and Liebmann in 1924. The latter brewery had been opened in 1868 by Samuel Liebmann and run by his two sons-in-law. After the repeal of Prohibition (q.v.), Liebmann Breweries, Inc., grew steadily and branched out with the purchase of the John Eichler Brewing Company in 1947, Trommer (q.v.) of Orange, New Jersey, and then two breweries in California that had been owned by Acme Breweries. Rheingold was the company's main brew dating from the 1880s, and that name was adopted for the company when Pepsi-Cola United Bottlers purchased Liebmann Breweries in 1964. In the meantime all but the Brooklyn and Orange plants had been sold. After a number of business shifts, amid declining sales, Chock Full O'Nuts Corporation bought the brewery in 1974 and then closed down the Brooklyn plant in January 1976. Two plants, in Orange and New Bedford, Massachusetts, remained open. In October 1977, C. Schmidt & Sons, Inc. (q.v.), of Philadelphia purchased the label and brewing rights for Rheingold.

SOURCES: Will Anderson, *The Breweries of Brooklyn* (New York, 1976); Stanley Baron, *Brewed in America* (Boston, 1962); *One Hundred Years of Brewing* (Chicago and New York, 1903; Arno Press Reprint, 1974); "A Rheingold with a Pepsi Chaser?" *Bev for Executives* (March 15, 1964).

Ripy, T. B., distilleries. Thomas Ripy established the Tyrone, Kentucky, distilleries in 1869. His plants were absorbed by the Kentucky Distilleries and Warehouse Company (q.v.) in 1902, but his sons, Ernest, Robert, Forest, and Ezra, opened another plant nearby and operated it as Ripy Bros. until the advent of Prohibition (q.v.). In the 1930s, Ezra and Robert resumed operations in the Hoffman (q.v.) distillery and Ernest organized a new business on the site of the old Ripy Bros. plant but evidently did not operate very long under the name. The Ripys became associated with the Wertheimers (q.v.).

SOURCES: *Kentucky's Distilling Interests* (Lexington, Ky., 1893); *Spirits* (April 1935 and May 1936); Art Williams, "The Kentucky Round-up," *Spirits* (August-September 1963).

Rochester brewing industry. Rochester was founded in 1812, and a few breweries were soon in operation. Among the more notable and long-lived breweries were Genesee (q.v.) and the American Brewing Company (q.v.).

A post-Prohibition firm that stayed in business until 1970 was the Standard Rochester Brewing Company, Inc. (q.v.), which was an amalgam of two older concerns. The city had about twenty breweries in the late nineteenth century, and by 1900 the population had grown to more than 150,000. In the 1930s only a few breweries reopened, and by the 1970s only the Genesee Brewing Company was still in business.

Roessle, John, Brewery. First of the lager beer (q.v.) brewers in Boston, Roessle opened his business in 1846. It was controlled by the family until it became part of a merger in 1890. The New England Breweries Company Ltd. (q.v.), a British syndicate, bought up stock in three Boston companies —one of which was the Roessle company.
SOURCE: One Hundred Years of Brewing (Chicago and New York, 1903; Arno Press Reprint, 1974).

Rosenstiel, Lewis S. (1891-January 21, 1976). Organizer of the modern Schenley Distillers Corporation (q.v.), Rosenstiel worked in Kentucky's Susquemac Distillery Company, which was managed by an uncle, David I. Johnson. During the early years of Prohibition (q.v.) in the 1920s, Rosenstiel sold bonds and whiskey stock and bought his first plant, the Schenley Company of Pennsylvania, in 1923. Other acquisitions followed, and when Prohibition was repealed, Schenley had a large stock of whiskey for U.S. distribution. The company continued to grow as Rosenstiel proved to be an innovative and capable businessman.
SOURCES: Cincinnati Post, January 22, 1976; "Lewis S. Rosenstiel," *Spirits* (December 1934); "Schenley," *Fortune* (May 1936).

Rueter, Henry H. (December 9, 1832-November 27, 1899). A German immigrant to the U.S., Rueter was a partner in the Boston brewery Rueter & Alley and then owner of Rueter & Company. He served as president of the U.S. Brewers' Association (q.v.) from 1875 to 1880.
SOURCE: One Hundred Years of Brewing (Chicago and New York, 1903; Arno Press Reprint, 1974).

Rueter & Alley. The Boston, Massachusetts, brewery was established in 1867 by Henry H. Rueter (q.v.) and John Alley. The company was the nation's fifteenth largest brewery in 1877. In 1885 Alley founded his own firm and entered the Massachusetts Breweries Company, Ltd., in 1900. Both breweries closed during Prohibition (q.v.). Rueter was president of the U.S. Brewers' Association (q.v.) from 1875 to 1880.
SOURCES: Manfred Friedrich and Donald Bull, *The Register of U.S. Breweries* (Trumbull, Conn., 1976); *One Hundred Years of Brewing* (Chicago and New York, 1903; Arno Press Reprint, 1974).

Ruh. The ruh is the storage period for bottom-fermentation (q.v.) beers after the main fermentation of the brew has taken place. Sometimes known as the secondary stage of fermentation, it is a rest period during which various substances settle out from the brew and the alcoholic content increases slightly. The length of the period ranges from ten days to a few weeks. The temperature of the cellars (later rooms) where the ruh casks are stored are kept just above the freezing point.

SOURCES: *One Hundred Years of Brewing* (Chicago and New York, 1903; Arno Press Reprint, 1974); Edward H. Vogel, Jr., et al., *The Practical Brewer* (St. Louis, Mo., 1946).

Rum. Produced from a fermented mash (q.v.) of molasses or sugar cane juice, rum must be distilled at less than 190 proof (q.v.). New England rum, which is heavy bodied and flavorful, may be advertised as straight rum and must be distilled at less than 160 proof. Rum, from the French *rumbullion*, meaning tumult or to boil again, is probably the oldest alcoholic beverage in America, dating to the colonies of the seventeenth century. In the eighteenth century it figured in the triangular trade: West Indian molasses was imported to New England and made into rum, which was shipped to Africa for slaves who were imported into the West Indies and the southern colonies. The drink was very popular in the colonial period and was largely supplied by Massachusetts and Rhode Island distillers. Colonial production was important enough for Parliament to pass the Molasses Act (q.v.) of 1733 in an effort to curtail the importation of non-British molasses. Rum continued to be more important than whiskey until the Revolution, but declined in the late eighteenth and early nineteenth centuries because of restrictions on the post-Revolutionary trade with West Indian ports, passage of the Embargo Act in 1807, and the abolition of the external slave trade in 1808. The former cut off foreign markets and the latter interfered with the triangular trade. But in the meantime the westward movement across the Appalachians encouraged the manufacture of a drink that could be made from locally produced grain—thus the growth of bourbon (q.v.), made from corn and other grains.

SOURCES: Gerald Carson, *The Social History of Bourbon* (New York, 1963); Victor S. Clark, *History of Manufactures in the United States*, vol. 1 (New York, 1929); Henry G. Crowgey, *Kentucky Bourbon* (Lexington, Ky., 1971); Esther Kellner, *Moonshine, Its History and Folklore* (Indianapolis, Ind., 1971).

Ruppert, Jacob, Jr. (ca 1880-January 13, 1939). Son of the founder of the Jacob Ruppert brewing company, Jacob, Jr., worked in the company, served in World War I, attaining the rank of colonel, and earned national attention by purchasing the New York Yankees baseball team. Although his motive was a love of baseball rather than advertising, his early involvement with sports encouraged brewers in the post-Prohibition era to consider the potential of linking beer with wholesome and popular social events. Col. Ruppert was also widely known in brewing circles as long-time president of the U.S. Brewers' Association (USBA) (q.v.). During the mid-1930s, Ruppert, as president of the USBA, opposed a spin-off group of western brewers who had formed a new group, Brewing Industry, Inc. (q.v.). He placed his support firmly behind the larger parent group but was also involved in organizing the United Brewers' Industrial Foundation within the USBA, which seemed to voice goals similar to those of the dissident organization. The groups merged not long after his death.

SOURCES: Will Anderson, *The Beer Book* (Princeton, N.J., 1973); Stanley Baron, *Brewed in America* (Boston, 1962); "The First Century: A History of the U.S.B.A.," *American Brewer* (February 1962).

Ruppert, Jacob, Brewery. The New York City brewing firm was established by Jacob Ruppert, Sr., in 1867. His father, Fritz, a German immigrant, had operated a brewery from 1850 to 1869, and Jacob, Sr., learned the business from him. Ruppert's brewery proved very successful and was one of the few non-national breweries to reach the 1-million-barrel output figure. His firm did so in 1916, even though the market area was primarily local and regional (New England). Jacob, Sr., who was born in 1842, married Anna Gillig in 1864. She was the daughter of George Gillig, a lager brewer also. Their son, Jacob, Jr. (q.v.), known as the Colonel because of his exploits and rank in World War I, was instrumental in continuing the business as a prominent nationally known brewery. He purchased the New York Yankees and ran the company successfully until his death in 1939. Following some difficult years in the 1940s, especially in 1948 and 1949 when damaging strikes hurt the brewery, the company revived somewhat in the early 1950s by virtue of the introduction of a new lighter beer called Knickerbocker. The brewery continued as one of the city's few brewing concerns until the plant was closed in 1965. Rheingold (q.v.) bought the brand name, but the outmoded plant was closed.

SOURCES: Will Anderson, *The Beer Book* (Princeton, N.J., 1973); Stanley Baron, *Brewed in America* (Boston, 1962); Herman A. Katz, "The Knickerbocker Story," *American Brewer* (July 1952); *One Hundred Years of Brewing* (Chicago and New York, 1903; Arno Press Reprint, 1974).

Rye whiskey. Rye is made from a fermented mash (q.v.) of at least 51 percent rye grain. Maryland and Pennsylvania were known for making rye whiskey, and because of that tradition blended whiskey is often referred to as "rye" in that region. Today, true rye whiskey accounts for a small portion of U.S. production, and is heavier and stronger in flavor and body than bourbon (q.v.).

S

Saccharometer. A specific form of the hydrometer (q.v.), this instrument measures the specific gravity or density of liquids. The saccharometer measures the amount of sugar in a solution, that is, the specific gravity of worts (q.v.) as compared with water. This device, and others, were introduced into the art of brewing in the 1780s and after. Various improvements were made over the years.

SOURCES: Thomas C. Cochran, *The Pabst Brewing Company* (New York, 1948); *One Hundred Years of Brewing* (Chicago and New York, 1903; Arno Press Reprint, 1974).

St. Louis Brewing Association. Eighteen of the approximately thirty St. Louis breweries were consolidated in 1889 by an English syndicate. Among those that merged were the Winkelmeyer (q.v.), Phoenix (q.v.), Wainwright (q.v.), Anthony & Kuhn, Bremen, Hyde Park, Schilling & Schneider, and Klausman plants. By 1902, seven of the breweries were closed and others would follow. Most of the remaining firms closed during Prohibition (q.v.), but at least two, the Columbia (q.v.) and Hyde Park breweries, reopened and the latter became part of the Griesedieck Western Brewery Company (q.v.). The Hyde Park Brewing Association was operated again in the post-Prohibition period by English investors.

SOURCES: Don Crinklaw, "The Battle of the Breweries," *St. Louis Post-Dispatch*, June 9, 1974; *One Hundred Years of Brewing* (Chicago and New York, 1903; Arno Press Reprint, 1974).

St. Louis brewing industry. Until 1840, virtually all the beer produced in St. Louis was ale (q.v.), porter (q.v.), or stout (q.v.)—a situation reflected across the nation until the advent of the German lager beer (q.v.) brewers of the 1840s. Apparently, the city's first lager brewer was the Lemp (q.v.) brewery, which brewed the distinctly German beer in the early 1840s. As the German population increased in the mid-nineteenth century, the city supported more and more breweries that found favorable water, shipping, and storage conditions. The Wainwright (q.v.), Louis Obert (q.v.), Joseph Uhrig (q.v.), Winkelmeyer (q.v.), and Phoenix (q.v.) breweries were among the early ones, and Anheuser-Busch (q.v.) was founded in 1860. In 1877, Lemp was still the largest company, with 61,000 barrels produced, and ranked nineteenth among the nation's breweries. But Anheuser-Busch was expanding rapidly under the leadership of August Busch and by 1895 would be second in production across the nation while Lemp was the eighth largest. In 1889, the St. Louis Brewing Association (q.v.), a British investment consolidate, bought up a number of local concerns, and reportedly offered $8 million to Busch. Although Busch refused (as did William Lemp and Louis Obert) to join the merger, the Wainwright, Winkelmeyer, and Poenix breweries joined fifteen other companies in the group. Among those who sold out was Anton Griesedieck (*see* Falstaff Brewing Corporation), who had bought the Phoenix brewery. Later, in 1907, the Griesediecks would merge their National brewery with another group, consisting of the Columbia (q.v.), American (q.v.), Empire, National (*see* Falstaff), Gast, and Home breweries in a consolidate known as the Independent Breweries Company (q.v.). On the eve of Prohibition (q.v.) in 1918, St. Louis was the home of about twenty-five breweries, but by 1935 the number would be down to eleven, and by 1960 to only three. In the late 1970s only the Anheuser-Busch and Falstaff companies operated breweries in the city.

SOURCES: Will Anderson, *The Beer Book* (Princeton, N.J., 1973); Don Crinklaw, "The Battle of the Breweries," *St. Louis Post-Dispatch*, June 9, 1974; James Lindhurst, "History of the Brewing Industry in St. Louis," unpub. M.A. thesis, Washington University, 1939; *One Hundred Years of Brewing* (Chicago and New York, 1903; Arno Press Reprint, 1974).

St. Vincent Abbey, Brewery of. The brewery near Latrobe, Pennsylvania, was founded in the mid-1850s as a source of beer for the Roman Catholic community of Benedictine priests and brothers. The religious group established the monastery in 1844 after migrating from Bavaria. The Pope originally allowed production for the monastery exclusively, but gradually the restrictions were lifted and the religious brewers sold their beer to a limited number of retailers. The monastery returned to exclusive production for the Benedictine Community in the 1890s because of the growth of prohibition sentiment within the Catholic Church. The brewery operation apparently became known as the Latrobe Brewing Company and ceased with Prohibition (q.v.).

SOURCES: Manfred Friedrich and Donald Bull, *The Register of U.S. Breweries* (Trumbull, Conn., 1976); *One Hundred Years of Brewing* (Chicago and New York, 1903; Arno Press Reprint, 1974).

Saladin, Jules Alphonse (active, 1870s-80s). A onetime associate of Nicholas Galland (q.v.), who patented a number of malting (q.v.) devices in the

1870s, Saladin, also a Frenchman, was noted for his compartment, or box, system of malting. His system improved temperature and moisture control and combined this feature with a mechanism for turning and stirring malt (q.v.). The system was introduced into the U.S. in 1887 by Ambrose Plamondon (q.v.), who organized the Saladin Pneumatic Malting Construction Company of Chicago.

SOURCES: Thomas C. Cochran, *The Pabst Brewing Company* (New York, 1948); *One Hundred Years of Brewing* (Chicago and New York, 1903; Arno Press Reprint, 1974).

San Francisco Breweries, Ltd. The consolidate of ten California breweries was formed by English investors with a capitalization of more than $7 million. The San Francisco companies in the merger were Wieland (q.v.), U.S. Brewing Company, Chicago Brewing Company, Willows Brewery, South San Francisco Brewery, and Pacific Brewery; the others were in Oakland and Berkeley. By 1902, only six of the plants still operated, and San Francisco Breweries, Ltd., was dissolved during Prohibition (q.v.) in the 1920s.

San Francisco brewing industry. The city's industry began in the late 1840s, probably 1849. Inevitably, identification of the first brewer is a matter of dispute, albeit a mild one. The Adam Schuppert Brewery (q.v.) is given credit by *One Hundred Years of Brewing* (1903), while the city directory indicated that William Bull's Empire Brewery was the first. Nevertheless, by the mid-1850s, about fifteen breweries operated in San Francisco, catering to a population approaching 40,000. Most of the early brewers produced "steam beer" (q.v.), a bottom-fermentation (q.v.) brew that was fermented at a higher temperature and more quickly than lager beer (q.v.). Lack of refrigeration made lagering (slow fermentation at lower temperatures) almost impossible, so that breweries either made top-fermentation (q.v.) ales and porters, or steam beer. When refrigeration devices became available in the late nineteenth century, many brewers switched to the brewing of the traditional lager. By 1880, San Francisco had almost forty breweries, most of them fairly small in comparison with the national brewers (q.v.), but the number declined gradually thereafter to ninteen by 1910 and four by 1935. By the 1970s, the Anchor Steam (q.v.) and New Albion (q.v.) breweries operated as independents, but Falstaff (q.v.) maintained a branch, as did Hamm (q.v.). Over the years the city witnessed trends similar to those of other brewing centers. English investors moved in during the 1890s and formed San Francisco Breweries, Ltd. (q.v.); mergers began in the period; and most concerns closed with Prohibition (q.v.) in the 1920s. Among the city's breweries were John Wieland (q.v.), National Brewing Company (q.v.), and Wunder (Acme/California Brewing Company) (*see* Wunder Brewing Company).

SOURCES: Will Anderson, *The Beer Book* (Princeton, N.J., 1973); Stanley Baron, *Brewed in America* (Boston, 1962); *One Hundred Years of Brewing* (Chicago and New York, 1903; Arno Press Reprint, 1974).

Schaefer, Rudolph J. (b. July 9, 1900). After graduation from Princeton, Schaefer took over the Schaefer brewing company (q.v.) of New York, of which he was president from 1924 to 1975.

SOURCE: Will Anderson, *The Breweries of Brooklyn* (New York, 1976).

Schaefer, F. & M., Brewing Company. Founded in 1842 by Frederick and Maximilian Schaefer, this New York City brewing concern is credited as being the oldest brewer of lager beer (q.v.) currently operating in the U.S. The brothers, who migrated from Wetzlar, Russia, bought a small plant and introduced the new lager beer. After a number of moves, they operated their brewery near Grand Central Station. Maximilian's son, Rudolph, took over as president in 1912 and moved the brewery to a new location in Brooklyn in 1915. During the Prohibition (q.v.) era in the 1920s, the company brewed near beer (q.v.) and manufactured ice. When Schaefer died in 1923 at the age of sixty, his two sons, Frederick M. E. and Rudolph J. (q.v.) continued the business, with Rudolph taking active control in 1927. Expansion followed in the 1930s and 1940s, and by 1963, Schaefer had acquired two additional plants, one in Albany and the other in Baltimore. In 1972, a modern plant was opened near Allentown, Pennsylvania, and the older Albany plant was closed soon afterward. In 1973, Schaefer bought Piel Brothers (q.v.), and then closed its Brooklyn plant in 1976.

SOURCES: Will Anderson, *The Breweries of Brooklyn* (New York, 1976); Stanley Baron, *Brewed in America* (Boston, 1962); *One Hundred Years of Brewing* (Chicago and New York, 1903; Arno Press Reprint, 1974); *Our One Hundredth Year* (Brooklyn, 1942).

Schell, August, Brewing Company. August Schell, a German immigrant, built the New Ulm, Minnesota, brewery in 1860. After becoming an invalid, Schell was succeeded by sons Otto and Adolph in 1877. August died in 1892 at the age of sixty-four. The brewery was incorporated in 1902 as the August Schell Brewing Company and continues in the 1970s as a small, local concern producing primarily for the local market.

SOURCE: One Hundred Years of Brewing (Chicago and New York, 1903; Arno Press Reprint, 1974).

Schenley Distillers Corporation. The origins of this huge distilling corporation date primarily from the 1920s when Lewis Rosenstiel (q.v.) acquired the Schenley Products Company of Schenley, Pennsylvania. Rosenstiel, who was from Cincinnati, worked in the Susquemac Distillery Company prior to Prohibition (q.v.). His uncle, David I. Johnson, was a company executive and encouraged Rosenstiel to learn the distilling business. But Prohibition in 1920 changed the plans, and Rosenstiel became, among other things, a whiskey broker disposing of whiskey stocks for medicinal purposes. In 1923, he began to buy up more whiskey stock and apparently became convinced that the Eighteenth Amendment (q.v.) would be of temporary duration. Thus he purchased the Schenley Products Company, a distillery dating from 1892, which had a license to produce whiskey for medicinal use. In 1924, he bought the Joseph S. Finch Distillery (q.v.) and its Golden Wedding rye in Schenley, Pennsylvania, and then the George T. Stagg (q.v.) plant of Frankfort, Kentucky, in 1929. Rosenstiel's strategy was to buy the concentration warehouses (*see* Liquor Concentration Act) of the companies, plus brands and "goodwill," or name of the distilleries. Other acquisitions included the Pepper distillery (q.v.) of Lexington, the Corning Distilling Company (q.v.) of Peoria, W. P. Squibb and Company of Lawrenceburg, Indiana, the New England Distilling Company (q.v.) of Covington, Kentucky, and the Bernheim Distilling Company (q.v.) of Louisville. The latter was known for its I. W. Harper and Old Charter brands. By the late 1930s, Schenley had control of more than thirty brands and distilleries, and one of the main brands was Old Quaker, which was made at a plant in Lawrenceburg, Kentucky. In the meantime, Rosenstiel had organized a strong management group that included Harold, Sanford, and Lester Jacobi, whom he had known in Cincinnati, Albert B. Blanton (*see* Stagg, George T., Distillery), president of the Stagg plant, and J. B. Deacon of Hoffman Beverage Company. During the 1940s and 1950s, Rosenstiel continued to expand through distillery acquisitions and diversification. An example of the latter was the acquisition of Blatz Brewing Company (q.v.) in 1945. It operated as a subsidiary until Schenley sold the firm to Pabst (q.v.) in 1958. One of the famous whiskey brand names was George Dickel (q.v.); Schenley had constructed a new plant in Tennessee to produce the whiskey. Other famous brands were J. W. Dant (q.v.) and Ancient Age. Among the imported brands controlled by Schenley are Dewar's White Label, Mateus, and Stock. Rosenstiel was not only a shrewd entrepreneur but also proved very capable as a lobbyist when he fought for extension of the bonding period (q.v.) in the 1950s. During the Korean War, many distillers built up stocks in anticipation of wartime restrictions. But the war remained relatively limited and Schenley especially was faced with large stocks of "hedge" whiskey, as was Publicker (q.v.). Because taxes had to be paid on whiskey in eight years whether or not it had been brought out of storage, Rosenstiel susccessfully campaigned for a 1958 extension of the bonding period to twenty years. In 1968 the Glen Alden Corporation acquired Schenley, and was then itself acquired by Rapid American Corporation in 1972.

SOURCES: "J. B. Deacon Retirement," *Spirits* (May 1946); Stan Jones, *Jones' Complete Barguide* (Los Angeles, 1977); "Lewis Rosenstiel," *Spirits* (December 1934); "Schenley," *Fortune* (May 1936); "Whiskey," *Fortune* (November 1933).

Schlitz, Joseph (May 15, 1831-May 7, 1875). Born in Mayence, Germany, Schlitz came to the United States with his parents in 1855. His father, Joseph, was a successful businessman and knew the art of brewing. Young Schlitz worked as a bookkeeper for the August Krug brewery, then managed the company for Krug's widow upon the owner's death in 1856. Two years later, Schlitz married Anna Krug and eventually incorporated the company as the Jos. Schlitz Brewing Company (q.v.). In 1875, while on a trip to Germany on the steamer *Schiller*, Joseph and Anna were drowned as a result of a shipwreck in the Irish Sea. Control of the company passed to their nephews, the Uihleins (*see* Schlitz, Jos., Brewing Company).

Schlitz, Jos., Brewing Company. This traditional and famous Milwaukee brewery uses as one of its long-standing slogans, "The Beer That Made Milwaukee Famous." The original founder was German immigrant August Krug, who built a small brewhouse to supply his Chestnut Street restaurant trade. The brewery grew, and when Krug died in 1856, Joseph Schlitz (q.v.), the company's bookkeeper, took over the business and subsequently married Krug's widow, Anna. In 1874 the name of the company was changed to Jos. Schlitz Brewing Company, but the next year Schlitz drowned in a shipwreck during a voyage to visit relatives in Mayence, Germany. Thus, in 1875, control of the company was assumed by the Uihlein family—more specifically, Schlitz's nephews, August, Henry, Edward, and Alfred Uihlein. Apparently, August Uihlein (q.v.) was the main figure in the business. He was the nephew of August Krug, and had been brought to Milwaukee by Krug's father in 1850. Uihlein completed his education, held management positions in other firms, and then returned to Schlitz in 1868. A turning point for the company came in 1871 with the Chicago Fire. Because water was scarce, the city became a ready market for beer. Edward Uihlein went to Chicago and successfully arranged for wide-scale distribution of Schlitz beer. Sales jumped nearly 50 percent, and by 1872 Schlitz was using the slogan, "The Beer That Made Milwaukee Famous." This event evidently encouraged Schlitz and the Uihleins to expand the company to the status of a national brewer (q.v.). Agencies (q.v.) were established across the U.S. as bottled and pasteurized beer was shipped, often by rail, to distant markets. In 1877 Schlitz ranked tenth among the nation's brewers in sales (about 78,000 barrels) but climbed to third in 1895, with about 650,000 barrels produced. Pabst (q.v.) and Anheuser-Busch (q.v.) ranked first and second. Schlitz reached the million-barrel mark around the turn of the century. In 1906, Joseph Uihlein, Sr., August's son, assumed management of the company, but it was Alfred, August's brother, who kept the brewing operation open during Prohibition (q.v.) in the 1920s. Alfred, the last of the original brothers, died in 1935 at the age of eighty-two. Joseph Uihlein went into the chocolate business and produced a candy, "Eline," but it did not prove very successful. The brewery engaged in producing yeast and malt syrups, and the company reopened upon the repeal of Prohibition. Erwin C. Uihlein, August's son, became president in 1933 and held the post until 1961 when Robert A. Uihlein (q.v.), Erwin's nephew, took over as chief executive. Erwin died in 1968 at the age of eighty-two. Upon Robert's death in November 1976, Daniel F. McKeithan became chairman. Eugene Peters became president in early 1976 although the Uihlein family retained control of the stock. Frank J. Sellinger, formerly of Anheuser-Busch, succeeded Peters in November 1977. Expansion of the business began in earnest in 1949 when Schlitz purchased the Ehret (q.v.) brewery in Brooklyn. Although this plant was later closed, other brewery acquisitions were made; but the main emphasis was on building new plants. By 1977, seven plants were in operation in cities such as Winston-Salem, Los Angeles, Tampa, and Honolulu, where Primo is produced. The Old Milwaukee brand was its 1960 answer to other popular-priced beers. By late 1978, Schlitz's advertising decisions, and other factors, apparently cost the company its No. 2 ranking, and there were rumors of a takeover by R. J. Reynolds. Yet Schlitz unquestionably has been an important company in the nation's and Milwaukee's brewing tradition.

SOURCES: "The Battle of the Beers," *Newsweek* (September 4, 1978); Wayne Kroll, *Badger Breweries* (Jefferson, Wis., 1977); *Milwaukee Journal*, May 21, 1978; *One Hundred Years of Brewing* (Chicago and New York, 1903; Arno Press Reprint, 1974); "Schlitz Through the Years" (brief company history, ca. 1977).

Schmidt, Leopold F. (ca. 1845-active ca. 1920). The founder of the Olympia Brewing Company (q.v.) of Olympia, Washington, Schmidt was one of many German immigrants to the U.S. He came to America in 1866, moved to Butte, Montana, and by 1876 had entered into a brewing partnership with Daniel Gamer. They named their company the Centennial Brewery. Later Schmidt was elected to the Montana legislature and was a member of a committee to aid in the building of the state capital. On a journey to inspect buildings in Olympia, he was impressed by the area's brewing potential, moved his family there, and opened the Capital Brewing Company in 1896. In 1902, the name was changed to Olympia, and Schmidt continued as a successful brewer. His firm was one of the first to adopt the "Crown" bottling method (*see* Bottled Beer), and the company was important as one of the first breweries to market bottled beer on a wide scale.

SOURCES: Will Anderson, *The Beer Book* (Princeton, N.J., 1973); Olympia Brewing Company, *Annual Report, 1976.*

Schmidt, Jacob, Brewing Company. Jacob Schmidt and a partner purchased the St. Paul, Minnesota, brewery in 1884. They purchased the Milwaukee Brewing Company in St. Paul and operated the company under that name until 1896, when it was renamed North Star Brewing Company. In 1901 Schmidt bought the St. Paul Brewing Company and closed his North Star plant; the new company was called the Jacob Schmidt Brewing Company. Schmidt, an immigrant from Bavaria, had worked in a number of breweries before buying his own. Among them were Chicago's Keeley (q.v.) brewery, Schell (q.v.) of New Ulm, and the Best (q.v.), Blatz (q.v.) and Schlitz (q.v.) companies. In 1962, Associated Brewing Company (q.v.) purchased Jacob Schmidt and was in turn purchased by G. Heileman (q.v.) in 1971.

SOURCES: One Hundred Years of Brewing (Chicago and New York, 1903; Arno Press Reprint, 1974); James D. Robertson, *The Great American Beer Book* (Ottawa, Ill., 1978).

Schmidt's, C., & Sons, Inc. Christian Schmidt founded this regional brewing company in Philadelphia in 1860. An immigrant from Wurtemberg, Germany, Schmidt acquired Courtenay's brewery and established what proved to be a long-lived family brewing company. Schmidt headed the company until his death in 1895, and then his son, Edward A., ran the company until 1944. Afterward, Frederick W. Schmidt, Christian H. Zoller, a grandson, and Carl E. von Czoernig ran the company. Then in April 1976, William H. Pflaumer bought the company, and William T. Elliott became president. By the late 1970s Schmidt's was the tenth largest American brewery and had established itself as a major regional brewer (q.v.), with plants in Cleveland, Ohio, and Philadelphia. Valley Forge Brewing Company was acquired in the 1960s, Duquesne Brewing Company (q.v.) in 1972, and label and brewing rights to Reading and Bergheim were purchased in 1976, Rheingold (q.v.) in 1977, and Erie Brewing Company (q.v.) with its Koehler brands in 1978. These purchases apparently followed the trend of much earlier acquisitions made by Edward A. Schmidt soon after the turn of the century. Under Edward's leadership, Schmidt's acquired the Robert Smith Ale Brewing Company (q.v.) and the Peter Schemm concern, but evidently neither plant was reopened after the repeal of Prohibition (q.v.). Schmidt's, which was one of Philadelphia's two operating breweries by 1979 (Henry Ortlieb [q.v.] being the other), based much of its mid- and late-1970s advertising on very positive taste tests conducted by the Philadelphia *Inquirer* and two other more scientific surveys. In each, Schmidt's beer was ranked as a clean-tasting beer, outscoring other more famous and prestigious brews.

SOURCES: Stanley Baron, *Brewed in America* (Boston, 1962); *One Hundred Years of Brewing* (Chicago and New York, 1903; Arno Press Reprint, 1974); "Schmidt's of Philadelphia: A Corporate Profile" (brief company history, June 1978).

Schoenhofen-Edelweiss (Brewery). Peter Schoenhofen founded this Chicago brewery with Matheus Gottfried in 1861. Schoenhofen had migrated from Germany to the U.S. in 1851 at the age of twenty-four. In 1867, he purchased Gottfried's share in the business and it became known as the Peter Schoenhofen Brewing Company. When Schoenhofen died in 1893, he was succeeded by son-in-law Joseph Theurer. The company continued to operate as Schoenhofen until 1934 when the name was changed to Schoenhofen-Edelweiss as a result of a merger with the National Brewing Company of Chicago. During the late 1940s, the firm was taken over by Atlas Brewing Company. Drewry's Ltd. (q.v.), U.S.A., of South Bend, Indiana, acquired control in 1951. Drewry's closed the Chicago operation in 1971.

SOURCES: Richard J. La Susa, "Nevermore the Local Lagers," *Chicago Tribune Magazine* (April 24, 1977); *One Hundred Years of Brewing* (Chicago and New York, 1903; Arno Press Reprint, 1974).

Schoenhofen, Peter, Brewing Company. *See* Schoenhofen-Edelweiss (Brewery).

Schoenling Brewing Company. Founded by E. Schoenling in 1933, the Cincinnati brewery has been managed by the Schoenling family. It has managed to establish a solid reputation as a local brewing company marketing brews such as Little Kings (ale) and Sir Edward Stout. By the late 1970s, Schoenling and Hudepohl (q.v.) were the only remaining Cincinnati breweries.

SOURCES: William L. Downard, *The Cincinnati Brewing Industry* (Athens, Ohio, 1973); James D. Robertson, *The Great American Beer Book* (Ottawa, Ill., 1978).

Schuppert, A., Brewery. Apparently this was California's first brewery. It was founded by Adam Schuppert in San Francisco in 1849. The firm remained in operation until about 1870.

Schwarz, Anton (February 2, 1839-September 24, 1895). A brewing chemist, Schwarz migrated from Germany to the U.S. in 1868. After writing for the *American Brewer*, a new brewery journal in New York, Schwarz became editor and the publisher. In 1882, after years of frustration, Schwarz established a successful brewers' college, the U.S. Brewers' Academy.

SOURCE: John P. Arnold and Frank Penman, *History of the Brewing Industry and Brewing Science* (Chicago, 1933).

Scotch whisky. Scotch is a malt whiskey (q.v.) made mainly from barley (q.v.), commonly in a pot-still (*see* Still). It is normally blended with grain whiskies and aged in uncharred oak barrels for at least three years, although most Scotches are eight to ten years old. The smokey flavor is the result of the barley malt being heated over a peat fire. There is evidence that the Scots were among the first distillers, possibly in the 1730s, to age their whisky. Before the mid-nineteenth century, however, Scotch whisky was straight malt whiskey. Then Andrew Usher & Company, and others, began blending malt whiskies with grain whiskies. The grain whiskies were made from corn and a small amount of barley malt and were distilled in a column or patent still (*see* Still), mainly in lower Scotland. The blended whisky became popular outside Scotland where there was a demand for a lighter whisky. Thus the Scotch blend contains about 20 to 50 percent malt whiskey (q.v.) and the balance is grain whisky. The differences among various Scotches stem from the blending of malt and grain whiskies. Highland whiskies are fairly light and considered to be the finest, especially from the Banffshire and Glen Livet regions. Lowland malts are mainly light in body, whereas the products of Campbelltown and Islay are fuller-bodied and smokier in flavor.

SOURCES: Alexis Lichine's New Encyclopedia of Wines & Spirits (New York, 1974); Harold J. Grossman, *Grossman's Guide to Wines, Beers, and Spirits* (New York, 1977); Frank Haring, ed., *Practical Encyclopedia of Alcoholic Beverages* (New York, 1959).

Seagram, Joseph E., and Sons, Inc. The world's largest distiller in the late 1970s was established in the U.S. in the early 1930s, just after repeal of Prohibition (q.v.), by Canadian Samuel Bronfman (q.v.). Prior to building a distillery in LaSalle, near Montreal, in the 1920s, Bronfman had been in the liquor mail order business. The name of his distilling firm was Distillers Corporation Ltd., and he increased inventory by merging with the Distillers Company Limited of Great Britain in 1926. Two years later, Joseph E. Seagram and Sons, Ltd., of Ontario was acquired. Seagram had been founded in 1857 and added additional prestige and stocks of whiskey. The parent company became known as Distillers Corporation-Seagrams Limited (DC-SL). By 1928, Bronfman believed it would be only a few years before U.S. Prohibition would be repealed, and he was interested in entering the American market. Distillers Company Limited of Great Britain chose not to be involved, and Bronfman's firm purchased the company's shares. In 1933, Bronfman established offices in New York and launched the American operation. The Lawrenceburg distillery in Indiana was the first purchase, followed by acquisition of Calvert (q.v.) in Maryland. The plants were expanded and commenced distilling, but in the meantime Bronfman imported part of his Canadian inventories, blended them at his plants and introduced Seagram Five Crown and Seven Crown, which proved very popular. Calvert Reserve and Special followed and also sold well. In 1936, the firm built a new plant in Louisville. During the 1930s, Seagram built a new distillery in Puerto Rico (Ronrico) and purchased Frankfort Distilling Company (q.v.) and its Four Roses brand in 1944. Another subsidiary was organized in the early 1930s as the Kessler Distilling Company, with Julius Kessler (q.v.) as president. Later, in 1950, Seagram bought the controlling interest in Fromm and Sichel (q.v.), in part because of Bronfman's earlier friendship with Franz Sichel. The interest in wine led to the purchase of Paul Masson Vineyards and the Browne Vintners Company. Among the other acquisitions were Chivas Brothers Ltd. in 1935, Carstairs in 1937, Mattingly and Moore (q.v.) in 1940, and Henry McKenna (q.v.) in 1941. Over the years, two important executives of Seagram were president, Gen. Frank R. Schwengel and Victor Fischel, who was made president of the House of Seagram in 1955 in charge of sales. Edgar and Charles, the founder's sons, were groomed in every facet of the business and took over the management of the company in stride. Edgar had been vice-president of DC-SL since 1955, and since 1957 president of Joseph Seagram & Sons, Inc. He became president of DC-SL in 1971 and later chairman and chief executive of the parent company. Charles, who had been vice-president and director, since 1958, of the House of Seagram, Ltd., responsible for DC-SL interests in Canada, Jamaica, and Israel, became executive vice-president of the parent company in 1971. DC-SL became the Seagram Co., Ltd., in January 1975. Edgar Bronfman, fifty, is the chairman and chief executive officer. Charles Bronfman, forty-eight, is chairman of the executive committee. Philip Beekman became president of Joseph E. Seagram and Sons, Inc., and president of the parent company in 1977. Distillers Corporation-Seagrams Ltd. proved to be very diverse and expansive moving into oil and gas production with purchase of Texas Pacific Oil Company in the mid-1960s. In 1978 the firm operated thirteen distilleries in the U.S. and Canada and twelve in other countries.

SOURCES: Samuel Bronfman, *From Little Acorns* (Montreal, 1970); *Forty Years of Repeal* (New York, 1973); Peter C. Newman, *King of the Castle, the Making of a Dynasty: Seagram's & the Bronfman Empire* (New York, 1979); "The Seagram Saga," *Bev/Executive* (February-June 1966).

Sedlmayr, Gabriel (active, 1830s). A pioneer scientific brewer of Munich, Sedlmayr, along with Anton Dreher, is credited with the introduction of bottom-fermentation (q.v.) and early use of the saccharometer (q.v.). He also established a course of brewing studies.

SOURCE: One Hundred Years of Brewing (Chicago and New York, 1903; Arno Press Reprint, 1974).

Seipp, Conrad, Brewing Company. Conrad Seipp, who migrated to the U.S. from Germany in 1848 at the age of twenty-three, founded a brewery in Chicago. In 1854, he rented the M. Best brewery, but built his own the following year after the Best plant had been destroyed in a fire. Frederick Lehmann joined him in a partnership from 1858 to 1872, when Lehmann died. The company was known as Seipp & Lehmann in this period, but became Conrad Seipp Brewing Company in 1876 when Seipp purchased the Lehmann shares. In 1877, Seipp was the nation's fifth largest brewer, with output of 95,000 barrels. Shortly after Seipp's death in January 1890, the company merged with the West Side and F. J. Dewes breweries and the L. C. Huck (q.v.) and George Biellen malthouses to form the Chicago Consolidated Brewery and Malting Company. Each company retained its name and organization. The companies jointly had sales of 350,000 barrels at the turn of the century, but Seipp was the largest producer. F. J. Dewes apparently closed in 1905, and the West Side and Seipp firms continued until Prohibition in the 1920s but did not reopen afterward.

SOURCES: Manfred Friedrich and Donald Bull, *The Register of U.S. Breweries* (Trumbull, Conn., 1976); *One Hundred Years of Brewing* (Chicago and New York, 1903; Arno Press Reprint, 1974); A. Seipp and Ernest C. Schmidt, "History of Conrad Seipp & Family," 1944, ms. in Chicago Historical Society.

Shaw, Alex D., Company. Alexander David Shaw founded this wine-importing company in 1881. The main import product was Duff Gordon Sherry. When Shaw died in 1913, his son, Munson, took over the company. In 1933 he aligned Shaw with National Distillers Products Company (q.v.) but formed the Munson G. Shaw Company Inc. in 1938. Munson Shaw died in 1951 at the age of seventy-three.

SOURCES: Spirits (July 1951); "Whiskey," *Fortune* (November 1933).

Sherley, Joseph Swagar (November 28, 1871-February 13, 1941). Attorney and Democratic congressman (1903-19) from Louisville, Kentucky, Sherley represented the blended whiskey (q.v.) producers in the dispute over the Pure Food and Drug Act (q.v.). A result was the "Taft decision" (q.v.) of 1909, which granted concessions to the blenders and rectifiers.

SOURCES: Biographical Directory of the American Congress, 1774-1961 (Washington, D.C., 1961); Gerald Carson, *The Social History of Bourbon* (New York, 1963).

Sherley, Thomas H. (December 31, 1843-ca. 1900). A Louisville, Kentucky, distiller, Sherley entered the whiskey business as a commission merchant (q.v.) in 1869. He was connected with the New Hope (q.v.) and E. Miles distilleries, and was also noted for preparing a plan whereby the many Kentucky distilleries might be organized into a more efficient and profitable enterprise. Sherley's plan was instrumental in the formation of the Kentucky Distilleries and Warehouse Company (q.v.) in 1899.

SOURCES: Sam Elliot, *Nelson County Record* (Bardstown, Ky., 1896); *Spirits* (April 1935).

Shufeldt, Henry H., & Company. This Chicago distilling company was founded in 1857. After considerable intimidation, and even violence, the company joined the Whiskey Trust (q.v.) in 1892. The plant was closed, then reopened in Peoria in 1904, became a food products company in the 1920s, and eventually became a part of the National Distillers' Products Company (q.v.) around 1930.

SOURCES: Distilleries file, Peoria Historical Society; Ernest E. East, "The Distillers' and Cattle Feeders' Trust, 1887-1895," *Journal of the Illinois Historical Society* 45 (Summer 1952).

Siebel, John Ewald (September 17, 1845-December 20, 1919). A German-born physicist, chemist, publisher, and educator, Siebel helped found the first scientific school for practical brewers in Chicago in 1882. The school closed, however, and in 1901 was replaced by the forerunner of the Siebel Institute of Technology. Dr. Siebel was an editor for the journal *Western Brewer* and the 1903 edition of *One Hundred Years of Brewing*.

SOURCES: John P. Arnold and Frank Penman, *History of the Brewing Industry and Brewing Science* (Chicago, 1933).

Sieben's Brewery. Michael Sieben, a German immigrant, founded this Chicago firm in 1865. He merged his company with the United Breweries Company in 1896, but the company remained in the family until closing in 1967. It was noted for a *bier stube* and beer garden, the latter dating from 1903. Joseph Sieben, a third-generation brewer, closed the business because of declining sales and the disintegration of the formerly solid German neighborhood.

SOURCES: Richard J. La Susa, "Nevermore the Local Lagers," *Chicago Tribune Magazine*, (April 24, 1977); *One Hundred Years of Brewing* (Chicago and New York, 1903; Arno Press Reprint, 1974).

Simon, William, Brewery. John Schusler founded the brewery in 1859 in Buffalo, New York. It was incorporated as the John Schusler Brewing Company in 1889; William Simon became proprietor in 1896, and in 1900 the company's name was changed to the William Simon Brewery. The firm survived Prohibition (q.v.) and eventually had an annual capacity of 250,000 barrels output before closing in 1972.

SOURCE: Manfred Friedrich and Donald Bull, *The Register of U.S. Breweries* (Trumbull, Conn., 1976); *One Hundred Years of Brewing* (Chicago and New York, 1903; Arno Press Reprint, 1974).

Small beer. A pre-1900 beer, it was generally home-brewed and made of malt (q.v.) and various other adjuncts (q.v.) such as ginger, sugar, molasses, and honey. The term was used to differentiate it from standard or strong beer (q.v.), usually brewed by the common brewer (q.v.). Small beer was used to describe colonial beers, which were generally fairly low in alcoholic content, and were top-fermented (q.v.). A 1737 recipe for small beer was found in a notebook kept by President George Washington.

SOURCES: John P. Arnold and Frank Penman, *History of the Brewing Industry and Brewing Science* (Chicago, 1933); Stanley Baron, *Brewed in America* (Boston, 1962); Robert Beverly, *The History of the Present State of Virginia* (London, 1705; ed. by Louis Wright, 1947).

Smith, Robert, Ale Brewing Company. This Philadelphia ale (q.v.) brewing company (q.v.) went out of business with national Prohibition (q.v.) in the 1920s. The original plant was established in 1774 by Joseph Potts, who was succeeded by Henry Pepper & Son, who were in turn succeeded by Pepper & Sickel. Smith, who had learned the brewer's business in the Bass brewery in England, took over in 1837.

SOURCES: John P. Arnold and Frank Penman, *History of the Brewing Industry and Brewing Science* (Chicago, 1933); *One Hundred Years of Brewing* (Chicago and New York, 1903; Arno Press Reprint, 1974).

Somerset Importers, Ltd. Known as the Wine & Spirits Division of Canada Dry Corporation from 1933 to 1968, the Somerset name was adopted in the latter year with the formation of a parent company, Norton Simon, Inc. Somerset became a subsidiary of Norton Simon, which emerged from the consolidation of Canada Dry Corporation, Hunt Foods and Industries, and McCall Corp. Since 1933, Somerset had increased and expanded its position as a spirits-importing firm with central offices in New York. The acquisition of U.S. distribution rights to Johnnie Walker Red Label and Black Label Scotches in 1933 were supplemented over the years with Johnnie Walker Swing Scotch (1944), Canada Dry Bourbon (1955), Canada Dry Gin and Vodka (1956), Crawford's Scotch (1963), and Tanqueray Gin (1972). Somerset also acquired the facilities of the Stitzel-Weller Distillery, Inc. (q.v.), in 1972 and changed the company name to Old Fitzgerald after the company's main brand. Other brands are Cabin Still, Rebel Yell, and W. L. Weller. Continuing its aggressive position as an importer and marketer of spirits, Somerset acquired U.S. distribution rights to Pimm's (1973), Mandarine Napolean Liqueur (1975), Hine Cognacs (1975), and Aalborg Akvavit of Denmark (1976). In 1975 the company acquired Bass Charrington Vintners, U.S. marketing rights to Alexis Lichine wines, and in 1977 purchased San Martin Vineyards in California. Somerset was the largest distributor for Distillers Company Limited (DCL), the huge British spirits conglomerate. In 1975 John E. Heilmann, an agressive entrepreneur who had been president of Four Roses and Seagram (q.v.), assumed the position of president and chief executive officer at Somerset.

SOURCES: "A Chronology of Somerset Importers, Ltd." (brief company history, 1978); "The Somerset Story," *Associated Beverage Publications* (September 1977).

Sour mash. In distilling (q.v.), sour mash is the result of adding some fermented mash (q.v.) from an earlier run to mash that is in fermentation (q.v.). About one-fourth of the previous day's mash, called "spent beer" (*see* Stillage), is mixed with the yeast (q.v.) and added to the next batch of fermenting grains. Therefore, the sour mash process is also known as the yeasting-back process, or formerly, as "sloppin back." Although some distillers use the term "sour mash" in labeling, most bourbon (q.v.) has been, and is, processed by this method rather than the sweet mash (q.v.) procedure. The sour mash technique aids a distillery in achieving uniformity of flavor and also adds character to the distillate. Because the spent beer is somewhat acidic in taste, the term sour mash evolved, although the whiskey is as sweet as the product of the sweet mash method. The mash is also cooked longer in the sour mash procedure as fermenting occurs between seventy-two and ninety-six hours.

SOURCES: Gerald Carson, *The Social History of Bourbon* (New York, 1963); Harold J. Grossman, *Grossman's Guide to Wines, Beers, and Spirits* (New York, 1977).

Southern Comfort Corporation. Southern Comfort, a St. Louis, Missouri, distilling company, was established in February 1934, just after Repeal, by Frances E. Fowler, Jr., and Philip B. Fouke. "Southern Comfort" is the firm's brand and Francis E. Fowler III is president of the company. Brown-Forman (q.v.) acquired the company in March 1979.

Sparging. This is the last step in the mashing (q.v.) of malt for brewing. After wort (q.v.) has been removed, or lautered, from the spent grains, additional hot water is sprayed over the remaining wort and solids in a rinsing or sparging process. The objective is to remove more sugar from the mash, as well as to dilute the wort.

SOURCES: *One Hundred Years of Brewing* (Chicago and New York, 1903; Arno Press Reprint, 1974); Edward H. Vogel, Jr., et al., *The Practical Brewer* (St. Louis, Mo., 1946).

Speakeasy. Speakeasy is a synonym for a saloon, or bar, which, while operating prior to Prohibition (q.v.) in 1920, maintained a discreet existence after passage of the Eighteenth Amendment (q.v.). The "underground" speakeasies often became associated with organized-crime syndicates that gained control of the illegal liquor trade in many U.S. cities.

Spent beer. *See* Stillage.

Spirit. An alcoholic beverage obtained from distilling (q.v.) a liquid that contains alcohol, a spirit is also any potable distillate from grain, sugar cane, and so forth. *See also*, Whiskey.

Spoetzl Brewery, Inc. A group of local businessmen established the Shiner, Texas, brewery in 1909. They survived a shaky beginning and sold out to Kosmos Spoetzl in 1915. He improved the brew and managed to withstand Prohibition (q.v.) by producing near beer (q.v.) and ice. Upon his death in 1950 at the age of seventy-seven, Cecelie (Miss Celie), his daughter, assumed ownership and control of this small brewery. In 1966 she sold the business to brewmaster William Bigler, who incorporated the company but kept the Spoetzl name. Two years later, the brewery was sold again and Archie A. Ladshaw became president. The only brand is Shiner Premium Beer.

SOURCES: *The Shiner Gazette,* July 29, 1971; *Brewers Digest* (September 1966 and July 1971).

Stagg, George T., Distillery. Known as the OFC (Old Fire Copper) Distillery, the Frankfort, Kentucky, distillery was built in 1869. Col. E. H. Taylor, Jr. (q.v.), founded the original plant, but George T. Stagg became principal owner in 1873. Taylor was general manager and sold his stock to Stagg in 1886. Stagg died in the early 1890s, and the plant was purchased by the W. B. Duffy family, known in the East for Duffy's Malt Whiskey. Albert B. Blanton bought the plant in the 1920s; he produced medicinal whiskey but sold the plant to Industrial Grain Products of Buffalo, New York, which in turn sold the works to Schenley Distillers Corporation (q.v.) in 1929. Blanton, who began his work with Stagg in 1897 as office boy, ultimately served as distiller, manager, and onetime owner. Lewis Rosenstiel (q.v.) of Schenley retained Blanton to manage the plant; Blanton was also vice-president and board member at Schenley from 1941 until retirement in 1952. The distillery was the largest Schenley plant in Kentucky but was apparently phased out in the early 1970s.

SOURCE: Art Williams, "In the Kentucky Tradition: History of the Albert B. Blanton Distillery," *Spirits* (August 1953).

Standard Distilling and Distributing Company. Standard was subsidiary or branch of the Whiskey Trust (q.v.) organized in 1898 in Peoria, Illinois, under the laws of New Jersey. It was formed to operate the plants of the former Whiskey Trust that had not been organized by American Spirits Manufacturing Company (q.v.). Joseph B. Greenhut, president of the trust, and Julius Kessler (q.v.) were involved in the leadership of the company. Standard bought the Atlas Distilling Company (q.v.) in 1898 and continued to operate until about 1915. Standard was part of Distillers' Securities Corporation, which was ultimately reorganized as National Distillers Products Company (q.v.).

SOURCES: Distilleries file, Peoria Historical Society; Ernest E. East, "Joseph B. Greenhut and Whiskey Trust Enter Peoria Field," *Arrow Messenger* (April 1937), and "Distillery Fires at Corning Plant," *Arrow Messenger* (March 1937).

Standard Rochester Brewing Company, Inc. This was the 1956 merger of the Standard Brewing and Rochester Brewing companies. The Standard company, formerly known as the Flower City Brewing Company (q.v.), was organized after the repeal of Prohibition (q.v.) in 1933; the Rochester company had formerly been the Moerlbach Brewing Company and was also organized after Repeal (q.v.). The company closed the Standard plant in 1955 and the Rochester plant in 1970. Two other companies also operated as Rochester and Standard before Prohibition, but closed during the 1920s.

SOURCE: Manfred Friedrich and Donald Bull, *The Register of U.S. Breweries* (Trumbull, Conn., 1976).

Standards of identity for distilled spirits. Federal definitions for distilled spirits date mainly from the "Taft decision" (q.v.) of 1909 when President William Howard Taft (q.v.) ruled on interpretations of the Pure Food and Drug Act (q.v.). Upon repeal of Prohibition (q.v.) in 1933, the Federal Alcohol Administration (q.v.) and succeeding federal agencies (*see* Federal Liquor Regulations) further defined and classified distilled spirits, setting "standards of identity" for the various beverages. Among the classes of spirits are: (1) neutral spirits or alcohol, (2) whiskey, (3) gin, (4) brandy, (5) blended applejack, (6) rum, (7) tequila, and (8) cordials and liqueurs. Specifications include definitions, and the standards and processes for production. Thus the many types of alcoholic beverages such as vodka, bourbon whiskey, corn whiskey, light whiskey, Scotch whisky, and Canadian whisky are defined and specified. Malt liquors are also defined. The Federal Alcohol Administration Act of 1936 set forth the most precise definitions for manufacture and aging and marks the genesis of modern regulations and standards.

SOURCES: Gerald Carson, *The Social History of Bourbon* (New York, 1963); Harold J. Grossman, *Grossman's Guide to Wines, Beers, and Spirits* (New York, 1977); *Red Book, 1955-56, Encyclopedic Directory of the Wine and Liquor Industries*; U.S., Department of Justice, *Proceedings . . . Concerning the Meaning of the Term "Whisky"* (Washington, D.C., 1909); U.S., Treasury Department, Internal

Revenue Service, Alcohol, Tobacco Products and Firearms, Title 27, *Code of Federal Regulations*, Part 5, "Labelling and Advertising of Distilled Spirits," 1978.

State liquor regulations. Colonial and state legislation to regulate and control the alcoholic beverage trade originated prior to statehood in many of the colonies. The main impetus behind early regulation was to raise revenue, but conservation of cereal crops at critical periods and temperance factors also figured in the passage of various laws. Other early laws, in the 1630s and 1640s, prohibited the sale of liquor to Indians and slaves. In 1650, Connecticut limited drinking to one-half hour at a time; and in 1658 Maryland passed a law whereby drunkards had to be confined in stocks for six hours. Governor James Oglethorpe of Georgia attempted to quell drunkenness in 1733 by prohibiting importation of hard liquor into the colony. One of the first prohibitory laws was passed in Indiana in 1816 when the legislature forbade Sunday liquor sales. As temperance (q.v.) agitation grew in the 1830s and 1840s, Georgia permitted local option (q.v.) in 1837, and Maine passed the first statewide prohibition law in 1846. Although the movement subsided in the 1860s and 1870s, it gained momentum again in the late nineteenth century and states passed more and more regulatory laws. With the enactment of national prohibition in 1919, the federal government superseded state controls; but upon repeal of Prohibition (q.v.) in 1933, the states once again were given wider prerogatives over liquor control. Although the states have secondary control, and laws may not conflict with federal legislation, state regulations may be more stringent than federal controls. There are currently two types of state control: (1) open-license states, in which private business makes sales of alcoholic beverages to on-premises and off-premises consumers; (2) control or monopoly states, which control the sale of all alcoholic beverages, or that of distilled spirits and certain wines in the state. In open-license states the business operates as a competitive enterprise and excise and sales taxes are collected, whereas in control states brands, prices, and revenues are controlled by the states. There has been, and is, a vast network of varying regulations in the states collectively and individually.

SOURCES: John P. Arnold and Frank Penman, *History of the Brewing Industry and Brewing Science* (Chicago, 1933); Stanley Baron, *Brewed in America* (Boston, 1962); Distilled Spirits Council of the U.S., *1975 Public Revenues from Alcohol Beverages* (Washington, D.C., 1977); Oscar Getz, *Whiskey: An American Pictorial History* (New York, 1978); Harold J. Grossman, *Grossman's Guide to Wines, Beers, and Spirits* (New York, 1977); Licensed Beverage Industries, *The Alcohol Beverage Industry and the National Economy* (New York, 1973); Morris Victor Rosenbloom, *The Liquor Industry* (Braddock, Pa., 1937).

Stave. The term applies to a narrow piece of wood used in making barrels (q.v.) or cooperage (q.v.) in brewing and distilling.

Steam beer. Originating on the Pacific coast, probably in California, this beer resulted from the necessity to ferment beer at higher temperatures than lager (q.v.). Whereas lager, a bottom-fermentation (q.v.) product, requires a cool temperature, steam beer could be fermented at all temperatures (about 65° Fahrenheit), but also with bottom-fermentation yeast. Thus beer similar to lager could be brewed on the West Coast even though natural ice supplies were unavailable in the warm climate. Special fermenters enabled the brewing of this beer, which was developed in the mid-nineteenth century. It was called steam beer because of the strong carbonation in the krauesening (q.v.) stage and resulting buildup of "steam" in the barrel, which was released when racking (q.v.). One popular feature of this beer was that it could be brewed and ready for consumption in just a few weeks. One source maintains that steam beer is the result of the only uniquely American brewing process. Today, the small Anchor Brewing Company (q.v.) of San Francisco lays claim to being the sole surviving steam beer brewery.

SOURCES: John P. Arnold and Frank Penman, *History of the Brewing Industry and Brewing Science* (Chicago, 1933); Michael Jackson, ed., *The World Guide to Beer* (Englewood Cliffs, N.J., 1977); *One Hundred Years of Brewing* (Chicago and New York, 1903; Arno Press Reprint, 1974); *The Western Brewer* 23 (February 15, 1898).

Steeping. Grain, usually barley (q.v.), is soaked in the malting stage for brewing and distilling, until it is softened and ready for germination (q.v.).

Stegmaier Brewing Company. Charles Stegmaier, an immigrant from Wurtemburg, Germany, established his brewery in Wilkes Barre, Pennsylvania, in the late 1850s. After working for a number of brewing firms, Stegmaier entered the bottling business and then went into a brewery partnership with George C. Baer. They closed as a result of the depression of 1873, and after a venture in the hotel business, Stegmaier rented the Bowkley Brewery before repurchasing the Baer and Stegmaier plant in 1880. Charles's son, Christian, joined the founder, and the company was known as C. Stegmaier and Son until 1896 when it was incorporated as the Stegmaier Brewing Company. The brewery survived Prohibition (q.v.) but closed in 1974.

SOURCES: Manfred Friedrich and Donald Bull, *The Register of U.S. Breweries* (Trumbull, Conn., 1976); *One Hundred Years of Brewing* (Chicago and New York, 1903; Arno Press Reprint, 1974).

Sterling Breweries, Inc. The Evansville, Indiana, firm was founded by Henry Schneider in 1863. After changing hands a number of times, John Hartmetz bought the brewery in 1877 and it carried his name. During the 1890s, an era of intense competition, the Hartmetz brewery merged with the

Evansville Brewery and the Fulton Avenue Brewery. The 1894 merger was known as the Evansville Brewing Association, and would later become Sterling, named after one of its brands of beer. To cope with Prohibition (q.v.) in the 1920s, the association formed two companies, Sterling Products Company and Sterling Refining Company. After repeal of Prohibition, Sterling Breweries, Inc., resumed operation as a brewery. The Hartmetz family continued to exercise an important role in management, but R. T. Riney was president from 1934 to 1963. Soon after he became chairman, Sterling became part of the Associated Brewing Company (q.v.), which was in turn acquired by G. Heileman (q.v.) in 1971.

SOURCES: *One Hundred Years of Brewing* (Chicago and New York, 1903; Arno Press Reprint, 1974); James D. Robertson, *The Great American Beer Book* (Ottawa, Ill., 1978); "The Sterling Story," *Brewers Digest* (July 1963).

Stevens Point Beverage Company. The origins of this Stevens Point, Wisconsin, brewery date to the late 1850s. Afterward it changed hands two times, and Gustav Kuenzel bought the company in the late 1890s, operating it as the Gustav Kuenzel Brewing Company. In 1902, the year after Kuenzel's death, the plant was incorporated as the Stevens Point Brewing Company. The company closed during Prohibition (q.v.) but reopened as the Stevens Point Beverage Company in 1933. The new president was Ludwig Korffman, who headed the company until the late 1940s when Calvin Korffman replaced him. In 1970, Felix Shibilski succeeded him. The brewery was the smallest in Wisconsin but remained a successful operation in the late 1970s.

SOURCES: Wayne Kroll, *Badger Breweries* (Jefferson, Wis., 1976); James D. Robertson, *The Great American Beer Book* (Ottawa, Ill., 1978).

Still. An apparatus used in the whiskey-making process (q.v.), the still separates alcohol and other volatile ingredients from the fermented wort (q.v.). The vapors are cooled and condensed and collected in liquid form. Alembic, deriving from Arabic terminology, was a very early name for a still, and was usually a pot for boiling. Early American pot-stills were normally made of copper and shaped like kettles. A long neck was attached for collecting the vapors, which were condensed in a spiral tube known as a worm (q.v.). The worm was placed in a tub of cold water that was circulated. After being drawn off, the low wine (q.v.) was distilled a second time in another pot-still, a doubler (q.v.). Other more primitive stills were made from hollowed logs about ten feet in length. The log would be split, hollowed, and then a copper tube was run through it and the two halves joined. Steam was sent through the pipe, and the low wine was carried to a doubler pot for the second distillation. This practice was known as "making it on a log" or "running it on a log." During the 1870s, the pot-still was gradually replaced by the three-chambered charge still and then by the continuous, or column, still, which is the most common type today. The continuous still evolved from Englishman Aeneas Coffey's "patent" still of the 1830s. Coffey made improvements on Scotsman Robert Stein's earlier still. Rather than a batch of fermented mash (q.v.) being put in, in the pot-still manner, the mash is fed into the top of the still continuously. The still contains a column of perforated plates, the mash flows down, is met by steam coming up from the bottom, and the alcohol is vaporized and flows into a condenser. Another improvement in distilling occurred in the early nineteenth century with the application of steam in raising the temperature of mash. The introduction of boilers would obviate the need for direct fire under the pot and thus the ever-present possibility of burning the mash. Steam distilleries grew in number after 1800.

SOURCES: Gerald Carson, *The Social History of Bourbon* (New York, 1963); Henry G. Crowgey, *Kentucky Bourbon* (Lexington, Ky., 1971); Harold J. Grossman, *Grossman's Guide to Wines, Beers, and Spirits* (New York, 1977); W. J. Rorabaugh, *The Alcoholic Republic* (New York, 1979); H. F. Willkie, *Beverage Spirits in America* (New York, 1949).

Stillage. A by-product resulting from the distilling of fermented mash (q.v.), stillage is also known as "spent beer." The highly nutritious grain is dried and used as feed supplements to livestock and poultry feeds.

Stitzel-Weller Distillery, Inc. The Louisville, Kentucky, firm resulted from a merger of two nineteenth-century firms. William LaRue Weller founded W. L. Weller & Sons in 1849. In the 1860s he was known for "selling honest whiskey at an honest price." The firm hired Julian Van Winkle (q.v.) in 1893 as a salesman. In 1908, he and fellow salesman Alex T. Farnsley bought the Weller company after Weller's death. The Stitzel firm was founded in 1872 by Philip Stitzel, who was joined by his brother, Frederick. A second plant was built in 1903 and soon after the firm became associated with the Weller company. Stitzel would supply Weller, which was noted for whiskey marketing, with several thousand barrels per year. Their association continued through Prohibition (q.v.) as Stitzel produced medicinal whiskey. Weller purchased a part interest, and the Stitzel-Weller Distillery, Inc., was established in a new plant in Shively, Kentucky, in 1935. The firm's most famous brand was, and is, Old Fitzgerald, a whiskey named after distiller John E. Fitzgerald, who became noted for his quality product in 1870. Van Winkle, president of Weller and then Stitzel-Weller, purchased the stock and brand names in the 1920s from Milwaukeean Sam Herbst, owner of the Old Fitzgerald distillery near Frankfort. Van Winkle brought his son, Julian, Jr., and son-in-law, King McClure, into the business. In 1972 the company became known as the Old Fitzgerald Distillery,

Inc., a move undertaken by Somerset Importers, Ltd. (q.v.), which purchased Stitzel-Weller in that year.

SOURCES: Dorothy L. Korell, "Bourbon Capital of the World," *Louisville* (October 20, 1965); Stan Jones, *Jones' Complete Barguide* (Los Angeles, 1977); "Van Winkle Sees Bourbon Boom," *Spirits* (May 1943).

Stout. A malt drink, similar to porter (q.v.) but darker and with a stronger malt (q.v.) flavor and taste, stout is made with the top-fermentation (q.v.) method.

Straight whiskey. This is whiskey (q.v.) distilled at no higher than 160 proof (q.v.) and aged in new charred oak barrels for at least two years. Upon bottling, water may be added to lower the proof to a minimum of 80 proof. Generally, straight whiskey is aged four years or more and distilled at under 160 proof, often between 110 and 130 proof. A minimum of 51 percent of a grain must be used, but straight whiskies may be bourbon (q.v.), rye (q.v.), corn (q.v.), wheat (q.v.), or Tennessee whiskey (q.v.). Only straight whiskies are bottled-in-bond (q.v.), although other distilled spirits such as rum (q.v.), gin (q.v.), and brandy (q.v.) may be if federal regulations are followed. Until the early twentieth century straight-whiskey producers usually referred to their product as "pure" whiskey. However, when the controversy over the definition of true whiskey emerged during the debate over the interpretation of the Pure Food and Drug Act (q.v.), the term "straight" was substituted for "pure." Producers of the drink changed the terminology because blended whiskey (q.v.) interests could lay better claim to the "pure" label, because their product contained fewer congeners (q.v.) and fusel oils (q.v.). *See also*, Taft Decision.

SOURCES: Gerald Carson, *The Social History of Bourbon* (New York, 1963); Harold J. Grossman, *Grossman's Guide to Wines, Beers, and Spirits* (New York, 1977); *Spirits* (August 1937).

Straub Brewery. John N. Straub founded the Pittsburgh brewery in 1831. In 1848 he moved to a new brewery in Allegheny City, but his son, Herman, continued to operate the Pittsburgh plant. The brewery became part of the consolidation known as the Pittsburgh Brewing Company (q.v.) in 1899.

SOURCES: *One Hundred Years of Brewing* (Chicago and New York, 1903; Arno Press Reprint, 1974); "Pittsburgh, History of Beer and a Market," *American Brewer* (June and July 1960).

Straub Brewery, Inc. The small brewery in St. Mary's, Pennsylvania, traces its origins to 1872. Known as the Peter Straub brewery until 1911, it was evidently called the Benjamin Spring Brewery from 1911 to 1913 and then Peter Straub Sons until the current name was adopted after Repeal (q.v.) in

1933. The company markets a local beer to a local populace, eschews advertising, and limits production.

SOURCE: James D. Robertson, *The Great American Beer Book* (Ottawa, Ill., 1978).

Stroh, Bernhard, Sr. (1822-June, 1882). A German-born brewer, Stroh migrated from Kirn in the Palatinate to the U.S. in 1848. Stroh had learned the brewer's trade from the family, especially his father, George Friedrich. Young Stroh apparently left home for political reasons, settled in Brazil for a time, but headed for Chicago. During a stop in Detroit, he decided to settle in the Michigan city and subsequently established a small brewery near the site of the present company. Known as B. Stroh (or Strow in some directories), Brewer, he personally delivered his light lager (q.v.) brew. He bought more land on Gratiot Avenue for the brewery in 1865, built a Victorian-style home nearby, and raised a family of five sons and two daughters. Stroh adopted the Lion Crest from Kyrburg Castle in Kirn, Germany, in 1870 and the crest has continued in company advertising. Stroh was succeeded in 1882 by Bernhard Stroh, Jr., his eldest son.

SOURCES: Will Anderson, *The Beer Book* (Princeton, N.J., 1973); *Brewers Digest* (September 1975).

Stroh Brewery Company. The regional Detroit, Michigan, brewery was founded in 1850 by German immigrant Bernhard Stroh (q.v.). The plant succeeded, and Stroh called it the Lion Brewery. The B. Stroh Brewing Company became the official name in 1882 and was changed to the present name, the Stroh Brewery Company, in 1909. Stroh had five sons; upon Bernhard, Sr.'s, death in June 1882, Bernhard, Jr., succeeded as president. Although remaining primarily a regional brewery, the company shipped a portion of its brew as far as Florida and Massachusetts. Pasteurization (q.v.) and refrigerated railcar transport permitted this late nineteenth-century development. Julius Stroh, a brother, succeeded Bernhard in 1908, and he is credited with returning to the fire-brewed process of brewing beer over direct fire rather than steam as was, and is, the more common process. During Prohibition (q.v.) in the 1920s, as the Stroh Products Company, Julius maintained the business by manufacturing near beer (q.v.), soft drinks, malt products, and ice cream—with the latter still being produced. Julius Stroh died in 1939 and his son, Gari Stroh, assumed the presidency and held the position until his death in 1950 at age fifty-four. John W. Stroh, his brother, took over as president and continued in the office until becoming chairman in 1967. John W. Shenefield, a company executive, was elected president and then was succeeded by Peter W. Stroh, Gari's son, in 1968. In 1964, in an expansion move, Stroh's acquired the Goebel Brewing Company (q.v.), a nearby Detroit brewery. By the late 1970s, Stroh's continued as a successful regional firm well-entrenched among the top ten, with more than 6 million barrels being produced.

SOURCES: *Brewers Digest* (September 1975); David T. Glick, "The Beverage of Moderation: Brief History of Michigan Brewing Industry," *Chronicle* (Summer 1977); *One Hundred Years of Brewing* (Chicago and New York, 1903; Arno Press Reprint, 1974); Stroh Brewery Company, "A History of the Stroh Brewery Company," (ca. 1977).

Strong beer. A commercial product of the colonial period in America, the beer was brewed by a common brewer (q.v.), was higher in alcoholic content than home-brewed beer, and was top-fermented.

Sunday, William Ashley (November 18, 1862-November 6, 1935). Popularly known as "Billy," the famous evangelist and revivalist gained fame in the early twentieth century. He became a staunch enemy of the liquor traffic and railed against the abuses of the saloon, which fostered gambling and prostitution among other vices.

SOURCE: *Dictionary of American Biography*, vol. 21.

Sunny Brook Distillery Company. The Rosenfield brothers opened the Louisville, Kentucky, firm in the early 1890s. They were commission merchants (q.v.) centered in Minneapolis, Minnesota. The plant was purchased by National Distillers Products Company as Prohibition (q.v.) came to a close in 1933.

SOURCES: "Great Names in Whiskey," *Spirits* (May 1937); "Whiskey," *Fortune* (November 1933).

Sweet mash. In this yeasting (q.v.) process employed in distilling (q.v.), virtually all fresh yeast (q.v.) is added to the mash (q.v.). It is also known as the yeast-mash method, in contrast to the sour-mash (q.v.) technique in which "spent beer" (*see* Stillage) from the previous day's mash is added back to the current mash. Relatively few distillers have used the sweet mash method over the years.

Swimmer. The term applies to a small metal container containing ice that was floated on bottom-fermentation (q.v.) lager beer (q.v.) during fermentation to hold the temperature under 45° Fahrenheit. Swimmers were officially known as attemperators. Patented in the late eighteenth century, these vessels were replaced after 1870 by more modern refrigeration methods and devices such as attemperating coils.

SOURCES: Thomas C. Cochran, *The Pabst Brewing Company* (New York, 1948); *One Hundred Years of Brewing* (Chicago and New York, 1903; Arno Press Reprint, 1974).

Syndicates, brewery. *See* Consolidations, Brewery.

Syracuse brewing industry. Syracuse, a city in western New York State, grew in population and breweries during the early nineteenth century. Johann Mang built the city's first commercial brewery in 1804, but his company lasted only a short time. By 1860 about twenty-two firms were operating because the city had grown as the result of westward expansion and the Erie Canal, which encouraged transport of people and products. Two of the more notable firms reopening in the 1930s after Repeal (q.v.) were Greenway (q.v.) and Haberle (q.v.), although Zett, Bartels, and Moore & Quinn also reopened. By the mid-1960s no brewery was operating in the city, however, as Haberle was the last to close in 1962.

SOURCES: Michael Gimigliano, "The Golden Age of Gambrinus—Brief History of Early Brewing in Syracuse," *Brewers Digest* (November 1975); *One Hundred Years of Brewing* (Chicago and New York, 1903; Arno Press Reprint, 1974).

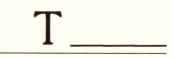

T. W. Samuel Distillery. *See* Maker's Mark Distillery, Inc.

Taft decision. In 1909 President William Howard Taft rendered a decision establishing "standards of identity" for various types of whiskey. The Pure Food and Drug Act of 1906 (q.v.) had been interpreted to consider whiskey as straight bourbon exclusively, whereas blended whiskey had to be labeled as "compound," "imitation," or "blended." At the urging of many liquor industry figures, mainly the blenders, Taft reopened a hearing on the issue. He ruled that both blended and straight whiskey could be defined as whiskey because, traditionally, virtually all beverage liquor distilled from grain had been considered as whiskey. Nevertheless, the differences among the types, such as bourbon, blended, straight, and so on, were to be spelled out and whiskey labeled as such. Taft's decision led to specifications for various liquor types based on methods of manufacture; subsequent federal regulations stem largely from the 1909 decision.

SOURCES: Gerald Carson, *The Social History of Bourbon* (New York, 1963); U.S. Department of Justice, *Proceedings . . . Concerning the Meaning of the Term "Whisky"* (Washington, D.C., 1909); H. F. Willkie, *Beverage Spirits in America: A Brief History* (New York, 1949).

Taft, William Howard (September 15, 1857-March 8, 1930). Born in Cincinnati, Ohio, Taft was the Republican president of the U.S. from 1909 to 1913. His involvement with the distilling industry stemmed from interpretations of the Pure Food and Drug Act (q.v.) that he modified in what became known as the "Taft decision" (q.v.) of 1909. Standards of identity were established, and various whiskey types in addition to straight whiskey were permitted to be marketed. Previously, the Kentucky interests had successfully lobbied for an interpretation that allowed only straight whiskey to be marketed legally as true whiskey, thus hampering sales of blended whiskey.

SOURCES: Gerald, Carson, *The Social History of Bourbon* (New York, 1963); H. F. Willkie, *Beverage Spirits in America: A Brief History* (New York, 1949).

Tap-tree. This is a round shaft of wood, with a wisp of straw wound around it. In brewing, the shaft acted as a plug for the mash tun (q.v.) and was loosened in order to permit the wort (q.v.) to run down into the underback (q.v.) as it was filtered from the mash (q.v.). The process was mechanized and improved during the nineteenth century as false bottoms, and, later, pumps, came into wider use and replaced the tap-tree. *See also*, Lauter Tun.

Taxation of distilled spirits and malt liquors, State. Since the 1600s, various forms of colonial and subsequently state taxation have been levied on distilled and malt liquors. The earliest laws were aimed primarily at control of the trade through the sale of licenses to taverns and other drinking houses. Even so, the Dutch colony of New Amsterdam levied an excise tax on spirits in the 1640s, mainly as a source of revenue, and a number of other colonies and states did put excise taxes on liquors. Generally, however, state taxes prior to Repeal (q.v.) were occupational in that distillers, brewers, and tavern keepers had to purchase licenses. Since Repeal in 1933 most states have levied per barrel taxes on beer that averaged $2.08 in 1948 and $3.70 in 1967. Distilled spirits were taxed an average of $0.66 per gallon in 1933, $1.53 in 1948, $2.09 in 1967, and $2.63 in 1976. Higher taxes on distilled spirits have traditionally reflected an attempt on the part of state (and federal) authorities to discourage consumption in relation to malt liquor products, which carry a lighter tax.

SOURCES: Stanley Baron, *Brewed in America* (Boston, 1962); Henry G. Crowgey, *Kentucky Bourbon* (Lexington, Ky., 1971); Distilled Spirits Council of the U.S., *Distilled Spirits Industry Annual Statistical Review, 1976* (Washington, D.C., 1977); Orba F. Traylor, "Taxation of Distilled Spirits in Kentucky and Other States," unpub. Ph.D. dissertation, University of Kentucky, 1948: U.S. Brewers' Association, *Brewers Almanac* (1968).

Taxation of distilled spirits, Federal. The Excise Act of 1791 (q.v.) was passed on March 3 and became effective July 1, 1791. Secretary of Treasury Alexander Hamilton, appointed by President George Washington, proposed in his Report on the Public Credit in January 1790 that an excise tax be levied on distilled spirits. Hamilton argued that the tax would provide a needed source of revenue and, in addition, would encourage the drinking of cider and malt liquors over ardent spirits. Thus the tax had a built-in temperance factor in an era of increasing consumption of hard liquor (*see* Temperance, and Prohibition). The tax, which ranged from $0.09 to $0.25 per gallon according to proof (q.v.), proved very unpopular, especially among the farmer-distillers (q.v.) of western Pennsylvania. Because of protests Congress modified the tax on July 1, 1792, incorporating gradual reductions from $0.02 to $0.07 per gallon and lower taxes on small stills. The attempt to pacify western distillers proved inadequate, however, and the tax ultimately resulted in the Whiskey Rebellion (q.v.) of 1794. In 1802, Congress repealed the tax as collection proved difficult and burdensome compared with net revenues, and the Jefferson administration opposed the tax anyway. Then, in order to pay off federal debts incurred in the War of 1812, Congress passed a new tax on distilleries and followed it with a tax of $0.20 per proof gallon. These taxes were in effect from January 1, 1814, to December 31, 1817. From 1818 to 1862 no internal revenue taxes were levied on distilled spirits. In September 1862 Congress reimposed the tax on distilled spirits as a means of financing the Civil War. The rate began at $0.20 per proof gallon and eventually reached $2 per gallon before being lowered to $0.50 in 1868. Illegal distilling had become so widespread that the tax was lowered as an incentive for payment. Between 1862 and 1894, federal taxes did not apply to whiskey stocks in storage. Thus a great deal of speculation and production occurred before the effective date of any tax. Those who held warehouse receipts (q.v.) or whiskey in storage benefited because the nonretroactive tax had the effect of increasing the value of their inventories. In 1894, the law was changed to include old, as well as new, whiskey. Thereafter the tax remained in existence, with gradual increases during wartime when the rate was normally increased more substantially. In 1951, as a result of the Korean conflict, Congress raised the rate to $10.50, a figure made "permanent" in 1964; it remains the current rate. *See also*, Appendix VII.

SOURCES: John P. Arnold and Frank Penman, *History of the Brewing Industry and Brewing Science* (Chicago, 1933); Gerald Carson, *The Social History of Bourbon* (New York, 1963); Henry G. Crowgey, *Kentucky Bourbon* (Lexington, Ky., 1971); Distilled Spirits Council of the U.S., *1977 Tax Briefs* (Washington, D.C., 1977); Oscar Getz, *Whiskey: An American Pictorial History* (New York, 1978); H. F. Willkie, *Beverage Spirits in America: A Brief History* (New York, 1949).

Taxation of malt liquors, Federal. The first direct federal internal revenue tax on malt liquors was passed in July 1862, to become effective on September 1. Congress passed the Internal Revenue Act of 1862 (q.v.) as a means of aiding the Civil War effort. Earlier duties had been imposed on imported malt liquors, but the 1862 tax was the initial taxation of the domestic industry. The Excise Act of 1791 (q.v.) included a provision for taxation of distilled spirits, but malt liquors were exempted, partially to encourage the consumption of the milder beverage. The 1862 law placed a tax of $1 per barrel on all beer sold plus a license fee for individual brewers. Brewers generally accepted the tax as necessary and responded with a sense of patriotism, but the law also prompted the organization of the U.S. Brewers' Association (USBA) (q.v.), which would enable the industry to respond to federal legislation with a degree of unity. The association achieved a reduction in the tax to $0.60 from March 1863 to March 1864, but the levy was raised once again to $1 at that time and remained there until 1898 when the Spanish-American War led to an increase to $2 per barrel. In 1901, the tax was reduced but then increased to $3 by 1919. After the repeal of Prohibition (q.v.) in 1933 the tax was set at $5 per barrel and was increased gradually until 1951 when the rate stabilized at $9 per barrel. When necessary, the USBA urged that changes be made in federal tax laws. An important change occurred in June 1890. The tax law had been imposed prior to the expansion of beer bottling and specified that a canceled stamp had to be placed over the bung-hole of the barrel to indicate payment of the tax. If the beer was to be bottled, the barrel had to be transported to separate bottling houses for filling the bottles. Capt. Fred Pabst (q.v.) and the USBA were instrumental in achieving the modification of 1890 permitting pipelines to carry the beer from cellars to bottling houses. Since 1933, federal taxing regulations have been modified to meet changing technology. *See also*, Appendix VI.

SOURCES: John P. Arnold and Frank Penman, *History of Brewing Industry and Brewing Science* (Chicago, 1933); Stanley Baron, *Brewed in America* (Boston, 1962); Thomas C. Cochran, *The Pabst Brewing Company* (New York, 1948); *One Hundred Years of Brewing* (Chicago and New York, 1903, Arno Press Reprint, 1974); USBA, *Brewers Almanac* (1974).

Taylor, Edmund H., Jr. (1832-1922). A noted distilling-industry figure, Taylor stressed the importance of quality "goods" and, as such, was a main factor in the passage of the Bottled-in-Bond Act of 1897 (*see* Bottled-in-Bond). He had been in banking in Versailles, Kentucky, and then entered the distilling business. One of his businesses was known as the J. Swigert Taylor distillery, and he marketed the famous Old Taylor. He also built the OFC and Carlisle distilleries but sold them to George T. Stagg (*see* Stagg, George T., Distillery). Colonel Taylor also operated E. H. Taylor, Jr., & Sons on Glenn's Creek near Frankfort. He was mayor of Frankfort, Kentucky, for a number of years. The Old Taylor brands and firm were purchased from his sons by National Distillers Products Company (q.v.) in 1929. During the 1909 hearing on the meaning of the term "whiskey," Taylor testified on behalf of the straight-whiskey producers. *See also*, Taft Decision.

SOURCES: Gerald Carson, *The Social History of Bourbon* (New York, 1963); *Kentucky's Distilling Interests* (Lexington, Ky., 1893); A. C. Stagg, "Report of Distilled Spirits, 1882-1884," unpub. list, 1950, Frankfort, Kentucky State Historical Society; U.S. Department of Justice, *Proceedings . . . Concerning the Meaning of the Term "Whisky"* (Washington, D.C., 1909).

Taylor, John, & Sons (Brewery). John Taylor and Lancelot Fiddler founded the Albany, New York, ale brewery in 1824. Taylor became sole owner later on and claimed by 1850 to have the largest brewery in the world. The company, known as Taylor Brewing & Malting Company after 1887, closed about 1905.

SOURCE: Stanley Baron, *Brewed in America* (Boston, 1962).

Taylor, K., Distilling Company. The Frankfort, Kentucky, distillery was established in 1934 by Kenner Taylor, son of Col. E. H. Taylor, Jr. (q.v.). Kenner Taylor died a short time after the opening of the business and A. L. Hinze, a longtime distillery executive, replaced him as president. The company was purchased by National Distillers Products Company (q.v.) in 1940 for approximately $2 million. The plant has since operated as the Old Grand Dad Distillery Company.

SOURCES: "Biographies," *Spirits* (May 1936); "K. Taylor Traces Line to Founders," *Spirits* (April 1935); *Spirits* (September 1940).

Taylor & Williams Distillery. *See* Dant, J. B., Distillery.

Temperance. The movement to discourage the use of alcoholic beverages began in the colonial era. Various laws were passed in colonial legislatures to discourage the use of intoxicants, and there were specific injunctions against selling or giving such drinks, notably spirits, to Indians or blacks. Liquor consumption was especially high in the late eighteenth and early nineteenth centuries as drinking alcoholic beverages was part of the lifestyle of Americans. Organized efforts for temperance—initially limitation rather than prohibition of drink—began in the 1820s, notably with the founding of the American Society for the Promotion of Temperance in 1826. The Washington Temperance Society (q.v.) and passage of the Maine Liquor Law (q.v.) in 1846 continued the early nineteenth-century drive, which was revived by the Women's Christian Temperance Union (q.v.), the Anti-Saloon League (q.v.), and other similar groups later in the century. The temperance movement became virtually synonymous with prohibition in the late 1800s as the sentiment for outlawing drink gained momentum and, of course, culminated in the Eighteenth Amendment (q.v.) in 1920. There is ample evidence that already in the colonial period, a distinction was being made between ardent spirits and malt, or fermented, beverages. Thus one aspect of temperance was to discourage the one and encourage the other —and the Excise Tax of 1791 (q.v.) was in part an example of such tendencies. Secretary of Treasury Alexander Hamilton, for instance, noted in his economic reports that beer and fermented beverages had a "moralizing tendency and salubrious nature." As prohibition advocates gained momentum in the early nineteenth century, temperance proponents often extolled the "moderate" virtues of beer. Whiskey consumption declined while beer consumption increased, in part, of course, owing to the influx of German immigrants. Brewing interests have stressed such differences also in an attempt to mute the forces of prohibition as regards beer—but, obviously, it had limited effect in the early 1900s as prohibition sentiment gained strength and culminated in nationwide Prohibition in 1920. *See also*, Prohibition, and with respect to liquor consumption *see* Appendixes I and II.

SOURCES: John P. Arnold and Frank Penman, *History of the Brewing Industry and Brewing Science* (Chicago, 1933); Jack S. Blocker, Jr., ed., *Alcohol, Reform and Society* (Westport, Conn., 1979); John A. Krout, *The Origins of Prohibition* (New York, 1925); W. J. Rorabaugh, *The Alcoholic Republic* (New York, 1979); Alice Felt Tyler, *Freedom's Ferment* (New York, 1962; 1st ed., 1944); Ian R. Tyrrell, *Sobering Up: From Temperance to Prohibition in Antebellum America, 1800-1860* (Westport, Conn., 1979).

Tennessee whiskey. This is a straight whiskey (q.v.) that must be distilled in Tennessee from a mash (q.v.) containing 51 percent of any grain. As in the case of bourbon (q.v.), however, corn is the primary grain used and the whiskey is distilled at less than 160 proof (q.v.). In 1941, Reagor Motlow (q.v.) of the Jack Daniel Distillery (q.v.) successfully argued to the Alcohol Tax Unit of the Treasury Department, that Tennessee's whiskey, in this case Jack Daniel's, was distinct from bourbon. Motlow claimed that unique production and special filtering methods (through maple charcoal) led to a distinctive product and, thus, justifiably distinct labeling. Originally, some of Tennessee's early drinkers had apparently added some maple syrup to their whiskey, and the filtering method built the additive into the process.

SOURCES: Ben Green, *Jack Daniel's Legacy* (Nashville, Tenn., 1967); Stan Jones, *Jones' Complete Barguide* (Los Angeles, 1971).

Thermometer. A device for measuring temperature, the thermometer, and other instruments, came into gradual and general use by American brewers and distillers toward the end of the eighteenth century. At first there was reluctance to utilize these "philosophic instruments," but by 1800 most had succumbed to scientific advances in instrumentation. The traditional method of determining temperature was the sensation of feeling. For example, one source instructed that the first mashing water should be "just hot enough to bite smartly on your finger," and as for the time the mash should be in the tub, the advice was to "let it remain until the steam is so far evaporated that you can see your face in it."

SOURCES: Henry G. Crowgey, *Kentucky Bourbon* (Lexington, Ky., 1971); *One Hundred Years of Brewing* (Chicago and New York, 1903; Arno Press Reprint, 1974).

Thieme & Wagner Brewing Company. John Wagner and D. Herbert established the Lafayette, Indiana, firm in 1858. Frederick A. Thieme bought Herbert's interest in 1862. The firm revived after Prohibition (q.v.) and became known as the Lafayette Brewery, Inc., until closing in 1952.

SOURCES: Manfred Friedrich and Donald Bull, *The Register of U.S. Breweries* (Trumbull, Conn., 1976); *One Hundred Years of Brewing* (Chicago and New York, 1903; Arno Press Reprint, 1974).

Thomann, Gallus (active, ca. 1840s-1920). Secretary of the U.S. Brewers' Association (q.v.) from 1898 to 1908, Thomann compiled a *Documentary History of the U.S.B.A.* He wrote numerous books and articles on brewing and brewing science during his tenure as secretary and manager of the Literary Bureau of the association.

SOURCE: *One Hundred Years of Brewing* (Chicago and New York, 1903; Arno Press Reprint, 1974).

Tivoli Brewing Company. (Detroit). This brewery was founded by Franz Brogniez in 1887, a somewhat disputed date (*One Hundred Years of Brewing* gives the date 1897). Brogniez had migrated from Brussels and brought in fellow Belgians Louis Schimmel and Bernhard Verstine as partners. The company survived Prohibition (q.v.) in the 1920s and became the Altes Brewing Company in 1948; National Brewing Company (q.v.) of Baltimore took it over in 1954 but continued to brew under the Altes label. In 1973 the Detroit brewery was closed, although National continued to brew Altes. When Carling (q.v.) and National merged in the mid-1970s, brewing of Altes commenced at the former's Frankenmuth plant.

SOURCES: David T. Glick, "The Beverage of Moderation: Brief History of the Michigan Brewing Industry," *Chronicle* (Summer 1977); *One Hundred Years of Brewing* (Chicago and New York, 1903; Arno Press Reprint, 1974).

Top-fermentation. The term refers to both a type of yeast (q.v.) and a fermentation (q.v.) procedure. Owing to the nature of the yeast, it rises to the top of the fermenting vats during fermentation and is used in the brewing of ale (q.v.), porter (q.v.), stout (q.v.), and what was called strong or common beer (q.v.). The length of the fermentation period is shorter than in the bottom-fermentation (q.v.) technique, lasting five to seven days because the brew is fermented at a higher temperature, about 50° to 75° Fahrenheit. Until the introduction in Germany in the early nineteenth century of a different yeast, which settled to the bottom of the fermenting vats, virtually all beer was of the top-fermenting variety.

SOURCES: Harold M. Broderick, ed., *The Practical Brewer* (Madison, Wis., 1977); *One Hundred Years of Brewing* (Chicago and New York, 1903; Arno Press Reprint, 1974).

Trademarks. The use of brand names for whiskies increased with the emergence of bottling in the 1880s and 1890s. Formerly, most whiskey was sold in saloons or stores in bulk form. The store had a barrel of whiskey, and the owner bottled the product on the spot. Some distillers began bottling and labeling their product before the Bottled-in-Bond Act of 1897 (q.v.), but afterward the practice grew rapidly. George Garvin Brown (q.v.) was one of the first to bottle and label whiskey—in this case, Old Forester.

Another was Hiram Walker's (q.v.) Canadian Club. By 1900 it was common practice for distillers to register brands under the Trademark Act. A similar trend occurred in the brewing industry in the 1870s as the market for beer expanded. Previously, many brewers identified their beers with a place (for example, Albany ale), or as a type of beer such as Pilsener, Dormunder, and Vienna. Many brewers registered their trademarks in the 1880s and 1890s. For example, Anheuser-Busch claimed the Budweiser name; Schlitz used a globe of the world, Pabst a blue ribbon, and Lemp the shield that Falstaff bought in the 1920s.

SOURCES: Stanley Baron, *Brewed in America* (Boston, 1962); Gerald Carson, *The Social History of Bourbon* (New York, 1963).

Treating. In early America, politicians regularly "treated" voters to hard liquors. Political candidates provided the drink, usually rum (q.v.) as voters went to the polls. Also known as "swilling the voters with bumbo," it was a common practice transplanted from England but adopted readily in America's frontier environment.

SOURCES: Henry G. Crowgey, *Kentucky Bourbon* (Lexington, Ky., 1971); Charles Sydnor, *Gentlemen Freeholders* (Chapel Hill, N.C., 1952).

Trommer's, John F. (Brewery). The Brooklyn brewery was founded by John F. Trommer, who had emigrated from Germany. He settled first in Maine, then worked in Boston, and finally settled in New York City. After working in a number of breweries, he purchased the recently built plant of Stehlin and Breitkopf in 1896. Known as the Evergreen Brewery, it grew gradually during the next two decades. Trommer died in 1898, but his son, George, continued the business. Somewhat atypically, George Trommer managed to expand business during the 1920s by lending money and giving support to potential owners of hot dog restaurants—which, of course, featured Trommer's White Label Near Beer. By 1930 he supplied more than 950 such places. In 1933, a second plant was opened in Orange, New Jersey, and both breweries proved very successful well into the late 1940s. The New York City strike of 1949 and loss of sales thereafter hurt the company, however, and the New Jersey plant was sold to Rheingold (q.v.) in 1950. And in 1951 Trommer announced the sale of the Brooklyn plant to Piel Brothers (q.v.). George Trommer died on November 6, 1956, at the age of eighty-three.

SOURCES: Will Anderson, *The Breweries of Brooklyn* (New York, 1976); *One Hundred Years of Brewing* (Chicago and New York, 1903; Arno Press Reprint, 1974).

Twenty-first Amendment. Congress passed the amendment in February, 1933, and it was ratified by the required number of states in December 1933.

The amendment repealed the Eighteenth Amendment (q.v.), which had authorized national prohibition of the manufacture and sale of intoxicating beverages. The Twenty-first Amendment resulted from the unpopularity of Prohibition (q.v.) and the activities of various "repeal" organizations such as the Association Against the Prohibition Amendment (q.v.), the Moderation League, and the Women's Organization for National Prohibition Reform. A wide spectrum of groups gradually voiced opposition to Prohibition and called primarily for some kind of alcoholic beverage reform short of total proscription. As ratified, the Twenty-first Amendment continued the idea of the Webb-Kenyon Act (q.v.), prohibiting interstate transport of intoxicating liquors in violation of a state's liquor laws. The amendment largely turned the question of liquor control back to the states.

SOURCES: Norman Clark, *Deliver Us from Evil* (New York, 1976); Fletcher Dobyns, *The Amazing Story of Repeal* (Chicago, 1940).

U

Uhrig, Joseph, Brewing Company. Joseph Uhrig and A. Kraut founded the St. Louis brewery in 1847. It was known as the Camp Spring Brewery and operated by Uhrig after Kraut's death in 1849. Uhrig died in 1874, and later, in 1880, the Excelsior Brewing Company (*see* American Brewing Company, St. Louis) acquired the company.

SOURCES: James Lindhurst, "History of the Brewing Industry in St. Louis, 1804-1860," unpub. M.A. thesis, Washington University, 1939; *One Hundred Years of Brewing* (Chicago and New York, 1903; Arno Press Reprint, 1974).

Uihlein, August (August 25, 1842-October 11, 1911). Secretary-treasurer and chairman of the Schlitz (q.v.) brewing concern, Uihlein played a major role in the company's expansion from 1871 to 1900. His son, Joseph, Sr., took over management from him in 1906.
SOURCE: Dictionary of Wisconsin Biography (Madison, Wis., 1960).

Uihlein, Robert A., Jr. (1916-November 12, 1976). Uihlein was president of the Schlitz Brewing Company (q.v.) in 1961 and also chairman from 1967 to 1976. As manager of the company, Uihlein expanded plants and sales firmly establishing Schlitz as the nation's second largest brewer until an onslaught by Miller (q.v.) in the mid-1970s. He was the son of Robert August and grandson of August Uihlein (q.v.).

Underback. Until mechanical improvements during the late nineteenth century, brewers filtered the wort (q.v.) from the mash (q.v.) by pulling a plug or shaft called a tap-tree (q.v.) from the mash tun (q.v.), permitting the liquor to run down to a lower floor in a tub known as a grant, or underback. *See also*, Lauter Tun.

U.S. Brewers' Association (USBA). Officially founded in Milwaukee on September 8, 1864, the organization first began in New York in 1862. Local brewers called a series of meetings in New York, then broadened the group to the national level. At the fourth convention in Milwaukee, the name U.S.

Brewers' Association was adopted. Brewers reacted to the Revenue Act of 1862, which levied a tax of $1 per barrel on beer that had already been consigned to bottles. The association sponsored a committee that argued the case before Congress and resulted in modification of the law in 1863. Instead of a tax of $1 per barrel, after March 3, 1863, it was reduced to $0.60 until April 1864 when the $1 would be reimposed. Over the years, the organization dealt with a variety of matters relating to the interests of the industry. Labor problems, federal and state taxation levels and techniques, ways to counteract prohibitionist forces, participation in the development of federal standards as in the Pure Food and Drug Act (q.v.), and industry concerns in general were among the activities of the association. Between 1916 and 1933, generally the years of Prohibition (q.v.), the association did not meet, but it resumed the annual convention in 1933. The association soon ran into trouble, however, this time within the brewing community. In 1936, a group of dissident brewers, largely from the West and Midwest and led by Anheuser-Busch (q.v.) and Pabst (q.v.), organized Brewing Industry, Inc. (q.v.). This trade organization believed that direct and more effective measures were necessary to neutralize "dry" activities—and that the USBA led by Col. Jacob Ruppert (q.v.) and other eastern companies, was not doing enough in that respect. Apparently responding to the break, the USBA announced in October 1936 that it was establishing a separate entity, the United Brewers' Industrial Foundation, as a public relations agency to educate the public and government as to the economic importance of the industry, and to promote internal industry responsibility. There was clearly some rancor between the two groups, but they met together, along with the American Brewers' Association (q.v.) (a near-beer association), in August 1938 to discuss a plan of action drawn up by Bernard Lichtenberg of the Institute of Public Relations. Lichtenberg had been retained by Brewing Industry, Inc., to map out a strategy to thwart the forces of prohibition. He came up with the Nebraska Plan (q.v.), which essentially stressed self-regulatory procedures. In the next few years, differences were worked out, and in January 1941 the three trade associations merged as the USBA, except that the Brewing Industry Foundation was continued as a separate public relations entity. Those two merged in 1944 as the U.S. Brewers' Foundation; the association reverted back to its original name, U.S. Brewers' Association, in 1961.

SOURCES: John P. Arnold and Frank Penman, *History of the Brewing Industry and Brewing Science* (Chicago, 1933); Stanley Baron, *Brewed in America* (Boston, 1962); "The First Century: A History of the U.S.B.A.," *American Brewer* (January and February 1962); Brewers' Association, *Documentary History of the United States Brewers' Association* (New York, 1896, 1898; comp. by Gallus Thomann).

U.S. Brewers' Foundation. *See* U.S. Brewers' Association.

U.S. Brewing Company (Chicago). U.S. Brewing was the merger of the Bartholomae & Leicht Brewing Company, the Michael Brand Brewing Company (q.v.), and the Ernst Brothers Brewery Company. The 1889 consolidation was extended in 1890 as the company merged with the Milwaukee and Chicago Breweries, Ltd., a British-American syndicate. The Val. Blatz Brewing Company (q.v.) was part of the merger. The U.S. Brewing Company revived after Prohibition (q.v.) and continued to operate until 1955.

SOURCE: Manfred Friedrich and Donald Bull, *The Register of U.S. Breweries* (Trumbull, Conn., 1976); *One Hundred Years of Brewing* (Chicago and New York, 1903; Arno Press Reprint, 1974).

U.S. Industrial Alcohol Company. The industrial alcohol company operated as a branch of the Distillers' Securities Corporation, the 1902 successor to the Distilling Company of America (q.v.). Distillers' Securities Corporation sold its controlling stock in U.S. Industrial Alcohol around 1915. The firm made a substantial profit during World War I. Also known as the Kentucky Alcohol Corporation, the company became part of National Distillers Products Company (q.v.) in the mid-1920s. It operated partly in the old Atlas Distillery (q.v.) of Peoria, Illinois. After National Distillers took over the company, an agreement was reached with the Commercial Solvents Corporation to produce the industrial alcohol. In the 1930s Commercial Solvents operated plants in Peoria (Woolner [q.v.]), Terre Haute, and Lawrenceburg, Indiana. National Distillers continues to operate the company, apparently as U.S. Industrial Chemicals.

SOURCES: H. W. Denny, "History and Modern Technology," *Spirits* (January 1936); Distilleries file, Peoria Historical Society; *Peoria Star*, December 28, 1924.

V

Van Winkle, Julian P. (1875-February 1965). Van Winkle was salesman, owner, and president of Stitzel-Weller Distillery, Inc. (q.v.). He joined the Weller firm as salesman in 1893, bought the company in 1908, and arranged to buy up Stitzel whiskies for resale. The association led to the merger in the 1920s. He was known as "Pappy."

SOURCES: "An Old Friend Remembers," *Bev/Executive* (March 1, 1965); *Spirits* (May 1936); "Van Winkle Sees Bourbon Boom," *Spirits* (May 1943).

Vassar, Matthew (April 29, 1792-June 23, 1868). A prominent brewer of Poughkeepsie, New York, Vassar helped found Vassar College. His father, James, came to the area from England in the 1790s and established an ale (q.v.) and porter (q.v.) brewery, which he managed until his death in 1810. Matthew Vassar then took over the business and managed it until 1867, when a nephew succeeded him. Over the years, M. Vassar and Company was known as the Eagle Brewery. Management problems led to its closing in 1896. The Vassars engaged in a number of businesses and built up a large fortune. In 1860 Matthew, who became a noted philanthropist, endowed the women's college in Poughkeepsie that is named after him. He contributed $400,000, becoming the main founder of the college.

SOURCES: Stanley Baron, *Brewed in America* (Boston, 1962); B. J. Lossing, *Vassar College and Its Founder* (New York, 1967); *One Hundred Years of Brewing* (Chicago and New York, 1903; Arno Press Reprint, 1974).

Vodka. The colorless, almost flavorless, alcoholic beverage is distilled from any grain material at 190 proof (q.v.) or above. It is bottled, without aging, usually between 80 and 100 proof. After distillation, vodka, which is essentially grain neutral spirits (q.v.), is charcoal-filtered to remove any flavor or aroma. Since 1950, U.S. consumption of vodka has grown from virtually zero to more than 20 percent of the distilled beverage output in the 1970s.

Voight Brewing Company. The Detroit firm was founded in 1866 by William Voight. E. W. Voight, his son, took over in 1871. The company reopened after the end of Prohibition (q.v.) but was in business for only four years, 1934-37.

Volstead, Andrew John (October 31, 1860-January 20, 1947). Republican congressman (1903-23) from Minnesota, Volstead, as chairman of the House Judiciary Committee in 1919, was primarily responsible for the formulation of the National Prohibition Act—later referred to as the Volstead Act (q.v.). The law was drafted as a means of enforcing the Eighteenth Amendment (q.v.). Largely because of his role, Volstead's name became nearly synonymous with Prohibition.

SOURCES: Dictionary of American Biography, Supplement 4 ; Andrew Sinclair, *Prohibition: The Era of Excess* (Boston, 1962).

Volstead Act. Formally known as the National Prohibition Act, Representative Andrew J. Volstead (q.v.) of Minnesota introduced the enforcement law for the Eighteenth Amendment (q.v.). It was passed in October 1919 and vetoed by President Woodrow Wilson on the grounds that continued wartime prohibition was unnecessary. Congress promptly overrode the veto. The legislation defined an intoxicating beverage as any drink containing 0.5 percent alcohol or more by volume. Penalties for liquor sales and search and seizure procedures were also included. Private stocks of liquor purchased before the act became effective could be retained; thus a high degree of "building up of supplies" occurred. Section 37 of the law also provided for the transportation and sale of medicinal spirits, but such liquor could only be purchased with a doctor's prescription. Federal licenses would be issued to selected applicants for the medicinal whiskey permits. The act was modified by the Cullen Act (q.v.) in 1933.

SOURCES: Norman Clark, *Deliver Us from Evil* (New York, 1976); Andrew Sinclair, *Prohibition: The Era of Excess* (Boston, 1962).

W _____

Wacker, Charles H. (August 29, 1856-October 31, 1929). A prominent Chicago entrepreneur and civic leader, Wacker started as a brewer. His father, Frederick Wacker, organized the Wacker and Birk Brewing and Malting Company in the early 1880s, and Charles succeeded his father as president in 1884. In 1889 the plant was sold to Chicago Breweries Ltd. (q.v.), which continued to operate the brewery in that name, as well as another brewery, the McAvoy (q.v.) plant. Wacker remained as manager of the company until 1901. He had numerous nonbrewing interests and business associations, had been a director of the World's Columbian Exposition of 1893, and was appointed chairman of the Chicago Plan Commission in 1909 by Mayor Fred A. Busse. He was mainly responsible for selling the idea of Chicago redevelopment to the public. Wacker Drive, formerly South Water Street, was named after him. After 1901, Wacker was involved primarily in real estate dealings.

SOURCES: Dictionary of American Biography, vol. 19; *One Hundred Years of Brewing* (Chicago and New York, 1903; Arno Press Reprint, 1974).

Wagner, John (active, 1840s). Generally accepted as the first lager beer (q.v.) brewer in the U.S., Wagner had a small home brewery on St. John Street in Philadelphia. The evidence that he introduced the first bottom-fermentation (q.v.) yeast (q.v.) to America is based largely on the recollection of Charles Wolf. Wolf, who had been involved in the Engel and Wolf (*see* Bergner & Engel) brewery of Philadelphia, submitted his version of the origins of lager to the compilers of *One Hundred Years of Brewing*, which was published by H. S. Rich & Company in 1903. In the absence of more concrete source material, his recollection, albeit sixty or so years after the fact, remains the most accepted.

SOURCES: Stanley Baron, *Brewed in America* (Boston, 1962); *One Hundred Years of Brewing* (Chicago and New York, 1903; Arno Press Reprint, 1974).

Wahl-Henius Institute. Dr. Robert Wahl and Dr. Max Henius founded the technical institute for brewers in 1886 in Chicago. Known also as a scientific station, the school reflected the trend of the period's emphasis on the art of brewing and instruction in scientific research.

Wainwright, Z. (Brewery). The Pittsburgh company was founded in 1818 by Joseph Wainwright, who was succeeded by his son in 1868. In 1891 the company was incorporated as Z. Wainwright & Company, and then joined the merger resulting in the formation of the Pittsburgh Brewing Company (q.v.) in 1899. *See also,* Wainwright Brewing Company.

SOURCE: "Pittsburgh, History of Beer and a Market," *American Brewer* (June and July 1960).

Wainwright Brewing Company. Ellis and Samuel Wainwright managed this St. Louis brewery beginning in 1846. Ellis had previously been involved with another partner, until Samuel, who learned the brewers' trade in his father's brewery in Pittsburgh (*see* Wainwright, Z.), joined him in the mid-1840s. When Ellis died in 1849, Samuel continued the brewery, which produced ale (q.v.) in the English tradition. Eventually, Wainwright's son, Ellis, took over the company and incorporated in 1883. In 1889 he sold the plant to the St. Louis Brewing Association (q.v.) and was named president of the English consolidation. Ellis also served as president of the U.S. Brewers' Association in 1891. The company closed during Prohibition (q.v.) in the 1920s.

SOURCES: James Lindhurst, "History of the Brewing Industry in St. Louis, 1804-1860," unpub. M.A. thesis, Washington University, 1939; *One Hundred Years of Brewing* (Chicago and New York, 1903; Arno Press Reprint, 1974).

Walker, Hiram (July 4, 1816-January 12, 1899). Hiram Walker was born in East Douglas, Massachusetts. His ancestors came to America in the seventeenth century. In the 1830 s he worked in a dry-goods store before making the six-day trip to Detroit, Michigan, in 1838. He ultimately entered the grocery business, and one of the commodities he sold was whiskey. The uncertain temperance laws of Michigan encouraged Walker, who was becoming a successful commission merchant (q.v.), to establish a business in Ontario, Canada, just across the Detroit River. He bought a 468-acre tract of land with some of the $40,000 he had accumulated and by 1858 had established a flour milling and distilling operation. When his sons joined him in the 1870s, the company became known as Hiram Walker and Sons. His Walker's Club Whisky was eventually renamed Canadian Club, and the distillery proved to be very successful. Walker maintained residence in Detroit and in 1880 built a ferry service across the river to his plant in Walkerville. Walker retired in 1895 after suffering a paralytic stroke; he died in 1899. *See also,* Walker, Hiram (Distillery).

SOURCES: Howard R. Walton, *Hiram Walker and Walkerville from 1858* (New York, 1958); "Through the Years . . . with Hiram Walker," *Canadian Beverage Review* (1952).

Walker, Hiram (Distillery). The prominent Canadian-based distilling company was founded by Massachusetts-born Hiram Walker (q.v.) in 1858.

Walker left Boston for the West in the 1830s, arrived in Detroit in 1838, and later established a grocery business. In the mid-1850s, after building a reputation as a successful grain commission merchant (q.v.), Walker built a flour mill and distillery on a large tract of land he had purchased in Walkerville, Ontario, on the Canadian side of the Detroit River. Concerns about prohibitionist activity and legal licensing in Michigan, coupled with the potential of Canada's markets and natural resources, encouraged Walker to establish his business in Canada. He bought 468 acres of land in 1856 and was producing flour and whisky by 1858. John McBride joined Walker in 1859 as a salesman, or "drummer," and Walker is supposedly the first such distillery to utilize a salesman. When McBride became a partner in 1863, the name of the business was changed to Hiram Walker and Company, but the name was changed again in 1867 when McBride left the enterprise. In 1871, Walker's son, Edward Chandler (1851-15), joined the firm; Hiram Walker and Son was the result. Franklin Harrington, another son, joined them in 1873; thus the firm became Hiram Walker and Sons. They introduced their Walker's Club Whisky (Canadian spelling normally omits the *e*) to the U.S. The whisky, a light blend of whiskies, proved popular enough that American competitors, led by Kentucky bourbon (q.v.) distillers, complained that American consumers could not determine whether "Club" was imported or a native American drink. Lobbying efforts followed, and Congress passed legislation in the late 1880s stipulating that the country of origin of the whisky had to be displayed on the label. Walker met the problem by changing his drink's name to Canadian Club; the tactic worked in his favor, and the trade name became a success. Subsequently, a number of producers and retailers falsely labeled their drink "Canadian" and Hiram Walker fought them legally and through public advertisements in newspapers and on billboards by accusing them of fraud, and warnings to the public. Walker received another American setback when the Pure Food and Drug Act (q.v.) of 1906 was initially interpreted as defining blended whiskey as being imitation whiskey. The "Taft decision" (q.v.) of 1909, however, clarified and reinterpreted the law, permitting blended whiskey to be defined as whiskey, although the type had to specified. After Hiram Walker's death in 1899, the family continued to manage the firm as Edward Chandler served as president from 1899-1915; then Franklin Hiram, James Harrington, and Harrington Walker ran the company. In 1926 they sold control to Harry C. Hatch (1883-1946), who had previously purchased Canada's oldest distillery, Gooderham and Worts of Toronto. Hatch and his associates paid $14 million for Walker's; $9 million of the price was for the "goodwill" associated with the Canadian Club trademark. Although Ontario had passed a prohibition law against retail sales, distilleries were permitted to operate to supply medicinal beverages and to produce for legal areas. Hatch's purchase paid off, and he expanded the company until his death in 1946. When

Prohibition (q.v.) was repealed in the U.S. in 1933, construction began on Walker's first American distillery at Peoria, Illinois. The plant opened in 1934. Other expansions of the parent company, Hiram Walker—Gooderham and Worts, Ltd., have included: (1) purchase of Ballantine and Son Ltd., a Scotch whisky-maker in 1936; (2) purchase of a distilling company in Buenos Aires in 1943; (3) building of a bottling plant in California in the mid-1940s; (4) various subsidiary distillery additions since 1950 in Europe, Scotland, and South America. Upon Hatch's death in 1946, Howard R. Walton became president and held the position until 1961 when he was succeeded by Burdettee E. Ford, who retired in 1964. H. Clifford Hatch became president of the parent company in 1964. Roy W. Stevens became vice-president in 1973 of Hiram Walker, Inc., the branch of the firm responsible for the U.S. market, and president in 1975. The firm, Canada's second largest distilling company, announced in early 1979 that it would phase out its Peoria distillery because the once modern plant had become comparatively outmoded. The company is currently constructing a modern blending and bottling facility at Fort Smith, Arkansas, to manufacture its line of cordials.

SOURCES: Gerald Carson, *The Social History of Bourbon* (New York, 1963); "Hiram Walker's Arrival in Detroit Heralds New Era" (brief company history, 1978); "Through the Years . . . with Hiram Walker," *Canadian Beverage Review* (1952); Howard R. Walton, *Hiram Walker and Walkerville from 1858* (New York, 1958); "Whiskey," *Fortune* (November 1933).

Wallerstein Laboratories. These brewing laboratories were established by Dr. Max Wallerstein in New York in 1902. His brother, Leo, joined him soon afterward, and the two developed numerous innovations in product improvements, receiving many patents in the areas of brewing waters, yeast, and fermented beverages. In 1910 the Wallersteins introduced an enzyme, Collupulin, which permitted chill proofing bottled beer and thus prevention of cloudiness and haziness in pasteurized bottled beer.

SOURCES: Wallerstein Laboratories, *You Can Take It With You: The Story of Bottled Beer* (ca. 1950).

Walter Brewing Company. John Walter founded the Eau Claire, Wisconsin, brewery in 1889. The company closed during Prohibition (q.v.) but reopened in 1933 and continues to operate in the 1970s as a small but successful local plant, marketing its beer mainly within seventy-five miles of the brewery. The company has been controlled and managed by the Walter family, which claims a long and varied history in brewing. In addition to the plant founded by John Walter, others were established by his brothers and thier sons. Among them were the Geo. Walter Brewing Company of Appleton, Wisconsin (1880-1972); Walter Bros. Brewing Company of Menasha, Wisconsin (1889-1956); Walter Brewing Company of Pueblo, Colorado

(1898-1975); and West Bend Lithia Company of West Bend, Wisconsin (1911-72). The latter plant was bought in 1911 by Martin and Charles, Sr. The Elau Claire brewery was the only plant in operation by the late 1970s and was managed by Charles Walter, Jr., who has held the position since 1973.

SOURCES: Company information; Wayne Kroll, *Badger Breweries* (Jefferson, Wis., 1976); "Walter Brewing Marks 65th Anniversary," *American Brewer* (September 1954).

Warehouse receipt. Issued by a warehouse supervisor, the receipt is a financial statement indicating that the owner of the goods (whiskey in this case) has stored his whiskey in the bonded warehouse (q.v.). Distillers used this device to finance tax payments that had to be made on whiskey that was still aging (q.v.), but at one time because of a bonding period (q.v.) of one to three years, had been liable for taxation before sale. Also, since large whiskey inventories are often built up, the warehouse receipt could be used as collateral for business loans. Such receipts were, and are, negotiable if the receipt indicates that the stock should be delivered to the holder, or any person named.

SOURCE: Gerald Carson, *The Social History of Bourbon* (New York, 1963).

Washington, George (February 1732-December 14, 1799). America's first president operated distilling operations at Mount Vernon in the 1780s and 1790s and specialized in peach brandy. The president also had a noted recipe for Cherry Bounce. Although much of his product was for home consumption, he did produce a large portion for commercial purposes. Porter was also a favorite drink as the president ordered supplies on a number of occasions from Robert Hare, and later, Benjamin Morris, of Philadelphia.

SOURCES: Stanley Baron, *Brewed in America* (Boston, 1962); *Beverages and Sources of Colonial Virginia* (New York and Washington, D.C., 1906); Oscar Getz, *Whiskey: An American Pictorial History* (New York, 1978).

Washington Temperance Society. Reformed drinkers founded the society in Baltimore, Maryland, in 1840. After attending a temperance lecture, largely as a joke, a group of six noted drinkers became convinced of the evils of alcoholic drink and formed the Washingtonian movement of reformed drunkards. They would help save others of their kind by holding meetings at which members would recount their personal problems because of liquor consumption.

SOURCES: John A. Krout, *The Origins of Prohibition* (New York, 1925); Alice Felt Tyler, *Freedom's Ferment* (New York, 1962; 1st ed., 1944); Ian R. Tyrell, *Sobering Up: From Temperance to Prohibition in Antebellum America, 1800-1860* (Westport, Conn., 1979).

Waterfill & Frazier Distillery Company. The firm dates from the 1860s. J. M. Waterfill and George Frazier purchased the plant, which was originally at Tyrone, Kentucky. John Dowling purchased the plant in 1903 and produced whiskey under the Waterfill & Frazier name. He moved the still to Mexico during Prohibition (q.v.) and produced the brand there. After Repeal in 1933, a new plant was built at Anchorage, Kentucky. Sometime later, the plant was moved to Bardstown, Kentucky; but the company was purchased by James Beam Distilling Company (q.v.) in 1974.

SOURCE: H. W. Coyte, "Anderson County Distilleries," unpub. paper, ca. 1979.

Wathen distilleries. The Wathen family traces its identification with Kentucky distilling to Henry Hudson Wathen's small plant of the late 1780s. His sons and grandsons continued in the distilling business. J. B. Wathen, Sr., established a plant under his name in the Louisville area in the early 1880s and the plant became part of the Kentucky Distilleries and Warehouse Company (q.v.) in the late 1890s. In the spring of 1900, J. B. Wathen's sons, R. E., O. H., and J. B., Jr., established a large distillery in Louisville, which became known as R. E. Wathen & Company. That plant became the largest in the American Medicinal Spirits Company (q.v.), which was formed by R. E. Wathen in the 1920s. In 1927, National Distillers Products Company (q.v.) absorbed American Medicinal Spirits and the Wathens assumed leadership roles in the National Distillers group. Another family member, Nace Wathen, a brother of J. B., was placed in charge of the Old Grand Dad Distillery Company, a small but well-known plant at Hobbs, Kentucky. The plant had been purchased by the Wathens in 1899 and had been operated for many years by R. B. Hayden, a pioneer Nelson County distiller credited with originating Old Grand Dad. This distillery was abondoned in 1920, and Old Grand Dad was later produced at the R. E. Wathen plant in Louisville by National Distillers. In the 1930s John A. Wathen of Lebanon, Kentucky, and others, established the John A. Wathen Distilling Company and rebuilt the old Mueller, Wathen, and Kobert distillery at Lebanon. It was eventually sold to Schenley (q.v.) and later dismantled. In all, the Wathens claim an impressive position among Kentucky distilling families.

SOURCES: Sam Elliott, *Nelson County Record* (Bardstown, Ky., 1896); *Kentucky's Distilling Interests* (Lexington, Ky., 1893); *Spirits* (April 1935 and May 1936); "Ten Years of Progress: Distillers," *Spirits* (November 1943); "Whiskey," *Fortune* (November 1933).

Webb-Kenyon Act. Congress passed legislation in March 1913 prohibiting the transportation of liquor in interstate commerce from a "wet" state into a state that had prohibited alcoholic beverages. Sponsors of the act hoped to promote more effective enforcement of state prohibition laws. The substance of the act was later included in the Twenty-first Amendment (q.v.), which repealed the Eighteenth Amendment (q.v.) to the Constitution.

Weiss beer. This is beer made primarily from wheat malt by the top-fermentation (q.v.) method. This beer, mainly a product of the Middle Ages in Europe, was very common in the period before the introduction of lager beer (q.v.) in the early nineteenth century. The brew goes through a second fermentation (q.v.) after being bottled. It is pale and very effervescent, and a number of small, specialized U.S. breweries marketed the beer in the late nineteenth century.

SOURCES: Will Anderson, *The Beer Book* (Princeton, N.J., 1973); *One Hundred Years of Brewing* (Chicago and New York, 1903; Arno Press Reprint, 1974); Edward H. Vogel, Jr., et al., *The Practical Brewer* (St. Louis, Mo., 1946).

Wertheimer distilling interests. Jacob Wertheimer began his whiskey brokerage business in Cincinnati in the late 1850s. His sons, Lee and Edward, Sr., incorporated as L. & E. Wertheimer in 1881. Their main brand was Old Spring, which was produced under contract by Hoffman & Hoekley (*see* Hoffman Distilling Company) of Lawrenceburg. They also opened a rectifying plant in Cincinnati about 1900. The Wertheimers continued as whiskey distillers and brokers after the repeal of Prohibition (q.v.) in 1933 and became associated with the Ripy family and the Hoffman Distilling Company. Jean Wertheimer was controller of that plant for a time. In 1963, the Wertheimer interests gained control of and enlarged the Ripy Bros. (q.v.) plant; Ernest W. Ripy, Jr., was to supervise the business. Edward Wertheimer was president of the Hoffman Distilling Company in the late 1970s.

SOURCES: *Spirits* (May 1939); Art Williams, "The Kentucky Roundup," *Spirits* (August and September 1963).

West End Brewing Company. The regional Utica, New York, brewery was founded in 1888 by F. X. Matt, a German immigrant who came to the U.S. in 1878. Matt became manager of Utica's Bierbauer brewery before helping to reorganize it in 1888. The new company became the West End Brewery, and Matt became president in 1905. In the period of Prohibition (q.v.) in the 1920s the company marketed the Utica Club brand of soft drinks, plus syrups and similar products. The name was later used in labeling the beers of the company. The Matt family has controlled the business over the years, and F. X. Matt, the founder, remained active up to his death in 1958 at the age of ninety-nine. His sons, Frank M. (who died in 1967) and Walter, were active in the business. Walter Matt is president, and his sons, F. X. II and J. Kemper, are vice-presidents of the company, as are two other descendants of the founder. Today the company is known especially for its replica of an 1888 tavern. The tavern, built in 1965, is famous as the Utica Club Brewery Tour Center.

SOURCES: Michael Jackson, ed., *The World Guide to Beer* (Englewood Cliffs, N.J., 1977); *Utica Club and the Brewing Industry* (Utica, N.Y., 1974); "West End's Ideal Little Brewery," *Beverage World* (November 1978).

Western Brewery (Stag). Philip Neu and Peter Gintz founded the brewery in the 1850s in Belleville, Illinois. After Gintz's death in 1873, the brewery was purchased by a corporate enterprise, led by William Brandenburger, which eventually sold out to one of its members, Adam Gintz. Called the Western Brewery company since 1873, the firm marketed Kaiser beer. In 1900 ownership passed to the Paul J. Sort Tobacco Company of Cincinnati and then to Henry L. Griesedieck of the St. Louis brewing family known for Falstaff (q.v.). Griesedieck continued the Stag brand of 1907 and manufactured root beer, soda water, and ice during Prohibition (q.v.). The name was modified to the Griesedieck Western Brewery Company in 1932; the firm bought the Hyde Park brewery of St. Louis in 1948 and continued successfully into the 1940s and 1950s. The Carling (q.v.) brewing interests bought the company in 1954 as part of an expansion program. In early 1979, G. Heileman (q.v.) purchased Carling National, and the Stag plant was part of the acquisition.

SOURCES: Belleville *Advocate*, March 6, and 8, 1907; Belleville *News-Democrat*, February 18, 1979; *One Hundred Years of Brewing* (Chicago and New York, 1903; Arno Press Reprint, 1974); "The Stag Brewery" (brief company history).

Wet. This term was most commonly used during the Prohibition (q.v.) era of the 1920s and the years leading up to passage of the Eighteenth Amendment (q.v.). A state, county, or local area that permitted the sale of alcoholic beverages was called "wet." A second common usage emerged in politics as politicians and public officials were referred to as being "wet," or against Prohibition. Likewise, opponents of prohibition laws were often called "wets."

Wheat whiskey. Made from a fermented mash (q.v.) of at least 51 percent wheat grain, wheat whiskey is distilled at not more than 160 proof (q.v.), and aged in new charred oak barrels (q.v.).

Wheeler, Wayne B. (November 10, 1869-September 5, 1927). An aggressive attorney and prohibition advocate, Wheeler joined the Anti-Saloon League (q.v.) in 1893—the year of its founding and his graduation from Oberlin College in Ohio. Wheeler became general counsel and later legislative superintendent. As the league's most powerful and noted lobbyist, he used political tactics and techniques known as "Wheelerism." A politician's vote was solicited not by a personal request but often by a flood of letters and telegrams from an aware public that would work to defeat the official in a subsequent election. Wheeler wrote most of the Volstead Act (q.v.) and helped write the Eighteenth Amendment (q.v.). Although he gained a reputation as a political manipulator, Wheeler also became known for his total dedication to the annihilation of the liquor traffic, and took no more than $8,000 as his annual salary.

SOURCES: Norman H. Clark, *Deliver Us from Evil* (New York, 1976); Peter Odegard, *Pressure Politics: The Story of the Anti-Saloon League* (New York, 1928); Justin Steuart, *Wayne Wheeler, Dry Boss* (New York, 1928).

Whiskey. Whiskey is a distilled alcoholic beverage made from grain that has gone through the various stages of the whiskey-making process (q.v.). The word derives from the Gaelic word *uisgebeatha* or *usquebaugh* (there are a number of spellings), meaning "water of life." The term "whiskey," which came into use during the Middle Ages in Europe, may be spelled *whiskey* or *whisky*, although the general practice is to use whiskey with the *e* when referring to American and Irish types. Whisky, omitting the *e*, is used normally in referring to Scotch and Canadian types. Straight (q.v.) and blended (q.v.) are the two main categories of whiskey, although there are many variations, based primarily on the type of grain used. Federal regulations (q.v.) define U.S. whiskey as "an alcoholic distillate from a fermented mash of grain distilled at less than 190 proof in such manner that the distillate possesses the taste, aroma, and characteristics generally attributed to whiskey, stored in oak containers (except that corn whiskey need not be so stored), and bottled at not less than 80 proof, and also includes mixtures of such distillates for which no specific standards of identity are prescribed." Until the 1890s, the only federal regulations dealing with whiskey were in the form of taxation. Then a series of acts, culminating in the Bottled-in-Bond Act (q.v.) of 1897, set minimum standards for production. The Pure Food and Drug Act (q.v.) of 1906 expanded the regulations, and then further refinement occurred with the "Taft decision" (q.v.), named after President William H. Taft (q.v.) in 1909. Current regulations date largely from 1933, when federal controls and standards were spelled out in detail. *See also*, Blended Straight Whiskey, Blended Whiskey, Bourbon Whiskey, Canadian Whisky, Corn Whiskey, Irish Whiskey, Light Whiskey, Malt Whiskey, Rye Whiskey, Scotch Whisky, Straight Whiskey, Tennessee Whiskey, and Wheat Whiskey.

SOURCES: *Alexis Lichine's New Encyclopedia of Wines & Spirits* (New York, 1974); Morris V. Rosenbloom, *The Liquor Industry* (Braddock, Pa., 1937); U.S., Treasury Department, Internal Revenue Service, Alcohol, Tobacco Products and

Firearms, *Code of Federal Regulations*, Title 27, part 5, Labelling and Advertising of Distilled Spirits, as of April 1978.

Whiskey-making process. Although the process might vary in some respects depending on local and individual practices, the essential elements in the making of whiskey (q.v.) are grain handling and milling, mashing (q.v.), fermentation (q.v.), distillation (q.v.), and maturation, or aging (q.v.). First, the grains are inspected and cleaned to remove all impurities. The most common grains are barley (q.v.), corn, and rye, and the proportion and type of grain used determines the whiskey type. After examination, the grain is ground into meal. In the mashing (q.v.) stage the grain is soaked in hot water (about eighteen to twenty gallons per bushel), and some starch is released during the process. Then malt (q.v.), usually barley, is added to the mash (q.v.), and the enzymes (q.v.) that are part of the malt convert the starch of the grain into sugar, maltose (q.v.). Afterward, the cooked mash is transferred to wooden or metal vats called fermenters. The water used is considered very important, and Kentucky bourbon (q.v.) distillers stress the importance of limestone water (q.v.) in their method. Yeast (q.v.) is then added to the fermenting vats to convert the fermentable sugars in the mash to alcohol, generally known as "distiller's beer" (q.v.). After fermenting for three to four days, the "beer," or fermented mash, is ready for distillation. Basically, whiskey is a distilled beer. During distillation, the mash, or "beer," is heated in a still (q.v.) to separate the alcohol from the mash. Alcohol boils at 173° Fahrenheit, whereas water must be heated to 212° Fahrenheit to induce boiling. Thus it is relatively easy to separate the alcohol from the water. In modern continuous stills, the mash is fed in near the top, and steam from the bottom vaporizes the alcohol which is drawn off, and condensed into a liquid in a condenser, formerly a "worm" (q.v.). The product of the first distillate is known as "low wine" (q.v.). This liquid is distilled again in a second still, known as a doubler (q.v.). The result is "high wine" (q.v.), or new whiskey, which is about 130 proof (q.v.), or 65 percent alcohol. Before aging, distilled water is added to the whiskey in the cistern room (q.v.) to reduce it to about 100-125 proof, depending on the distiller's method. Any of the fermented mash that has not vaporized is drained off as "spent beer" (*see* Stillage) and part of it is added to fresh and yeast in the process of making sour mash (q.v.) in a "yeasting back" procedure. This is a common process. Sweet-mash (q.v.) whiskey is made without any stillage being returned to the fermenters. The by-product of distillation, the spent beer, is called stillage (q.v.) and is marketed as feed for cattle and other livestock. Finally, after transfer to the cistern room, the whiskey is poured into special whiskey barrels (q.v.) to be aged for at least two years. Aging takes place in warehouses of the open-air type, "open-rick" (q.v.), or enclosed warehouses in which temperature and humidity are carefully controlled. During aging, the whiskey increases in alcoholic content because of the evaporation, outage (q.v.), of water owing to warm, dry, conditions; therefore, distilled water is added to lower the proof prior to bottling. Until 1959, when federal regulations were changed, whiskey had to be bottled and taxes paid on it after eight years; but the 1958 law (which went into effect July 1 of the next year) increased the bonding period (q.v.) to twenty years.

SOURCES: *Bourbon, the World's Favorite Whiskey* (New York, ca. 1970); Gerald Carson, *The Social History of Bourbon* (New York, 1963); Harold J. Grossman, *Grossman's Guide to Wines, Beers, and Spirits* (New York, 1977); *In Olde Kentucke* (Frankfort, Ky., ca. 1970); James Boone Wilson, *The Spirit of Old Kentucky* (Louisville, Ky., 1945).

Whiskey Rebellion. In 1791, the federal government, following Secretary of Treasury Alexander Hamilton's proposal for raising funds to meet federal debts, levied an excise tax (*see* Excise Act, 1791) on distilled spirits. This tax especially hurt the farmers of southwestern Pennsylvania, who not only consumed so-called farmer whiskey in large amounts but also converted their corn and rye into whiskey for the transmontane trip by pack animal to eastern markets. A packhorse could carry about four bushels of grain, but it could transport the equivalent of twenty-four bushels of grain in the form of alcohol. In 1794, opposition to the tax ultimately resulted in refusal to pay the levies and a boycott of tax officials. To enforce federal law, President George Washington called out a militia force of some 13,000 men. With Hamilton himself accompanying the army, the massive force marched into western Pennsylvania but found virtually no resistance and only a few rebels. Two of the leaders were convicted of treason, but President Washington later pardoned each of them. Federal authority was maintained, but the incident was part of a series of events that widened the breach between the Jeffersonian and Hamiltonian political factions. Even the president was convinced that the rebellion had been fomented by the French-supporting Democratic societies.

SOURCES: Leland D. Baldwin, *Whiskey Rebels: The Story of a Frontier Uprising* (Pittsburgh, 1939); Gerald Carson, *The Social History of Bourbon* (New York, 1963); Jacob E. Cooke, "Whiskey Insurrection," *Pennsylvania History* 30 (1963).

Whiskey Ring. A group of western distillers and Internal Revenue Service officials conspired to evade the 1868 whiskey tax of $0.50 per gallon. The agents simply overlooked large portions of taxable whiskey and then divided the potential revenues with the distillers. In 1874, new Secretary of Treasury Benjamin Bristow began an investigation of the "Ring," which led to its demise. The activities led to political scandal because President Ulysses S. Grant's private secretary, Gen. Orville E. Babcock, was among those indicted. Charges abounded that the group intended to use part of the funds to help reelect Grant. Although Babcock was acquitted and no final proof of political scandal came to light, the Grant administration weakened public confidence in the government. Gen. John McDonald, an area supervisor in the Internal Revenue Service, and a main figure in the "Ring," was convicted of conspiring to defraud the government. McDonald entered a federal prison in 1875 to serve a three-year sentence but was pardoned by President Rutherford Hayes in 1877. Soon after, McDonald published *Secrets of the Great Whiskey Ring* (1880), which implied that President Grant himself had been involved in the scandal.

SOURCE: Gerald Carson, *The Social History of Bourbon* (New York, 1963).

Whiskey Trust. Officially known as the Distillers' & Cattle Feeders' Trust, the combine was organized in Peoria, Illinois, in May 1887. The group also supplied nutritious sour-mash grain residue (slop) to cattle feed companies —thus the name. It was an extension of various pools of the 1870s and 1880s. The "Peoria Pool" of the early 1870s had been promoted by H. B. "Buffalo" Miller, a Peoria distiller. That organization gave way to the Western Export Association of 1881, which failed in 1882. Other pooling arrangements, designed to reduce production and raise prices, were worked out yearly, but each suffered from the basic problem of pooling—that is, an illegal organization finds it almost impossible to enforce its rules. Individual members might intermittently overproduce, cut prices, or withdraw from the association. Intimidation is the only tactic the organization can use to keep members in line; and there are, of course, drawbacks to such methods. The trust, conversely, would be a formal business arrangement under corporate auspices. Sixty-five distilleries joined the trust, which elected Joseph B. Greenhut (q.v.) of Peoria as president. The association's members turned over their stock to trustees who would manage the combine. Most of the distilleries were closed, but the company operated ten plants in Peoria— a city noted for cool limestone water, good river transportation, and proximity to coal, corn, and railroads (*see* Peoria Distilling Industry). Of the original members, most were in Illinois and Indiana. The region's alcohol output, consisting largely of industrial alcohol and neutral spirits, totaled more than 40 million gallons per year, more than two-thirds of the total U.S. output. Among the Peoria companies in the trust were Great Western (q.v.), Woolner Distilling Company (q.v.), Monarch (q.v.), Clarke Bros. (q.v.), and Great Eastern (q.v.). One goal of the backers of the trust was to respond to changing federal tax policies by effective pricing. In 1892, for example, anticipating an increase in the internal revenue tax, the trust bought up more distilleries and whiskey stocks and raised prices $0.20 cents per gallon on its alcohol. When the tax was not enacted, the trust was faced with both an excess of whiskey and public disfavor because of its recent price increase. Meanwhile, the trust manipulated prices at the expense of independents, sold watered stock (stock representing more than the value of actual assets), and on occasion was implicated in the use of violence against a recalcitrant independent. In fact, the secretary of the trust, George J. Gibson of Peoria, was arrested in 1891 on charges of attempting to destroy the property of the H. H. Shufeldt & Company (q.v.). His case did not come to trial and Gibson remained on the trust's payroll, although he did resign his post. In 1890 the trust incorporated with a new name, Distilling and Cattle Feeding Company, because of the unpopular image resulting from the word "trust." During the early 1890s, the company purchased a number of distilleries in Kentucky, but the association encountered increasing financial and legal problems, notably from Illinois and federal antitrust authorities for buying plants simply to shut them down. In 1895 the company went into receivership (q.v.). Greenhut left the trust in that year. Afterward, the trust's history became a maize of corporate entities and titles. Numerous new alignments were formed, each appearing to be autonomous, but evidence suggests centralization was still the goal. Among the new distillery associations that emerged were: the Kentucky Distilleries and Warehouse Company (q.v.), with Julius Kessler (q.v.) as president; American Spirits Manufacturing Company (q.v.); and the Standard Distilling and Distributing Company (q.v.). Each of the three associations controlled a number of distilleries and were semiautonomous but merged in 1899 to form the Distilling Company of America (q.v.). Sources indicate that Kessler was also an officer in the Distilling Company of America and Standard Distilling and Distributing. Greenhut also appears to have had a strong interest in Standard Distilling and Distributing. A committee of the U.S. House of Representatives conducted an intensive investigation in 1899. The parent company became known as Distillers' Securities Corporation about 1902, but other subsidiaries apparently continued to operate. After 1900, dividends rose and fell, and the remnants of the trust received substantial competition from small distillers. One of its companies, U.S. Industrial Alcohol (q.v.), was sold in 1913, and that firm proved very successful during World War I. During Prohibition (q.v.), Distillers' Securities Corporation changed its name to U.S. Food Products Company, then went into receivership in 1921. In 1924 it was reorganized as National Distillers Products Company (q.v.), with Seton Porter (q.v.) as the chief executive. *See also*, Peoria Distilling Industry.

SOURCES: Gerald Carson, *The Social History of Bourbon* (New York, 1963); Victor S. Clark, *History of Manufactures in the U.S.*, vol. 3 (New York, 1929); H. W. Coyte, "The Whiskey Trust," unpub. paper, 1977; Ernest E. East, "The Distillers' and Cattle Feeders' Trust, 1887-1895," *Journal of the Illinois State Historical Society* 45 (Summer 1952); Jeremiah W. Jenks and Walter E. Clark, *The Trust Problem* (New York, 1929); "Whiskey," *Fortune* (November 1933).

Wickersham, George W. (September 19, 1858-January 25, 1936). In 1929 President Herbert Hoover appointed Wickersham chairman of a commis-

sion to study enforcement problems surrounding the Eighteenth Amendment (q.v.). Wickersham had previously served as attorney general under
President William Howard Taft. The Wickersham commission (q.v.) submitted its report in 1931. The report supported the continuance of the
Volstead Act but found that there was no effective enforcement of the law.
Increased appropriations to provide for enforcement would be the only
solution.

SOURCES: Norman H. Clark, *Deliver Us from Evil* (New York, 1976); *Dictionary of American Biography*, Supplement 4.

Wickersham Commission. President Herbert Hoover appointed the commission in 1929. It was to study the enforcement of law in general, and the
Eighteenth Amendment (q.v.) in particular. Under the chairmanship of
George Wickersham (q.v.), the commission, formally known as the Commission on Law Enforcement and Observance, submitted its report in 1931.
The report noted in part that 15,370 distilleries and 1,140,063 gallons of
spirits had been seized by agents in 1929. Also, the great volume of hops in
production indicated an increasing malt liquor production. The conclusion
was that the Volstead Act (q.v.) should be continued even though no effective enforcement seemed possible unless huge federal appropriations could
support the enforcement effort. At a time when the nation had sunk to the
depths of the Depression, such expenditures appeared improbable. Thus the
Wickersham commission reported on an unfortunate situation that seemed
to have no solution.

SOURCES: Norman H. Clark, *Deliver Us from Evil* (New York, 1976); National
Commission on Law Observance and Enforcement, *Report on the Enforcement of
the Prohibition Laws of the United States* (Washington, D.C., 1931); Andrew
Sinclair, *Prohibition: The Era of Excess* (Boston, 1962).

Wiedemann, George, Brewing Company. The Newport, Kentucky, brewery, was located just across the Ohio River from Cincinnati. George
Wiedemann bought an interest in the Butcher brewery in 1870, but assumed
sole ownership in 1878. The family continued to manage the brewery until
1927, closed for a time, and reorganized and reopened in 1937, with George
Wiedemann's grandson, H. Tracy Balcom, as president. In 1964, the firm
was acquired by G. Heileman (q.v.) of LaCrosse, Wisconsin.

SOURCES: William L. Downard, *The Cincinnati Brewing Industry* (Athens,
Ohio, 1973); *One Hundred Years of Brewing* (Chicago and New York, 1903; Arno
Press Reprint, 1974).

Wieland, John, Brewing Company. John Wieland, a German immigrant,
established the San Francisco brewing firm in 1855. He bought into the
August Hoelscher & Company brewery and then took over his own plant
in 1856. Calling it the Philadelphia Brewery because of his earlier association with the city, Wieland expanded his company into the West Coast's

largest firm. In 1881, the company produced about 59,000 barrels. Upon his death in 1885, three sons took over the company, but in 1890 they sold it to the San Francisco Breweries Ltd. (q.v.), one of the many English brewing syndicates (*see* Consolidations, Brewery) in the U.S. It operated under the Wieland name, producing about 120,000 barrels in 1917, until it was closed during Prohibition (q.v.) in the 1920s.

SOURCES: Will Anderson, *The Beer Book* (Princeton, N.J., 1973); *One Hundred Years of Brewing* (Chicago and New York, 1903; Arno Press Reprint, 1974).

Wiley, Harvey W. (October 18, 1844-June 30, 1930). Chief of the Department of Agriculture's Bureau of Chemistry, Wiley was known as a vehement supporter of pure food and drug legislation. As such he was the primary author of the Pure Food and Drug Act of 1906 (q.v.). Wiley used *The Pharmacopoeia of the United States* as the guide for definitions of various drugs and medicines. The eighth revision of the work, which appeared in 1905, included a definition of whiskey (q.v.) that seemed to exclude blended or rectified whiskey as being the genuine product. Wiley used the source to side with the straight bourbon whiskey producers who portrayed blends as adulterations of pure whiskey. The controversy continued from 1906 to 1909 when President Taft (q.v.) rendered the "Taft decision" (q.v.). Dr. Wiley disagreed with the decision, resigned from government service, and eventually became a prohibitionist. Wiley authored a number of works; among them, *The History of a Crime Against Food* (1926).

SOURCES: Oscar E. Anderson, Jr., *The Health of a Nation: Harvey W. Wiley and the Fight for Pure Food* (Chicago, 1958); Gerald Carson, *The Social History of Bourbon* (New York, 1963).

Willard, Frances (September 28, 1839-February 18, 1898). A reformer and educator, Willard served as president of the Evanston College for Ladies (Illinois) in the early 1870s. In 1874 she resigned to become secretary of the Women's Christian Temperance Union (q.v.). She became president in 1879. Although she alienated some women, she was able to bring most conservatives, moderates, and radicals together in the cause of temperance.

SOURCES: *Dictionary of American Biography*, vol. 20; Norman H. Clark, *Deliver Us from Evil* (New York, 1976).

Willett, Thompson (b. January 27, 1909). President of the Willett Distilling Company (q.v.) of Bardstown, Kentucky, Willett, and his brother, John L., established the company in 1936. Their father, Lambert, had been a distiller, and the sons entered the industry after the repeal of Prohibition (q.v.). Thompson Willett has been the only president of the family-owned and operated company, which markets Old Bardstown Bourbon.

SOURCE: Jay Hall, "Bardstown: Where Bourbon Is King," *Mid-South*, January 8, 1978.

Willett Distilling Company. The Bardstown, Kentucky, distillery traces its origins to the late 1860s when John David Willett, Thomas S. Moore, and another partner established their plant. Willett had married Moore's sister-in-law, and Willett's sister, Catherine, married Ben F. Mattingly (*see* Mattingly & Moore Distilling Company). Willett's son, Lambert, continued in the whiskey business after his father's death. He was a partner in the Clear Springs Distilling Company, but he and his associates sold the plant during the Prohibition (q.v.) period, and it was eventually absorbed by National Distillers Products Company (q.v.). After engaging in nonwhiskey-related pursuits in the 1920s, Lambert Willett became superintendent of the Bernheim Distilling Company (q.v.) in 1933. Thompson Willett (q.v.), Lambert's son, joined his father at Bernheim in 1933, but he and his brother, John, formed their own company, the Willett Distilling Company, in 1936. When Lambert retired from Bernheim in 1942, he became active in the Willett firm. The company has been managed and owned by the Willett family, and Thompson Willett has been the sole president of the distillery, which markets Old Bardstown as its main brand. Thompson Willett's sons, Richard F. and John David, actively participate in running the company, the latter as an associate of a sales agency that merchandises the firm's products. Paul and Robert Willett, Thompson's brothers, serve as vice-presidents.

SOURCES: "Willett Distilling Company," *Kentucky Beverage Journal* (March 1957 and April 1963); Thompson Willett, "The Willett Distilling Story," unpub. paper, September 1974.

Wilson Act, 1890. According to this piece of federal legislation, alcoholic beverages shipped into a state from another state became subject to local law upon entry into the receiving state. The act represented the first in a string of victories for "dry" advocates who were pushing for state, rather than federal, jurisdiction over the interstate commerce in alcoholic beverages. The Webb-Kenyon Act (q.v.) in 1913 was a similar achievement.

Windisch-Muhlhauser Brewing Company. Founded in 1867 by Conrad Windisch and the Muhlhauser brothers, Gottlieb and Henry, this Cincinnati brewery was one of a number of firms referred to as the Lion Brewery. The founders, all German immigrants, had come to the U.S. in the late 1840s and early 1850s. The company proved very successful and could be described most accurately as a regional brewery (q.v.) with a very large local trade. The Windisch and Muhlhauser families controlled the firm. During Prohibition (q.v.) in the 1920s, the company first attempted to stay open by producing various malt products and soft drinks but closed in 1922. In 1933, Charles Windisch sold the plant, which eventually was reopened as the Burger Brewing Company (q.v.).

SOURCES: William L. Downard, *The Cincinnati Brewing Industry* (Athens, Ohio, 1973) and "When Gambrinus Was King," *Cincinnati Historical Society Bulletin* (Winter 1969); *One Hundred Years of Brewing* (Chicago and New York, 1903; Arno Press Reprint, 1974).

Winkelmeyer, Julius, Brewing Association. The St. Louis brewery was founded in 1843 by Frederick Stifel and Julius Winkelmeyer, both of whom were immigrants from Germany. They were very successful, and the brewery expanded rapidly. When Stifel died in a cholera epidemic in 1849, Winkelmeyer took over the business. After he died in 1867, his wife ran it. In 1879 the official name of the company, which was known as the Union Brewery, became the Julius Winkelmeyer Brewing Association. In 1889 it was sold to the St. Louis Brewing Association (q.v.), which renamed the plant Excelsior. It was closed in 1916.

SOURCES: Don Crinklaw, "The Battle of the Breweries," *St. Louis Post-Dispatch*, June 9, 1974; *One Hundred Years of Brewing* (Chicago and New York, 1903; Arno Press Reprint, 1974).

Winter, M., Brothers Brewing Company. The company was founded in 1883 in Pittsburgh by German immigrant M. Winter, who had worked previously at the Chicago brewery of Conrad Seipp (q.v.). Winter rented the Reichenbach facilities and built up a successful business, apparently the third largest in Allegheny County by the late 1890s. In February 1897, however, the company joined the merger of twenty-one area brewery concerns known as the Pittsburgh Brewing Company (q.v.).

SOURCE: "Pittsburgh, History of Beer and a Market," *American Brewer* (June and July 1960).

Witte, F. W., Brewing Company. Frederick W. Witte founded this Brooklyn brewery in 1874. The brewery was fairly small but continued until 1903. It was known for production of Weiss beer (q.v.), which is mild and pale and normally brewed from wheat. This beer was somewhat popular before Prohibition (q.v.) but since then has practically disappeared from the American market.

SOURCE: Will Anderson, *The Breweries of Brooklyn* (New York, 1976).

Wolf, Fred W. (active ca. 1870s). An architect and brewers' engineer in Chicago, Wolf designed many late nineteenth-century midwestern breweries. He also patented Weinig and Wolf's Malt Kiln Floors and Steep Tank Valves.

SOURCE: *Western Brewer* 2 (May 15, 1877).

Women's Christian Temperance Union. Generally known as the WCTU, the National Women's Christian Temperance Union was founded in 1874 in Cleveland, Ohio. Its objectives centered on promoting total abstinence from alcoholic beverages and suppressing the liquor traffic. Frances Willard (q.v.) was one of the founders and became president in 1879. The organization supported the Anti-Saloon League (q.v.) and proved instrumental in passage of the Eighteenth Amendment (q.v.).

SOURCE: Jack S. Blocker, ed., *Alcohol, Reform and Society: The Liquor Issue in Social Context* (Westport, Conn., 1979).

Woolner Distilling Company. The Peoria, Illinois, company was organized in the mid-1870s by the Woolner brothers, who immigrated from Hungary. Adolph, Samuel, and Ignatius bought the Grove Distillery from Richard Gregg and were joined by two other brothers, Jacob and Morris. They incorporated in the mid-1880s. The company was part of the Whiskey Trust (q.v.) for a time, and Adolph Woolner was vice-president of the trust until his death in 1891. The Woolners operated a variety of distilleries under the name until the advent of Prohibition (q.v.) when the remaining company was sold to U.S. Food Products (*see* National Distillers Products Company). From 1891 to 1898 the Woolners operated a plant called the Atlas Distillery (q.v.), which was sold to Standard Distilling and Distributing Company (q.v.), a trust subsidiary.

SOURCES: Distilleries file, Peoria Historical Society; Ernest E. East, "Distillery Fires in Corning Plant," *Arrow Messenger* (March 1937).

Worm. Normally a coiled copper tube leading from the head of the still (q.v.), the worm is water-cooled and the hot alcoholic vapors condense in the worm. Formerly, cooling was done by placing the worm, or condenser, in a drum or barrel known as a flakestand (q.v.). After the repeal of Prohibition (q.v.), more modern methods of cooling appeared utilizing methods of mechanical refrigeration. Previously, distilling had to be done during cool-weather periods when spring, river, or pond water was necessary.

SOURCES: Carl J. Kiefer, "Planning a Modern Distillery," *Spirits* (October 1933); Harry A. Tuer, "Vacuum Refrigeration for the Distillery," *Spirits* (December 1936).

Wort. The syrupy liquid results from boiling a mash (q.v.) of grain. The spent grains are strained off and rinsed, or sparged, to extract more sugar and water from the wort. The remaining wort is cooled; yeast is added; and then fermentation begins. The term is used in making both whiskey (q.v.) and beer (q.v.) but is more common in brewing technology. *See also*, Brewing Process, and Whiskey-Making process.

Wunder Brewing Company. Founded by Philip Frauenholz and Jacobi Gundlach in 1852, this San Francisco steam beer (q.v.) brewery was known as Philip Frauenholz Company until 1896, then as Frederick Schultz & Sons until the mid-1890s when J. C. Wunder bought the plant. From 1905 to 1916 it was known as the Acme Brewing Company, and then joined the California Brewing Association in 1916. In the years following the repeal of Prohibition (q.v.) the plant was known as Acme Breweries, California Brewing Association, or California Brewing Company until closing in 1957.

XYZ

Yeast. Yeast is the basic biological fermenting agent used in brewing and distilling to convert the sugars in the wort (q.v.) or mash (q.v.) into alcohol and carbon dioxide. Brewers and distillers usually employ a yeast grown from their own pedigreed strain, that is, cultured yeast. The particular strain is important in producing a unique product, and thus much care is taken in developing, maintaining, and protecting the unique qualities of individual yeasts. In brewing, certain yeasts rise to the top of the brewing vats in what is known as the top-fermentation (q.v.) process, whereas other yeasts settle at the bottom in the bottom-fermentation (q.v.) process. Ale (q.v.) is the primary product of the former, and lager (q.v.) of the latter. Emanating from experiments with yeast in Denmark in the late nineteenth century, American brewers gradually adopted pure cultured yeast. Emil Christian Hansen, a Danish biochemist, is credited with introducing the first such yeast that would work as the brewer desired, permitting greater control of fermentation (*see* Pasteurization). The first U.S. brewer to adopt the Hansen method was Schlitz (q.v.). William Uihlein (*see* Schlitz, Jos., Brewing Company), who had studied in Denmark, introduced pure cultured yeast at the Milwaukee brewery in the mid-1880s. For whiskey-making, two types of yeasting (q.v.) processes are followed. The most common one is called the yeast-back, or sour-mash (q.v.), method, and the yeast-mash or sweet-mash (q.v.) method is the other, but less common technique.

SOURCES: John P. Arnold and Frank Penman, *History of the Brewing Industry and Brewing Science* (Chicago, 1933); Stanley Baron, *Brewed in America* (Boston, 1962); Thomas C. Cochran, *The Pabst Brewing Company* (New York, 1948); Harold J. Grossman, *Grossman's Guide to Wines, Beers and Spirits* (New York, 1977); James Boone Wilson, *The Spirit of Old Kentucky* (Louisville, Ky., 1945).

Yeasting. Yeast (q.v.) is added to mash (q.v.) in the fermentation (q.v.) of whiskey (q.v.). Two techniques—the sour-mash (q.v.), or yeast-back, method and the sweet-mash (q.v.), or yeast-mash, method—are used. In the brewing process, the addition of yeast is called "pitching" (q.v.).

Yuengling, D. G., and Son, Inc. (Brewery). David G. Yuengling founded what is America's oldest brewery under continuous management. Yuengling came to the U.S. from Germany in 1828 at the age of twenty-two. He opened a brewery in Pottsville, Pennsylvania, in 1829 and operated the business until his death in 1876. His son, Frederick G., had entered the business in 1873, and the company has been under Yuengling management throughout its long history. Frank D. assumed directorship in 1900, and he was later succeeded by Richard L. Yuengling, Sr., who was born in 1915. The company marketed near beer (q.v.) during the 1920s and was probably the first company to award President Franklin Roosevelt with a case of 3.2 percent beer in 1933, just after modification of the Volstead Act (q.v.). The company is known for its variety of beers, among them ale, porter, bock, and lager. In 1873 David G. Yuengling, Jr., established another brewery operation in New York City. The primary business was in ale, but another plant was opened to produce lager beer (q.v.) in Richmond, Virginia. The plants did well at the outset but had financial troubles generally and were closed in 1897.

SOURCES: Will Anderson, *The Beer Book* (Princeton, N.J., 1973); *One Hundred Years of Brewing* (Chicago and New York, 1903; Arno Press Reprint, 1974); James D. Robertson, *The Great American Beer Book* (Ottawa, Ill., 1978).

Zymase. An enzyme (q.v.) by-product of yeast (q.v.), zymase acts as the primary fermenting agent in the making of alcoholic beverages. *See also*, Fermentation.

APPENDIXES

Appendix I: Alcoholic Beverage Consumption, 1710-1975
(Absolute Alcohol for Each Beverage, per Capita of Total
Population, in U.S. Gallons)

	Spirits		Wine		Cider		Beer		Total
Year	Beverage	Absolute Alcohol	Beverage	Absolute Alcohol	Beverage	Absolute Alcohol	Beverage	Absolute Alcohol	Absolute Alcohol
1710	2.0	0.9	0.1	0.05	18	1.8	—	—	2.7
1770	3.7	1.7	0.1	0.05	18	1.8	—	—	3.5
1785	3.0	1.4	0.3	0.1	18	1.8	—	—	3.3
1790	2.7	1.2	0.3	0.1	18	1.8	—	—	3.1
1795	3.1	1.4	0.3	0.1	18	1.8	—	—	3.3
1800	3.8	1.7	0.3	0.1	17	1.7	—	—	3.5
1805	4.3	1.9	0.3	0.1	16	1.6	—	—	3.6
1810	4.6	2.1	0.2	0.05	16	1.6	0.7	0.05	3.7
1815	4.4	2.0	0.2	0.05	16	1.6	—	—	3.6
1820	4.7	2.1	0.2	0.05	15	1.5	—	—	3.6
1825	5.0	2.2	0.2	0.05	15	1.5	—	—	3.7
1830	5.2	2.3	0.3	0.1	15	1.5	—	—	3.9
1835	4.2	1.9	0.3	0.1	8.5	0.8	—	—	2.8
1840	3.1	1.4	0.3	0.1	2	0.2	1.3	0.1	1.8
1845	2.1	0.9	0.2	0.05	—	—	1.4	0.1	1.0
1850	2.1	0.9	0.2	0.05	—	—	1.6	0.1	1.0
1855	2.2	1.0	0.2	0.05	—	—	2.7	0.1	1.1
1860	2.3	1.0	0.3	0.1	—	—	3.8	0.2	1.3
1865	2.1	0.9	0.3	0.1	—	—	3.5	0.2	1.2
1870	1.9	0.9	0.3	0.1	—	—	5.2	0.3	1.3
1875	1.7	0.8	0.5	0.1	—	—	6.2	0.3	1.2
1880	1.5	0.7	0.6	0.1	—	—	6.9	0.3	1.1
1885	1.4	0.6	0.5	0.1	—	—	11.4	0.6	1.3
1890	1.4	0.6	0.4	0.1	—	—	13.3	0.7	1.4
1895	1.2	0.5	0.4	0.1	—	—	15.2	0.8	1.4
1900	1.2	0.5	0.4	0.1	—	—	15.5	0.8	1.4
1905	1.3	0.6	0.5	0.1	—	—	17.3	0.9	1.6
1910	1.4	0.6	0.6	0.1	—	—	19.8	1.0	1.7
1915	1.2	0.5	0.5	0.1	—	—	20.2	1.0	1.6
1920	1.4	0.6	—	—	—	—	—	—	0.6
1925	1.4	0.6	—	—	—	—	—	—	0.6
1930	1.4	0.6	—	—	—	—	—	—	0.6
1935	1.1.	0.5	0.3	0.1	—	—	10.9	0.5	1.1
1940	1.0	0.4	0.7	0.1	—	—	12.9	0.6	1.1
1945	1.1	0.5	0.8	0.1	—	—	17.9	0.8	1.4
1950	1.1	0.5	0.8	0.1	—	—	17.6	0.8	1.4
1955	1.1	0.5	0.9	0.2	—	—	16.2	0.7	1.4
1960	1.3	0.6	0.9	0.2	—	—	15.2	0.7	1.5
1965	1.5	0.7	0.9	0.2	—	—	16.0	0.7	1.6

Year	Spirits		Wine		Cider		Beer		Total
	Beverage	Absolute Alcohol	Beverage	Absolute Alcohol	Beverage	Absolute Alcohol	Beverage	Absolute Alcohol	Absolute Alcohol
1970	1.8	0.8	1.3	0.2	—	—	18.4	0.8	1.8
1975	1.8	0.8	1.6	0.2	—	—	21.4	1.0	2.0

SOURCE: W. J. Rorabaugh, *The Alcoholic Republic: An American Tradition* (New York: Oxford University Press, 1979). Rorabaugh cautions that this table represents consumption estimates and approximations that tend "to suggest a precision that is lacking." Nevertheless, the figures are based on often solid evidence and indicate the general trend in drinking.

Appendix II: Alcoholic Beverage Consumption, 1710–1975
(Absolute Alcohol for Each Beverage, per Capita of
Drinking-Age (15 +) Population, in U.S. Gallons)

Year	Spirits Beverage	Spirits Absolute Alcohol	Wine Beverage	Wine Absolute Alcohol	Cider Beverage	Cider Absolute Alcohol	Beer Beverage	Beer Absolute Alcohol	Total Absolute Alcohol
1710	3.8	1.7	0.2	0.05	34	3.4	—	—	5.1
1770	7.0	3.2	0.2	0.05	34	3.4	—	—	6.6
1785	5.7	2.6	0.6	0.1	34	3.4	—	—	6.1
1790	5.1	2.3	0.6	0.1	34	3.4	—	—	5.8
1795	5.9	2.7	0.6	0.1	34	3.4	—	—	6.2
1800	7.2	3.3	0.6	0.1	32	3.2	—	—	6.6
1805	8.2	3.7	0.6	0.1	30	3.0	—	—	6.8
1810	8.7	3.9	0.4	0.1	30	3.0	1.3	0.1	7.1
1815	8.3	3.7	0.4	0.1	30	3.0	—	—	6.8
1820	8.7	3.9	0.4	0.1	28	2.8	—	—	6.8
1825	9.2	4.1	0.4	0.1	28	2.8	—	—	7.0
1830	9.5	4.3	0.5	0.1	27	2.7	—	—	7.1
1835	7.6	3.4	0.5	0.1	15	1.5	—	—	5.0
1840	5.5	2.5	0.5	0.1	4	0.4	2.3	0.1	3.1
1845	3.7	1.6	0.3	0.1	—	—	2.4	0.1	1.8
1850	3.6	1.6	0.3	0.1	—	—	2.7	0.1	1.8
1855	3.7	1.7	0.3	0.1	—	—	4.6	0.2	2.0
1860	3.9	1.7	0.5	0.1	—	—	6.4	0.3	2.1
1865	3.5	1.6	0.5	0.1	—	—	5.8	0.3	2.0
1870	3.1	1.4	0.5	0.1	—	—	8.6	0.4	1.9
1875	2.8	1.2	0.8	0.1	—	—	10.1	0.5	1.8
1880	2.4	1.1	1.0	0.2	—	—	11.1	0.6	1.9
1885	2.2	1.0	0.8	0.1	—	—	18.0	0.9	2.0
1890	2.2	1.0	0.6	0.1	—	—	20.6	1.0	2.1
1895	1.8	0.8	0.6	0.1	—	—	23.4	1.2	2.1
1900	1.8	0.8	0.6	0.1	—	—	23.6	1.2	2.1
1905	1.9	0.9	0.7	0.1	—	—	25.9	1.3	2.3
1910	2.1	0.9	0.9	0.2	—	—	29.2	1.5	2.6
1915	1.8	0.8	0.7	0.1	—	—	29.7	1.5	2.4
1920	2.1	0.9	—	—	—	—	—	—	0.9
1925	2.0	0.9	—	—	—	—	—	—	0.9
1930	2.0	0.9	—	—	—	—	—	—	0.9
1935	1.5	0.7	0.4	0.1	—	—	15.0	0.7	1.5
1940	1.3	0.6	0.9	0.2	—	—	17.2	0.8	1.6
1945	1.5	0.7	1.1	0.2	—	—	24.2	1.1	2.0
1950	1.5	0.7	1.1	0.2	—	—	24.1	1.1	2.0
1955	1.6	0.7	1.3	0.2	—	—	22.8	1.0	1.9
1960	1.9	0.8	1.3	0.2	—	—	22.1	1.0	2.0
1965	2.1	1.0	1.3	0.2	—	—	22.8	1.0	2.2

	Spirits		Wine		Cider		Beer		Total
Year	Beverage	Absolute Alcohol	Beverage	Absolute Alcohol	Beverage	Absolute Alcohol	Beverage	Absolute Alcohol	Absolute Alcohol
1970	2.5	1.1	1.8	0.3	—	—	25.7	1.2	2.5
1975	2.4	1.1	2.2	0.3	—	—	28.8	1.3	2.7

SOURCE: W. J. Rorabaugh, *The Alcoholic Republic: An American Tradition* (New York: Oxford University Press, 1979). Rorabaugh cautions that this table represents consumption estimates and approximations that tend "to suggest a precision that is lacking." Nevertheless, the figures are based on often solid evidence and indicate the general trend in drinking.

Appendix III: Number of Breweries, Population, and Production in Urban Brewing Centers, ca. 1890

City	Approximate No. of Breweries	Population	Production (barrels)
Main Brewing Centers			
Boston	21	448,477	838,365
Brooklyn	38	(included in New York)	1,402,415
Buffalo	20	255,664	482,473
Chicago	41	1,099,850	1,566,392
Cincinnati	24	296,908	1,068,594
Detroit	33	205,876	269,203
Milwaukee	14	204,468	1,472,096
New York	77	2,507,414	4,247,851
Philadelphia	91	1,046,964	1,387,004
St. Louis	29	451,770	1,538,369
San Francisco	26	298,997	489,145
Secondary Brewing Centers			
Albany	16	94,923	377,411
Baltimore	38	434,439	486,778
Cleveland	28	261,353	323,465
Louisville	23	161,129	—
Newark	30	181,830	943,805
Pittsburgh	34	238,617	307,866
Rochester	15	133,896	423,669
Syracuse	15	88,143	—

SOURCES: Will Anderson, *The Beer Book* (Princeton, N.J., 1973); Manfred Friedrich and Donald Bull, *The Register of U.S. Breweries, 1876–1976* (Trumbull, Conn., 1976); U.S., Bureau of the Census, *Abstract of the Twelfth Census of the United States, 1900*, 3rd ed. (Washington, D.C., 1904); *Western Brewer* (February 1890).

NOTE: See Boston Brewing Industry, Brooklyn Brewing Industry, and so on, for a brief article on each brewing center listed.

MAIN BREWING CENTERS

Boston

Haffenreffer & Co.
New England Breweries, Ltd.
Massachusetts Breweries Co., Ltd.
John Roessle Brewery

Brooklyn

Consumer's Park Brewing Corp.
Peter Doelger Brewing Corp.
Edelbrew Brewery, Inc.
Nassau Brewing Co.
Piel Brothers Brewery
Rheingold Breweries, Inc. (S. Liebmann)
F. & M. Schaefer
John F. Trommer's Brewery
F. W. Witte Brewing Co.

Buffalo

Magnus Beck Brewing Co.
William Simon Brewery

Chicago

Best Brewing Co. of Chicago
Birk Brothers Brewing Co.
Michael Brand Brewing Co.
Canadian Ace Brewing Co.
Chicago Breweries, Ltd.
Peter Hand Brewing Co.
John A. Huck Brewery
Keeley Brewing Co.
Lill and Diversey
McAvoy Brewing Co.
Schoenhofen-Edelweiss
Conrad Seipp Brewing Co.
Sieben's Brewery
United States Brewing Co.

Cincinnati

Burger Brewing Co.
John Hauck Brewing Co.

Hudepohl Brewing Co.
Christian Moerlein Brewing Co.
Red Top Brewing Co.
Schoenling Brewing Co.
George Wiedemann Brewing Co.
Windisch-Muhlhauser Brewing Co.

Detroit

Detroit Brewing Co.
E. & B. Brewing Co.
Goebel Brewing Co.
Philip Kling Brewing Co.
Koppitz-Melchers Brewing Co.
Pfeiffer Brewing Co.
Stroh Brewery Co.
E. W. Voight Brewing Co.

Milwaukee

Val. Blatz Brewing Co.
Cream City Brewing Co.
Adam Gettelman Brewing Co.
Miller Brewing Co.
Pabst Brewing Co.
Jos. Schlitz Brewing Co.

New York

Beadleston & Woerz
Bernheimer & Schmid
H. Clausen & Son
Peter Doelger Brewing Corp.
George Ehret's Hell Gate Brewing Co.
James Everard Brewing Co.
Flanagan, Nay & Co.
Jacob Ruppert Brewery
F. & M. Schaefer Brewing Co.

Philadelphia

Louis Bergdoll Brewing Co.
Bergner & Engel Brewing Co.
John F. Betz & Son, Inc.
Esslinger Brewing Co.
Liebert & Obert
William Massey & Co.
Henry F. Ortlieb Brewing Co.
Francis Perot's Sons (Malting Co.)
F. A. Poth & Sons, Inc.

C. Schmidt & Sons, Inc.
Robert Smith Ale Brewing Co.

St. Louis

American Brewing Co.
Anheuser-Busch, Inc.
Columbia Brewing Co.
Falstaff Brewing Corp.
Independent Breweries Co.
William J. Lemp Brewing Co.
Louis Obert Brewing Co.
Phoenix Brewery
St. Louis Brewing Association
Joseph Uhrig Brewing Co.
Wainwright Brewing Co.
Julius Winkelmeyer Brewing Association

San Francisco

Anchor Brewing Co.
National Brewing Co.
New Albion Brewing Co.
San Francisco Breweries, Ltd.
A. Schuppert Brewery
John Wieland Brewing Co.
Wunder Brewing Co.

SECONDARY BREWING CENTERS

Albany

Albany Brewing Co.
Peter Ballantine & Sons
Beverwyck Brewing Co.
Dobler Brewing Co.
Hedrick Brewing Co.
John Taylor & Sons

Baltimore

Dukehart Brewing Co.
Gottlieb-Bauernschmidt-Strauss Brewing Co.
Maryland Brewing Co.
National Brewing Co.

Cleveland

Cleveland & Sandusky Brewing Co.

Louisville

> Central Consumers Brewing Co.
> Falls City Brewing Co.
> Frank Fehr Brewing Co.
> John F. Oertel

Newark

> Peter Ballantine Brewing Co.
> Christian Feigenspan, Inc.
> Gottfried Krueger Brewing Co.

Pittsburgh

> C. Baeuerlein Brewing Co.
> Duquesne Brewing Co.
> Eberhardt & Ober
> Ft. Pitt Brewing Co.
> Phoenix Brewing Co.
> Pittsburgh Brewing Co.
> Straub Brewery
> Z. Wainwright
> M. Winter Bros. Brewing Co.

Rochester

> Genesee Brewing Co.
> Standard Rochester Brewing Co.

Syracuse

> Greenway Brewery
> Haberle Brewing Co.

NOTE: See individual entries for each brewing center and firm listed.

Appendix V: Currently Operating Brewing and Distilling Firms (1979)

BREWERIES

Anchor Brewing Co.
Anheuser-Busch, Inc.
Champale, Inc.
Cold Spring Brewing Co.
Adolph Coors Brewing Co.
Dixie Brewing Co.
Duncan Brewing Co.
Eastern Brewing Corp.
Erie Brewing Co.
Falls City Brewing Co.
Falstaff Brewing Corp.
General Brewing Co.
Genesee Brewing Co.
Geyer Bros. Brewing Co.
G. Heileman Brewing Co.
Horlacher Brewing Co.
Jos. Huber Brewing Co.
Hudepohl Brewing Co.
Hull Brewing Co.
Jones Brewing Co.
Fred Koch Brewery, Inc.
Latrobe Brewing Co.
Jacob Leinenkugel Brewing Co.
Lion, Inc.
Miller Brewing Co.
New Albion Brewing Co.
Olympia Brewing Co.
Henry F. Ortlieb Brewing Co.
Pabst Brewing Co.
Pearl Brewing Co.
Jos. Pickett & Sons, Inc.
Pittsburgh Brewing Co.
Prinz Brau Alaska, Inc.
F. & M. Schaefer Brewing Co.
August Schell Brewing Co.
Jos. Schlitz Brewing Co.
C. Schmidt & Sons, Inc.
Schoenling Brewing Co.
Spoetzl Brewery, Inc.
Stevens Point Beverage Co.
Straub Brewery, Inc.
Stroh Brewery Co.
Walter Brewing Co.

West End Brewing Co.
D. G. Yuengling and Son, Inc.

DISTILLERIES

Ambur Distilled Products, Inc.
American Distilling Co.
Austin, Nichols & Co., Inc.
Barton Brands, Ltd.
James B. Beam Distilling Co.
A. Smith Bowman Distillery
J. T. S. Brown Distillers Co.
Brown-Forman Distillers Corp.
R. L. Buse Co.
Calvert Distillers Co.
Jack Daniel Distillery
Fleischmann Distilling Co.
Florida Distillers Co.
Glenmore Distillers Co.
Heaven Hill Distilleries, Inc.
Heublein, Inc.
L. Hirsch & Co.
Hoffman Distilling Co.
Kasser Distillers Products Corp.
McCormick Distilling Co.
Majestic Distilling Co.
Maker's Mark Distillery, Inc.
Medley Distilling Co.
Michter's Distillery, Inc.
National Distillers Products Co.
Publicker Distillers Products
Schenley Distillers Co.
Jos. E. Seagram and Sons
Somerset Importers, Ltd. (Old Fitzgerald)
Southern Comfort Corp.
Hiram Walker Distillery
Willett Distilling Company

> *NOTE:* See individual entries for each firm listed. The list does not include all plants oper-
> ated as subsidiaries of the larger companies—nor is it a complete list of operating
> firms. Information was unavailable on a few distilling firms.

Appendix VI: History of the Federal Excise Tax on Beer

Congress subjected beer to taxation by enacting a law on July 1, 1862, which became effective in August 1862. The following table indicates the federal excise tax rate on malt beverages from 1862 to 1980:

Period	Tax per Barrel
August 1862—March 3, 1863	$ 1.00
March 4, 1863—March 31, 1864	0.60
April 1, 1864—June 13, 1898	1.00[a]
June 14, 1898—June 30, 1901	2.00[a]
July 1, 1901—June 30, 1902	1.60
July 1, 1902—October 22, 1914	1.00
October 23, 1914—October 3, 1917	1.50
October 4, 1917—February 24, 1919	3.00
February 25, 1919—October 28, 1919	6.00
April 7, 1933—January 10, 1934	5.00[b]
January 11, 1934—June 30, 1940	5.00
July 1, 1940—October 31, 1942	6.00
November 1, 1942—March 31, 1944	7.00
April 1, 1944—October 31, 1951	8.00
November 1, 1951—1980	9.00

SOURCE: U.S. Brewers Association, *Brewers Almanac 1974* (Washington, D.C., 1974).

[a]There was a 7½ percent discount for leakage.

[b]This was the tax on beer containing not more than 3.2 percent of alcohol by weight, the sale of which was relegalized by the act of March 27, 1933. The tax on beer of greater alcoholic content remained at $6 and was not reduced to $5 until the Liquor Taxing Act of 1934.

Appendix VII: History of Federal Liquor Excise Taxes

Period From	To	Rate	Notes
July 1, 1791	June 30, 1792	9¢ to 25¢ per gallon according to proof	Alternative tax—annual tax of 60¢ per gallon on still capacity
July 1, 1792	June 30, 1802	7¢ to 18¢ per gallon according to proof	Alternative tax on still capacity reduced to 54¢ annually
July 1, 1802	Dec. 31, 1814	No tax	All liquor excise taxes abolished
Jan 1, 1814	Jan. 31, 1815	No tax per gallon	Tax on distilleries was substituted for a tax per gallon
Feb. 1, 1815	Dec. 31, 1817	20¢ per proof gallon	Added to tax on distilleries
Jan. 1, 1818	Aug. 31, 1862	No tax	Internal Revenue tax was abolished entirely in 1818, remaining non-existent until 1862
Sept. 1, 1862	March 6, 1864	20¢ per proof gallon	All distilled spirits
March 7, 1864	June 30, 1864	60¢ per proof gallon	All spirits
July 1, 1864	Dec. 31, 1864	$1.50 per proof gallon	All spirits except grape brandy
Jan. 1, 1865	July 19, 1868	$2.00 per proof gallon	All spirits except grape, peach and apple brandy
July 20, 1868	July 31, 1872	50¢ per proof gallon	Illegal distilling activity became so prevalent that Bureau of Internal Revenue requested Congress to reduce the tax to 50¢
Aug. 1, 1872	March 2, 1875	70¢ per proof gallon	All spirits
March 3, 1875	Aug. 26, 1894	90¢ per proof gallon	All spirits
Aug. 27, 1894	Oct. 2, 1917	$1.10 per proof gallon	All spirits
Oct. 3, 1917	Dec. 31, 1926	$2.20 per proof gallon	Medicinal rate
Oct. 3, 1917	Feb. 24, 1919	$3.20 per proof gallon	Spirits diverted to beverage use
Feb. 25, 1919	Jan. 11, 1934	$6.40 per proof gallon	Spirits diverted to beverage use
Jan. 16, 1920	Jan. 11, 1934		National Prohibition
Jan. 1, 1927	Dec. 31, 1927	$1.65 per proof gallon	Reduction of medicinal rate
Jan. 1, 1928	Jan. 11, 1934	$1.10 per proof gallon	Reduction of medicinal rate
Jan. 12, 1934	June 30, 1938	$2.00 per proof gallon	Permanent on all spirits, beverage rate of $6.40 no longer applied to legal production, end of Prohibition
July 1, 1938	June 30, 1940	$2.25 per proof gallon	All spirits except brandy
July 1, 1940	Sept. 30, 1941	$3.00 per proof gallon	All spirits except brandy, designated as temporary defense tax increase to expire June 30, 1945
Oct. 1, 1941	Oct. 31, 1942	$4.00 per proof gallon	The Revenue Act of October 1941 increased the tax to $4.00 and made it permanent

Period From	To	Rate	Notes
Nov. 1, 1942	March 31, 1944	$6.00 per proof gallon	"Permanent Rate" only temporary, as tax was again increased
April 1, 1944	Oct. 31, 1951	$9.00 per proof gallon	Increase designated as temporary rate change with termination after World War II. Became permanent by act of March 11, 1947[a]
Nov. 1, 1951		$10.50 per proof gallon	The act of October 20, 1951, made provision that tax increase be temporary reverting to $9.00 rate April 1954. Rate extended.[b]
June 30, 1964	The 1951 "temporary" tax made permanent.		

SOURCE: Distilled Spirits Council of the U.S., 1977 Tax Briefs (Washington, D.C., 1977).

[a]Preceding the increase from $6.00 to $9.00 per proof gallon, the House Ways and Means Committee stated: "Ordinarily, such a high tax rate might increase the amount of bootlegging," and it wrote into the Revenue Act of 1943 that the $9.00 rate was to expire ". . . on the first day of the first month which begins six months or more after the date of the termination of hostilities in the present war." This provision was stricken by the act of March 11, 1947.

[b]The increase from $9.00 to $10.50 per proof gallon was enacted despite the fact that the Committee on Federal Tax Policy recommended no further increases. In its report "Financing Defense," the committee stated: "In the case of alcoholic beverages, even the present taxes provide a substantial incentive to illicit manufacture, and any further material increase would offer still greater inducement. We do not recommend increases above the present rates, which are still at the highest levels attained during World War II."

NOTE: A "proof" gallon is a gallon of 100 proof spirits. Thus a gallon of 80 proof bourbon is assessed $8.40 in federal excise tax ($10.50 × .80 = $8.40).

Appendix VIII: Partial List of Firms in the Kentucky Distilleries and Warehouse Company[a]

Year	Distillery	Location
1898	Peacock Distillery	Kaiser Station
1899	J. M. Atherton Distilleries (JK)	Athertonville
1899	Normandy Distillery	Louisville
1899	Paris Distilling Co.	Paris
1899	John Cochran's Spring Hill Co.	Frankfort
1900	Coon Hollow & Big Spring	Coon Hollow
1900	Boldrick & Callaghan	Calvery
1900	J. B. Wathen & Bros.	Louisville
1901	G. G. White Chickencock Distillery	Paris
1901	J. N. Blakemore	Alton
1901	Crab Orchard Distillery	Crab Orchard
1901	W. H. McBrayer's Cedar Brook (JK)	Lawrenceburg
1901	J. G. Roach Old Log Cabin (JK)	Louisville
1902	Ashbrook Bros.	Cynthiana
1902	G. R. Sharpe's Old Lewis Hunter	Lair
1902	T. B. Ripy	Tyrone
1902	J. G. Mattingly & Sons	Louisville
1904	Ashland Distillery	Lexington
1904	Bond & Lillard	Lawrenceburg

SOURCES: H. W. Coyte, "The Whiskey Trust," unpub. personal paper, 1977; "The Trust," *Spirits* (April 1935).

[a]JK indicates that the firm was purchased by Julius Kessler & Company, a subsidiary of Kentucky Distilleries and Warehouse Company.

Appendix IX: The Largest Breweries in 1877, 1895, and 1973

Largest Brewers (1877)	Production (Barrels)
George Ehret, New York, N.Y.	138,449
Ph. Best, Milwaukee, Wis.	121,634
Bergner & Engel, Philadelphia, Pa.	119,807
P. Ballantine & Sons, Newark, N.J.	107,592
Conrad Seipp, Chicago, Ill.	95,167
H. Clausen & Son, New York, N.Y.	90,642
Flanagan & Wallace, New York, N.Y.	88,677
Jacob Ruppert, New York, N.Y.	84,432
Beadleston & Woerz, New York, N.Y.	79,658
Jos. Schlitz Brewing Company, Milwaukee, Wis.	79,538
Wm. Massey & Co., Philadelphia, Pa.	75,193
Albany Brewing Co., Albany, N.Y.	72,723
Christian Moerlein, Cincinnati, Ohio	72,588
Frank Jones, Portsmouth, N.H.	71,471
Rueter & Alley, Boston, Mass.	67,121
Clausen & Price, New York, N.Y.	64,896
Boston Beer Co., Boston, Mass.	62,881
Yuengling & Co., New York, N.Y.	62,740
W. J. Lemp, St. Louis, Mo.	61,229
Windisch, Muhlhauser & Bro., Cincinnati, Ohio	59,475

SOURCE: *One Hundred Years of Brewing* (Chicago and New York, 1903; Arno Press Reprint, 1974).

Largest Brewers (1895)	Production (Barrels)
Pabst Brewing Co., Milwaukee, Wis.	900-1,000,000
Anheuser-Busch Brewing Assn., St. Louis, Mo.	700,000- 800,000
Jos. Schlitz Brewing Co., Milwaukee, Wis.	600,000- 700,000
George Ehret, New York, N.Y.	500,000- 600,000
Ballantine & Co., Newark, N.J.	500,000- 600,000
Bernheimer & Schmid, New York, N.Y.	400,000- 500,000
Val. Blatz Brewing Co., Milwaukee, Wis.	350,000- 400,000
Wm. J. Lemp Brewing Co., St. Louis, Mo.	300,000- 350,000
Conrad Seipp Brewing Co., Chicago, Ill.	250,000- 300,000
Frank Jones Brewing Co., Portsmouth, N.H.	250,000- 300,000
Peter Doelger, New York, N.Y.	250,000- 300,000
Ruppert, New York, N.Y.	250,000- 300,000
James Everard, New York, N.Y.	250,000- 300,000
Christian Moerlein Brewing Co., Cincinnati, Ohio	250,000- 300,000
Bergner & Engel, Philadelphia, Pa.	250,000- 300,000
Bartholomay Brewing Co., Rochester, N.Y.	250,000- 300,000

SOURCE: *Brewers Guide for the United States, Canada and Mexico* (1896).

Largest Brewers (1973)	Production (Barrels)
Anheuser-Busch, Inc.	29,887,000
Jos. Schlitz Brewing Co.	21,343,000
Pabst Brewing Co.	13,128,000
Adolph Coors Co.	10,950,000
Miller Brewing Co.	6,919,000
Falstaff Brewing Corp.	6,009,000
F. & M. Schaefer Brewing Co.	5,000,000
Stroh Brewery Co.	4,646,000
G. Heileman Brewing Co.	4,420,000
Carling Brewing Co.	3,800,000
Olympia Brewing Co.	3,637,000
C. Schmidt & Sons, Inc.	3,520,000
Theo. Hamm Brewing Co.	3,400,000
Rheingold Breweries, Inc.	2,675,000
National Brewing Co.	2,196,000
Genesee Brewing Co.	1,850,000
Pearl Brewing Co.	1,611,000
Grain Belt Breweries, Inc.	1,100,000
Lone Star Brewing Co.	1,066,000
Rainier Brewing Co.	860,000

SOURCE: Manfred Friedrich and Donald Bull, *The Register of U.S. Breweries, 1876-1976* (Trumbull, Conn., 1976).

Appendix X: Operating Breweries by States in Selected Years, 1876-1973

State	1876	1880	1890	1895	1900	1910	1914	1919	1935	1940	1945	1950	1955	1960	1965	1973
AL	4	—	1	4	5	1	2	—	—	—	—	—	—	—	—	—
AK	1	—	3	4	15	5	4	3	3	2	—	—	—	—	—	—
AZ	7	11	4	2	3	2	2	—	1	1	1	1	1	1	1	1
AR	—	—	—	—	1	1	1	—	—	—	—	—	—	—	—	—
CA	206	186	145	120	117	82	74	65	41	32	21	17	16	12	12	10
CO	36	27	21	18	15	13	12	—	5	4	4	4	3	3	3	2
CT	31	20	23	20	21	21	20	19	12	9	5	2	2	1	1	1
DE	2	4	4	5	5	6	4	3	1	2	2	2	2	—	—	—
DC	16	10	7	5	5	5	4	4	2	1	1	1	1	—	—	—
FL	—	—	—	—	1	1	2	1	10	6	6	6	6	7	3	6
GA	2	1	3	6	6	4	4	4	1	1	1	1	—	1	1	2
HI	—	—	—	—	1	1	1	—	6	7	2	5	5	4	3	2
ID	10	12	30	18	19	10	6	—	5	4	3	3	1	—	—	—
IL	165	110	112	122	114	113	100	93	62	52	39	31	21	15	12	3
IN	105	66	48	49	45	41	39	33	17	16	13	11	6	4	4	3
IA	132	118	23	27	28	20	18	—	4	3	3	3	3	2	1	1
KS	34	30	2	2	2	—	—	—	—	—	—	—	—	—	—	—
KY	35	32	28	25	30	22	19	17	7	8	6	6	5	5	4	2
LA	10	9	8	7	9	12	12	11	7	6	6	5	4	4	3	3
ME	4	—	—	—	—	—	—	—	—	—	—	—	—	—	—	—
MD	70	57	43	29	29	24	19	15	11	9	7	7	6	6	6	4
MA	28	31	33	35	47	40	39	32	14	15	14	13	8	7	4	3
MI	147	117	107	98	87	74	70	59	45	37	23	19	13	10	7	5
MN	112	103	100	95	85	71	66	60	24	22	19	18	15	13	10	5
MO	87	64	59	47	52	52	53	46	19	17	13	10	9	6	6	4

MT	22	19	18	16	26	22	21	21	10	9	8	7	5	3	1	—
NB	15	26	23	22	22	14	14	13	5	5	4	4	3	3	2	1
NV	30	32	17	8	5	5	3	—	2	2	2	1	1	—	—	—
NH	6	5	5	6	5	4	4	4	1	1	1	1	—	—	—	1
NJ	69	51	47	45	51	40	40	36	15	14	13	9	9	8	6	5
NY	393	334	290	274	270	194	165	153	69	61	44	36	24	18	13	7
NC	1	—	—	—	—	—	—	—	—	1	1	1	1	—	—	1
ND	—	—	6	1	—	—	—	—	—	—	—	—	—	—	—	—
OH	216	164	133	122	124	120	118	104	54	50	38	33	15	12	8	5
OK	—	—	—	1	—	—	—	—	2	3	2	2	1	1	1	—
OR	30	32	33	25	26	20	13	—	6	6	4	2	1	1	1	1
PA	361	297	266	221	220	248	233	209	107	72	63	53	32	26	24	18
RI	6	5	3	5	8	8	7	6	6	3	2	2	2	1	1	1
SC	3	2	1	2	1	1	1	1	—	—	—	—	—	—	—	—
SD	—	—	8	5	5	4	4	4	1	1	—	—	—	—	—	—
TN	6	2	4	4	4	5	4	—	1	3	2	2	1	—	—	1
TX	47	21	9	13	12	15	16	14	10	8	7	7	6	6	7	7
UT	22	14	9	8	7	6	5	4	2	2	2	2	2	2	1	—
VT	1	1	1	—	1	—	—	—	2	—	—	—	—	—	—	—
VA	5	2	2	4	8	6	6	6	2	4	4	4	3	2	2	2
WA	13	29	31	29	33	34	26	—	18	15	11	11	8	7	5	4
WV	16	—	7	8	9	14	10	—	4	2	1	1	1	1	1	—
WI	157	205	171	168	163	140	138	131	86	74	61	48	43	33	27	11
WY	8	6	7	3	5	3	2	3	3	3	3	2	—	—	—	—
	2,685	2,266	1,902	1,732	1,751	1,498	1,404	1,179	703	592	462	392	283	225	182	122

SOURCE: Manfred Friedrich and Donald Bull, *The Register of U.S. Breweries, 1876–1976* (Trumbull, Conn., 1976).

NOTE: Mississippi never had a brewery.

Appendix XI: Statement of the Number of Grain and Molasses Distilleries in Operation, January 1, 1891, and Their Daily Capacities

States	No. of Distilleries		Capacity of Grain Distilleries		Capacity of Molasses Distilleries	
	Grain	Molasses	Bushels	Gallons	Gallons	Spirits
Alabama	2		12	31		
Arkansas	12		88	216		
California	2		435	1,670		
Colorado	1		9	31		
Connecticut	3		575	2,284		
Georgia	72		864	2,174		
Illinois	14		33,623	180,627		
Indiana	7		4,591	19,259		
Iowa						
Kentucky	172	1	36,265	142,035	522	444
Maryland	13		2,684	10,680		
Massachusetts	1	7	68	239	10,078	8,566
Minnesota	1		2,210	9,947		
Nebraska	2		2,317	10,025		
New Hampshire		1			152	129
New Jersey	1		400	1,600		
New York	2		1,901	7,603		
North Carolina	273		1,073	2,773		
Ohio	13		8,268	35,970		
Oregon						
Pennsylvania	62		7,139	27,994		
South Carolina	15		89	219		
Tennessee	47		848	2,608		
Texas	9		72	206		
Virginia	51		318	900		
West Virginia	1		559	2,336		
Wisconsin	3		496	2,027		

SOURCE: "Statement of Distillers in 1891," *The Wine and Spirit Bulletin: Devoted to the Interest of the Wine Trade* 5, no. 3 (February 3, 1891).

SELECTED BIBLIOGRAPHY _____

The sources listed represent a portion of the material used in compiling this dictionary. Because most entries are followed by source citations, the works cited here are more general in nature, although certain sources of special interest have also been included. The following works contain extensive bibliographies:

Stanley Baron, *Brewed in America* (Boston, 1962);

Gerald Carson, *The Social History of Bourbon* (New York, 1963);

Thomas C. Cochran, *The Pabst Brewing Company* (New York, 1948);

Henry G. Crowgey, *Kentucky Bourbon* (Lexington, Ky., 1971).

ARTICLES

Angle, Paul. "Michael Diversey & Beer in Chicago." *Chicago History* (Spring 1969). Diversey was one of Chicago's first brewers and distinguished himself as a civic leader.

"Beer Bottle, Its History, The." *American Brewer* (March 1963). Brief account of the origins and history of beer bottling.

Bigger, Jeanne Ridgway. "Jack Daniel Distillery and Lynchburg." *Tennessee Historical Quarterly* (Spring 1972). Brief account of the famous distillery, written in a topical rather than chronological style.

Carson, Gerald. "Bourbon: Amber Waves of Grain—100 Proof." *American Heritage* (February 1974). Survey of the origins of bourbon, centering on its Kentucky birthplace and the popularity it enjoyed across the nation.

Crinklaw, Don. "A Saga: The Lemps of St. Louis." *St. Louis Post-Dispatch*, December 2, 1973. Brief account of the famous St. Louis brewing family.

"Distilleries of Old Kentucky." *Spirits* (April 1935). Series of articles on the Kentucky distilling industry. Although most of the information is credible and reliable, some portions contain contradictions and inaccuracies. It is, on balance, a very valuable set of articles.

Fine, Steven M. "King of Suds." *The Pittsburgher* (October 1977). Brief history of the Pittsburgh brewing industry.

"The First Century: A History of the United States Brewers Association, 1862-1962." *American Brewer* (January and February 1962). History of the USBA by the editors of the *American Brewer*, a journal established by the association.

Gimigliano, Michael. "The Golden Age of Gambrinus—A Brief History of Early Brewing in Syracuse." *Brewers Digest* (November 1975). Brief survey of the breweries of Syracuse, New York.

"Kentucky's Sons: Family Trees of Noted Distillers." *Spirits* (May 1936). Lengthy article on the personalities involved in and the history of the Kentucky distilling industry.

Kirkpatrick, Woodward. "Kentucky Saga." *Spirits* (January 1934). Review of the industry and the impact of concentration and Prohibition by the secretary of the Old Lewis Hunter distillery.

Korell, Dorothy L. "Bourbon Capital of the World." *Louisville* (October 20, 1965). Brief account of the Louisville distilling industry, primarily in the post-Prohibition era.

La Susa, Richard J. "Nevermore the Local Lagers." *Chicago Tribune Magazine* (April 24, 1977). Valuable summary history of Chicago's brewing industry from its early-nineteenth-century origins to its demise in the 1960s.

Lynch, Charles A., and John Ward Willson Loose. "A History of Brewing in Lancaster County, Legal and Otherwise." *Journal of the Lancaster County Historical Society* 70 (1966). Summary history of the Pennsylvania county's many breweries.

McMillen, Harlow. "Staten Island's Lager Beer Breweries, 1851-1962." *Staten Island Historian* (July-September 1969). Company-by-company history of the New York island's brewing industry.

Packowski, George W. "Beverage Spirits, Distilled." *Kirk-Othmer, Encyclopedia of Chemical Technology*. Third ed., vol. 3 (1978). Article centering on the chemical aspect of distilling with a historical background on the industry.

"Rare Jack Daniel's." *Fortune* (July 1951). Brief article on the appeal, based on quality and scarcity, of Jack Daniel whiskey.

Renner, Richard Wilson. "In a Perfect Ferment: Chicago, the Know-Nothings and the Riot for Lager Beer." *Chicago History* (Fall 1976). Account of a so-called beer riot in 1855 against discrimination and taxation mainly affecting the German community.

"The Seagram Saga." *Bev/Executive* (February-June 1966). In-depth study and history of the Bronfman firm. The series spans nearly one-half of volume 3 of *Bev*, an industry trade journal.

Sifford, Darrell. "Bourbon Whiskey: Kentucky's All-American Drink." Louisville *Courier-Journal Magazine* (March 27, 1966). General overview of the post-Repeal Kentucky distilling industry.

"Through the Years . . . with Hiram Walker." *Canadian Beverage Review* (1952). Brief history of Hiram Walker, Inc., including colorful material on the founder and the history of the firm after 1926 when it was purchased by Harry C. Hatch.

BOOKS

Alexis Lichine's New Encyclopedia of Wines & Spirits. New York: Alfred A. Knopf, 1974. Valuable directory emphasizing the types of spirits and processes in making them. It contains historical information as well.

Anderson, Oscar E., Jr. *The Health of a Nation: Harvey W. Wiley and the Fight for Pure Food*. Chicago: University of Chicago Press, 1958. Biography of Dr. Harvey Wiley, the nation's chief chemist in 1906, who became the primary interpreter of the Pure Food and Drug Act.

Anderson, Will. *The Beer Book, an Illustrated Guide to American Breweriana.* Princeton, N.J.: The Pyne Press, 1973. A general guide to breweriana, illustrating beer cans, labels, and so on, including valuable historical information on many breweries and brewing areas.

———. *The Breweries of Brooklyn: An Informal History of a Great Industry in a Great City.* Croton Falls, N.Y., 1976. Study of the Brooklyn breweries, primarily in the late nineteenth and early twentieth centuries.

Arnold, John P. *Origins and History of Beer and Brewing.* Chicago: Alumni Association of the Wahl-Henius Institute of Fermentology, 1911. General and international survey of beer and brewing from prehistoric times through the European Middle Ages and the discovery of America to 1800.

———, and Frank Penman. *The History of the Brewing Industry and Brewing Science in America.* Chicago: privately printed, 1933. History of the industry and technical advances including material on Prohibition, brewers' associations, and individual breweries.

Asbury, Herbert. *Carry Nation.* New York: Alfred A. Knopf, 1929. Biography of the famous prohibitionist portraying her as a suffering, emotional person with a broken nervous system.

———. *The Great Illusion: An Informal History of Prohibition.* Garden City, N.Y.: Doubleday & Company, Inc., 1950. Social history of the Prohibition era written in a colorful style.

Baron, Stanley. *Brewed in America: A History of Beer and Ale in the United States.* Boston: Little, Brown and Company, 1962. First-rate study of the industry from the colonial period to 1961.

Birmingham, Frederic. *Falstaff's Complete Beer Book.* New York: Award Books, 1970. Informal work containing a brief history of the industry, but with valuable information on brewing and brewing terminology.

Blocker, Jack S., ed. *Alcohol, Reform and Society: The Liquor Issue in Social Context.* Westport, Conn.: Greenwood Press, Inc., 1979. A sourcebook of essays on the history and social context of alcohol, temperance, and Prohibition.

Broderick, Harold M., ed. *The Practical Brewer: A Manual for the Brewing Industry.* Madison, Wis.: Master Brewers Association of the Americas, 1977. An update of the 1946 publication (*see* Edward Vogel et al., *The Practical Brewer*) featuring technical articles on the various processes involved in brewing.

Bronfman, Samuel. . . . *From Little Acorns* . . . Montreal: Distillers-Corporation-Seagram's Ltd., 1970. History of Seagram by the founder of the modern company, which dates from the 1920s.

Byrne, Frank L. *Prophet of Prohibition: Neal Dow and His Crusade.* Madison, Wis.: State Historical Society of Wisconsin, 1961. Biography of the Maine prohibitionist of the mid-nineteenth century.

Cannon, James, Jr. *Bishop Cannon's Own Story.* Durham, N.C.: Duke University Press, 1955. Autobiography of the famous prohibition crusader of the early twentieth century.

Carson, Gerald. *The Social History of Bourbon: An Unhurried Account of Our Star-Spangled American Drink.* New York: Dodd, Mead & Company, 1963. Informal and somewhat light-hearted history that is, however, very valuable and sound. It is one of the few comprehensive histories of the industry.

Channing, Steven A. *Kentucky*. New York: W. W. Norton & Company, Inc., 1977. General history of the state briefly recounting the history and importance of the distilling industry. It is a volume in the State and the Nation Series.

Cherrington, E. H. *The Evolution of Prohibition in the United States of America.* Westerville, Ohio: American Issue Press, 1920. General history of temperance by the Anti-Saloon League's head of educational and propaganda publications.

Clark, Norman H. *Deliver Us From Evil: An Interpretation of American Prohibition.* New York: W. W. Norton & Company, Inc., 1976. Insightful and balanced scholarly history of Prohibition and its demise.

Clark, Victor S. *History of Manufactures in the United States, 1607-1928.* 3 vols. New York: McGraw-Hill, 1929. Classic history containing especially helpful information on the Whiskey Trust.

Cochran, Thomas C. *The Pabst Brewing Company: The History of an American Business.* New York: New York University Press, 1948. The only full-scale scholarly history of an American brewing company; an excellent study that is broader in scope than the title indicates.

Colvin, D. Leigh. *Prohibition in the United States.* New York: George H. Doran Company, 1926. An account of the origins and history of the Prohibition party, as well as the prohibition movement.

Crowgey, Henry G. *Kentucky Bourbon, The Early Years of Whiskeymaking.* Lexington: The University Press of Kentucky, 1971. Scholarly and balanced history of the Kentucky distilling industry from the 1790s to about 1850.

Current, Richard N. *Wisconsin: A History.* New York: W. W. Norton & Company, Inc., 1977. A volume in the States and the Nation Series. It is a concise, readable, but comprehensive study of the Badger state and includes a brief but very well done history of Milwaukee's brewing industry.

Dabney, Virginius. *Dry Messiah: The Life of Bishop Cannon.* New York: Alfred A. Knopf, 1949. Balanced account of the noted Virginia political and religious leader who headed the Anti-Saloon League in the late 1920s.

De Clerck, Jean. *A Textbook of Brewing.* Vol. 1. London: Chapman and Hall, Ltd., 1957. Essentially a technical account of the brewing process.

Downard, William L. *The Cincinnati Brewing Industry: A Social and Economic History.* Athens: Ohio University Press, 1973. Study of an urban brewing industry focusing on the social place of the industry and business aspects within the industry.

Ehret, George. *Twenty-five Years of Brewing.* New York, 1891. Brief history of the brewing industry in America and Ehret's Hell Gate brewery.

Elliot, Sam Carpenter. *Nelson County Record: An Illustrated Historical and Industrial Supplement.* Bardstown, Ky.: Record Printing Co., 1896. A late-nineteenth-century industrial history including summary histories of many Kentucky distilleries.

Engelmann, Larry. *Intemperance: The Lost War Against Liquor.* New York: The Free Press, 1979. Account of the origins and repeal of Prohibition, focusing on the state of Michigan.

Friedrich, Manfred, and Donald Bull. *The Register of United States Breweries, 1876-1976.* Trumbull, Conn.: Donald Bull Publisher, 1976. A comprehensive list of more than 2,000 brewing firms with name changes and dates of operation. Volume 1 includes breweries by location, and volume 2 is an alphabetical list.

Furnas, J. C. *The Life and Times of the Late Demon Rum.* New York: G. P. Putnam's Sons, 1965. Social history of temperance and Prohibition.

Getz, Oscar. *Whiskey: An American Pictorial History.* New York: David McKay Company, Inc., 1978. General and informative survey of the distilling industry by a distiller who established the Barton Museum of Whiskey History in Bardstown, Kentucky.

Green, Ben A. *Jack Daniel's Legacy.* Nashville, Tenn.: Rich Printing Co., 1967. A folksy and entertaining history of Jack Daniel's.

Grossman, Harold J. *Grossman's Guide to Wines, Beers, and Spirits.* Revised by Harriet Lembeck. New York: Charles Scribner's Sons, 1977. General guide to alcoholic beverages, especially valuable for technical processes and the origins of the industries.

Hofmeister, Rudolph A. *The Germans of Chicago.* Champaign, Ill.: Stipes Publishing Co., 1976. History of the Germans of Chicago, with a brief treatment of Germans and brewing.

Isaac, Paul E. *Prohibition and Politics: Turbulent Decades in Tennessee, 1885-1920.* Knoxville: The University of Tennessee Press, 1965. Scholarly account of Prohibition in one state.

Jackson, Michael, ed. *The World Guide to Beer.* Englewood Cliffs, N.J.: Prentice-Hall, Inc., 1977. General account of brewing and beer, with one chapter on American brewing in the 1970s.

Jenks, Jeremiah W., and Walter E. Clark. *The Trust Problem.* New York: Doubleday, Doran & Company, Inc., 1929. Economic study of the trust movement including a treatment of the Whiskey Trust.

Jones, Stan. *Jones' Complete Barguide.* Los Angeles: Barguide Enterprises, 1977. Popular account of beverages containing a valuable lengthy historical introduction to the liquor industry and individual companies in the U.S.

Kane, Frank. *Anatomy of the Whiskey Business.* Manhasset, N.Y.: Lake House Press, 1965. Survey of trade aspects on the distilling industry, and state legislation and control.

Kelley, William J. *Brewing in Maryland.* Baltimore: John D. Lucas Printing Co., 1965. Comprehensive account of the breweries in the state.

Kellner, Esther. *Moonshine, Its History and Folklore.* Indianapolis, Ind.: Bobbs-Merrill Co., 1971. Social history of moonshine in the U.S.

Kentucky's Distilling Interests: An Illustrated History Containing Sketches and Announcements of the Most Celebrated Brands in the State. Lexington: Kentucky Distillers' Bureau, 1893. Late-nineteenth-century industrial survey of the state's major distilleries.

Kobler, John. *Ardent Spirits: The Rise and Fall of Prohibition.* New York: Putnam, 1973. General survey of the prohibition movement from the seventeenth through the twentieth centuries.

Kostka, William, Sr. *The Pre-Prohibition History of Adolph Coors Company, 1873-1933.* n.p., n.d. Short, informal history of the noted Golden, Colorado, brewery.

Krebs, Roland, and Percy J. Orthwein. *Making Friends Is Our Business: 100 Years of Anheuser-Busch.* Anheuser-Busch, Inc., 1953. A general survey of the company containing much colorful detail.

Kroll, Harry Harrison. *Bluegrass, Belles, and Bourbon.* New York: A. S. Barnes & Co., 1967. Light, informal account of Kentucky's distilleries.

Kroll, Wayne L. *Badger Breweries, Past and Present.* Jefferson, Wis., 1976. Primarily written for beer can collectors. The book is well-researched and contains brief histories of the bulk of Wisconsin's breweries. A short history of beer packaging is very useful.

Krout, John Allen. *The Origins of Prohibition.* New York: Alfred A. Knopf, 1925. Noted history of the prohibition movement.

Maurer, David W. *Kentucky Moonshine.* Lexington: University Press of Kentucky, 1974. Social history of illegally produced spirits in Kentucky.

Merz, Charles. *The Dry Decade.* New York: Doubleday, Doran & Company, Inc., 1931 (American Library ed., Seattle, 1969). A view of the Prohibition era seeing repeal as the natural result of America's refusal to obey an unpopular law.

Newman, Peter C. *King of the Castle, the Making of a Dynasty: Seagram's & the Bronfman Empire.* New York: Atheneum, 1979. Comprehensive, well researched and written history of the Bronfman enterprises and family.

Odegard, Peter H. *Pressure Politics: The Story of the Anti-Saloon League.* New York: Columbia University Press, 1928. Classic study of pressure politics focusing on the tactics of the Anti-Saloon League, which lobbied for Prohibition.

One Hundred Years of Brewing. Chicago and New York, 1903; Arno Press Reprint, 1974 (Originally published by H. S. Rich & Co.). A 700-plus page history of the industry published by the editors of the trade journal *Western Brewer.* The work is indispensable for the history of brewing and brewing technology and contains capsule summaries of hundreds of late-nineteenth-century brewing firms.

Pearce, John Ed. *Nothing Better in the Market.* Louisville, Ky.: Brown-Forman Distillers, 1970. Company-authorized history containing valuable information on the Kentucky industry and the Brown-Forman distillery.

Pierce, Bessie L. *A History of Chicago.* 3 vols. New York: A. A. Knopf, 1937-57. Classic history of Chicago containing important information on the brewing industry and the Whiskey Trust.

Red Book, 1955-56 and 1961-62. Encyclopedic Directory of the Wine and Liquor Industries. New York, 1955-56 and 1961. Compilation of statistical, legal, and general industrial information on the two industries.

Robertson, James D. *The Great American Beer Book.* Ottawa, Ill., and Thornwood, N.Y.: Caroline House Publishers, Inc., 1978. Survey of individual breweries, primarily those currently operating. The format is a series of brief articles on the firms.

Rorabaugh, W. J. *The Alcoholic Republic: An American Tradition*. New York: Oxford University Press, 1979. History of American drinking patterns and habits from 1790 to 1830. It is concluded that the society resorted to drink in large part because of social changes.

Schlüter, Hermann. *The Brewing Industry and the Brewery Workers' Movement in America*. Cincinnati: Union of United Brewery Workmen of America, 1910. History of the labor movement written from the perspective of labor. The work contains important historical information and statistics.

Sinclair, Andrew. *Prohibition, The Era of Excess*. Boston: Little, Brown and Company, 1962. Comprehensive history of the Prohibition era, attempting to answer why the "Noble Experiment" was such a failure.

Steuart, Justin. *Wayne Wheeler, Dry Boss*. New York: Fleming H. Revell Company, 1928. Biography of the Anti-Saloon League's legislative superintendent and most noted lobbyist for Prohibition.

Storms, Roger C. *Partisan Prophets: A History of the Prohibition Party*. Denver, Colo.: National Prohibition Foundation, Inc., 1973. Brief chronicle of the party's origins, history, and tactics from 1854 to 1972.

Taft, Philip. *Organized Labor in American History*. New York: Harper & Row, 1964. History of the labor movement, with a brief treatment of organized labor in the brewing and distilling movements.

Taylor, Robert Lewis. *Vessel of Wrath: The Life and Times of Carry Nation*. New York: New American Library, 1966. Well-written biography of the famous prohibitionist.

Timberlake, James H. *Prohibition and the Progressive Movement, 1900-1920*. Cambridge, Mass.: Harvard University Press, 1963. Interpretive study of the Prohibition era emphasizing the relationship with the period's "progressive" impulse.

Tyrell, Ian R. *Sobering Up: From Temperance to Prohibition in Antebellum America, 1800-1860*. Westport, Conn.: Greenwood Press, Inc., 1979. A history of temperance and Prohibition focusing on the early-nineteenth-century social and economic climate which fostered the movement.

Vogel, Edward H., et al. *The Practical Brewer: A Manual for the Brewing Industry*. St. Louis, Mo.: Master Brewers' Association of America, 1946. Technical manual on brewing.

Walden, Howard T. *Native Inheritance: The Story of Corn in America*. New York: Harper & Row Publishers, 1966. General history of corn and its history in America. One chapter is devoted to the use of corn in the making of distilled liquor.

JOURNALS

American Brewer. Journal published by the U.S. Brewers' Association. It was initiated in 1868. The journal focused on trade matters within the industry, but often carried articles on the history of the industry and individual breweries.

Brewers' Almanac. Annual reports beginning in the 1940s on the brewing industry. Statistical information on state laws is stressed. The U.S. Brewers' Association published the journal.

Brewers Digest. Trade journal published from 1926 to 1934 as the *Siebel Technical Review* and from 1934 to 1938 as the *Brewers Technical Review.* Since 1938 the journal has been published monthly as *Brewers Digest*; it contains various feature-style histories in addition to industry information.

Brewers Journal. See *Western Brewer.*

Spirits. Trade journal of the wine and liquor industries. Publication began in 1933, and the journal absorbed the *American Wine and Liquor Journal* in 1942, and the *Liquor News* in January 1943. In October 1963 it became known as *Bev for Executives.* During the 1930s, there was much information on the history of the companies in the industry. Generally, the publication stressed topics of interest to those in the industry, that is, market reports, status of government laws and regulations, technical discussions, and so on.

Western Brewer. Journal published by J. M. Wing and Co. of Chicago. The first volume appeared January 1, 1876, and volumes continued under that title until 1920. General brewers' trade information including market reports, prices of barley, hops, and similar commodities was included. Also, topical and historical information on brewers and companies was featured periodically. From 1920 to 1932 the publication was known as the *Beverage Journal,* then again was referred to as the *Western Brewer* from January 1933 to May 1934 when it was finally renamed *The Brewers' Journal.*

Wine and Spirit Bulletin: Devoted to the Interest of the Wine and Spirit Trade. Trade journal edited by George R. Washburne and issued from 1886 to 1918. The journal was published in Louisville, Kentucky, and is helpful for contemporary arguments on the bonding period, growth of prohibition sentiment, and general statistical items related to distilling.

U.S. GOVERNMENT PUBLICATIONS

Federal Trade Commission, *The Brewing Industry.* Washington, D.C.: Government Printing Office, 1978. Study of the industry from 1945 to 1976, with special emphasis on the trend toward fewer firms.

Udell, Gilman, compiler. *Liquor Laws.* Washington, D.C.: U.S. Government Printing Office, 1978. Guide to federal liquor laws passed after 1890.

U.S. Department of Justice. *Proceedings Before and by Direction of the President Concerning the Meaning of the Term "Whisky."* Washington, D.C.: Government Printing Office, 1909. Report of Solicitor-General Lloyd Bowers on the meaning of whiskey. The hearing, ordered by President William H. Taft, resulted in some 1,300 pages of documentation, and was held to determine the proper interpretation of the Pure Food and Drug Act of 1906.

PAMPHLETS, BRIEF HISTORIES, DISSERTATIONS AND DIRECTORIES

Bourbon, the World's Favorite Whiskey. New York: Bourbon Institute, ca. 1970. Twenty-four-page pamphlet describing the origins and development of bourbon, with a brief description of the process of making the drink.

Cooper, Isabella Mitchell. *References, Ancient and Modern, to the Literature on Beer and Ale*. New York: United Brewers' Industrial Foundation, 1937. General bibliography of works on beer and ale.

Distilled Spirits Council of the U.S. *Distilled Spirits Industry Annual Statistical Review*. Washington, D.C.: DISCUS, 1977. Statistical survey of the industry with tables on consumption, internal revenue income, state laws, production, and so on.

Forty Years of Repeal: The Story of an Industry. New York: Jobson Printing Corp., 1973. Brief history of the distilling industry after 1933. Histories of the major companies, Schenley, Seagram, National Distillers, Brown-Forman, and Hiram Walker, are included.

History of Packaged Beer and Its Market in the United States. New York: American Can Company, 1969. Brief article on beer packaging by American Can Company.

In Olde Kentucke. Frankfort: Kentucky Distillers Association, ca. 1970. Brief account of Kentucky distilling and the steps in whiskey-making.

Jillson, Willard Rouse. *Early Kentucky Distillers, 1783-1800*. Louisville, Ky.: Standard Printing Co., 1940. Sixty-page account of the origins of Kentucky's distilling industry.

Lindhurst, James. "History of the Brewing Industry in St. Louis, 1804-1860." Unpub. M.A. thesis, Washington University, 1939. Academic survey of the early years of brewing in St. Louis, Missouri.

Maurer, Fleisher, & Associates. *Union with a Heart: International Union of United Brewery, Flour, Cereal, Soft Drink, and Distillery Workers of America: 75 Years of a Great Union, 1886-1961*. Washington, D.C.: National Publishing Company, 1961. Brief and comprehensive account of the union.

Nelson, James L. "Business History of the San Antonio Brewing Association." Unpub. M.A. thesis, Trinity University, 1976. Well-researched and written history of the Texas brewery.

Our One Hundredth Year. Brooklyn, N.Y.: F. & M. Schaefer Brewing Co., 1942. Company history of the New York firm.

Persons, Warren M. *Beer and Brewing America*. U.S. Brewers' Foundation, 1941. Brief history of the industry concentrating on trends after repeal of Prohibition in 1933. Valuable statistical data are included.

Plavchan, Ronald Jan. "A History of Anheuser-Busch, 1852-1953." Unpub. Ph.D. dissertation, Saint Louis University, 1969. Well-written history of the nation's largest brewery.

Rosenbloom, Morris Victor. *The Liquor Industry*. Braddock, Pa.: Ruffsdale Printing Co., 1937. Brief survey of the distilling industry, mainly in the post-Repeal era. Surveys of the major companies are included.

Tovey's Directory: Official Brewers and Maltsters' Directory, 1882 and 1891. New York: A. E. J. Tovey, 1882, and *Brewers' Journal*, 1891. General directory to the firms in the two industries.

Walton, Howard R. *Hiram Walker (1816-1899) and Walkerville from 1858.* New York: Newcomen Society in North America, 1958. Pamphlet biography and history of approximately twenty-five pages by the president of Hiram Walker-Gooderham & Worts, Ltd.

Willkie, H. F. *Beverage Spirits in America: A Brief History.* New York: Newcomen Society of England, American Branch, 1949. Newcomen address surveying the history of the distilling industry in the U.S.

Wilson, James Boone. *The Spirit of Old Kentucky.* Louisville, Ky.: Glenmore Distilling Company, 1945. Pamphlet of more than thirty pages especially detailing the process of making bourbon.

INDEX ⎯⎯⎯

About the Author

WILLIAM L. DOWNARD is Professor of History at St. Joseph's College in Rensselaer, Indiana. He is the author of *The Cincinnati Brewing Industry: A Social and Economic History*.